What sort of minds do animals have? Do they have feelings, desires, or beliefs? Are they capable of self-awareness, language, or autonomy? Do animals have moral standing, and if so, how seriously should we take their interests when they conflict with human interests?

This book distinguishes itself from the sometimes polemical literature on these issues by offering the most judicious and balanced exploration yet available of animals' moral standing and of related questions concerning their minds and welfare. Transcending the overplayed debate between utilitarians and rights theorists, the book employs a fresh methodological approach in defending highly progressive conclusions regarding our treatment of animals. David DeGrazia provides the most thorough discussion yet of whether equal consideration should be extended to animals' interests, and he examines the issues of animal minds and animal welfare with an unparalleled combination of philosophical rigor and empirical documentation.

Taking animals seriously

Taking animals seriously

Mental life and moral status

DAVID DeGRAZIA

GEORGE WASHINGTON UNIVERSITY

CAMBRIDGE
UNIVERSITY PRESS

Published by the Press Syndicate of the University of Cambridge
The Pitt Building, Trumpington Street, Cambridge CB2 1RP
40 West 20th Street, New York, NY 10011-4211, USA
10 Stamford Road, Oakleigh, Melbourne 3166, Australia

First published 1996

Printed in the United States of America

Library of Congress Cataloging-in-Publication Data
DeGrazia, David.
Taking animals seriously : mental life and moral status / David
DeGrazia.
p.   cm.
Includes bibliographical references and index.
ISBN 0-521-56140-x (hc).—ISBN 0-521-56760-2 (pbk.)
1. Animal welfare—Moral and ethical aspects.   2. Animal
psychology.   I. Title.
HV4708.D44   1996
179'.3—dc20   95-46689
CIP

A catalog record for this book is available from the British Library.

ISBN 0-521-56140-x hardback
ISBN 0-521-56760-2 paperback

To the memory of David Hamovit

Contents

Acknowledgments   *page* ix

1   A short primer on animal ethics   1

2   The coherence model of ethical justification   11

3   Animals' moral status and the issue of equal
    consideration   36

4   Motivation and methods for studying animal minds   75

5   Feelings   97

6   Desires and beliefs   129

7   Self-awareness, language, moral agency, and autonomy   166

8   The basics of well-being across species   211

9   Back to animal ethics   258

    Index   299

Acknowledgments

In writing this book, I have incurred many debts. Most of the book was drafted during a two-semester leave of absence made possible by a fellowship from the American Council of Learned Societies. I am very grateful to the ACLS. I am equally grateful to the College of Arts and Sciences, George Washington University, which granted me, in effect, an early sabbatical and provided crucial financial support (including a Junior Scholar Incentive Award). In a day when support for the humanities is in jeopardy and funding is increasingly politicized, it is heartening to me that these two institutions supported, without prejudice, a project in such a controversial area. I would also like to thank my wonderful colleagues in the Department of Philosophy and in the Program in Bioethics at G.W.U. Their decency and professionalism have made working life a pleasure since I arrived in 1989; they were also very supportive during my leave in the 1993–4 school year.

Many academic friends read drafts of chapters and provided valuable feedback, leading to innumerable revisions. Each of the following individuals read and commented on at least one chapter: Andy Altman, Tom Beauchamp, Marc Bekoff, Jeff Blustein, Steve Fleishman, Margaret Holmgren, Hugh LaFollette, Tom Mappes, Madison Powers, Tom Regan, Andrew Rowan, Steve Sapontzis, Wayne Sumner, and Gary Varner. Among those who commented on more than one chapter, Andy Altman deserves special thanks for reviewing four of them and, more importantly, for rekindling my spirits with encouragement on several occasions. Some of my embryonic attempts to work out problems in animal ethics profited from the comments of fellows and scholars at the Kennedy Institute of Ethics, Georgetown University. In various stages of writing, I also benefitted from unpublished manuscripts by David Pears, John Searle, Wayne Sumner, and Gary Varner, who kindly permitted me to cite their works. I thank Andrew Rowan both for going over a number of scientific points about animal mentation with me and for letting me draw heavily from an article we coauthored, "Pain, Suffering, and Anxiety in Animals and Humans." Thanks are also due to Marty Stephens and other friends at the Humane Society of the United States for providing some useful literature about animals.

I am very grateful to Cambridge University Press for its interest in my manuscript and especially to Terence Moore for his professionalism and encouragement as editor. The manuscript was read by two anonymous reviewers. Both were very insightful; one went well beyond the call of duty in furnishing specific comments, including many helpful suggestions.

My philosophical reflections about animals considerably predate the present book. I wrote my dissertation on the same topic, so this is a good time to thank my committee: Ray Frey and Tom Regan, who generously served as outside readers, and Wayne Davis and Tom Beauchamp of Georgetown University. Tom Beauchamp was an especially helpful mentor and has given me valuable advice several times since my graduation.

Many other teachers are partly responsible for my pursuing a career in philosophy. I would especially like to thank Larry Thomas, who taught my first class in philosophy at the University of Maryland; Arthur Adkins, my bachelor's thesis advisor at the University of Chicago; Jim Griffin and David Pears, my teachers at Oxford; and Bob Veatch, who has been extraordinarily helpful and supportive since the day he told me about Georgetown's graduate school program.

Closer to home, I thank Liz and Lane, Chris, Belinda and Craig, Gus (who first encouraged me to study philosophy), Mom and Zelda, and Dad and Lora, for their love. I am also grateful for many friendships—several dating back to elementary school—which have nourished me all these years; this book is dedicated to one of those old friends. Finally, and most of all, I thank my wife, Kathleen, who renews my faith in humanity on a daily basis.

Chapter 1

A short primer on animal ethics

Lately, nonhuman animals have been the topic of a great deal of social and professional discussion. Open questions concern animals' *moral status* as well as their *mental lives*. On the moral front, the animal protection movement in the past quarter-century has questioned traditional assumptions about animals—that they have little or no moral status, and that they may be used for practically any human purpose. But some have taken this movement to deny obvious moral differences between humans and animals. Spokespersons for professions that use animals have sometimes angrily asserted a fundamental, unquestionable gulf between humans and other animals. Who is right? How are we to understand the moral status of animals? Among the obvious differences between humans and animals, which, if any, are morally important? We have nothing resembling a consensus on these issues.

The jury is also out with respect to animal minds. As the scientific study of animal mentation gains respectability, the public is increasingly fascinated by this topic. Note the popular books speculating about waking and dreaming states of various domestic species (not to mention television commercials featuring cute animals drinking beer or driving trucks). While some see the increased attention to animal minds as hopelessly sentimental anthropomorphism, others take it to reflect the overdue demise of a prejudice against animals.

While intriguing and important in its own right, the mental life of animals is also crucial to the ethical study of animals—*animal ethics*, as it is now called. That is because what sorts of mental capacities we attribute to animals have a great deal to do with how we think they should be treated. If an animal is thought to be a sort of organic wind-up toy, people are unlikely to go far out of their way for it. But if an animal is believed to be self-aware or rational, or to have a rich emotional life, different responses are likely.

This book is based on the premise that philosophical work is essential to understanding animals. Untutored "common sense" is insufficient in areas such as this, where there is much fundamental disagreement and where traditional or common assumptions are questioned for their adequacy. Philosophy offers critical reflection that can help to distinguish good insights from the products of prejudice, as well as certain kinds of analytical tools. Examining the moral status of animals in a careful, disciplined manner requires some measure of theorizing, taking us to the area of philosophy known as *ethical theory*. Similarly, examining animal minds in light of empirical evidence requires trekking through thickets of conceptual issues and questions about what sorts of inferences are justified by what sorts of evidence. This means investigations in what is known as the *philosophy of mind*.

While this book is animated by philosophical investigations, it is by no means written exclusively for philosophers. It is written for thoughtful people who are interested in animals and are willing to work patiently through complex issues regarding them.

THE FIRST GENERATION

Since the mid-1970s, philosophers have contributed substantially to animal ethics. It will be worthwhile to highlight some leading contributions—even if briefly and somewhat impressionistically—in order to achieve a sense of what has been done and what remains to be done.[1] My review focuses on the book-length discussions that, in my opinion, have contributed the most to the philosophical discussion of animal ethics.[2] As we will see, this discussion depends heavily on theses about the mental lives of animals, so that animal ethics necessarily involves the philosophy of mind and the natural sciences. (Readers who are unfamiliar with the literature reviewed here should note that their introduction to animal ethics will, in effect, continue as specific issues are taken up in later chapters.)

More than any other work, Peter Singer's *Animal Liberation* brought questions about the moral status of animals into intellectual respectability.[3] In this work, Singer argues on the basis of behavioral, physiological, and evolutionary evidence that many animals (at least vertebrates) have interests—at the very least an interest in not suffering.

---

[1] Parts of the review that follows draw from my "The Moral Status of Animals and Their Use in Research: A Philosophical Review," *Kennedy Institute of Ethics Journal* 1 (1991), esp. pp. 49–56.

[2] Of course, one might not agree with all my judgments here. For example, one might argue for the inclusion of Bernard E. Rollin, *Animal Rights and Human Morality* (Buffalo, NY: Prometheus, 1981) or Michael P. T. Leahy, *Against Liberation: Putting Animals in Perspective* (London: Routledge, 1991).

[3] *Animal Liberation* (New York: New York Review of Books, 1975)

Indeed, he identifies *sentience,* the capacity to suffer, as the admission ticket to the moral arena. Nonsentient beings have no interests, and where there are no interests, there is nothing morally to protect. On the other hand, all sentient beings have interests and therefore moral status.

Noting that leading ethical theories assume some principle of *equal consideration of interests,* Singer argues that there is no coherent reason to exclude (sentient) animals' interests from the scope of equal consideration. Including animals does not entail precisely equal *treatment.* Dogs have no interest in learning to read and write, so equal consideration does not require providing them an education even if we hold that humans are entitled to an education. However, it does mean that if a human and a rat suffer equally in duration and intensity, their suffering has the same moral weight or importance. Singer employs this simple thesis in a scathing critique of common uses of animals for human purposes. He gives particularly detailed attention to factory farming and the use of animals in biomedical research, calling for the abolition of the former and the near-abolition of the latter.

Singer's contribution has much to recommend it. His arguments are presented with unusual clarity. The wealth of information about common uses of animals is truly eye-opening. And Singer manages in very few pages to demolish some popular rationalizations for the status quo while writing at a level that practically any adult reader can understand.

But the book also has disadvantages. The cost of wide accessibility is some degree of philosophical superficiality. (Indeed, I think a major problem in animal ethics is that several philosophers seem to have used the goal of accessibility as an excuse to avoid some difficult philosophical issues.) Singer slips by many issues that philosophers find it natural to flag. Examples include the possible relevance of social relationships to a determination of moral status, the nature of suffering and its relation to other mental states, and whether there should be a burden of proof on one who denies that equal consideration should extend to animals. Other problems include (1) difficulties with the theory of utilitarianism, which lurks in the background and sometimes drives his arguments, and (2) an untenable defense of a very important claim—namely, that equal consideration for animals is compatible with the judgment that the lives of normal humans are ordinarily more valuable than the lives of animals.

Like Singer, R. G. Frey embraces *utilitarianism,* the ethical theory that states that the right action is that which maximizes good consequences. His *Interests and Rights* is philosophically more in-depth than most works in animal ethics.[4] Unlike Singer, Frey argues in this early work

---

[4] *Interests and Rights: The Case Against Animals* (Oxford: Clarendon, 1980)

that animals have no interests (and therefore cannot be harmed). To reach this conclusion, he begins by contending that all morally relevant interests are based on desires. Then he argues that one cannot have a desire (say, to own a book) without a corresponding belief (that I lack a book or that the statement "I lack a book" is true). He makes the case that a belief—which always amounts to a belief that a certain sentence is true—requires language. Because animals lack language, they lack the beliefs requisite for desires and therefore lack desires. Thus, animals have no interests. Lacking interests, animals have no significant moral status.

Frey's book has received considerable attention, in part because for over a decade it was the only well-known philosophical book making the moral case against animals. Its chief merit is that it recognizes the philosophical issues implicated in exploring animals' minds and moral status and gives these issues energetic philosophical treatment. Its chief demerit is that it is largely mistaken.

For example, among the more dubious premises in the foregoing argument are that beliefs are always beliefs that some sentence is true, and that they require language. (In Chapter 6, I will argue that language is not necessary for having desires and beliefs.) Frey's view also has some incredible implications. It is hard to believe that kicking a cat does not harm her—causing her to suffer—and that doing so is not contrary to her interests. We should not be surprised, then, to find considerable strain at the end of the book when he almost entirely avoids the word *suffering* (which he apparently ties to harm and interests). Frey states instead that "higher" animals can experience "unpleasant sensations" and that gratuitously causing such sensations is wrong.[5] Moreover, it is unclear why it is not in one's interests to avoid unpleasant sensations. (Frey apparently agrees because he now allows that many animals have interests and can suffer and be harmed.[6])

I will comment further on Frey's work in later chapters. Here it is worth noting that his version of utilitarianism (like Singer's) implies that not only animals—but humans—lack moral rights, because *there is no such thing* as a moral right; the only ultimate moral standard is the principle of utility, the principle that we should maximize good consequences. This principle might require us, in some circumstances, to override individuals' interests in ways that seem clearly unjust (that is, seem to violate their rights), such as framing an innocent man to prevent a riot.

---

[5] ibid, pp. 170–71
[6] Frey has been most forthcoming with these concessions in public lectures and in conversation. But see, e.g., Frey, "The Significance of Agency and Marginal Cases," *Philosophica* 39 (1987): 39–46.

Seizing on such problems, Tom Regan argues for an alternative. His *Case for Animal Rights* is perhaps the most systematic and explicitly worked-out book in animal ethics.[7] His moral position begins by rejecting utilitarianism. Regan argues that because it is committed to maximizing the good with no prior commitment to how the good is to be *distributed,* utilitarianism fails to respect the moral importance of individuals *as individuals.* If slavery is wrong, according to the utilitarian, it is only because the institution fails to maximize the good, not because of the inviolability of persons. It is not even clear that the painless, carefully concealed killing of one unconsenting person to retrieve organs to save a few other persons is wrong on utilitarian reasoning.

Regan proposes that we regard individuals as possessing *equal inherent value.* Who are "individuals"? They are beings who have a welfare, who can fare well or badly over time. Thus animals who have beliefs, desires, and a psychophysical identity over time—*subjects-of-a-life*—have inherent value. This includes at least normal adult mammals. Inherent value implies a basic Respect Principle, which in turn implies a prima facie duty not to harm "subjects." Importantly, Regan includes both inflictions and deprivations as harms, so that death, which deprives one of life's opportunities, is ordinarily a harm to "subjects"— even those lacking the concepts of life and death. A careful examination of the Respect Principle leads Regan to the thesis that "subjects" have *a right not to be harmed* that is not to be overridden for utilitarian or other reasons (except in very rare circumstances in which those whose rights are to be overridden would be harmed even if no action were taken). Applying his rights view to various problem areas, Regan calls for the abolition of animal agriculture, hunting and trapping, and the harmful use of animals in research.

Regan's classic book continues to represent an important position in animal ethics. On the whole, *The Case for Animal Rights* is carefully argued and thorough. The position laid out is far more coherent than traditional thinking about animals, and Regan impressively integrates his moral reasoning about humans and other species. The work on animal minds was very good for its time (the early 1980s). Moreover, the assertion of nearly absolute rights allows Regan to avoid a notorious conundrum in animal ethics that will be introduced in Chapter 3: the "problem of marginal cases."

At the same time, Regan's rights view seems underdetermined by his arguments. In particular, the postulate of equal inherent value merits a much more vigorous defense than he has supplied; he has not answered the best arguments against ascribing such equal value to all "subjects." His view also has some incredible results—for example, that

[7] *The Case for Animal Rights* (Berkeley: University of California Press, 1983)

it would be wrong to cause a minor unconsented harm to one individual who would not otherwise be harmed in order to prevent a major catastrophe. (Utilitarianism does not have a monopoly on counterintuitive implications.) In addition, his handling of the rare cases in which rights may be overridden (e.g., when every rightholder on a lifeboat will drown if none is sacrificed) is at best incompletely defended and at worst inconsistent with his strong interpretation of inherent value, his abolitionist position on animal research, or both. Further, his account of *positive duties*—which concludes that we have a prima facie duty to assist *victims of injustice* but no such duty to help others in need—is almost certainly unsustainable.[8]

Singer, Frey, and Regan have made important contributions. Much of the animal ethics literature comes close to suggesting that they have mapped out *the* major views in this debate; it is not unusual for an article or anthology to represent "the utilitarian view," "the rights view," and no other. This suggests that their views are very different from each other. *The first generation* of major scholars in animal ethics has supported this impression with their extraordinary emphasis, in their books and articles, on the utility-versus-rights debate.

Yet the views of the first generation—especially with Frey now conceding that animals have interests—are strikingly similar. All fit comfortably within the tradition of liberal individualism: The moral focus is on the individual, whether as rights-bearer or as bearer of interests to be counted in utility maximization. Thus, they largely ignore approaches (such as Midgley's, discussed in the next section) that ground obligations in social relations more than in individuals' characteristics, such as sentience. They also favor highly systematic, unified ethical theories. This is not a trivial concurrence; philosophers today are increasingly doubtful that any simple, unified theory can corner the market on ethical insight. An example of a more pluralistic approach is that of Sapontzis (see next section).

One of the most remarkable facts about the first generation is that they all agree on the basic idea of extending equal consideration to animals. For the utilitarians, animals' interests count equally in maximizing the good. For Regan, animals' interests are somewhat more rigorously protected by rights. The vast majority of humanity—and most philosophers, for that matter—do *not* grant animals' interests equal consideration. Thus, the issue of whether to do so is emphatically more important than the utility-versus-rights debate.

---

[8] The points made in the last two sentences are powerfully argued by Dale Jamieson, "Rights, Justice, and Duties to Provide Assistance: A Critique of Regan's Theory of Rights," *Ethics* 100 (1990): 349–62.

THE SECOND GENERATION

The work of what I call *the second generation* of major scholars in animal ethics has been more diverse and greatly underappreciated. It begins with Mary Midgley's *Animals and Why They Matter*.[9] Much of Midgley's book is devoted to discrediting the view that animals are morally unimportant. In this effort, she profitably distinguishes several ways in which thinkers have dismissed the interests of animals. In arguing against such dismissal, she stops short of entirely rejecting the idea that the needs of those socially closer to us have moral priority over the needs of those less close. Indeed, in a qualified endorsement of such a perspective, she departs from the individualist mainstream and invokes social-bondedness, and the emotions connected with them, as morally paramount. By way of analogy, she goes on to argue that a preference for one's own species is acceptable *within limits*, in no way justifying the dismissal of animals' interests. (She deplores contemporary methods of meat production, for example.) Rather than portraying the moral concerns of family, kin, nation, species, and so on as forming concentric circles with oneself in the middle, she portrays them as overlapping concerns. Her book is also notable for a sustained, historically informed critique of the traditional views that (1) reason is the basis for moral status, and (2) reason alone, not emotion, is authoritative in ethics.

Midgley's work brings theoretical fresh air into the debate. Her contribution constitutes a challenge to the extension of equal consideration to animals that is significant both for its constructiveness and for the feminism-influenced insights that drive it. I will critically examine her view in Chapter 3.

In *Morals, Reason, and Animals*, S. F. Sapontzis, like Midgley, eschews efforts to ground ethics in ahistorical, reason-derived norms.[10] Sapontzis treats ethics as a pragmatic endeavor rooted in cultural traditions but capable of progress within a tradition. He contends that while the Western tradition does not question our casual consumption of animals, certain fundamental elements of that tradition point in the direction of animal liberation. In view of the lack of a clearly authoritative ethical theory, and suspicious of relatively simple frameworks (like utilitarianism and Regan's view), he treats three major goals of our moral tradition as on a par: reducing suffering, being fair, and developing moral virtues. Thus, his view is an amalgam of considerations of utility, rights, and virtue. In the end, he condemns current animal-

---

[9] *Animals and Why They Matter* (Athens, GA: University of Georgia Press, 1983)
[10] *Morals, Reason, and Animals* (Philadelphia: Temple University Press, 1987)

consuming practices, although he is not quite an abolitionist with respect to animal research.

Sapontzis' book is one of the very best in the field. His probing discussions of, for example, the harm of death, the environment, the possibility of animal virtue, and the so-called "replacement argument" are outstanding. His pragmatic, pluralistic approach avoids some of the pitfalls of monolithic ethical theories. My impression, however, is that the argumentation is unevenly rigorous. I also wonder why just the above three prongs of our tradition are the ones we should appeal to in ethics. And do we really have a shared conception of fairness? More troublingly, couldn't one argue that a fourth prong is the idea that human interests deserve vastly more weight than animal interests? After all, this idea is as old as our tradition itself and seems to enjoy majority support today.

The least systematic of the books discussed in this overview, Rosemary Rodd's *Biology, Ethics, and Animals* is nevertheless a very important contribution.[11] Combining competence in both philosophy and biology, Rodd explores animal ethics equipped with something the other authors lack: a superior scientific understanding of animals generally (in terms of evolutionary theory and scientific methodology) and of different species of animals. This allows her, for example, to rebut effectively various sceptical claims about animal mentation, comment knowledgeably about the animal-communication debate, and cast serious doubt on the assumed human monopoly on self-awareness and moral agency. Her constructive discussion of conflicting human and animal interests contains fresh insights and creative proposals; it features discussions of neglected topics, such as pest control, and one of the best discussions of animal research in the literature.

In the end, her view might best be described as a modified animal-liberation view that endorses some partiality toward humans but seeks to minimize conflicts between humans and animals through better understanding of the latter. She holds that the harmful use of animals is justified only when (1) the animals are compensated by benefits that make up for the harms they endure, or (2) harming animals is the only way to prevent death or substantial harm to humans (in which case, harms to the animals must be kept to an absolute minimum).[12] Perhaps the book's chief weakness is that in places, one might expect more extensive argumentation on distinctively philosophical issues—such as the comparative value of different sorts of lives and the status of duties of assistance. Another difficulty is that rambling prose sometimes makes it hard to follow lines of argument.

---

[11] *Biology, Ethics, and Animals* (Oxford: Clarendon, 1990)
[12] ibid, p. 175

Our tour of the second generation ends with Peter Carruthers' *The Animals Issue*, which I consider the most important published case against animals.[13] A lively, provocative book, it challenges not only the extension of equal consideration to animals but even the more modest thesis that animals have *some* moral status—that their interests matter morally in their own right and not just because of effects on human interests. Employing the coherence model of ethical justification (which I elaborate and defend in Chapter 2), Carruthers argues that morality is best understood in terms of an imaginary social contract constructed by rational agents. He contends that only humans are rational agents and therefore covered by the terms of morality, but he maintains that, for several reasons, *even nonrational humans* should be covered by these terms. In the last chapter, he somewhat tentatively advances the thesis that the mental states of animals are all unconscious (which, if true, makes the case against animals much easier).

Carruthers' concise and thoughtful book is an important challenge to the philosophical arm of the animal protection movement. But I suspect that the book would have been stronger had the last chapter simply been omitted. And discussions (in several chapters) of animals' mental capacities are vitiated by very little engagement with relevant empirical literature (in stark contrast to Rodd's work, for example). In Chapters 3 and 5, I devote a section each to undermining Carruthers' contract approach to animal ethics and his skepticism about animal consciousness, respectively.

THIS BOOK

Where does the present book fit in? In part, it is a response to my perception of some gaps and weaknesses in the existing animal ethics literature. It is also a response to growing (and partly independent) interest in the mental life of animals—an offering of the sort of conceptual and philosophical work that is needed to interpret empirical data responsibly in marshalling theses about animal minds. My overarching purpose in *Taking Animals Seriously* is to explore the mental life and moral status of animals in a philosophically penetrating, empirically well-informed way. Under the umbrella of this general aim are several more specific ones.

First, I want to transcend the utility-versus-rights debate and offer a well-developed methodology, a version of the coherence model, for fruitful pursuit of questions in animal ethics. I employ that methodology in arguing that many animals have moral status and that much of

---

[13] *The Animals Issue: Moral Theory in Practice* (Cambridge: Cambridge University Press, 1992)

our current use of animals is ethically indefensible. I also argue in favor of equal consideration for animals but take pains to explain what that means and, just as importantly, what it does not mean (since the idea is often misunderstood). In sum, on the ethical front, I try to show that prevalent ethical attitudes about animals are largely *incoherent* (in a broad sense of that term). At the same time, I draw attention to some morally interesting *differences* among bearers of moral status; those who champion animal protection often downplay such differences. Second, in exploring the mental life of animals, I strive for both philosophical rigor and empirical richness. I try to demonstrate, among other things, that a large class of animals have feelings, desires, and beliefs and that some interesting mental properties (e.g., self-awareness) and other phenomena of interest (e.g., language) are neither all-or-nothing nor exclusively human. Third, I endeavor to explore the basic features of animal well-being and related notions, especially in comparisons with humans—drawing from the study of animal minds and contributing to the project of animal ethics—in a more detailed and penetrating way than has been accomplished before.

The plan of the book is as follows. In Chapter 2, I describe, develop, and defend my methodology in ethics. This chapter is less centrally about animals than are the other chapters; readers who are not so concerned about methodology may wish to skim it. In Chapter 3, I distinguish the fundamental questions about the moral status of animals, argue that animals have basic moral status, establish a burden of proof in favor of equal consideration for animals, and argue that the best attempts to carry this burden fail. It is explained that further understanding of what equal consideration would amount to, and of the moral status of particular animals, requires work in value theory (which explores the basic features of individual well-being), which in turn requires a decent grasp of animals' mental life. Chapter 4 further motivates the study of animal minds and explains the pluralistic method to be used in this study. (The method for studying animal minds can be seen as part of the broader methodology for ethics, the coherence model.) In Chapter 5, I argue that most or all vertebrates, and probably some invertebrates, have feelings; in Chapter 6, I argue that these same animals have desires and beliefs. Chapter 7 investigates self-awareness, language, moral agency, and autonomy in relation to animals. Drawing from the work on animal minds, Chapter 8 explores animal well-being. Particular emphasis is given to the question of whether death ordinarily harms humans more than it harms other sentient animals—a crucial issue in unpacking equal consideration. We return to animal ethics in Chapter 9, which specifies numerous principles and other moral conclusions of interest to animal ethics, before confronting the issues of eating animals and keeping them in zoos.

Chapter 2

The coherence model
of ethical justification

This chapter describes and defends my methodology in ethics: a version of the *coherence model of ethical justification*. The chapter begins with a contrasting picture of foundational views of ethics. It proceeds to a preliminary characterization of the coherence model and two major theoretical challenges: the problems of initial credibility and bias. In the remainder of the chapter, the model is further characterized and developed in a way that addresses these problems.

FOUNDATIONALISM

Foundational views of ethics maintain that ethics has a foundation of some kind. Some claim that ethics has a *normative* foundation—that is, a privileged norm or set of norms (whether principles, rules, or specific judgments)—by which all other norms may be justified. Other foundational views assert that ethics has a *metaethical* foundation—that there are nonmoral considerations or facts that make ethics, or a particular ethical view, rationally necessary.

As I use the term, *ethical rationalism* (hereafter, simply *rationalism*) is the view that ethics has a metaethical foundation.[1] *Deductivism* is the view that ethics has a normative foundation that can be expressed as a supreme principle (or perhaps as an explicitly related—say, hierarchically arranged—set of principles). The structure of a deductivist theory is sufficiently defined that all correct moral judgments are supposedly, in principle, derivable from that structure, given relevant factual information.

---

[1] Under the rubric of *rationalism,* I include not just views that claim that the rational necessity of being moral can be shown *discursively* (say, by appeal to noncontradiction or to self-interest) but also views that claim that some moral norms are literally *self-evident.* See, e.g., W. D. Ross (*The Right and the Good* [Oxford: Oxford University Press, 1930], p. 29).

As an example, R. M. Hare's metaethical theory is rationalist because it purports to show how the logic of moral language rationally compels us to accept a certain ethical theory. That ethical theory is utilitarianism, which is deductivist because it states that all correct moral judgments are derivable from a certain normative foundation, the principle of utility.[2] Using our terminology, Ross' ethical theory is not deductivist because, while it has a normative foundation in a set of basic *prima facie* duties (each of which, by definition, is an *actual* duty in the absence of conflicts), such duties are not related in any explicit way that would allow the derivation of specific ethical judgments in conflicts. Also, Ross is careful not to claim completeness for his list of prima facie duties.[3]

Rationalism and deductivism are often confused or conflated, but they are distinct and neither entails the other. Nevertheless, they form a natural pair, both being motivated by the general attractions of foundations. Such a rationalist-deductivist theory, if successfully defended, would be the most theoretically adequate approach. It would, in principle, provide a definite method for justifying all correct moral judgments.

Unfortunately, for various reasons well-known to philosophers, the adequacy of ethical foundationalism has been placed in doubt. It is not among the goals of this book to refute foundationalism. Let me simply assert several working assumptions. The first assumption is that the history of moral philosophy strongly suggests that hopeful rationalists are expecting too much of reason. The second is that there is no compelling reason to assume that ethics has a simple, unified normative foundation of the kind deductivists claim. I also take it that normative ethics is worth pursuing even in the absence of a convincing argument for foundationalism, because normative ethics does not need foundationalism and because (to state a final assumption) moral skepticism—the thoroughgoing rejection of morality and moral argument—is wrongheaded. Note that any work in normative ethics assumes that moral skepticism is wrongheaded.

THE COHERENCE MODEL INTRODUCED

The most promising model of ethical justification is the coherence model, also known as the model—or method—of *reflective equilibrium*. (I will sometimes speak of a version of this model as *a* coherence model.) The coherence model avoids the pitfalls of foundationalism while providing an alternative to moral skepticism. Later we will see

[2] *Moral Thinking: Its Levels, Method, and Point* (Oxford: Clarendon, 1981)
[3] *The Right and the Good*, p. 20

that it is not defeated by its two strongest challenges. But the model's major proof will be in the pudding—the way it allows fruitful pursuit of animal ethics later in this book. For now, let us content ourselves with a sketch of what a coherence model would look like.

In a coherence model, no set of ethical norms is granted epistemic privilege such that all justification is to be based, ultimately, on those norms. Deductivism, as we have seen, treats a supreme principle as foundational. Inductivism treats particular ethical judgments about cases, actions, persons, or something else as foundational; more general norms are justified on the basis of those particular judgments.

In the present model, justification occurs at all levels of generality: judgments about cases, actions, persons, or the like, principles and rules of differing degrees of generality, and perhaps theories.[4] Judgments at any level can be used to revise judgments at any other level. For example, one might initially believe it justified to test drug addicts in hospitals for HIV without their consent, because seeking consent might interfere with gaining data that would be useful for treating future HIV-infected patients. But one might accept the principle that we should never treat persons merely as means, which arguably suggests that one should reject this initial judgment. Such patients, the argument goes, are not treated as ends in themselves unless they are given the option to

---

[4] The more general epistemological idea that there is no indubitable foundation to knowledge, which instead takes the form of a coherent system, has roots in Peirce, Dewey, Goodman, Quine, Sellars, Davidson, and Wittgenstein (though his antipathy toward system requires qualifying the attribution to him). For starters, see J. Buchler (ed.), *Philosophical Writings of Peirce* (New York: Dover, 1955); John Dewey, *Reconstruction in Philosophy* (Boston: Beacon, 1948); Nelson Goodman, *Fact, Fiction, and Forecast* (Cambridge, MA: Harvard University Press, 1955); W. V. Quine, *Word and Object* (Cambridge, MA: MIT Press, 1960); Wilfred Sellars, *Science, Perception and Reality* (London: Routledge and Kegan Paul, 1963); Ludwig Wittgenstein, *On Certainty* (Oxford: Blackwell, 1969); and Donald Davidson, *Inquiries into Truth and Interpretation* (Oxford: Clarendon Press, 1984). One can take anti-foundationalism to differing degrees of departure from philosophical tradition. Richard Rorty, in my view, takes it to an extreme, denying any role for epistemological methods, believing them to be rationalist residue (see, e.g., *The Consequences of Pragmatism* [Minneapolis, MN: University of Minnesota Press, 1982]). I agree with many of Kai Nielsen's criticisms of Rorty's view (see, e.g., *After the Demise of the Tradition* [Boulder, CO: Westview: 1991], Part II).

Use of a coherence model in ethics was made famous by John Rawls, who called the model *reflective equilibrium*. See his "Outline for a Decision Procedure for Ethics," *Philosophical Review* 60 (1951): 177–97; and *A Theory of Justice* (Cambridge, MA: Harvard University Press, 1971). Not often noted is that Rawls cites someone before him as bringing this conception of justification to ethics (*Theory of Justice*, p. 579, note 33): Morton White, *Toward Reunion in Philosophy* (Cambridge, MA: Harvard University Press, 1956). For an important early exploration of the model, see Norman Daniels, "Wide Reflective Equilibrium and Theory Acceptance in Ethics," *Journal of Philosophy* 76 (1979): 256–82.

refuse testing. This revision of judgments moves "downward" (from principle to case). But, in the coherence model, one may also revise "upward." For example, confronted with the case of a psychiatric patient who threatens to kill an identified person, we might revise a principle of patient confidentiality to allow exceptions in this sort of case.

An important feature of most versions of the coherence model—one worth preserving—is that its norms are never considered final. One must always be open to the possibility that our ethical convictions will require modification in light of further considerations. Thus, while we strive for a state of equilibrium in our total set of ethical convictions upon due reflection (hence the term *reflective equilibrium*), we are never finished with moral inquiry. New problems arise. Fresh information and novel insights make us question old judgments. Moral reasoning is viewed as dynamic and is not expected to produce a final, rationally necessary theory.

How do we know which judgments or norms to revise in a conflict? In the foregoing examples, why not (1) reject or revise the prohibition against treating persons as means, or (2) retain confidentiality as an exceptionless principle—instead of the other way around? How can we justify our resolution of conflicts? In brief, conflicts are to be settled by making revisions that increase coherence in one's system of ethical convictions. But the term *coherence* here is used very broadly—perhaps reconstructively—to cover numerous theoretical virtues.

THEORETICAL VIRTUES TO BE SOUGHT IN THE COHERENCE MODEL

What are the specific theoretical virtues packed into the possibly reconstructed term *coherence* when we say our model directs us to strive for coherence among ethical beliefs? Most obviously, the broad notion of "coherence" includes a more narrow usage of the term. But even this narrower sense is difficult to pin down. It is sometimes treated as just *logical consistency*, but I think that is an error. Logical consistency is not much to ask of a theorist. In fact, probably any theory meets, or can be massaged enough to meet, this test. That is because one can always produce ad hoc distinctions in order to avoid outright contradiction— as long as there is no quality control on the production of distinctions. "Why is it OK to upset your baby if I say it's not OK for you to upset mine? My baby has brown hair." There is no logical contradiction here, but lacking a plausible story about why hair color is relevant, it is surely incoherent. Indeed, there is no contradiction per se in asserting that it is wrong to upset my baby because she is mine but not wrong to upset other babies because they are not mine. Yet this sort of special-exemptions judgment is the paradigm of moral judgments that we try to rule out as unjustified.

Coherent positions are not only consistent. They also enjoy *argumentative support*. What is offered as an argument or reason for a distinction or other judgment must at least be recognized as such. In ethics, mere numerical differences are not recognized as reasons for differences in treatment or entitlement. That you are you is no reason why you should be permitted into the Redskins' locker room; that you are a reporter, whose job includes locker-room interviews, is a reason. One advantage of requiring justifying reasons is that reasons that count (unlike numerical differences) can be generalized, so that the judgment, the reason offered, and all their logical implications can be tested for consistency with other judgments that the speaker affirms. While bare consistency is easy to maintain, consistency among a wide array of judgments under constraints of adequate reason giving is more challenging. But there can be considerable disagreement about what counts as an adequate reason in many contexts.

Suppose that someone can give plausible reasons for her moral judgments. Not for all of them, let us say—since that would imply either an infinite regress, circularity, or rationalism (which terminates in a non-moral foundation)—but for a respectable number. Suppose that all of these judgments and justifications are mutually consistent. Is the package coherent?

Following Shelly Kagan, I hold that the parts of a coherent system must hang together and the system must explain how the parts hang together. There must be a tolerable amount of illumination over the whole. Different lines of judgments plus supporting reasons must not seem disjointed or unconnected—disparate parts of an ad hoc totality. For example, if different moral principles apply to our treatment of humans and to our treatment of animals, this division should be explained. I call the theoretical virtue in question *global illumination*. These words from Kagan explain much of the point (although he does not explicitly distinguish what I call *argumentative support* and *global illumination*):

> [Even if our] maxims form a mutually consistent set, we *still* want our theory to provide an *account* of the distinctions, goals, restrictions, and the like, which they embody as well. An adequate justification for a set of principles requires an *explanation* of those principles—an explanation of why exactly these goals, restrictions, and so on, should be given weight, and not others.[5]

---

[5] *The Limits of Morality* (Oxford: Clarendon, 1989), p. 13

So much for coherence in a relatively narrow sense. What other theoretical virtues are there? For one, a theory should be *simple,* other things equal. If a large number of considerations can be reduced to a smaller number, without sacrifice in terms of other virtues, the smaller set is preferable. Sometimes simplicity even helps us to understand complexity. For example, we might start with a doctrine of informed consent in medicine for adults, acknowledging exceptions for incompetent adults, and another doctrine of best interests for minors, with exceptions for mature minors in some circumstances. A simpler picture would illuminate these two doctrines: a theory of the role of autonomy in medical decision making, which explains exceptions to both doctrines. While simplicity is a theoretical virtue, it is possible to give it too much weight. Deductivists may sometimes prize simplicity too highly in conflicts with plausibility.

Two other theoretical virtues are *clarity* and *power.* Specificity tends to make norms clearer but runs some risk of overgeneralizing. "Respect all human beings" is somewhat vague but arguably exceptionless. "Keep your promises" is more specific and clear but implausible without qualifications. A theory displays power if it yields judgments beyond the moral considerations taken into account in forming the theory. For example, a theory of business ethics exhibits power to the extent that it illuminates new cases of ethical interest in business as they arise; it has even more power if it sheds light on a different area of interest, such as computer ethics. A theory displays maximum power if it is fully comprehensive of the moral domain, being able to generate answers to all moral questions.

Another virtue—which is crucial to coherence theories but often downplayed by foundationalists—is *plausibility.* A judgment, rule, principle, distinction, or exception is plausible to the extent that it is believable in its own right. I use the terms *intuitions* and *intuitive judgments* to mean judgments made simply because they seem correct, whether or not they are supported by further considerations. It is important to note that *intuitions* in this sense does not imply the use of a special moral faculty, the existence of a metaphysical realm of moral facts, or any other epistemological or metaphysical thesis. A coherence model takes intuitions seriously, which is to say that it counts plausibility as a theoretical virtue.

The methodological challenge is to avoid excessive reliance on this sometimes problematic virtue. As we will see, several prominent philosophers are hostile toward the notion of plausibility as a theoretical virtue. But a complete rejection of intuitions as a methodological tool requires deductivism and rationalism. The weaknesses of such foundationalism motivate the rejection of extreme anti-intuitionism.

A final theoretical virtue for which a system of moral beliefs should strive is sometimes neglected: *compatibility (or coherence) with whatever else we know or reasonably believe.* Suppose that Descartes' conviction that it was morally permissible to perform surgery on unanesthetized dogs depended on his belief that dogs were not conscious creatures and therefore could not suffer. The falsity of his factual belief would then undermine his ethical judgment, since the latter depended on the factual assumption. If someone held that women should not be given positions of responsibility in society because they are less intelligent as a class than men, the normative judgment would be undermined by the falsity of the factual premise. While obvious, this theoretical virtue is enormously important both in theory and practice, and it will be explored further in a later section.

OBJECTIVITY IN ETHICS, AND WHY WE SHOULD CARE ABOUT COHERENCE

Before turning to major objections to the coherence model, let me comment briefly on the underlying conception of objectivity and on the importance of coherence. Ethics or morality involves the making of moral judgments, and these judgments imply standards that are, to some degree, general in form. For ethics to be intelligible as both a practice and a subject of (nonskeptical) philosophical exploration, it must admit of some kind of objectivity. But there are many senses of "objectivity," and probably different ones are appropriate in different domains.[6]

I think the appropriate conception of objectivity in ethics is one of *intersubjectivity,* one that appeals to the concepts of *reasonableness* and *making sense.* Such concepts are embedded in our practices of moral deliberation, persuasion, and reflection (including philosophizing). None of these concepts is inherently metaphysical. They are also independent of rationalism, because claims of reasonableness and making sense can be fallibilistic and contextual.[7]

---

[6] For example, perhaps an empirical belief is objective (or true) if its content is partly the outcome of an appropriate causal process involving our senses. But it is hard to see how the objectivity of logic could be understood this way.

[7] One might be tempted to say that the *foundation* of ethics is reasonableness (or making sense). But that is hardly worth saying, because standards of reasonableness, unlike "reason" traditionally construed, do not—as far as we know—come out of "the view from nowhere" but ultimately out of human practices. Nor does such a conception lend itself to the foundationalist program of rational deduction for the solution of ethical problems. Finally, the concept of reasonableness is already moral (and prudential), whereas the idea of a rational foundation for ethics is usually taken to mean something entirely nonmoral. A reviewer of this book suggested that the coherence model itself is a form of foundationalism. That is true if we use *foundationalism* so broadly that it applies to *any* methodology in ethics, but I made clear

In effect, I have been building my case for a coherence model of ethical justification within a broader philosophical pragmatism. By *pragmatism* I mean, roughly, the view that the best way to approach philosophical and moral problems is not to try to get behind appearances and glimpse things as they are in themselves—an approach that assumes there is a "God's-eye" view of things—but to understand theories as tools for dealing with the world, and to use (and fashion) them accordingly.[8] Unlike some pragmatists, I do not positively deny that there is a "God's-eye" view. I hold that such a view, if it exists, is beyond our grasp, making it an inappropriate goal for those of us hoping to make progress on the problems that confound us. But then why care about coherence, since it is not taken to point us to moral truth in a robust sense (morality as seen from the "God's eye" view)?

Some will press this question from an antitheoretical angle. Coherence, they think, is a theoretical value out of place in ethics, because moral practices do not need tidying up by the methods of philosophy. These practices are fine as they are. Any attempt to increase their coherence is the artificial imposition of pseudo-objectivity—the last gasp of philosophers nostalgic for the traditional philosophical notion of objective moral truths. Coherence has no intrinsic value and, if self-consciously pursued in ethics, threatens to rob moral living of some of its integrity.

This anti-theoretical attitude is highly problematic. Ethics is, again, connected with being reasonable and making sense. If someone's position on an issue is unreasonable or does not make sense, either in its own right or given other things she believes, she has reason to revise her beliefs.[9] Now, *coherence is a constraint on reasonableness.* An incoherent opinion, position, or theory is not reasonable; it does not make sense. The aforementioned theoretical virtues, which together provide standards of coherence in our broad sense, are all widely recognized as improving the quality of a body of ethical beliefs.

It might be objected that coherence in the broad sense is not required for a set of ethical beliefs to be reasonable. All that is required, according to the objection, is coherence in a narrow sense—say, logical consistency plus argumentative support. It is true that, in practice, we do not ordinarily require the achievement of all the theoretical virtues embodied in broad coherence for a set of ethical beliefs to count as

---

that I am using the term in a more specific sense, one that does not characterize my model.

[8] Cf. Richard Rorty, "Introduction: Pragmatism as Anti-Representationalism," in John P. Murphy, *Pragmatism: From Peirce to Davidson* (Boulder, CO: Westview Press, 1990), p. 2.

[9] Cf. Allan Gibbard, *Wise Choices, Apt Feelings: A Theory of Normative Judgment* (Cambridge, MA: Harvard University Press, 1990), pp. 6–7.

reasonable. But in critical reflection, we do recognize the theoretical virtues as improving a set of ethical beliefs, as making them more reasonable or sensible, for reasons explained previously. For example, a set of ethical beliefs that is at odds with our best factual thinking in some area clearly has a problem. An ethical view fragmented into different parts with no illumination over the whole seems ad hoc and invites suspicion of arbitrariness or some other problem.

The last claim will meet with some resistance. Why strive for *system*—as demanded by global illumination, fully achieved—rather than contenting ourselves with piecemeal ethical argumentation, left unconnected to some broader system? Some of the classical pragmatists, such as Dewey, and some modern pragmatists and antitheorists, including Rorty, favor a piecemeal approach, unconstrained by the goal of a greater system. It is no doubt true that we will usually "do" ethics— as philosophers or just reflective persons—piecemeal, working on particular issues or areas of concern, not explicitly connected to a greater system. But there is value in holding the idea of a complete system as an *ideal* and seeking global illumination, as Gibbard argues:

> Stories about ideal coherence tell us where responses to piecemeal challenges could lead. Inferences that seem attractive one by one can be strung together to reach suspect conclusions. If we have some idea of what might be ideally coherent, that can guide our responses to piecemeal challenges.[10]

There are compelling reasons, then, for seeking broad coherence in ethics and resisting the strongly anti-theoretical stance favored by some philosophers.[11] Appeals to coherence in our sense give content to the intersubjective conception of ethical objectivity.

THE PROBLEMS OF INITIAL CREDIBILITY AND BIAS

We have achieved a preliminary understanding of what it would be to have a coherent set of ethical beliefs (and why we should care about coherence). But where do we start? Does one just take one's convictions as they are and then theorize and revise until they form a coherent set? Not exactly. As stressed by Rawls, we begin with a set of judgments that we have good reason to consider *reliable,* dropping judgments formed

---

[10]ibid, pp. 230–31
[11]See, e.g., Bernard Williams, *Ethics and the Limits of Philosophy* (Cambridge, MA: Harvard University Press, 1985); Rorty, *The Consequences of Pragmatism;* and Alasdaire MacIntyre, *After Virtue* (Notre Dame, IN: University of Notre Dame Press, 1981). For a collection of essays providing an overview, see Stanley G. Clarke and Evan Simpson (eds.), *Anti-Theory in Ethics and Moral Conservatism* (Albany, NY: SUNY Press, 1989).

in circumstances known to make judgments unreliable. Thus, we discount wavering judgments, ones formed in a rage or in a knee-jerk way, ones likely to be biased by self-interest, and so on. We begin with *considered judgments:* moral judgments about which we have great confidence upon reflection—that is, after scrutinizing them carefully, hearing counterarguments, checking for bias, and so on. As examples, Rawls mentions the judgments that racial discrimination and religious intolerance are unjust.[12]

But considered judgments are not immune to being revised or dropped. Starting with a set of considered judgments, one is to try to formulate principles that account for at least most of them. (Some considered judgments may themselves be principles.) One may find that a sturdy set of principles accounts for almost all of the original considered judgments, and that those not accounted for now seem less credible than the principles (in view of their support). In that case, the recalcitrant judgments may be dropped. Thus, our moral convictions are pruned in two ways: (1) our initial set includes only those judgments thought to be reasonably reliable, and (2) from that set judgments may be dropped that do not match principles formulated to account for most of them.[13]

A number of philosophers have been deeply dissatisfied with this proposal.[14] R. B. Brandt represents the dissatisfaction well. He asks why we should be impressed with the process just described, unless we have good reason to believe that "some of the beliefs are initially *credible*—and not merely initially believed—for some reason other than their coherence" within our system of ethical judgments.[15] Even if filtered in the two ways described, the fact remains, these critics charge, that the process begins with certain judgments that are just believed, and not justified in any further way. That a judgment is believed is not a reason

---

[12] *A Theory of Justice,* p. 19

[13] Tom Beauchamp asked me whether there is a problem of consistency, or coherence, among considered judgments themselves. If so, the problem would be very small. Considered judgments will rarely conflict because of criteria for what is to count as a considered judgment. They are to be unwavering, unlikely to be biased, and so on. If there are conflicts, one should strive to eliminate them by applying the criteria of coherence discussed above, dropping considered judgments that cohere least well with the total set. If it is ever really necessary to prune in this way, then this is a third way of pruning our moral convictions.

[14] See, e.g., R. M. Hare, "Rawls' Theory of Justice" (in two parts), *Philosophical Quarterly* 23 (1973): 144–55, 241–52; Peter Singer, "Sidgwick and Reflective Equilibrium," *Monist* 58 (1974): 490–517; R. B. Brandt, *A Theory of the Good and the Right* (Oxford: Clarendon, 1979), ch. 1; Joseph Raz, "The Claims of Reflective Equilibrium," *Inquiry* 25 (1982): 307–30; and David Copp, "Considered Judgments and Moral Justification: Conservatism in Moral Theory," in David Copp and David Zimmerman (eds.), *Morality, Reason and Truth* (Totowa, NJ: Rowman & Allanheld, 1985), pp. 141–68.

[15] *A Theory of the Good and the Right,* p. 18

to believe it. Rawls and his followers may claim to throw out unreliable judgments, these critics continue, but in the absence of any reason to believe the surviving ones, there is no justification for considering them reliable. As Daniels puts it, "Coherent fictions are still fictions, and we may only be reshuffling our prejudices."[16] In effect, the critics are challenging the assumption that the intuitive plausibility of a moral judgment counts in favor of accepting that judgment.

According to such critics, the situation is even worse for these "modern intuitionists" (coherence theorists) than for the old-fashioned intuitionists who claimed that we could perceive moral facts with a special moral faculty. Modern intuitionists think they are better off, for disavowing both epistemological claims about a faculty of intuition and metaphysical claims about moral facts to be perceived. But at least the old intuitionists provided a reason to believe the intuitions, which were taken to be true and foundational:

> With some pomp and circumstance, the earlier intuitionist at least outfitted his intuitions with the regal garb of epistemic priority, even if this later turned out to be the emperor's clothes. The modern intuitionist . . . allows his naked opinions to streak their way into our theories without benefit of any cover story.[17]

The coherence model assumes that our considered judgments have some initial credibility. Is there any basis for this assumption? Or are Rawls and company mistaken in holding that judgments formed in conditions thought to be conducive to reliability *are* really reliable?

Let me reframe the question by focusing on some judgments that are very plausible in their own right. Consider "Gratuitous torture is wrong," "Killing human beings for no reason is wrong," and "Rape is, in anything like normal circumstances, wrong." The qualifiers "gratuitous," "for no reason," and "in anything like . . ." sound defensive and may distract, so let me reformulate the moral ideas in a way that makes them virtually indubitable: "Torture is prima facie wrong," "Killing human beings is prima facie wrong," and "Rape is prima facie wrong." These considered judgments are far more credible, *in their own right,* than any moral theory. They have initial credibility. It would be easy to add others.

What is behind the critics' theoretical concern? How could one question the credibility of judgments like "Rape is prima facie wrong"? The critics believe that no moral judgments are really credible or justified unless part of, or derivable from, a moral foundation that can be known

---

[16] "Wide Reflective Equilibrium and Theory Acceptance in Ethics," p. 269. Daniels does not endorse this objection.
[17] ibid, p. 268. Daniels is paraphrasing the critics here.

with certainty. "You don't even know that rape is prima facie wrong," they might say, "unless you (or someone) can prove it!"—where "prove it" means provide rationally necessary foundations that justify the judgment. But the fact that none of these rationalist-deductivist critics has provided the foundations for which they are holding out takes some of the wind out of their critical sails. Rejection of their foundationalism makes it seem quite impossible that one could make "Rape is prima facie wrong" more credible by way of philosophical argument than it already is.

The difficulties of rationalism and deductivism strengthen the case for the coherence model. Indeed, they may seem to leave no alternative to taking our most reflectively plausible moral beliefs to be credible (even if, in principle, not immune from revision). But there is an alternative: One can always be a moral skeptic and deny that any moral judgment is credible or correct. Now, again, it is a premise of this book that moral skepticism is mistaken, a premise shared by all who engage in normative ethics. From this standpoint, considered judgments have initial credibility. (Indeed, the credibility of such judgments as "Rape is prima facie wrong" provides a powerful argument against skepticism.)

Nevertheless, legitimate worries remain. There are not terribly many general judgments that are virtually certain and therefore confidently counted as considered judgments. We want to be able to assert with confidence judgments that are less prima facie obvious. A theory about the moral status of animals should say more than "It is prima facie wrong to cause animals to suffer"! Can we show that some less-than-totally-obvious moral judgments have initial credibility?

We might expand our base of initial judgments beyond the virtually indubitable ones exemplified previously. Doing so would provide more material from which to build a theory. But as soon as we try to do so, the risk of infection from bias becomes significant. Most Americans, for example, probably think that there is a moral right to own property, but their belief may be the product of culture. Probably most persons believe that the harmful use of animals for good purposes is essentially unproblematic—the problems simply concerning the details of how much, in what circumstances, and in what ways. Yet a pro-human bias is very likely here. While Rawls rightly cautions us about bias, the task is to locate it.[18]

---

[18] Peter Carruthers' failure to take species bias seriously enough leads him, in my opinion, to use the coherence model incorrectly. He sometimes treats intuitions that are likely to be soaked with species bias (e.g., "our common-sense belief that human and animal lives cannot be weighed against one another") as if they were considered judgments (*The Animals Issue: Moral Theory in Practice* [Cambridge: Cambridge University Press, 1992], p. 9).

An adequate coherence model needs to deal with the problem of bias. On the assumption that moral skepticism is wrong, judgments that clearly qualify as considered judgments have substantial credibility in their own right. How might we show that a wider range of moral judgments are credible? Well, membership in a more-or-less coherent set of judgments that includes some clearly credible ones (these considered judgments) does, to some extent, increase a judgment's credibility; coherence in our sense includes argumentative support and other virtues, not mere consistency, so judgments in such a set tend to be mutually supporting. But this may offer limited assurance if there is good reason to believe that many judgments in the set are biased.[19] We need more of a story about our moral judgments taken together. This story is told well only if it is part of a larger story.

THE ROLE OF BACKGROUND THEORIES (OR THINKING)

The two most reknowned proponents of the coherence model, Rawls and Daniels, sometimes seem to concede that even considered judgments have limited initial credibility. The sort of pruning and adjusting process I described earlier affords only *narrow reflective equilibrium* (NRE), they would say. Much more credible are considered judgments in *wide reflective equilibrium* (WRE).[20] This is achieved when ethical judgments in NRE are in some way tested against various *conceptions* (Rawls' term for full-blown moral views) or background theories (a concept stressed by Daniels and explained in a moment). Purporting to develop Rawls' idea of WRE, Daniels wrote numerous articles that have greatly influenced the literature on coherence theorizing.[21] I doubt, however, that what Daniels developed was quite what Rawls had in mind or that it was ever perspicuously laid out. (Nor was Rawls very clear.) Unfortunately, much of the sympathetic follow-up literature

---

[19] Complicating matters is the fact that the likelihood of bias does not *entail* that a judgment is wrong. The judgment that one has special obligations to one's children is likely to be biased, given natural affections for one's own offspring, yet this judgment is almost certainly correct.

[20] See Daniels, "Wide Reflective Equilibrium and Theory Acceptance in Ethics," p. 258, note 4. Cf. Rawls, *A Theory of Justice,* p. 49, although here the distinction between NRE and WRE is only implicit. Rawls explicitly distinguishes them in "The Independence of Moral Theory," *Proceedings and Addresses of the American Philosophical Association 1974–75* 48 (1975), p. 8.

[21] See especially "Wide Reflective Equilibrium and Theory Acceptance in Ethics"; "Moral Theory and the Plasticity of Persons," *Monist* 62 (1979): 265–87; "Reflective Equilibrium and Archimedean Points," *Canadian Journal of Philosophy* 10 (1980): 83–103; "On Some Methods of Ethics and Linguistics," *Philosophical Studies* 37 (1980): 21–36; and "Two Approaches to Theory Acceptance in Ethics," in Copp and Zimmerman, *Morality, Reason, and Truth,* pp. 120–40.

seems to parrot Daniels and is just as obscure about what WRE amounts to and how it is supposed to improve upon NRE.[22]

Rather than recapitulate the Daniels-inspired WRE literature, I will briefly explain the importance of background theories, or thinking, in the coherence model. In an earlier section, it was noted that one of the theoretical virtues to be sought in this model is compatibility of our moral beliefs with whatever else we know or reasonably believe. Foundational moral theorists have often spoken of the relevance of the "facts" to ethics, but coherence theorists sometimes take what we know or reasonably believe as somewhat more theory-laden than the word *facts* might suggest. Background theories may be understood as those theories—nonmoral theories but perhaps also moral ones—that represent our best efforts in different areas of thought, providing us with whatever we know or reasonably believe besides our considered (moral) judgments. The basic picture picks up on Quine's idea that our beliefs form an enormous, interconnected whole, so that changes in one part of the system can have repercussions elsewhere in the system.[23] There are several ways in which background theories or thinking can affect our moral judgments—in a manner that helps to protect against bias, thereby adding credibility to those judgments.

First, focusing on nonmoral background theories or thinking— rather than blandly acknowledging the need to take "facts" into account—can help to identify and root out bias-infected empirical assumptions.[24] A vigorous awareness and exploration of nonmoral background thinking is paramount. For example, an ideological bias might encourage Americans to assume, uncritically, that a government-financed ("single-payer") health-care system would be less efficient than a market-driven system. But an examination of available evidence dramatically fails to support this assumption.[25] Assuming that one of

---

[22] See, e.g., Michael R. DePaul, "Reflective Equilibrium and Foundationalism," *American Philosophical Quarterly* 23 (1986): 59–69. Margaret Holmgren argues convincingly that the relationship between NRE and WRE has been systematically misunderstood ("The Wide and Narrow of Reflective Equilibrium," *Canadian Journal of Philosophy* 19 [1989]: 43–60).

[23] For a classic statement, see W. V. Quine, "Two Dogmas of Empiricism," *Philosophical Review* 60 (1951): 20–43.

[24] Kai Nielsen rightly stresses the importance of empirical background theories to the coherence model (*After the Demise of the Tradition*, chs. 9–11). For a more recent summary statement, see "Relativism and Wide Reflective Equilibrium," *The Monist* 76 (1993): 316–32.

[25] See, e.g., David U. Himmelstein and Steffie Woolhandler, "A National Health Program for the United States: A Physicians' Proposal," *New England Journal of Medicine* 320 (1989): 102–8; Robert G. Evans, Jonathan Lomas, Morris L. Barer et al., "Controlling Health Expenditures—the Canadian Reality," *New England Journal of*

the major moral goals of health-care reform is efficiency or cost containment, attention to nonmoral background theories (of health-care economics, for example), or even just an open-eyed look at empirical evidence, can make a difference in our moral reasoning about this issue.

Another advantage to vigorously engaging nonmoral background theories is that doing so may inspire us, in practice, to reconsider certain moral assumptions (which may be bias-infected). Conceptual components of feminist theory might change one's thinking about what constitutes respect and what counts as oppression. A philosophical theory of informed consent may alter one's view of when consent is meaningful. Empirical data in the psychological literature might better inform one of circumstances that now strike one as oppressive and problematic for meaningful consent. As a result of several shifts "in the background," one might reconsider one's assumption that there is nothing morally objectionable about men paying women to dance in the nude. As another example, information gathering and social-sciences theorizing might lead one to reexamine the assumed moral importance of the combatant–civilian distinction (especially when combatants are coerced by a dictator and surrender whenever given a chance), or of the distinction between all forms of "terrorism" and "legitimate state force" (especially when the former is used by those lacking power, and the latter is used to terrorize).

There is no clear line between nonmoral "correction," as we find in the example of health-care finance, and nonmoral thinking that inspires a reconsideration of moral assumptions, as in the last two examples. Moreover, the connection between nonmoral background theories and our moral judgments is as much psychological and practical as it is

Medicine 320 (1989): 571–77; John Iglehart, "The United States Looks at Canadian Health Care," *New England Journal of Medicine* 321 (1989): 1767–72; Milton J. Roemer, "Prudence in International Comparisons," *International Journal of Health Services* 21 (1991): 681–84; Richard J. Botelho, "Overcoming the Prejudice Against Establishing a National Health Care System," *Archives of Internal Medicine* 151 (1991): 863–69; Kevin Grumbach, Thomas Bodenheim, David U. Himmelstein, and Steffie Woolhandler, "Liberal Benefits, Conservative Spending," *JAMA* 265 (1991): 2549–54; Dan E. Beauchamp, "Universal Health Care, American Style: A Single Fund Approach to Health Care Reform," *Kennedy Institute of Ethics Journal* 2 (1992): 125–35; Marcia Angell, "How Much Will Health Care Reform Cost?", *New England Journal of Medicine* 328 (1993): 1778–79; and Jim McDermott, "The Case for a Single-Payer Approach," *JAMA* 271 (1994): 782–84. Impressively, the U.S. Congressional Budget Office, which can hardly be accused of ideological bias against the free market, concluded that a single-payer system in the U.S.A. could achieve universal coverage while saving billions of dollars annually in comparison with current spending (which leaves 37 to 39 million people uncovered). The CBO has judged no other plan submitted to Congress to be likely to save money while achieving universal coverage ("In Poor Health" [editorial], *The Nation* 259 [July 11, 1994]: 39–40).

logical. Such theories can be engaged to challenge our moral thinking in practice, ultimately affecting which moral judgments we consider worthy of systematizing. In doing so, they can help to root out biases that infect our moral convictions.

Here is one more example. Evolutionary theory, if taken to heart, might knock some of the metaphysical wind out of the conviction that humans are fundamentally and without exception—essentially!— different from nonhuman animals, a conviction that tends to underlie traditional moral beliefs about animals. Evolutionary theory does not *refute* the metaphysics, much less the ethics; it makes it more difficult to provide a convincing rationale for the traditional ethics, which seemed to fit so well with the idea of essential differences.[26]

Do *moral* background theories have any role in a well-developed coherence model? In practice, they might. Perhaps just as nonmoral components of, say, feminist theory can inspire revisions of belief, moral components of such theory should be even more likely to do so. But now suppose that an insight from such a theory is convincing enough to cause a revision in our moral beliefs. What is the difference between that insight's coming from a moral background theory and upsetting our moral beliefs, and that insight's simply being one of our moral judgments as we attempt to think broadly? If we bought some moral "background theory" wholesale, it would be our ethical theory, and we wouldn't need to worry about background theories. We do not buy any moral background theory wholesale. If such a theory has anything to offer, we will find some of its judgments compelling, on reflection.

The important point is that we should simply think as broadly as possible (striving for theoretical power and global illumination) when identifying and working with considered judgments—and imagine utilitarian, Kantian, feminist, socialist, "Billbuckleyan," and other interlocuters presenting their best moral arguments. Some of those arguments will persuade us, and some will not.[27] This preserves the point of moral background theories.

The combination of these moral and nonmoral challenges to our thinking should go a long way toward eliminating previously undetected biases, thereby increasing the credibility of a more-or-less coherent set of beliefs that contains considered judgments. But fully meeting the problem of bias requires additional work.

---

[26] This argument is powerfully developed in James Rachels, *Created from Animals: The Moral Implications of Darwinism* (Oxford: Oxford University Press, 1990).
[27] There is no need to restrict the set of imagined interlocuters. Unreasonable ones will not spoil the process, because their arguments won't be convincing.

ADDRESSING THE REMAINING CONCERN
ABOUT BIAS

Universalizability or impartiality: Initial pros and cons

In view of our interest in ensuring sufficient critical edge and protection against bias, it is important to see that a system of beliefs in reflective equilibrium would include a principle of universalizability or impartiality, suitably interpreted. Acknowledging such a principle hardly suggests a deductivist model in which all correct moral judgments are to flow from this principle. Indeed, the notion I have in mind is too formal to serve as the foundation for a moral theory. Yet appeals to *universalizability* or *impartiality* (I will use the terms interchangeably) can offer enough critical force to play an important role in theory formation. Moral judgments that we are inclined to make—even considered judgments—may be challenged by the apparent implications of universalizability (and vice versa). In Chapter 3, a precise formulation of universalizability will be necessary. For now, an informal characterization in the context of a preliminary defense will be more useful.

The familiar idea that in ethics we should try to be impartial, much as we expect a judge to be impartial, is arguably itself a considered judgment. Traditionally, most moral theorists have held that the moral point of view itself involves impartiality. Utilitarians have held this view, as have Kantians. Many less traditional theorists, such as Baier and Gert, have as well.[28] Even Rawls, who bucked tradition with the coherence theory, believes that his method vindicates the use of a contract heuristic designed to achieve impartiality. For all of these theorists, to say a moral judgment is partial is tantamount to saying it is prejudiced. In morality, they think, we aspire to make judgments that are, in some way, universally valid. There is something right about this contention, but it requires defense, especially when our coherence model rejects so many other features common to traditional theories.

Consider a related reason to take impartiality seriously. As a social phenomenon, morality involves the practices of moral justification, and justification requires some significant agreement on standards, so that people do not just talk past each other. An action or judgment is considered justified if, among other things, it is backed by reasons that are recognized as good reasons—not just by the agent but by agents generally. Thus, the practices of moral justification suggest an impartial standpoint. The most adequate justification counts as a justification from everyone's perspective, not just one's own; the justifying reasons

---

[28] Kurt Baier, *The Moral Point of View* (Ithaca, NY: Cornell University Press, 1958); Bernard Gert, *Morality: A New Justification of the Moral Rules* (New York: Oxford University Press, 1988)

could be accepted from any point of view. (Of course, by "everyone" I mean everyone who is morally serious and committed to achieving a coherent ethical view.) In this sense, partiality—say, giving Fred a supposedly merit-based award because he is your neighbor—amounts to a failure to achieve the sort of social validity sought in morality. That is not to say that certain forms of partiality—such as giving special attention to your own family—could not be accepted from everyone's point of view (more on this later), but we now have a second argument for including a principle of universalizability within the coherence model.

Such a principle is important for animal ethics. Some have charged that common attitudes about animals amount to *speciesism,* unjustified discrimination against animals. Appeals to universalizability could help to root out such a bias, if that is what common attitudes toward animals represent; if not, then the sort of partiality that humans tend to feel for other humans could receive validation from an impartial (intersubjective) standpoint.

Recently, the idea that impartiality or universalizability is essential to morality, or even morally desirable, has faced vigorous challenges. Casuistry (a kind of case-based reasoning in historical context), the ethics of care, feminist ethics, virtue ethics, and various forms of historicism and anti-theory in ethics have all challenged the idea of a universal perspective in ethics. The relevant literature is rich, complex, and diverse. I will sketch a few leading ideas, just enough to clarify the challenges.[29]

One challenge to impartiality is the claim that (1) no rational foundation for such a moral perspective has been, or is likely to be, discovered.[30] More strongly, one might argue that (2) the ideal of impartiality is not a coherent notion, that there is no "view from nowhere." A third challenge stems largely from the work of Carol Gilligan and the vast literature it has inspired: (3) Impartiality is a moral perspective that tends to characterize the thinking of males; but a more contextualized, care-based approach is very common among females, and there is no good reason to think it less valid.[31] Another comes from casuists, classi-

---

[29] In addition to the sources cited in the footnotes that follow, I draw broadly from Jonsen and Toulmin, *The Abuse of Casuistry;* Williams, *Ethics and the Limits of Philosophy;* MacIntyre, *After Virtue;* Annette Baier, *Postures of the Mind* (Minneapolis, MN: University of Minnesota Press, 1985); Mary Jeanne Larrabee (ed.), *An Ethic of Care: Feminist and Interdisciplinary Perspectives* (New York: Routledge, 1993); Eva Feder Kittay and Diana T. Meyers (eds.), *Women and Moral Theory* (New York: Rowman & Littlefield, 1987); and Helen Bequaert Holmes and Laura M. Purdy (eds.), *Feminist Perspectives in Medical Ethics* (Bloomington, IN: Indiana University Press, 1992).
[30] See, e.g., MacIntyre, *After Virtue,* chs. 4 and 5.
[31] See Carol Gilligan, *In a Different Voice* (Cambridge, MA: Harvard University Press,

cal pragmatists, and feminists: (4) A principle of impartiality or universalizability is almost useless for lack of content and remoteness from concrete problems; ethics must be contextualized and detailed. This challenge comes from diverse camps, including Ross and the feminists: (5) Much of the moral life flows from special relationships (such as parent-to-child, friend-to-friend, and doctor-to-patient), which ground actions and attitudes that can only be described as partial. The following challenge is found in much of the literature on ethical issues involving race and gender: (6) Impartiality is excessively abstract insofar as it erases some morally salient experiences, such as being gendered or being a minority. A final challenge is common in the ethics of care and virtue ethics literature: (7) Impartialist perspectives typically fail to account for affective components of moral action, most importantly (a) the moral sensibilities (such as attunement) that are needed to bring general norms appropriately to bear in complex and delicate situations, and (b) the expressive qualities that are integral to appropriate behavior within personal relationships (such as showing that you care in the way you give condolences).[32] These are, I think, the strongest arguments against impartiality in ethics.

Retaining a modest notion of impartiality

I believe that the collective force of the foregoing seven arguments is considerable. Nevertheless, I contend that numerous critics advancing these arguments have underestimated the compatibility between the "partialist" perspectives that they favor and the "impartialist" ones that they criticize. Also, I think some of the criticisms miss the mark. Let me respond to each challenge.

I agree with challenge (1). Rationalism has not delivered a metaethical foundation for an impartialist perspective. I doubt it will. That doesn't mean that discursive, suggestive arguments within the methods of reflective equilibrium cannot vindicate impartiality—especially if it is taken not as some sort of complete moral foundation but rather as an important critical tool. Indeed, I am advancing such arguments. As for challenge (2), *perhaps* perfect impartiality, a view from nowhere that makes no reference to the contingencies of human existence, is inco-

---

1982). For diverse discussions of this thesis, see essays in Larrabee, *An Ethic of Care*, and in Kittay and Meyers, *Women and Moral Theory*. For an excellent effort to develop and clarify the ethics of care, see Jeffrey Blustein, *Care and Commitment* (New York: Oxford University Press, 1991).
[32]See Lawrence A. Blum, "Gilligan and Kohlberg: Implications for Moral Theory," in Larrabee, *An Ethic of Care*, pp. 59–61.

herent. But we are after nothing so rigorous; the relevant sense of impartiality appeals to intersubjectivity. Furthermore, we can acknowledge even toned-down impartiality as an ideal that may be very difficult or impossible to achieve fully in practice, yet worth pursuing as
best we can.

As a psychological thesis, maybe impartiality is more typically respected by males, whereas females tend somewhat more to think in
terms of caring relationships. (Actually, there is a vigorous debate over
the nature and epistemic status of the available data, but it need not
concern us here.[33]) The important point is that the highly suggestive
findings of Gilligan in challenge (3) (let us assume that they are not
wildly off the mark) give good reason not to denigrate the care perspective. But the use I propose for impartiality does not suggest that the care
perspective is invalid, just that it is insufficient. Owen Flanagan and
Kathryn Jackson plausibly say this about the case of the husband who
cannot afford medication for his critically ill wife and whose pharmacist
will not give it away free: "*Heinz,* after all, should steal the drug because
it is *his* wife [caring partiality]; and his wife should get the drug because
any human life is more important than any avaricious pharmacist's
desire to make some extra money [impartiality]."[34]

These points also help with challenge (4). It is worth emphasizing
how important detail and context are to normative ethics. Still, theory—
and, I argue, impartiality—are also needed, and impartiality and rich
contextualization do not exclude each other.

According to challenge (5), certain special relationships justify partiality. For example, a parent not only may, but should, pay far more
attention to his or her own children than to other children. But partiality
in action and deliberation is often compatible with impartiality at the
level of ultimate justification. Whether the obligations that flow from
the parent–child relationship are ultimate (as Ross contends), or
grounded in something more basic (as the utilitarian holds), certain
forms of partiality can be regarded as impartially valid. *Any* parent—
absent special circumstances, such as giving up a child for adoption—
should regard the child as demanding his or her special care and attention.[35] (The compatibility of partiality in practice and impartiality at a
theoretical level will prove important in Chapter 3.)

[33] See, e.g., Larrabee, *An Ethic of Care,* esp. Part III and Carol Gilligan, "Reply to
Critics", pp. 207–14.
[34] "Justice, Care, and Gender: The Kohlberg–Gilligan Debate Revisited," in Larrabee,
An Ethic of Care, p. 74
[35] George Sher, "Other Voices, Other Rooms?: Women's Psychology and Moral Theory," in Kittay and Meyers, *Women and Moral Theory,* p. 186. For an excellent effort to
reconcile partiality and impartiality, see Christina Hoff Sommers, "Filial Morality,"
in Kittay and Meyers, *Women and Moral Theory,* pp. 69–84.

Challenge (6) states that impartiality is too abstract insofar as it erases morally salient experiences, like being a minority. But this is no criticism of impartiality per se, just of some impartialist perspectives that overlook such experiences. A plausible impartialist ethics will recognize the salience of salient relationships, but, given global illumination, it will do so in a way that explains why some experiences are salient in certain contexts whereas others are not. For example, that someone is a black American may call for special sensitivity in discussing with her recent research on the relationship between race and intelligence (even in the context of debunking such research). On the other hand, that I am white does not automatically disqualify my opinions on affirmative action. A good theory will illuminate these points.

As for challenge (7), even if impartialist perspectives typically fail to account for the affective components of moral action, there is no reason why they must fail in this way. Perhaps they cannot account for these affective components *by appeal to impartiality*. If so, an independent discussion of moral sensibilities would be required.

The general need, in justification or theorizing, for more gritty tools than abstract principles or impartial reasoning explains why I favor a coherence theory that gives impartiality its due, rather than a deductivist theory that purports to flow out of impartiality alone. To deny that impartiality has any place in ethics seems odd at best and very possibly incoherent.[36]

I believe that appeals to universalizability can help to provide the sort of critical edge that is lacking in contemporary casuistry and at least most other forms of inductivism, while avoiding the relativism and irrationalism that threatens overly contextualized feminist approaches.[37] This critical edge cuts against the bias (unjustified partiality) of some of the judgments that we might be inclined to affirm. If such judgments are tainted by an unnoticed nationalistic, ideological, or even "speciesist" bias, appeal to universalizability can help to detect it.

In conclusion, the coherence model can provide reasonable checks against bias, as this book as a whole should demonstrate.

---

[36] Although feminism has inspired many critics of impartiality, a number of feminist writers have argued in favor of retaining impartiality. See Laura M. Purdy, "A Call to Heal Ethics," in Holmes and Purdy, *Feminist Perspectives in Medical Ethics,* p. 11; Susan Sherwin, "Feminist and Medical Ethics: Two Different Approaches to Contextual Ethics," ibid, p. 24; and Virginia Held, "Feminism and Moral Theory," in Kittay and Meyers, *Women and Moral Theory,* pp. 119–20.

[37] For a highly insightful, constructive critique of some recent feminist philosophy, see Martha Nussbaum, "Feminists and Philosophy," *New York Review of Books* (October 20, 1994): 59–63.

SPECIFICATION AS A USEFUL METHOD IN THE COHERENCE MODEL

The method of specification

A method that has received some recent attention in the literature, and that will prove useful in our coherence model, is *specification*. (A method that is in a sense the opposite of specification—call it "abstraction"— involves the inferring of general norms from analysis of particular cases. I will not elaborate on this more familiar, inductive method here.) Specification has, I think, been used in much work in practical ethics, but an article by Henry Richardson brought it into theoretical prominence.[38] The essay's first sentences indicate that this method is intended as a way forward once we have seen the shortcomings of deductivism and of intuitive balancing in conflicts:

> Starting from an initial set of ethical norms, how can we resolve concrete ethical problems? We may try to *apply* the norms to the case, and if they conflict we may attempt to *balance* them intuitively. The aim of this paper is to show that a third, more effective alternative is to *specify* the norms.[39]

Let us turn now to a case that Richardson uses to illustrate his thesis.

Consider this seemingly reasonable initial norm and the uncertain conclusion to which it leads: (1) It is wrong for lawyers not to pursue their clients' interests by all lawful means; and (2) in this case of defending an accused rapist, it would lawfully promote the client's interest to cross-examine the victim about her sex life in such a way as to make sexist jurists think that she consented; therefore, (3) it would be wrong not to cross-examine the victim in this way. A different, equally plausible norm leads to a conflicting conclusion: (4) It is wrong to defame someone's character by knowingly distorting her public reputation; and (5) to cross-examine the victim about her sex life in such a way as to make sexist jurists think she consented would be to defame her character by knowingly distorting her public reputation; therefore, (6) it would be wrong to cross-examine the victim in this way. How can the dilemma be resolved, since applying both norms would be contradictory, and intuitive balancing would leave the conclusion without argumentative support?

---

[38] Henry S. Richardson, "Specifying Norms as a Way to Resolve Concrete Ethical Problems," *Philosophy and Public Affairs* 19 (1990): 279–310. I discuss the importance of this method to bioethics in "Moving Forward in Bioethical Theory: Theories, Cases, and Specified Principlism," *The Journal of Medicine and Philosophy* 17 (1992): 511–39. In the present section, I draw from this article.
[39] "Specifying Norms," p. 279

Richardson's suggestion is to tailor one of the norms to make it more specific. For example, (1) might be replaced with (1'): It is wrong for lawyers not to pursue their clients' interests by all means that are *both* lawful *and ethical*. This amendment by itself does not settle the conflict, but it motivates a reexamination of the scope of (4). While attacking a witness's character is common practice among lawyers, perhaps a rape victim needs special protections for her allegations. So we might replace (4) with (4'): It is always wrong to defame *a rape victim's* character by knowingly distorting her public reputation. With the specifications expressed in (1') and (4'), the conflict seems to be settled.[40] Specified norms, such as (1') and (4'), need not be absolute; they may be qualified by "generally" or "for the most part." And they are subject to future revision.[41]

How are particular specifications justified? Richardson rightly criticizes the model of intuitive balancing for forfeiting any claim to discursive justification or argumentative support.[42] How does specification do any better? Other specifications were possible in the case about the rape victim. If all we can say is that we made the intuitively most attractive specification, it is unclear how that is better than—or even different from—intuitive balancing of conflicting norms.

The answer is to hook the method of specification right into the coherence model, which affords the possibility of reasoned criticism.[43] As a concluding remark, Richardson summarily notes that specification

benefits from a considerable degree of casuistical flexibility without sacrificing a potentially intimate tie to guiding theories; and it is able to proceed from norms looser and hence more acceptable than the completely universal ones required by the deductivist to reach a conclusion through a [formal] syllogism.[44]

Interestingly, the coherence model incorporates casuistry or case analysis even in specifying norms, because case analysis—underdetermined by general principles that are already accepted—is a large part of the theoretical engine. But by making use of and specifying general principles and rules that are interconnected within a larger system, the present model avoids the anti-theoretical excess that mars much of contemporary casuistry.

[40] ibid, pp. 281–83
[41] ibid, pp. 294–95
[42] ibid, pp. 285–87
[43] ibid, p. 299
[44] ibid, p. 308

Some comments about the method

Let us back up and ask what the advantages of specification amount to, if anything. Richardson criticizes intuitive balancing and judgment, associating this approach with the work of Ross and many contemporary bioethicists. But why couldn't a sophisticated intuitionist recommend the method of intuitive balancing *within a coherence model*? If ultimately it is appeals to coherence (in our broad sense) that justify particular specifications, why couldn't one similarly justify particular intuitive balancings in terms of coherence? Indeed, what is the difference?[45]

One difference is that *intuitive* balancing does not appeal to background considerations of coherence. The balancing act—say, favoring autonomy over beneficence in a particular conflict—is justified by appeal to its intuitive plausibility. The problem here is lack of discursive justification; the appeal is inarticulate, failing to provide reasons where reasons are needed as material for reasonable discussion. It is true that, at some point, justificatory reasons run out, but they should not run out so soon; otherwise, one's theory threatens to be almost completely ad hoc. One tries to apply certain norms, but whenever there is a conflict—that is, nearly whenever there is need for serious ethical reflection—one favors whichever norm seems weightier in the circumstances and offers no further reason! This common approach fails to live up to the theoretical virtue of argumentative support.

On the other hand, there is no logical bar to using balancing within a coherence model. Rather than appealing to the intuitive plausibility of a particular balancing, one would appeal to the superior overall coherence of the resulting set of norms. Indeed, in a certain formal sense, this approach is the same as specification within a coherence model. Because it relies for justification on background considerations of coherence, the model requires that particular balancings be made for reasons. But any balancing plus supporting reason is equivalent to a specification. For example, suppose that one balances "Keep patients from unnecessary harm" and "Seek competent adult patients' informed consent before performing medical interventions" in favor of the former in emergencies—the reason being that one can reasonably presume consent. That is tantamount to this specification: "Seek competent adult patients' informed consent before performing medical interventions when you cannot reasonably presume consent."

---

[45]Some of these questions were pressed on me by Jim Childress and Tom Beauchamp in conversation. What follows is my response to these questions and to our differences, as noted in Beauchamp and Childress, *Principles of Biomedical Ethics*, 4th ed. (New York: Oxford University Press, 1994), p. 34.

While in a certain formal sense specification and balancing are the same if each is embedded in a coherence model, there are at least three reasons for thinking in terms of specification. (1) Specification *avoids potentially confusing associations* with old-fashioned intuitive balancing. (2) It *produces something to use in the future*: a more specific norm that, while subject to future revision, is found useful in a certain kind of case. Biomedical ethics has thrived on further and further refinements (specifications) of general norms; consider case law and the related bioethics literature on withdrawing treatment. Specifications, in effect, *make explicit* the reasons that could enlighten particular balancings within a coherence model. (3) Specifications can often *preserve and even clarify the point of the norm specified*. The point of the doctrine of informed consent, for example, is not to provide an arbitrary imposition on the work of health professionals. It is to ensure that competent adult patients consent (or would consent) to medical treatment given to them. The specification "Seek . . . when you cannot reasonably presume consent" preserves and even clarifies this point. Thus, used rightly, specification often draws out the moral content of general norms. Balancing does not do this in any clear way.

Enough about method. Let us turn to normative ethics.

Chapter 3

Animals' moral status and the issue of equal consideration[1]

INTRODUCTION

How are we to understand the moral status of animals? Are animals due any moral consideration at all? If not, why not? If so, do animals deserve consideration simply because of the way our treatment of animals affects *us humans*? Or is it because animals' interests have moral importance *in their own right*? If animals' interests matter in their own right, how much do they matter? Should they be given as much consideration as human interests? If so, what does that mean, exactly? What would such equal consideration amount to? And if not, in what ways— or how much—do animals' interests matter?

Sometimes importantly different questions regarding the moral status of animals are not clearly enough distinguished. Failure to distinguish different questions often leads to misunderstanding of opponents' arguments and then to proud refutations of views no one holds. (For example, the medical literature contains numerous arguments against the view that animals—sometimes, *all* animals—and humans are alike in *every* morally significant respect.[2] But no one, to my

---

[1] In a few places in this chapter, I draw from ideas published in my "Equal Consideration and Unequal Moral Status," *Southern Journal of Philosophy* 31 (1993): 17–31.
[2] For example, in an article much praised by the medical community but severely criticized by philosophers, Carl Cohen writes that

> [t]he first error is the assumption, often explicitly defended, that all sentient animals have equal moral standing. Between a dog and a human being, according to this view, *there is no moral difference*. . . . ("The Case for the Use of Animals in Biomedical Research," *New England Journal of Medicine* 315 [1986], p. 867) (italics added).

Cohen also claims the following:

> If all forms of animate life—or vertebrate animal life?—must be treated equally, and if therefore in evaluating a research program the pains of a rodent

knowledge, holds that view.) For the sake of clarity, the basic questions asked in the previous paragraph may be broken down somewhat more formally as follows:

1. Does the treatment of animals raise ethical issues at all?
2. If not, why not?
   3. If so, do animals' interests matter in their own right?
   4. If not, why not? How should we treat them, and why?
      5. If so, should the interests of animals be given moral weight equal to that given to relevantly similar human interests?
      6. If not, why not? How much consideration should animals' interests be given, and why?
      7. If so, what does such equal consideration amount to?

A few concepts are worth introducing here. While probably most people in our society would answer question 1 affirmatively, at least on reflection, those who would not would take the view of *absolute dismissal*.[3] Among persons who think animals raise ethical issues, those who believe animals' interests have moral importance independently of human interests confer some degree of *moral status* on animals (at least, as I use the term). To believe animals' interests matter so much that they should be given moral weight equal to that given to our relevantly similar interests is to subscribe to some *principle of equal consideration* that extends to animals. I will sometimes speak of "equal consideration" or "equal consideration for animals" as elliptical for such mouthfuls as "consideration for animals' interests that is equal to that given to relevantly similar human interests."

Equal consideration (at least as construed here) is not what many people take it to be. I believe the present construal is faithful to what scholars in animal ethics have meant by the term, but they have generally left it without explicit analysis. As we will see, giving as much moral weight to animals' interests as we give to relevantly similar human interests does *not* entail (1) identical rights for humans and animals, (2) a moral requirement to treat humans and animals equally, or (3) the absence of any morally interesting differences between animals

count equally with the pains of a human, we are forced to conclude (1) that neither humans nor rodents possess rights, or (2) that rodents possess all the rights that humans possess (ibid).

That Cohen conflates numerous issues will soon be apparent. For a brief discussion of deficiencies in Cohen's arguments, see my "The Moral Status of Animals and Their Use in Research: A Philosophical Review," *Kennedy Institute of Ethics Journal* 1 (1991), pp. 61–62.

[3] For a good discussion of this position and its problems, see Mary Midgley, *Animals and Why They Matter* (Athens, GA: University of Georgia Press, 1983), ch. 4.

and humans.[4] (This should not be surprising. Equal consideration for humans does not entail, for example, identical rights; adults have some capacities and interests that ground rights—such as the right to refuse medical treatment—that young children do not have.) Moreover, equal consideration is a very rough working notion that can be interpreted in various ways.

Nevertheless, the issue of equal consideration *may* be the most crucial in animal ethics. To be sure, the issue of animals' basic moral status—the question of whether animals' interests matter in their own right—is extremely important to animal ethics, and a sizable part of this chapter is devoted to it. As with the issue of moral status, a great deal normatively turns on the issue of equal consideration (on any plausible interpretation of this idea). But the equal-consideration issue, as we will see, is much more difficult to settle than the moral-status question. If, in the end, equal consideration *is* to be granted to animals, then many common attitudes about animals—and at least most of our animal-exploiting practices—are wrong. Thus, resolution of this issue is potentially revolutionary. One would think, then, that the philosophical literature would be packed with in-depth explorations of equal consideration. But one finds, in fact, very few sustained discussions of this issue. Singer's *Animal Liberation*, for example, contains little argument for extending the principle to animals, beyond claiming that there is no good reason to restrict it to humans, and that to do so is analogous to racism and sexism.[5]

In this chapter, a preliminary set of arguments gets animals "in the door," by establishing that animals' interests matter, and in their own right. (Which animals have interests cannot be determined without further empirical and philosophical work.) After the notion of equal consideration is sufficiently clarified, another set of arguments establishes a presumption in favor of equal consideration, such that those opposing the extension of this principle to animals shoulder a burden of proof. Five major attempts to carry this burden are carefully considered and defeated, supporting the conclusion that equal consideration should extend to animals. But what exactly this amounts to requires a good deal of work in value theory (and therefore the philosophy of mind) and, of course, ethical theory—at least some of which is done in the remaining chapters of this book.

---

[4] Cf. Peter Singer, *Animal Liberation*, 2d ed. (New York: New York Review, 1990), pp. 2, 5.
[5] ibid, p. 5

GETTING ANIMALS "IN THE DOOR"

Animals as having interests; ethics as concerning interests

Why believe that animals raise ethical issues at all? What's wrong with absolute dismissal of animals? One short answer is that animals have interests, and ethics is centrally concerned with interests, so that, prima facie, it would seem that ethics should be concerned with animals. While this argument is meant only to be suggestive, some might not even find it that. Assuming they are not simply in the grip of a powerful bias against animals, they probably fail to recognize the place of interests in ethics or misunderstand the relevant conception of interests.

Interests (or, collectively, welfare or well-being) form a large part of the subject matter of ethics. Ethical systems generally, to some degree, protect or even promote individuals' interests, at least their most important ones. Rights theories protect one's interest in life, self-determination, physical security, and the like. Utilitarianism regards one's interest, or welfare, as counting equally within the overall good to be promoted. Even theories that take the ultimate reason for ethical action to be the agent's self-realization or growth are unlikely to be considered ethical theories unless the actions that they require are generally respectful of others' most important interests.

But what is meant by "interests"? For now we need only a rough conception. Two common expressions are that someone *has* an interest in something and that something *is in* someone's interests. One is generally understood to have an interest in something (say, getting a job) if one wants, desires, prefers, or cares about—that is, takes an interest in—that thing. And something (such as food) is ordinarily understood to be in someone's interest if that thing has, or might have, a positive effect on that individual's good, welfare, or well-being. Following Regan, we might call these two general types of interests *preference interests* and *welfare interests,* respectively.[6] For those who see an individual's welfare as closely tied to the satisfaction of her preferences or desires, these two kinds of interests are very close. For, on that assumption, even if one does not actually prefer what is in one's interest (say, getting enough sleep), one should—because what is in one's interest generally satisfies the bulk of one's preferences (even if not every one of them). It will be convenient to use the general term *interests* to cover both sorts of interests, and to speak of *having interests* in the case of either sort, not just for preference interests.

[6] Tom Regan, *The Case for Animal Rights* (Berkeley: University of California Press, 1983), pp. 87–88

Animals have interests. By saying this, I do not mean that every member of the animal kingdom from humans to protozoa have interests, but that many animals, at least sentient ones, do. Later chapters will take on such issues as what sentience is and which animals may reasonably be considered sentient. For now, we may content ourselves with the claim that animals who have desires, preferences, or concerns, or who are capable of suffering and enjoyment, have interests. Ordinarily, at least mammals and birds are thought to have such mental life (although we will examine evidence for this supposition only later). Since ethics concerns interests, which animals have, it would seem, prima facie, that the treatment of animals is part of the subject matter of ethics.

REFLECTIONS ON SOME THOUGHT-EXPERIMENTS

Reflections on some thought-experiments should add enough force to the foregoing argument to give us a compelling case not only that animals raise ethical issues but that their interests matter in their own right—that is, that animals have moral status. Consider a passage from *Crime and Punishment*:

> With the cry of "now," the mare tugged with all her might, but far from galloping, could scarcely move forward; she struggled with her legs, gasping and shrinking from the blows of the three whips which showered upon her like hail. The laughter in the cart and in the crowd was redoubled, but Mikolka flew into a rage and furiously thrashed the mare, as though he supposed she really could gallop.
>
> "Let me get in, too, mates," shouted a young man in the crowd whose appetite was aroused.
>
> "Get in, all get in," cried Mikolka, "she will draw you all. I'll beat her to death!" And he thrashed and thrashed at the mare, beside himself with fury. . . .
>
> All at once laughter broke into a roar and covered everything: the mare, roused by the shower of blows, began feebly kicking. . . .
>
> Two lads in the crowd snatched up whips and ran to the mare to beat her about the ribs. . . .
>
> . . . He ran beside the mare, ran in front of her, saw her being whipped across the eyes, right in the eyes! . . . She was almost at the last gasp, but began kicking once more.
>
> "I'll teach you to kick," Mikolka shouted ferociously. He threw down the whip, bent forward and picked up from the bottom of the cart a long, thick shaft, he took hold of one end with both hands and with an effort brandished it over the mare. . . .
>
> And Mikolka swung the shaft a second time and it fell a second time on the spine of the luckless mare. She sank back on her haunches, but lurched forward and tugged forward with all her force, tugged first on

one side and then on the other, trying to move the cart. But the six whips were attacking her in all directions, and the shaft was raised again and fell upon her a third time, and then a fourth, with heavy measured blows. . . .

"I'll show you! Stand off," Mikolka screamed frantically; he threw down the shaft, stopped down in the cart and picked up an iron crowbar. "Look out," he shouted, and with all his might he dealt a stunning blow at the poor mare. The blow fell; the mare staggered, sank back, tried to pull, but the bar fell again with a swinging blow on her back and she fell on the ground like a log.

"Finish her off," shouted Mikolka and he leapt, beside himself, out of the cart. Several young men, also flushed with drink, seized anything they could come across—whips, sticks, poles—and ran to the dying mare. Mikolka stood on one side and began dealing random blows with the crowbar. The mare stretched out her head, drew a long breath, and died.[7]

In a testy response to a series of articles on animal ethics run by the *Hastings Center Report*, Robert White, a neurosurgeon, asserts that "[a]nimal usage is not a moral or ethical issue. . . . "[8] *If such absolute dismissal is correct, then none of the actions described in the foregoing passage raises any ethical issues whatsoever.* It is difficult to imagine a less plausible position.

Our treatment of animals raises ethical issues. But perhaps that is only because of the effects of such treatment on *us*. Kant thought so, maintaining what is today called the *indirect duty view*. On this view, we have duties regarding our treatment of animals, but such duties derive from, and are entirely dependent on, certain duties we have to humans, the sole possessors of moral status. For Kant, we should avoid cruelty to animals simply because cruelty to them is likely to foster character traits in the agent that make her *more likely to mistreat humans*.[9] Put another way, we have indirect duties to animals based on direct duties to humans. Another indirect view (another way to deny moral status to animals without absolute dismissal) is to argue that our treatment of animals demonstrates, or perhaps shapes, our *moral character*—and that this is a sufficient reason to treat them well. It is virtuous to be kind, vicious to be cruel, one might say.

[7] Fyodor Dostoevski, *Crime and Punishment*, trans. Constance Garnett (New York: Bantam Classics, 1982), pp. 50–52
[8] *Hastings Center Report* 20 (November–December 1990), Letters: 43. The series of articles was "Animals, Science, and Ethics," *Hastings Center Report* (May–June 1990), Special Supplement: 1–32. For a rebuttal to White, see my letter, *Hastings Center Report* 21 (September–October 1991): 45.
[9] Immanuel Kant, *Lectures on Ethics*, trans. Louis Infield (New York: Harper and Row, 1963), p. 239

Indirect views do not hold up under careful scrutiny. Robert Nozick challenges such views in the following way:

> Some say people should not do so because such acts brutalize them and make them more likely to take the lives of [we can add "or otherwise harm"] *persons*, solely for pleasure. These acts that are morally unobjectionable in themselves, they say, have an undesirable moral spillover. (Things then would be different if there were no possibility of such spillover—for example, for the person who knows himself to be the last person on earth.) But why *should* there be such spillover? If it is, in itself, perfectly all right to do anything at all to animals for any reason whatsoever, then provided a person realizes the clear line between animals and persons and keeps it in mind as he acts, why should killing animals tend to brutalize him and make him more likely to harm or kill persons? Do butchers commit more murders? (Than other persons who have knives around?) If I enjoy hitting a baseball squarely with a bat, does this significantly increase the danger of my doing the same to someone's head? Am I not capable of understanding that people differ from baseballs, and doesn't this understanding stop the spillover? Why should things be different in the case of animals? To be sure, it is an empirical question whether spillover does take place or not; but there is a puzzle as to why it should.[10]

Nozick asks why we should assume there would a spillover of the kind assumed by indirect theories. He also implies that pulverizing animals for no morally weighty reason would seem wrong even if spillover were impossible. Imagine that Mikolka were the only one abusing the horse and were the last person on Earth—or were himself about to die and predictably would not come into contact with other humans. It is absurd to say that in either of these circumstances abusing the animal would not be wrong.

Our certainty that abusing animals is wrong is very great; we think ourselves perfectly justified in believing this considered judgment. Yet any putative empirical connection between such actions and harmful acts to other persons would be an unsure basis for asserting the wrongness of abusing animals. We cannot claim to have compelling evidence for such a connection; even if we did, the connection would admit of exceptions (say, when spillover was impossible), but the wrongness of such behavior would not. Indeed, sometimes abusing animals might lead to a *positive* spillover for humans, removing any claim that the wrongness of the abuse reduces to its effects on humans. A shepherd might convince us that he treats people better when he is permitted to work off his ill temper by beating up his dogs.[11]

[10] *Anarchy, State, and Utopia* (New York: Basic Books, 1974), p. 36
[11] Midgley, *Animals and Why They Matter*, p. 52

As noted earlier, the indirect-duty theorist may base her argument on considerations of character or virtue, arguing that cruelty to animals is wrong because it manifests a bad character. But while cruelty to animals does manifest a bad character, this consideration does not fully account for the wrongness of such cruelty. First, actions such as Mikolka's seem wrong, at least in part, because of what they do to the animal; the animal impresses us as a being who is wrongfully harmed, not simply a practicing ground for virtue. It might be responded that, although virtuous agents act compassionately and avoid cruelty toward animals for the sake of animals (with animals, not character, in mind), the ultimate ground of the relevant duties is virtue.[12] In my view, this reply does not adequately account for the conviction that the animals themselves are wronged. But, more decisively, the present position leaves entirely unexplained *why* cruelty to animals is a vice and compassion to them a virtue—if, as the position assumes, animals lack moral status and therefore cannot be directly wronged. If a horse has no more moral status than a newspaper, why should butchering a horse for fun reveal a defect in character any more than does tearing up a newspaper for fun? (We have already found inadequate the appeal to spillover effects.) The only viable account of cruelty acknowledges the moral status of its victims.

Moral agents have direct duties to animals. Animals' interests matter in their own right, which is to say some animals have some degree of moral status. (From now on, "animals" should be taken to refer to animals with interests, unless otherwise stated.)

As an aside, it is very reasonable to identify at least part of what is wrong with gratuitously pulverizing animals as the causing of needless *suffering*. If the poor mare had never died, the series of actions would hardly have been justified, so it is not as if killing animals is all that is wrong with abusing them. (In fact, it is a significant philosophical problem whether killing animals is even prima facie wrong; note our conflicting beliefs about painless killing.) And it cannot be plausibly argued that the wrongness of causing such suffering depends on the species of animal. Imagine any animal believed capable of suffering to be in a position as similar as possible to the horse's—the act seems as surely to be wrong. This brings us to a considered judgment as solid as any with implications for animals: *It is prima facie wrong to cause suffering (regardless of who the sufferer is).* That it was relatively straightforward to arrive at this thesis reflects the fact that avoiding suffering is the interest most readily attributable to animals. What other interests animals have will be considered in later chapters.

---

[12]Peter Carruthers, *The Animals Issue: Moral Theory in Practice* (Cambridge: Cambridge University Press, 1992), p. 154

Less generous views easily explicable as bias

The fact that animals have interests (with which ethics is concerned), and the impossibility of making sense of certain considered judgments without attributing moral status to animals, together support this attribution. No argument of which I am aware should undermine our confidence in it. Then how can we explain the fact that some people find either absolute dismissal or the indirect approach plausible? (My answer will in effect be an "error theory," an account of how a widely held belief—that animals lack moral status—could be mistaken.)

As for absolute dismissal, I do not assume even Robert White really holds this view, and I have never met anyone who does. But I assume *some* people do. And a look at history makes it likely that many more people have been absolute dismissers. (After all, our culture has changed.) But I don't think their beliefs about animals require special explanation any more than the existence of white supremacists does. Absolute dismissers and white supremacists are deeply prejudiced against individuals whom they perceive to be outside their group (species or race). They tend to believe that their own group's interests conflict sharply with those of outsiders, so their prejudice is partly rooted in (unenlightened) self-interest.

Less obviously, supporters of the indirect approach have also, I think, missed its obvious weaknesses due to the distorting lens of prejudice. It is easy to see how there could be such prejudice. Common practices include the everyday use of animals for food, clothing, and entertainment. The way of life incorporating such practices is a deeply entrenched part of our culture. Thus, it requires considerable independence of thinking to engage in a thorough questioning of this lifestyle. Because people tend to think that such everyday use of animals is in their interests, and because animals—who cannot stand up for their own interests—have had virtually no advocates until recently, the assumption that they lack moral status has been entirely natural. But once we put the reality of animals' interests into focus, and subject our thinking to critical scrutiny, matters begin to look very different.

Animals have some moral status. But how much, relative to humans? To get a handle on this question, let us consider equal consideration and what it would be like, roughly, to extend it to animals. Then we can consider arguments for and against doing so.

THE BASIC IDEA OF EQUAL CONSIDERATION

The idea of equal consideration was brought into the forefront of animal ethics by Peter Singer:

[T]he leading figures in contemporary moral philosophy have shown a great deal of agreement in specifying as a fundamental presupposition of their moral theories [a] requirement that works to give everyone's interests equal consideration—although these writers generally cannot agree on how this requirement is best formulated.

It is an implication of this principle of equality that our concern for others and our readiness to consider their interests ought not to depend on what they are like or on what abilities they may possess. Precisely what our concern or consideration requires us to do may vary according to the characteristics of those affected.[13]

Singer rightly notes that a principle of equal consideration is widely assumed or defended, although it is formulated in different ways. Indeed, the idea of equal consideration is sufficiently vague and loose that very different theories are compatible with it.[14] Despite its vagueness, this principle is far from trivial, for to extend any version of it to animals would constitute a revolution in attitudes. There is little question that such practices and institutions as factory farming, hunting for sport, trapping, and common methods of cosmetics testing involve less-than-equal consideration for animals.

Several examples of ethical theories that assume equal consideration will aid in unpacking its meaning. First, utilitarians assume this principle. As Jeremy Bentham put it, "Each [is] to count for one, and no one for more than one," in evaluating the likely consequences of possible actions. Bentham and John Stuart Mill after him were especially consistent utilitarians in making a radical departure from common thinking. They noted that this principle applies to animals, since they too are subject to pleasure and pain, contentment and misery.

Contract theorists also assume equal consideration. Typically, they understand those subject to equality to be human and to have equal rights. For John Rawls, equality takes a decidedly anti-utilitarian form: "Each person possesses an inviolability founded on justice that even the welfare of society as a whole cannot override."[15] In contract theory, those and only those individuals subject to the terms of the contract enjoy equal consideration.

Libertarianism is another theory that is generally understood to issue in equal rights for humans only. Despite taking animals very seriously when few philosophers did, Nozick attributes rights only to persons (although he uses the neutral word *individuals* here): "INDIVIDUALS

---

[13] *Animal Liberation,* p. 5

[14] For a historically well-informed discussion of the concept of equality as applied to humans, see William B. Griffith, "Equality and Egalitarianism: Framing the Contemporary Debate," *Canadian Journal of Law and Jurisprudence* 7 (1994): 5–26.

[15] *A Theory of Justice* (Cambridge, MA: Harvard University Press, 1971), p. 3

have rights, and there are things no person or group may do to them (without violating their rights)."[16]

Finally, consider Regan's rights view, which attributes nearly absolute rights to all "subjects-of-a-life": "like us, animals have certain basic moral rights, including in particular the fundamental right to be treated with the respect that, as possessors of inherent value, they are due as a matter of strict justice."[17] If equal consideration is at the heart of such a variety of theories as utilitarianism, contract theory, libertarianism, and Regan's animal-rights view, what does this principle amount to?

Equal consideration, whether for humans or animals, means in some way giving equal moral weight to the relevantly similar interests of different individuals. Now, if an ethical theory did not affirm this principle even for humans, it would regard different humans as having differential moral status. In other words, it would amount to a form of moral hierarchy or elitism within humanity. If that sounds feudalistic or aristocratic, it is. Classical utilitarianism and the libertarian contract theories of Hobbes and Locke were, in fact, self-consciously pitted against the alleged divine right of kings, as well as other feudalistic and aristocratic residue in law, politics, and popular religion. We liberal democrats have become so comfortable with the idea of basic equality among humans that we sometimes forget how substantial a moral principle it is.

What is in question for us is whether equal consideration should apply to animals. What would be ruled out, if we took this course? Would equal consideration rule out some partiality, in practice, toward human beings? Would it preclude stronger moral protections for some human interests? Would it mean that we should be aggressively involved in trying to benefit animals, as opposed to largely leaving them alone? Applied to animals, the basic idea of equal consideration—the very general idea at the heart of the theories discussed earlier—entails none of these things. A great deal of interpretation and additional theorizing is needed to fill out an ethical theory.

What is ruled out, at the level of theory, is *a general discounting of animals' interests*. By "discounting" I do not mean complete dismissal but an across-the-board devaluing of their interests relative to ours (the extreme case of which is complete dismissal). To extend less-than-equal consideration to animals is to assert that their interests matter less than ours, just because it is animals (or some defined set of beings coextensive with animals) who have those interests. So, for example, a monkey's interest in avoiding pain of some amount matters less, intrinsically, than a human's interest in avoiding pain of the same amount.

[16] *Anarchy, State, and Utopia*, p. ix
[17] *The Case for Animal Rights*, p. 329

At a practical level, equal consideration for animals would rule out, most importantly, *the routine overriding of animals' interests in the name of human benefit*. While equal consideration is compatible with different ethical theories, it is incompatible—if extended to animals—with all views that see animals as essentially resources for our use. Equal consideration may be compatible with *some* use of animals (and perhaps even humans—think of conscription) for human purposes. But unequal consideration implies that animals and humans have such fundamentally different moral standing that the two exist in a hierarchy in which those at the top may regard those beneath them as resources for bettering their own lives. To proponents of equal consideration, unequal consideration is a form of feudalism and aristocracy that persists in contemporary liberal democracy.

One more point—a rather subtle one—needs to be made about this principle. Since equal consideration for animals involves giving their interests equal moral weight, a puzzle arises. For it is obvious that different animals and humans have some very different interests. Women have an interest in competent gynecological care in a way that men do not. Children have an interest in becoming literate whereas dogs do not. Chimpanzees have an interest in frequent social interactions with other chimps, while some primates prefer to go it alone. And competent adult humans have an interest in making decisions about their own medical care, but mice have no such interest.

If equal consideration is extended to animals, then each animal's interests are in some way to be equally taken into account. But since what is to be taken into account can differ so greatly from individual to individual, can we say anything meaningful about the implications of equal consideration for particular interests?

I believe a common interpretive move has been made by most of the leaders in animals ethics (including Feinberg, Frey, Hoff, Rachels, Regan, Singer, Sumner, and VanDeVeer). While Singer, for example, makes a few remarks gesturing in the direction of this interpretation, none of these theorists makes it very explicit.[18] Equal consideration, again, means attributing equal moral weight or importance to relevantly similar interests. The crucial concept here is that of *relevantly similar interests*. We tend to think that what is at stake for me in avoiding pain—considered just in terms of its unpleasantness—is similar to what is at stake for another person in avoiding pain. Similarly, regardless of whether it should carry just as much moral weight (an ethical question), what is at stake for Lassie in avoiding qualitatively similar pain (a prudential question) would presumably be the same. This illus-

---

[18] See my "Equal Consideration and Unequal Moral Status" for an early attempt to clarify this interpretive move.

trates the basic idea of relevantly similar interests. Sentient animals, including humans, have a relevantly similar interest in avoiding pain, taken in terms of its unpleasantness[19]—whether or not we should extend equal consideration and therefore give equal moral weight to their interests in avoiding pain.

Consider some examples of relevantly different interests. The availability of worms (or some other fishfood) may be vital to a fish but is ordinarily much less important to humans. Generally, the availability of worms is a relevantly different interest for fish and humans. Interestingly, all of the philosophers just mentioned regard *life,* staying alive, as relevantly different for normal humans and animals. Other things equal, they believe, a normal human loses more in dying than does an animal.[20] Thus, for them, equal consideration is compatible with giving greater moral weight to a normal human's life (taken simply in its prudential aspect, its value to the human in question) than to an animal's life (taken in its prudential aspect, its value to the animal). The only way to make sense of this judgment—which I find perfectly *intelligible,* whether or not correct—is to interpret it in this way: Although we use the same word, "life," to denote their respective interests, a normal human's interest in life, other things equal, is relevantly different from an animal's interest in life. Different things are at stake for the human and animal.

Equal consideration for animals entails giving equal moral weight to their relevantly similar interests. It forbids generally devaluing their interests relative to ours just because the interest-bearers are animals. We cannot say much about what interests are relevantly similar— whether, for example, human and animal lives, freedom, or functioning should be equally weighty—without a lot of work in value theory.

---

[19] The qualification is meant to set aside the complicating fact that pain can have, in addition to its *intrinsic* disvalue to the subject (its unpleasantness), *instrumental* disvalue to her. For example, pain can prevent us from pursuing valued projects and can lead to future unpleasant feelings, such as resentment or painful memories. The instrumental disvalue of pain will be taken up in a later chapter.

[20] See Joel Feinberg, *Rights, Justice, and the Bounds of Liberty* (Princeton: Princeton University Press, 1980), p. 200; R. G. Frey, "Animal Parts, Human Wholes," in James M. Humber and Robert F. Almeder (eds.), *Biomedical Ethics Reviews 1987* (Clifton, NJ: Humana Press, 1987), p. 93; Christina Hoff, "Immoral and Moral Uses of Animals," *New England Journal of Medicine* 302 (1980): 115–18; James Rachels, "Do Animals Have a Right to Life?," in Harlan B. Miller and William H. Williams (eds.), *Ethics and Animals* (Clifton, NJ: Humana Press, 1983), p. 254; Regan, *The Case for Animal Rights,* p. 324; Singer, *Animal Liberation,* p. 20 and *Practical Ethics,* 2d ed. (Cambridge: Cambridge University Press, 1993), pp. 105–9, 117–31; L. W. Sumner, "Animal Welfare and Animal Rights," *Journal of Medicine and Philosophy* 13 (1988), p. 169; and Donald VanDeVeer, "Interspecific Justice and Animal Slaughter," in Miller and Williams, *Ethics and Animals,* pp. 156–62.

Thus, further unpacking of equal consideration will be postponed until later.

ESTABLISHING A PRESUMPTION IN FAVOR OF EQUAL CONSIDERATION

Equal consideration for animals a possibility

By now the title of this section may seem rather obvious. But I think that, historically, philosophers and others have generally missed the fact that equal consideration, some basic notion of equality, could meaningfully be extended to animals. When a Benjamin Franklin or a Jeremy Bentham suggested that we look at animals in a radically different way, the suggestion was probably greeted not with a refutation but with a laugh or sneer. Until animals are taken seriously enough that this possibility is clearly in mind, intelligent discussion of the reasons for and against equal consideration is impossible.

Many people today dismiss this issue before they even understand it. It is a sad statement about prevailing levels of intellectual integrity that uncomprehending, automatic dismissal of the possibility of equal consideration is deemed worthy of publication in many medical journals.[21] Quite a few philosophers, including some contemporary ones, demonstrate similar closemindedness in the face of this issue.[22] Since it is a central task of their speciality to engage in intelligent questioning of moral assumptions, such automatic dismissal by philosophers is ironic. In any event, once the logical possibility of equal consideration for animals is in view, the question becomes whether it is right.

For now I assume that equal consideration could not extend beyond animals—meaning, again, animals who have interests—to include nonsentient animals, plant life, or inanimate things. That is because what equal consideration takes into account are individuals' interests, and these other entities have none. Some will challenge that last claim. "Deep ecologists" will argue that a being need not be sentient to have

[21] See, e.g., C. S. Nicoll and S. M. Russell, "Analysis of Animal Rights Literature Reveals the Underlying Motives of the Movement: Ammunition for Counteroffensive by Scientists," *Endocrinology* 127 (1990): 985–89; J. M. Maharry, "The Issue of Animal Rights and Human Rights," *American Journal of Obstetrics and Gynecology* 164 (1991): 1543–48; and Herbert Pardes, Anne West, Harold Alan Pincus, "Physicians and the Animal-Rights Movement," *New England Journal of Medicine* 324 (1991): 1640–43.
[22] For an historical overview, see Tom Regan and Peter Singer (eds.), *Animal Rights and Human Obligations*, 2d ed. (Englewood Cliffs, NJ: Prentice Hall, 1989), Part I. For a contemporary example, see Stanley Benn, "Egalitarianism and the Equal Consideration of Interests," in J. Roland Pennock and John W. Chapman (eds.), *Equality* (New York: Atherton Press, 1967), p. 69.

interests or a welfare. I disagee that nonsentient beings can have "interests" or a "welfare" in any sense relevant to morality, but I will not tackle this issue until Chapter 8. For now, we need only note that the set of beings to whom equal consideration should be extended *may* be as wide as the set of sentient animals; the claim that equal consideration should be extended this far is perfectly *intelligible*. This is the first step in my effort to establish a presumption in favor of equal consideration for animals.

Universalizability and relevant differences

The second move invokes impartiality or universalizability. In Chapter 2, we used both terms to denote a single principle that is subject to slightly different interpretations; I argued that such a principle was defensible and important within a coherence model. Following up on some relevant literature, here I will favor the term *universalizability*.

As emphasized by such philosophers as Kant and R. M. Hare, while moral judgments may be particular, each implies a general judgment. Thus "He should not lie" implies something like "People should not lie in situations relevantly similar to his." After all, there is presumably some reason why he shouldn't lie, and this reason will apply in cases other than this one. To claim that he should not lie but she should, according to the principle of universalizability, one would have to hold that there is a relevant difference between his and her circumstances (or between him and her)—on pain of unintelligibility.[23]

For present purposes, universalizability may be taken as doing the same work as the formal principle of justice or equality, traditionally attributed to Aristotle: Equals should be treated equally, and unequals unequally.[24] The principle is formal because it does not specify the respects in which individuals are to be considered equals, just as universalizability provides no criteria of relevant similarity. But formal justice implies that individuals should be treated equally unless they are unequal in some relevant respect (perhaps their circumstances or a more basic fact about them).

What universalizability and formal justice imply about equal consideration and animals' interests is a bit confusing, because two kinds of relevant similarity come into play. The first kind of relevant similarity concerns beings themselves and whether they are subject to equal con-

[23]See R. M. Hare, *Moral Thinking: Its Levels, Method, and Point* (Oxford: Clarendon, 1981), pp. 107–16.
[24]Aristotle, *Nicomachean Ethics* V.3.1131a10–b15. For a highly detailed and scholarly discussion of this formal principle, see Peter Westen, *Speaking of Equality* (Princeton: Princeton University Press, 1990), ch. 9.

sideration. But, as stressed earlier, there is also the matter of what equal consideration would come to: What interests count as relevantly similar (and are therefore to be given equal weight, in terms of rights, utility, or something else)? *Universalizability and formal justice imply that we should grant equal moral weight or importance to everyone's (relevantly similar) interests, unless there is a relevant difference between the beings in question.* Of course, the principle of equal consideration asserts that there is no relevant difference among beings—or some set of beings, such as humans—that justifies giving their (relevantly similar) interests unequal weight. In making this claim, it qualifies as a substantive moral principle.

Setting aside for now the question of what equal consideration would come to, are animals to be extended equal consideration in the first place? The *inegalitarian* (let's make that a technical term) says no, implying that there is a relevant difference between humans and animals that justifies giving less-than-equal consideration to animals. Does the inegalitarian bear a burden of proof? Universalizability implies that there must *be* a relevant difference between humans and animals if only humans should receive equal consideration. But it does not strictly follow that the inegalitarian must *identify* such a difference and *convincingly argue* that it is relevant.[25] Put another way, it doesn't follow that we should assume equal consideration for animals unless the inegalitarian refutes the assumption.

No, but we are getting closer to a reasonable presumption. Because animals have interests, equal consideration *could* be meaningfully extended to them. Universalizability suggests that, if some beings to whom equal consideration could be extended should not be covered by the principle, there must be a relevant difference among beings that justifies excluding some. So where should the burden of proof lie? As explained next, there should be a rebuttable presumption in favor of equal consideration.

Completing the case for a presumption

Permitting unequal consideration in the absence of any justification (rebuttal) would be (1) highly unfair, and (2) given the likelihood of pro-human bias, too inviting of error.[26] Let me explain both points.

If animals are not due the consideration we grant to humans (that is, if their relevantly similar interests are to be given less weight), there

[25] Jorge Garcia pointed this out to me. Westen carefully explains why a presumption of equality is not logically entailed by Aristotle's formal principle of justice (*Speaking of Equality,* pp. 233–36).

[26] In general, rebuttable presumptions appear to be justified by the factors of gravity of error and its probability (ibid, p. 249).

must be a relevant difference between animals and humans. Now suppose we judged that the inegalitarian need *not* provide a convincing argument that there is a relevant difference. In that case, certain individuals (namely, animals) could be subjected to considerable harms—including confinement, injury, suffering, and death—in the absence of any justification whatsoever for the claim that these individuals, unlike other individuals (namely, humans), are appropriately subjected to such harms. To harm some individuals in the name of unequal consideration, without ensuring that the harmful treatment is justified, simply seems unfair. Indeed, it is difficult to imagine what could be less fair. (Many human groups have felt the brunt of such unfairness.)

Second, a burden of proof is needed to protect against error. In clarifying the general idea of equal consideration, we found that utilitarianism, contract theories, libertarianism, and Regan's rights view all embrace this principle, as applying at least to humans. In fact, all serious contenders among ethical theories have this egalitarian feature, reflecting the fact that morally serious people today accept some principle of equality for human beings. Our question is whether it should extend to animals.

Here, the fact of bias against animals is important. Even if, in the end, unequal consideration for animals is justified, there can be no denying that Western civilization reveals a history of substantial bias against animals. Until recently (with very few exceptions), their moral status was not taken seriously at all, a fact reflected in the embarrassingly superficial dismissals of animals by most of the great moral philosophers.[27]

How much bias remains today? Since the extent of animals' moral status is far from settled in the public mind, and since many people today do take animals seriously, it is risky to venture generalizations. Nevertheless, while a historical overview of moral attitudes suggests considerable progress in recent centuries (and, quite notably, in recent decades), we can be sure that the possibility of significant bias against animals is very high.

People often harbor biases against those who are relatively defenseless (such as children, the elderly, and the handicapped) and those perceived to be different (such as homosexuals, foreigners, and members of other ethnic groups). Animals are both relatively defenseless and very different from us. Moreover, their interests are typically thought to conflict significantly with ours—activating another source of prejudice. And, in general, one need not be jaded to perceive in human history the tendency of those possessing power to discriminate

---

[27] For some of the great dismissers as well as some exceptions, see Regan and Singer, *Animal Rights and Human Obligations,* Part I.

against, and oppress, the powerless until physical force or the psychological force of popular sentiment causes a change in attitude and practice. While growing in influence, the animal-protection movement is hardly so powerful as to eradicate bias against animals.

Since prejudice may affect our moral thinking about animals, including our reasoning about equal consideration, we should require the inegalitarian to justify giving less-than-equal consideration to animals. Otherwise, we make it too likely that we will get matters wrong, that we will accept unequal consideration when equal consideration is right. Such a burden of proof on the inegalitarian makes sense from the perspective of coherence theorizing, as laid out in Chapter 2. For we give much less weight to judgments that seem highly likely to be biased. Indeed, no such judgment counts as a considered judgment. In the same methodological spirit, we should require moral positions that are likely to be infected with bias (such as unequal consideration) to be defended explicitly and convincingly. This means a burden of proof.

The cumulative force of the preceding arguments is sufficient to establish a burden of proof for the inegalitarian. *Unless and until unequal consideration for animals is successfully defended, we should regard equal consideration as more reasonable.* Unlike Singer, Frey, and Regan (see Chapter 1), I believe that the strongest arguments against equal consideration for animals are quite powerful. In my opinion, these authors have not been very imaginative in considering arguments against equal consideration. On the other hand, few who assume less-than-equal consideration for animals explicitly defend their assumption. Drawing from arguments that I have either read, heard, or made up myself, in the remainder of this chapter I present and criticize five of what I take to be the seven strongest challenges to equal consideration: (1) contractarianism; (2) the "sui generis view"; (3) the argument from social bondedness; (4) the argument from moral agency; and (5) the argument from coherence. (The sixth challenge cannot be adequately explained before Chapter 8; the seventh is more naturally discussed in Chapter 9.)

FIVE CHALLENGES TO EQUAL CONSIDERATION FOR ANIMALS

Contractarianism

1. The position. Perhaps the inegalitarian position can be supported by a plausible contract theory, according to which one's moral rights and duties flow from the terms of an agreement reached by contractors in a hypothetical bargaining situation. Drawing from the work of Rawls and Scanlon,[28] Peter Carruthers argues that contractarianism provides the most adequate framework for a moral theory. Because animals are not rational agents of the sort who can participate in designing a contract, Carruthers argues, animals lack moral status.[29] If Carruthers is right that animals lack moral status, it follows that they are not due equal consideration. I take Carruthers' challenge as representative of contractarianism because it is by far the most developed contractarian case against animals.

2. Critique. The contractarian case against equal consideration for animals falters on two major points: (1) The thesis that animals lack moral status has very implausible implications and cannot be coherently defended (as we saw earlier); and (2) the thesis that rational agency is the basis for moral standing has very implausible implications regarding nonrational humans. Carruthers anticipates these objections and responds in detail, but his replies are inadequate.

In response to charge (1), Carruthers argues that contractarianism can allow some moral restrictions on our treatment of animals, such as a prohibition of gratuitously causing animals to suffer. Such restrictions are based not on animals' rights or moral status (he conflates the two concepts), but on (a) respect for the feelings of animal lovers or (b) considerations of moral character.[30]

But we have already seen that indirect duty views cannot adequately account for our obligations to animals. Argument (a) is analogous to the argument from moral spillover and is subject to analogous rebuttal. Egregious instances of animal abuse, such as Mikolka's treatment of the horse, would be wrong even if no human's feelings could possibly be affected.[31] Moreover, our judgment that such actions are wrong is virtually certain, but the empirical claim that gratuitously harming animals will, in fact, negatively affect animal lovers' feelings is much less secure—especially if the harm is privately inflicted. (Besides, why don't sadists' feelings—which should be positively affected by knowledge of such actions—count?) And we have seen that appeals to character, as in (b), are insufficient. Once again, no ethical theory that entirely withholds moral status from animals is adequate.

Carruthers also counters (2), the charge that contractarianism cannot

[28] Thomas Scanlon, "Contractualism and Utilitarianism," in Amartya Sen and Bernard Williams (eds.), *Utilitarianism and Beyond* (Cambridge: Cambridge University Press, 1982)

[29] *The Animals Issue*, chs. 1–6

[30] ibid, chs. 5, 7

[31] Carruthers acknowledges this point (ibid, pp. 108–9), holding that the appeal to character is therefore required to account for our duties to animals.

deal satisfactorily with humans who are not rational agents, such as babies, very senile persons, and the profoundly retarded. How to deal plausibly with such humans, on any theory whose criteria for moral status seem to leave them out, is known as *the problem of marginal cases*. Carruthers argues that *all* (postnatal) humans have moral rights or status. The contract would establish the rights of nonrational humans based on (a) slippery-slope considerations, and (b) considerations of social stability.

Regarding (a), Carruthers argues that failure to confer rights on nonrational humans in drawing up the contract will invite errors about who has moral rights and will expose some humans to abuse:

> [T]here are no sharp boundaries between a baby and an adult, between a not-very-intelligent adult and a severe mental defective, or between a normal old person and someone who is severely senile. . . . In contrast, there really is a sharp boundary between human beings and all other animals.[32]

In practice, we have no trouble distinguishing between humans and even our closest animal relatives, chimpanzees, whereas discriminations between rational and nonrational humans would be a very subtle matter. Thus, contractors had better decide that all humans have basic rights, lest we slide down the slope to abuse.

This is an important argument, but I do not think it fully withstands scrutiny. Consider a human who would clearly fail to satisfy the criterion of rational agency: someone with an I.Q. of 10. That it would be wrong to use him in extremely painful toxicity tests for cosmetics is quite clear. But the empirical claim—that any criterion excluding him from the circle of rights holders would have slippery-slope troubles— while not unreasonable is less than certain. And regarding a hypothetical society where people were such accurate and honest judges of others' rationality that there would be no realistic worries about a slippery slope, it would still seem wrong to use the profoundly retarded in toxicity tests. The wrongness of such exploitation seems independent of the empirical premise that Carruthers would have it stand upon.[33]

---

[32] ibid, pp. 114–15

[33] The slippery-slope argument may also founder on its exclusion of fetuses from the status granted to "all humans." Carruthers takes fetuses to be very different from other members of our species in terms of the reactions they evoke:

> It is natural to be struck by the suffering of senile old people or babies, in a way that both supports and is supported by assigning direct rights to these groups. It is not so natural for us to respond similarly towards a foetus, however, especially in the early stages, unless we already have prior moral beliefs about its status. (ibid, p. 117)

Carruthers' second argument on behalf of nonrational (postnatal) humans is that contractors would want to confer rights on them to avoid the social instability that would otherwise result due to people's natural affections: Many people would be psychologically incapable of complying with a rule withholding moral status from nonrational humans.[34] This argument, like some of the others we have considered, is only as strong as the empirical premise on which it rests: Are we so certain that social instability would result? Even if we are, it seems quite possible that some societies *could* have—indeed, some *have* had—rather different attitudes about newborns or the severely mentally ill, for example. In such societies, these humans would not have moral status (at least on the basis of this argument). I would argue, however, that regardless of likely effects on social stability, these humans have moral status and should not be used as mere playthings, objects of experimentation, or the like. Carruthers, in my view, simply has the wrong basis for moral status: What is crucial is not rational agency, or one's social and psychological relations to rational agents, but the possession of interests.

In conclusion, Carruthers' handling of the moral status of animals clearly fails, whereas his handling of nonrational humans' moral status, though somewhat stronger, probably fails as well. Contractarianism certainly has not fared well enough to displace the presumption in favor of equal consideration.

The "sui generis view"

1. The position. One of the subtler challenges to equal consideration is what I call the *sui generis view*. Although rarely acknowledged by philosophers, it captures what I believe to be a common conviction about

---

The last phrase suggests that those who have "prior moral beliefs" about the status of fetuses may well respond sympathetically toward them. Perhaps Carruthers feels that such a response to fetuses does not require accommodation because it is based on prior moral beliefs, rather than being a "natural" response independent of moral beliefs. But how is Carruthers in a position to determine that (1) sympathetic responses to fetuses are caused by moral convictions, whereas (2) people assuming a morally neutral stance do not naturally respond in this way? It is not unusual for persons who do not have "prior moral beliefs" about the fetus' status—that is, who are not strongly anti-abortion—to be struck by the resemblance of a late fetus (in a sonogram) to a newborn baby. (Indeed, premature births suggest that late fetuses *could be* newborn babies.) Now Carruthers does stress the early stages of pregnancy in his argument, so perhaps he could work out his position by drawing some line during the course of pregnancy. In any event, it seems fair to say that his exclusion of fetuses, or some fetuses, from the realm of rights requires more defense than he has provided.

[34] ibid, p. 117

the moral status of humans. Moreover, this position enjoys the support of an important line of philosophical thinking about the nature of justification.

Justifications for what counts as a morally relevant characteristic (and for anything else), the argument begins, have to end somewhere.[35] Logic alone cannot decide what counts as relevant. The inegalitarian and the champion of equal consideration simply differ on what characteristics are morally relevant. Some examples will clarify the general point being made about moral justification.

Rationalists believe that reasons justifying correct moral judgments, including judgments about relevance, can be provided all the way to the point at which it can be shown that denying the judgment would involve a logical error or some other form of irrationality. Others doubt that rationality is capable of grounding moral judgments but hold that there are certain objective moral axioms that one either recognizes or does not.[36] Beauchamp notes the possibility of this position in the present context:

> We seem here to encounter a metaphysical dispute about the universe of values. . . . Regan's conviction is that humans and animals "have value of the same kind." The metaphysical problem of whether dogs, chickens, and lizards have less value than humans, and indeed whether there is relatively more or less value across species . . . is not a matter that can be decided by formal justice or equality. . . . While I shall here assume, in disagreement with Regan, that there are different levels of value that attach to creatures in nature, I do so as a presupposition.[37]

For the present sort of inegalitarian, being human—that is, homo sapiens—*just is*, sui generis, a morally relevant characteristic that grounds special moral status. The argument for the relevance of being human goes no farther than that. It is not a contradiction to deny the relevance of being human; nor is being human relevant because all and only humans possess some further characteristic (e.g., rationality) that can be shown to be relevant. While champions of equal consideration invoke traits that cut across species lines, like sentience, the former cannot logically demonstrate that species membership per se is morally irrelevant.

---

[35] That justifications for an assertion eventually run out is a familiar Wittgensteinian thought. See, e.g., Ludwig Wittgenstein, *Philosophical Investigations*, trans. G. E. M. Anscombe (New York: Macmillan, 1953), sec. 217.

[36] The view that there are *self-evident* moral axioms can count as a form of rationalism (see Chapter 2, note 1).

[37] Tom L. Beauchamp, "Problems in Justifying Research on Animals," in National Institutes of Health, *National Symposium on Imperatives in Research Animal Use* (NIH Publication No. 85–2746, 1985), p. 87

2. Critique. It is hard to refute a view that, by its nature, almost cuts off further debate. My strategy is to press the thesis that species membership is morally relevant by revealing (1) the oddity of the thesis itself, and (2) the implausibility of its implications.

First, the sui generis view suffers from a "problem of queerness." The claim that falling within a certain genetic range (being a member of our species) is necessary and sufficient for full consideration is just exceedingly odd, especially when we consider the presumably gradual emergence of new species from old. Assuming that *Homo erectus* is the species from which we evolved, it seems highly arbitrary to suggest that if some members of that hominid species somehow survived today, their interests would deserve less consideration than the interests of all *Homo sapiens*.

Indeed, a clear genetic line between "them" and "us" is more something to draw than something to find. There was no magic moment when *Homo erectus* mutated into *Homo sapiens*. Of course, there are no surviving hominid intermediaries—such as *Homo erectus, Homo habilis, Australopithecus afarensis*, or *Australopithecus ramidus*—who would bridge the genetic gap between us and our nearest living relatives, the Great Apes.[38] This historical accident might make the gap, the discontinuity, between us and chimpanzees (the closest ape to us) seem greater than it is.

While chimpanzees are very different from us in many ways, they are surprisingly close to us genetically—that is, in terms of percentage of shared DNA. Indeed, chimps are more closely related to *Homo sapiens* than they are to the next closest primate, gorillas.[39] Actually, there are two chimpanzee species—common chimps and pigmy chimps—and our difference from each (about 1.6%) is barely double the difference between the two kinds of chimps (0.7).[40] Our common ancestor with chimps lived in Africa between 5 and 7 million years ago, not a long time by evolutionary standards.[41] Although chimps are classified as among the Great Apes—along with gorillas and orangutans—there is arguably no natural, genetics-based grouping that includes these species but no hominid species.[42] In fact, while biology textbooks have

[38] For a helpful summary of hominid history as it is currently understood, see Stephen Jay Gould, "So Near and Yet So Far," *New York Review of Books* (October 20, 1994): 24–26.

[39] R. Lewin, "DNA Reveals Surprises in Human Family Tree," *Science* 226 (1984): 1179–83

[40] Jared Diamond, "The Third Chimpanzee," in Paola Cavalieri and Peter Singer (eds.), *The Great Ape Project: Equality Beyond Humanity* (New York: St. Martin's, 1993), pp. 94–95

[41] Richard Dawkins, "Gaps in the Mind," in Cavalieri and Singer, *The Great Ape Project*, p. 82

[42] ibid

traditionally taught that hominids and the Great Apes are in different *families*—namely, Hominidae and Pongidae—use of criteria based on genetic relatedness suggests that hominids, the two chimp species, and perhaps even gorillas are members of the same *genus*.[43]

The following passage from Rosemary Rodd underscores the genetic closeness between humans and our nearest living neighbor:

> Human and chimpanzee differ mainly in their control genes, which comprise a relatively small proportion of the total DNA. Human specialties are achieved by, for example, a delayed cut-off time for brain growth and changes in body proportions. . . . Suppose we were to alter the DNA of an embryonic chimpanzee so that his brain continued to grow after birth, or even to alter all the control genes which distinguish human and ape. Would the resulting child be human or animal? Since chimpanzee and human have 98 per cent of their DNA in common, he could either be said to be genetically 100 per cent human . . . or 98 per cent chimp, 2 per cent human (by inheritance). Or are present-day African apes 98 per cent human by virtue of common inheritance? Presumably it would be possible to modify those same control genes in human embryos to increase the period of brain growth, and brain-weight. One wonders how such an infant would be entitled to view his human progenitors when he became adult.[44]

While the technical competence required to perform such genetic manipulations may be a long way off, another sort of manipulation dramatizing the genetic closeness between humans and chimpanzees—impregnating chimps with human sperm—may already be possible. There have been two reports of successful human–chimp fertilization. In one case, the pregnant chimp was alleged to have died; in the other, it was claimed that an abortion terminated the experi-

---

[43] Diamond, "The Third Chimpanzee," pp. 96–97

[44] *Biology, Ethics and Animals* (Oxford: Clarendon Press, 1990), pp. 37–38. In light of facts such as those adduced by Rodd, and by others cited previously, statements like the following by Willard Gaylin border on the unintelligible:

> The order of change between the chimpanzee and the human being is of such a magnitude as to represent a break, a discontinuity. We are not the next step, or even a giant leap forward. We are a parallel and independent entity; a thing unto ourselves; in a class of our own; *sui generis* . . . . The distance between man and ape is greater than the distance between ape and ameba. (*Adam and Eve and Pinocchio* [New York: Viking, 1990], p. 5)

On the other hand, it is not clear that Gaylin is interested in the relevant facts. For he later admits that his claims come from "my bias," from "my world" (ibid, p. 12). Why persons concerned about animal ethics should be interested in this "Gaylocentric" position is not explained.

ment.[45] The cautious reader will not accept these reports without further documentation. But one should not dismiss them as impossible. Members of different species can sometimes reproduce, although their offspring are infertile. For example, a mule is the infertile offspring of a female horse and male donkey.

In light of all of these considerations, even if genes were so morally important—which is hard to fathom—why would the *species* line be so crucial? Why wouldn't moral importance attach, sui generis, to members of the genus homo? Or to the family that includes us and the other Great Apes? Or to all primates—or mammals? Put into clear light, the thesis of the sui generis moral relevance of species is very peculiar.

The sui generis view also has some highly implausible implications. Suppose that we genetically engineered a species of whale to produce an animal with a far more massive brain, and greater intelligence, than we have.[46] According to the sui generis view, because such superintelligent whales would not be members of our species, they would be subject to less-than-equal consideration. But the matter of species seems irrelevant here.

Species differences also seem irrelevant in the imaginary case in which highly intelligent, social aliens arrive on our planet. While they would not be of our species, I cannot see why—on genetic grounds—they should be entitled to less consideration than human beings are due.[47] (And appeal to metaphysical grounds here is simply mystifying.)

Acceptance of the sui generis view has another problematic implication. If we allow species to count morally without any further grounds, there would seem to be no principled reason not to let sex, race, sexual preference, or intelligence count without any further grounds. Even if most of us are convinced that these latter grounds are morally irrelevant, what could we say to the person who claims intelligence (or whatever) affects moral status, sui generis, if we allow the species factor to be invoked without any justifying argument?[48]

One might protest that the preceding arguments wrongly take the sui generis view as asserting that certain genetic properties justify special status absolutely—that is, from the point of view of any moral

[45]These cases are discussed in Clive Hollands, "Trivial and Questionable Research on Animals," in Gill Langley (ed.), *Animal Experimentation: The Consensus Changes* (New York: Chapman and Hall, 1989), pp. 139–40. Hollands cites *The Daily Telegraph* (December 13, 1980) and *The London Evening Standard* (May 11, 1987). The *Telegraph* article cites a Shanghai newspaper, *Wen Hui Bao.*

[46]The idea comes from Rodd, *Biology, Ethics and Animals,* pp. 40–41.

[47]Cf. James Rachels, *Created from Animals: The Moral Implications of Darwinism* (Oxford: Oxford University Press, 1990), pp. 183–84.

[48]Cf. Singer, *Animal Liberation,* p. 9.

agent. Instead, one might argue, species membership is relevant only for members of that species. But this move turns the sui generis view into a different approach, according to which *genetic relatedness* is a morally relevant characteristic that homo sapiens have—from the human standpoint. Now the view is similar to the social-bondedness view (discussed in the next subsection), which, as we will see, shares its difficulty of drawing just the right line between "us" and "them." For, again, being *Homo sapiens* is just one case of genetic relatedness to "us." Additionally, the argument from genetic relatedness suffers from essentially the same problem of queerness as discussed previously: Genes don't seem so important.

Once properly exposed, the sui generis view has very little to recommend it. If being human has special moral significance, it must be in some respect other than mere species membership.

The argument from social bondedness

1. The position. One of the most powerful challenges to equal consideration for animals involves appealing to widely accepted cases of partiality based on social bonds, and arguing that partiality toward humans is similarly grounded. No one has developed this argument better than Mary Midgley.[49] According to Midgley, species, unlike race, is a significant grouping:

> Race in humans is not a significant grouping at all, but species in animals certainly is. It is never true that, in order to know how to treat a human being, you must first find out what race he belongs to. (Cases where this might seem to matter always really turn on culture.) But with an animal, to know the species is absolutely essential. A zoo-keeper who is told to expect an animal, and to get a place ready for it, cannot even begin to do this without far more detailed information. . . . Even members of quite similar and closely related species can have entirely different needs about temperature and water-supply, bedding, exercise-space, solitude, company and many other things.[50]

The species difference is crucial. Perhaps surprisingly, the same

> is also true, though less drastically, for age and sex. Certainly these distinctions have been misunderstood and misused, but they are real. One can be different without being inferior. Serious injustice can be done to

---

[49] *Animals and Why They Matter*. See also, e.g., Leslie Pickering Francis and Richard Norman, "Some Animals are More Equal Than Others," *Philosophy* 53 (1978): 507–27.
[50] *Animals and Why They Matter*, pp. 98–99

women or the old by insisting on giving them exactly the same treatment as men or the young.[51]

Our tendency to favor other humans is, like so many other forms of partiality, not a prejudice, but an appropriate discrimination based on social—and, at some level, biological—bonds:

> The special interest which parents feel in their own children is not a prejudice, nor is the tendency which most of us would show to rescue, in a fire or other emergency, those closest to us sooner than strangers. . . . There is good reason for such a preference. We are bond-forming creatures, not abstract intellects.[52]

The species preference is so natural that we cannot eliminate it. It is the business of morality to manage conflicts between such justified special claims and the more impartial considerations of justice:

> These preferences [based on social bonds] do indeed cause problems. By limiting human charity, they can produce terrible misery. On the other hand they are also an absolutely central element in human happiness, and it seems unlikely that we could live at all without them. . . . Morality shows a constant tension between measures to protect the sacredness of these special claims and counter-measures to secure justice and widen sympathy for outsiders. To handle this tension by working out particular priorities is our normal moral business.[53]

There is much truth, Midgley argues, for the following common conviction:

> An emotional, rather than rational, preference for our own species is . . . a necessary part of our social nature, in the same way that a preference for our own children is, and needs no more justification. . . . The natural preference for one's own species [is not] a product of culture. It is found in all human cultures, and in cases of real competition it tends to operate very strongly.[54]

Overall, Midgley holds that while justice requires us to take animal welfare much more seriously than we commonly do, and while we should try to widen human sympathies for animals, human beings have special claims on other humans that justify some partiality in their favor.

[51] ibid, p. 100
[52] ibid, p. 102
[53] ibid, p. 103
[54] ibid, p. 104

2. Critique. Appeals to social bondedness are supported by a conviction that no one is prepared to abandon—namely, that some significant degree of partiality toward family and other loved ones is justified. Of course, the justifiability of such partiality does not imply that we may violate others' basic rights, treat people unfairly, or even ignore the important claims of others. Social bonds justify some *favoring*. But does this seemingly innocuous contention justify a general *discounting* of animals' interests, giving them less weight than we give relevantly similar human interests? In arguing for a negative answer, I take up Midgley's major claims one by one.

First, Midgley claims that, unlike race, but to some extent like age and gender, species is a significant difference. We cannot know how to treat an animal without knowing its species, unlike the case of persons and race (though we may need to know about a person's culture). And we might be treating women and the aged very badly if we treat them like men and the young.

While these particular claims are very plausible, Midgley's inferences about partiality turn on a failure to distinguish *equal treatment* and *equal consideration*. Of course, we should not treat turtles like birds or people, or treat old ladies like young men. But we shouldn't grant less consideration to the interests to old ladies. We have to understand their special needs to know how to treat them. Midgley, in effect, conflates the issue of *what interests members of a group have* with the issue of *how much weight their interests should receive*. Of course, species differences are important in understanding the various interests of animals. But if they are also important for determining the weight that their interests should receive, Midgley has not shown us why.

Midgley is on safe ground in asserting that parents rightly favor their children's interests, and that people are justified in saving those close to them in an emergency. But these assertions are not incompatible with equal consideration.[55] The principle of equal consideration is somewhat loose and subject to varying interpretations and specifications. The most demanding interpretation is probably that of versions of utilitarianism that require very substantial self-sacrifice in working to benefit others.[56] Even with these interpretations, parents are expected to pay special attention to their children, since local efforts tend to be more beneficial.[57] And the point about saving those closest to us in an emergency is no serious challenge to equal consideration. We have to save

[55] Nor are they incompatible with an impartial perspective. For an interesting discussion, see Madison Powers, "Contractualist Impartiality and Personal Commitments," *American Philosophical Quarterly* 30 (1993): 63–72.
[56] See, e.g., Shelly Kagan, *The Limits of Morality* (Oxford: Clarendon, 1989).
[57] See Frank Jackson, "Decision-theoretic Consequentialism and the Nearest and Dearest Objection," *Ethics* 101 (1991): 461–82.

someone first, giving us some discretion about rescue order. Moreover, all the benefits of maintaining close relationships support an obligation to favor those close to one in such circumstances.

Furthermore, as we saw earlier, equal consideration is compatible with theories that (1) grant equal rights and therefore (2) do not regard everyone's interests as collectively something to maximize, even in principle. These views can easily accommodate certain widely recognized forms of partiality (which are compatible with the asserted rights). What equal consideration clearly rules out, again, is the general discounting of animals' interests, such that they count for less just because of who has them. In places, Midgley seems to support this view, and in other places, she does not. But it requires argument.

Midgley is quite right that morality must work out the relative weights of claims based on special relationships and those based on justice—a point granted, on some level, by virtually every egalitarian theory. Now while bonding-based preferences do seem centrally important to human happiness, Midgley exaggerates in saying that we could not live without them, if "them" includes or entails a general discounting of animals' interests. The existence of many animal liberationists who practice what they preach proves the point.

Midgley claims that an emotional preference for our own species is a necessary part of our social nature and is analogous to a preference for our own children. If this species preference is thought to include across-the-board discounting of animals' interests, again, she is wrong that such a preference is necessary. If this preference is truly analogous to favoring one's own children over other children and saving loved ones in emergencies, the analogy may well be valid, but, again, it does not challenge equal consideration (a point developed in Chapter 9).

Despite the truth and importance of many of Midgley's insights, she has not made a case that overturns equal consideration. Moreover, unless she adopts some principle of equal consideration, her view may be vitiated by too much emphasis on partiality and its supposed rootedness in social bonds. Can appeals to social bondedness in justifying partiality toward humans be convincingly likened to family-based preferences but contrasted with bigotry? Why are racism and sexism unjustified, if species-based partiality is justified? According to Midgley, the "natural preference for one's own species . . . is not, like race-prejudice, a product of culture."[58]

This response worries me, because it seems *possible* that a little bit of racial and ethnic discrimination *is* natural for human beings; fear of what strikes one as *different* is not foreign to human psychology. Indeed, culture may be necessary to correct for this natural tendency, if it exists.

[58] *Animals and Why They Matter*, p. 104

Besides, at the risk of stating the obvious, there is no reason to assume that actions expressing our natural tendencies are right. (One shudders to imagine the use of this assumption by a sex-deprived rapist.)

Midgley's view might best be strengthened by deemphasizing the claims about what is natural and by more explicitly adopting a reasonably interpreted principle of equal consideration. She does, anyway, acknowledge that claims of justice compete with bonding-based claims. She even says this about equality:

> [The term *equality of consideration*] is still misleadingly quantitative. We are not called on to give equal amounts of time and energy to all human beings. We have to deploy our very limited powers selectively. The notion of equality does not displace intelligent selection, but exists to guide it. It prevents us from overlooking certain urgent claims which lie outside our ordinary interests. In the case of human beings, therefore, it is not a stultifying principle, spraying out an unmanageable infinite range of diluted equal duties. . . . Its first function is to point out certain definite duties which we would otherwise not see. Its second, which is subtler and wider, is to change the way in which we look at human beings in general, including those with whom we have no practical concern at all. It reminds us (in Kantian language) that they too are persons, not things, that they are entitled to respect because they exist as ends in themselves. . . . There is somebody inside there.[59]

I couldn't agree more. But, unless a convincing argument defeats equal consideration for animals, we should make corresponding points for them. Equal consideration for animals would not entail an infinite number of equally diluted duties. It would point out certain important direct duties, such as a prima facie duty not to cause suffering. And it would have most of us make a gestalt shift in our view of animals. Sentient animals are not resources to be exploited for human benefit, but beings whose interests matter in their own right. There is, after all, "somebody inside there."

The argument from moral agency

1. The position. Some thinkers explicitly employ what I call *the argument from moral agency* to justify special moral status for human beings.[60] I believe it also underlies many people's pretheoretical think-

[59] ibid, p. 94
[60] See, e.g., Cohen, "The Case for the Use of Animals in Biomedical Research"; Tibor R. Machan, "Do Animals Have Rights?," *Public Affairs Quarterly* 5 (1991), p. 170; H. J. McCloskey, "Moral Rights and Animals," *Inquiry* 22 (1979): 25–35; Bonnie Steinbock, "Speciesism and the Idea of Equality," *Philosophy* 53 (1978), pp. 252–53; and Mary

ing about animals. Moreover, it can motivate and bolster contractarianism's case against equal consideration for animals (as suggested by Carruthers' arguments).

The argument from moral agency takes different forms, emphasizing different overlapping properties that characterize normal adult human beings: moral agency, autonomy, rationality, or the like. Because these properties tend to come together in normal adult humans, and because the arguments for the relevance of these properties seem fundamentally similar, I will simplify matters by focusing on just one of them: moral agency.

According to the position, all and only moral agents are entitled to equal consideration. This criterion is assumed to cover humans (at any rate the vast majority of them) but not animals. What is the relevance of moral agency?

I believe there are, at bottom, two important arguments for the relevance of moral agency. The first may be called *the argument from dignity.* Moral agents, the argument goes, possess what Kant called *dignity* simply in virtue of being moral agents. There is something inherently valuable about a being who can, to put it in Kantian idiom, determine her own will in accordance with moral law. Now the only moral agents are human beings. Animals, though sensitive creatures, lack the relevant property and therefore are not entitled to equal consideration—even if, contra Kant, they are thought to have some moral status. (While I have never found this argument compelling, I have been impressed by how many thoughtful, well-informed persons—including some moral philosophers—are convinced by it. I comment later on where my intuitions about moral relevance diverge from theirs, before trying to break the impasse.)

The second argument for the relevance of moral agency is based on a *principle of reciprocity.* According to this principle, it is impossible for A to have duties to B unless B has duties to A. In the present context, since animals presumably cannot have duties to humans, humans cannot be thought to have duties to animals. (Since the duties in question are direct duties—see "Reflections on some thought-experiments," earlier in the chapter—this position denies that animals have any moral status.) Moral agents have duties only to other moral agents, meaning human beings.

Why accept the principle of reciprocity?[61] One defense is that this principle is simply *self-evident.* A second, perhaps more plausible

Ann Warren, "Human and Animal Rights Compared," in Robert Elliot and Arran Gare (eds.), *Environmental Philosophy* (University Park, PA: Penn State University Press, 1983): 112–123.

[61] For an early discussion of this principle and its implications for animals, see W. D. Ross, *The Right and the Good* (Oxford: Oxford University Press, 1930), pp. 48–50.

defense is that the principle is grounded in *fairness*. To have and act in accordance with moral duties is to restrict one's freedom and forgo certain benefits; it is therefore a burden. But it is unfair for some to incur a burden for the benefit of others—those to whom they have duties—unless those others also incur a burden for the benefit of members of the first group. If humans had duties to animals, they would bear a moral burden while animals enjoyed a free ride, as it were. This would be unfair, according to the argument.

2. Critique. I believe three stumbling blocks prevent the argument from moral agency from meeting the burden of proof shouldered by the inegalitarian: (1) the problem of relevance, (2) the problem of marginal cases, and (3) the gradualist thesis about moral agency.

The *problem of relevance* is the problem of convincingly establishing the moral relevance of a particular characteristic present in humans but not in animals. Here the problem may be seen as the argumentative move from premise (p1) to conclusion (c):

(p1) All and only humans are moral agents.
Ergo (c) all and only humans are due full (equal) consideration.

On the face of it, this is quite a jump—from a factual claim to a profound moral conclusion. At least this additional moral premise about relevance is needed:

(p2) All and only moral agents are due full (equal) consideration.

The reasoning is still not transparent. *Why* are all and only moral agents due full (equal) consideration? Here's where either the argument from dignity or the principle of reciprocity comes in.

According to the argument from dignity, all and only moral agents are due equal consideration because moral agency confers an exclusive dignity on the agent. But how does one get from the claim that A is a moral agent to the conclusion that A has a dignity such that A's interests carry more weight than the relevantly similar interests of nonagents?

As far as I can make out, to have dignity just means to be the sort of being who deserves full moral consideration or who has full moral status. (Note that having full moral status—enjoying full moral protection in some sense—would entail deserving full, equal consideration; whether deserving equal consideration entails full moral status is uncertain and will be considered in Chapter 8.) I do not get any clear sense that dignity is some distinct nonmoral fact that is supposed to have moral relevance. The term *dignity* seems to be a rhetorical flourish announcing a being's moral status. (Interestingly, sounding this flourish might be self-defeating, for one might find it plausible to follow Regan in asserting that all subjects-of-a-life have dignity.[62]) Thus, we are left, in effect, with the earlier claim that moral agency is per se morally relevant.

Does the principle of reciprocity establish the relevance of agency? No, because there is no good reason to accept the principle. Many do not find it self-evident, especially after considering the fact that human babies, who are not moral agents, seem to be the recipients of some duties (such as our duty not to abuse them). And the fairness argument seems question-begging. How could we say, in advance of working out our moral relationship to animals, whether moral agents might not have duties to beings who have no reciprocal duties? If the argument is intuitive—it seems unfair that the moral burden could be so unevenly distributed—note that this sense of fairness does not prevent us, again, from taking human babies to be the recipients of duties. (And not all of them have the potential for moral agency.) Moreover, it seems at least as unfair that some individuals might be permitted routinely to harm other individuals, without compensation, for the first group's benefit—as permitted by most views that assume unequal consideration.

Any tendency to find the principle of reciprocity either self-evident or grounded in fairness probably results from a reduction of all morality to contractual arrangements. As we saw earlier, such a reduction is probably unable to deal plausibly with humans who are not moral agents. Worse, the principle of reciprocity implies that we have no direct duties to animals at all—a thesis we have seen collapse under careful scrutiny.[63]

Let us consider the problem of relevance from another angle. Clearly, the fact that A (say, your sister) is a moral agent, whereas B (say, your baby) is not, is relevant to regarding A as responsible for her actions but

---

[62] Regan uses the term *inherent value* in lieu of *dignity*. He begins with the safer claim that moral agents have equal inherent value before arguing that restricting such value to moral agents is arbitrary (*The Case for Animal Rights*, pp. 235–41). That Regan speaks of inherent value as a "postulate" is consistent with my claim that *inherent value* and *dignity* are used to announce moral status rather than to describe some fact upon which a being's moral status is supposedly based.

[63] It might be argued that I have interpreted reciprocity too strongly. Rather than implying that animals cannot be the recipients of *duties,* the argument goes, reciprocity implies that animals cannot be the recipients of (do not deserve) *equal consideration*. This more modest thesis is not vulnerable to the charge of having wildly implausible implications. But this move is undermined by the logic driving the idea of a reciprocity requirement, which seems to lead back to the stronger thesis. For (according to the argument from moral agency) animals are not moral agents and therefore cannot reciprocate *any* duties we might have to them. This modified position also shares with the unmodified reciprocity view the other difficulties under discussion.

not so regarding B. Clearly, the fact that C (a bird) is sentient, while D (a boulder) is not, is relevant to taking care not to drop a rock on C (thereby causing her pain and distress) without being so concerned about D. But how is the fact that A is a moral agent whereas B (who is sentient) is not, relevant to the claim that, say, A's pain of some duration and intensity should carry more moral weight than B's pain of the same duration and intensity?[64] The connection is dark. Indeed, I suspect there is no connection.

Perhaps some of the appeal of the present position stems from a Midgley-like confusion between (1) what interests a being has, and (2) how much moral weight to give whatever interests a being has. Moral agency and related properties can crucially affect item (1)—for example, giving rise to autonomy-based interests—with the result that we should treat moral agents differently from nonagents. For example, paternalistic acts may be helpful to a dog or baby but quite inappropriate in the case of a moral agent. But what is at issue is item (2).

Now one might respond that equal consideration for (sentient) animals also makes an arbitrary connection between sentience and moral status. This is a confused accusation, however. Sentience is a condition for having interests (a claim defended in Chapter 8), the protection of which is the business of morality. To treat those lacking any interests at all as having moral status makes little sense. Moreover, in a way, the principle of equal consideration does not deny equal consideration for nonsentient things like rocks. You could say that equal consideration is extended to all things, but in the case of rocks, there are no interests to take into account.[65]

Nevertheless, moral justifications do give out somewhere, and there may be room for reasonable disagreement about where it gives out in a given context. For many people, apparently, moral agency per se really does seem relevant to how much one's interests count. No further connection needs to be made explicit because the relevance of agency, according to the argument, is basic.

This position is stronger than the sui generis view. It seems much more likely that moral agency is relevant to how much consideration one is to be given than that species per se is relevant. Species, a somewhat arbitrary genetic matter, seems a remote consideration once clearly in focus; moral agency—which, after all, is a moral concept—is more plausible. While I do not find the proposed connection compelling, I will not be dogmatic in claiming its irrelevance. So far, our intuitive sense of moral relevance seems indeterminate with respect to this

---

[64] Cf. Rachels, *Created from Animals*, pp. 177–78.
[65] Singer, *Animal Liberation*, pp. 7–8

characteristic. I will undermine the argument from moral agency with further critique.

First, there remains the *problem of marginal cases*. Not all human beings are either actually, potentially, or formerly moral agents. Yet it is very hard to believe that those humans who fail to meet this standard are not entitled to equal consideration. One might argue that the consequences of giving them less-than-equal consideration are so pernicious as to justify giving them, in practice, equal consideration. (Carruthers' slippery-slope argument and argument from social stability are versions of this claim.) As noted in our critique of contractarianism, that move has problems involving the implication that their status depends on contingencies in a way that other humans' status does not, and involving the possibility that we are wrong about the existence of such contingencies. Any position that avoids the problem of marginal cases has an advantage over theories hounded by it. Equal consideration for animals has this advantage over inegalitarianism based on the argument from moral agency.

The latter position is also vitiated by the fact that moral agency is most reasonably viewed as a *matter of degree that is not exclusively human*.[66] As argued more fully in Chapter 7, nature does not endow humans with all of the characteristics that make up moral agency and endow other creatures with none of them. The capacities to project into the future, to learn from experience, to keep multiple considerations in mind, to feel for others, to make decisions, and so on are found, to some degree at least, in many mammals. Such capacities are more highly developed in animals who are generally more complex. But it is oversimplified to say that only humans are moral agents.

Of course, one could stipulate some degree of moral agency as a *threshold*, claiming that only humans meet it. But the fact that any such line would be somewhat arbitrary, given the *gradualist thesis*, puts in question any attempt to place great weight on it. We are to believe that everyone on one side of this arbitrary line should receive full (equal) consideration, while everyone on the other side should receive less consideration. Even if there are different kinds of moral agency as well as degrees (as I myself argue in Chapter 7), it is hard to see why only one kind would be so morally crucial.

In addition, if a threshold is drawn low enough to catch the vast majority of humans, we will probably have to grant some animals full moral status. (This is true even if we shuttle in the very young on claims of potential, and the very old with a "can't lose it" thesis.) Dolphins and Great Apes quite arguably demonstrate as much moral agency as, say,

---

[66] See, e.g., S. F. Sapontzis, *Morals, Reason, and Animals* (Philadelphia: Temple University Press, 1987), ch. 3; and Rachels, *Created from Animals*, ch. 4.

the moderately retarded[67] (see Chapter 7)—but we had better count the latter as moral agents, lest the problem of marginal cases spin completely out of control. (Open-minded inegalitarians might not mind bucking tradition and bringing a few nonhuman species into the circle of full moral status.)

In conclusion, the argument from moral agency makes a debatable case for the relevance of moral agency, is plagued by the problem of marginal cases, and is rendered somewhat more doubtful by the gradualist thesis. In light of these arguments—in conjunction with the likelihood of bias here (namely, the desire to confer unique standing on human beings)—it is most reasonable to regard the argument from moral agency as failing to overturn the presumption in favor of equal consideration. Indeed, it is perhaps most reasonable to regard the intuition that moral agency is necessary for equal consideration as itself a product of bias.

The argument from coherence

1. **The position.** A fifth challenge to equal consideration attempts to turn the tables on our coherence theorizing. It argues that the thesis that animals are due less-than-equal consideration is part of a moral position that is more coherent than a position adopting equal consideration. In light of the problem of marginal cases, the problem of relevance, and the gradualist thesis, the inegalitarian thesis is admittedly somewhat ad hoc. But further considerations of coherence more than make up for this theoretical imperfection, according to the argument.

Taking up the anti-foundationalist metaphor of a ship, no single plank of which is indispensable, Flanagan points out that "logical elegance is not all we care about. There is also the matter of staying afloat. Some constructions provide roomier, more comfortable lodgings and overall happier, safer, less treacherous and rough trips."[68] It may be logically a little messy, but otherwise desirable, to brush off the burden of proof on the inegalitarian. Considering the radical revisions that would be entailed for our institutions and practices, it is best to sacrifice some logical elegance by accepting unequal consideration without a thoroughly worked-out, perfectly consistent argument justifying the presumed difference between humans and animals.

This argument reveals the significant tie between classical pragmatism (as represented by Peirce, James, and Dewey) and contemporary

---

[67] See, e.g., the numerous discussions of chimpanzees and dolphins in Rodd, *Biology, Ethics and Animals.*
[68] Owen J. Flanagan, Jr., "Quinean Ethics," *Ethics* 93 (October 1982), p. 72

coherentist theorizing.[69] One challenge that the present approach shares with classical pragmatism is that any assumed account of *what works* or *what is practical*—understood as a criterion for ethical conduct—cannot take into account consequences for humans while discounting consequences for animals, without begging the question.[70] But a modest amount of question-begging is the sort of logical price that this position claims to be worth paying. It builds on classical pragmatism by exploiting the flexibility of the coherence model.

Alternatively, the present approach can jettison the appeal to pragmatic considerations and lean on the point about people's actual moral convictions. Equal consideration for animals would do too much violence to our moral beliefs to be worth the theoretical price. Better to accept the admittedly ad hoc sharp division in status between humans and animals in order to stem the tide of a massive upheaval of people's beliefs. For, in coherence theorizing, we have to start where we are and make revisions only if doing so increases overall coherence. Where we are is most decidely in an outlook that regards animals—especially those not among the "higher animals"—as fundamentally less deserving of moral consideration than are fellow humans.

2. Critique. The only way to take on this coherence-based approach is head on, by showing clearly that the theoretical virtues of the coherence approach (see Chapter 2) do not vindicate unequal consideration. Let us begin with the inegalitarian's strongest appeal here, which implicitly invokes the virtue of plausibility. The most prevalent beliefs about animals seem to vindicate the inegalitarian position; extending equal consideration to animals would be highly revisionist, tearing much of the fabric of popular moral thought.

But notice that those intuitions have little if any probative force. First, they conform to pro-human bias and may simply reflect it. Second, people who have grappled long and hard with the philosophical problems associated with the moral status of animals have much more mixed intuitions than those who have not subjected their views to vigorous scrutiny and challenge. Some evidence for that claim is the animal ethics literature. Those persons who have worked through these issues sufficiently to publish on them do not vindicate inegalitarianism. Their intuitions are mixed, and quite a few end up supporting equal consideration (see Chapter 1). Where bias is as likely as it is here, we must be very wary of prereflective intuitions. They certainly don't qualify as considered judgments.

---

[69] For a historical discussion of this tie, see John P. Murphy, *Pragmatism: From Peirce to Davidson* (Boulder, CO: Westview, 1990).
[70] John Dewey's moral philosophy, for example, begs the question in this way. See James Gouinlock (ed.), *The Moral Writings of John Dewey* (New York: Hafner, 1976).

Now that it is clear that the inegalitarian does not enjoy an advantage in terms of plausibility, it is quite easy to show that unequal consideration (in the absence of some unknown compelling argument) is less coherent than equal consideration for animals. First, the problem of marginal cases remains. If some humans are denied equal consideration, then the position suffers in terms of plausibility. If these humans are protected only by appeal to contingencies such as side effects, there is perhaps some sacrifice in plausibility and surely some uncertainty about the empirical basis for the move. If all humans are claimed to be covered by equal consideration *in principle,* then the view suffers in terms of argumentative support. For, as we have seen, no argument has explained this radical demarcation of standing between all humans and all animals. If the inegalitarian claims that some property justifies equal consideration for all humans, even though some humans in fact lack the property, the view fails in terms of logical consistency. If the inegalitarian gets really ad hoc and claims that we have two different moralities—one for humans and one for animals—without explaining how they relate, why they are different, and so on, then the position lacks global illumination.

I believe that unequal consideration for animals, in the absence of a well-argued defense, also entails a sacrifice in terms of another virtue: compatibility or coherence with whatever else we know or reasonably believe. Radical demarcation between humans and animals seems to fit better with a world view in which we did not evolve from other species but were created more or less in our present form. That picture makes the idea of a human essence more congenial. And while it certainly takes argument to move from the factual claim about a human essence to the moral claim about unique moral status, perhaps such an argument could be provided. But in virtue of the facts of evolution, the inegalitarian's view is shakier. This position is not logically incompatible with evolution; the two certainly do not contradict each other. But it is hard to see how unique moral standing for humans can fit well with the facts of evolution.[71]

A further factual challenge to inegalitarianism comes from our increasing understanding of animals' mental capacities and social living. The next four chapters are devoted to the mental life of animals. To anticipate a conclusion, many animals reveal far more cognitive, emotional, and social complexity than scientists have traditionally granted. The complexity of animals supports gradualist theses not only about moral agency but also about other properties that may be morally salient (such as sociability and self-awareness). As we saw earlier, it is

[71] See Rachels, *Created from Animals,* chs. 2 and 3.

difficult to square such gradualism with the sharp discontinuity of moral status proposed by the inegalitarian.

In conclusion, unless and until a solid argument is found to support unequal consideration, the theoretical virtues of the coherence model favor equal consideration for animals.

Chapter 4

Motivation and methods
for studying animal minds

We have now investigated methodology in ethics, animals' basic moral status, and the issue of equal consideration. In this and the following three chapters, we will explore the mental lives of animals, before returning to ethics. This detour may seem abrupt. Why turn from morals to mind?

REASONS TO EXPLORE THE MENTAL LIFE OF ANIMALS

Confronting the scientific and philosophical issues pertaining to animal mentation is an essential part of taking animals seriously and is best done before pushing further into ethics. This is so for several reasons.

First, exploring animals' mental lives is necessary for determining which animals have *basic moral status*. As was explained in Chapter 3 (and will be elaborated on in Chapter 8), only beings with interests have moral status, and only sentient beings—who, by definition, have certain mental states (see Chapter 5)—have interests. What exactly are these mental states and which animals have them?

But we want to know more than which animals have moral status. Perhaps (even from an equal-consideration view) there are some morally significant *differences* among beings with moral status. Thus, we want to know (1) whether there are morally important differences among beings with moral status, and, if so, (2) what factual variables underlie such differences, and, in general, (3) which morally relevant traits particular animals have. As we will see in Chapter 8, to determine all this requires work in value theory. And since (as we will also see) any plausible value theory cashes prudential value at least partly in terms of mental states—such as enjoyment and suffering, or desires—value theory across species requires us to learn about animal minds. (For convenience, I will use *mental states* as a shorthand for mental states, events, processes, or the like.[1])

So both the assignment of moral status and value theory make animal minds matter. Now it was argued in Chapter 3 that we should extend equal consideration to animals—that is, give equal moral weight to their relevantly similar interests. But even those who believe (however mistakenly!) that they can justify *unequal* consideration for animals have reason to explore animal mentation. For they are likely to justify their views on the basis of different mental capacities. Some people, for example, believe that moral agency is necessary and sufficient for deserving equal (full) consideration. Some give a similar role to autonomy, while others stress such traits as self-awareness and linguistic competence. As we will see in Chapter 7, plausible analyses of these traits make reference to mental capacities. Assuming such theorists do not go in for the completely indefensible view that only, say, moral agents have any moral status at all, they will presumably acknowledge that some other characteristics are relevant to *how much* weight a being's interests should receive. A proponent of unequal consideration might hold, for example, that (1) only autonomous beings are due full consideration, and (2) the degree of (less-than-equal) consideration other animals are due is correlated to the complexity of their consciousness. Such a view would motivate an examination of animal mentation, in order to determine which animals are autonomous, and to determine the complexity of the consiousness of nonautonomous conscious beings.

Thus, for several reasons and even from different ethical viewpoints, the path to the ethical treatment of animals runs through their minds. In terms of the theoretical virtues embraced by the coherence model (see Chapter 2), we need to ensure that our moral claims about animals are compatible or coherent with the rest of what we know or reasonably believe—in particular, regarding what animals are like.

Ironically, statements by researchers and others who work regularly with animals frequently suggest far less understanding of animals than one might expect. Often these instances of intellectual error converge with moral failings. Here is an example of a wildly implausible claim about monkeys' mental lives in the context of unethical treatment of the monkeys (treatment inconsistent with equal consideration, or probably any serious consideration, for the monkeys):

> The Defense Nuclear Agency confirmed that, over a five-year period, 1,379 primates—nearly all of them rhesus monkeys—had been used in its tests. In one set of tests, the animals had been subjected to lethal doses of

---

[1] An everyday understanding of what is to count as *mental* will suffice for now. The complexities of defining this concept rigorously will be discussed in Chapter 5.

radiation and then forced by electric shock to run on a treadmill until they collapsed. Before dying, the unanesthetized monkeys suffered the predictable effects of excessive radiation, including vomiting and diarrhoea. After acknowledging all this, a DNA spokesman commented: "To the best of our knowledge, the animals experience no pain."[2]

Surprisingly, many researchers and veterinarians do not distinguish between anesthesia and chemical restraint. The latter immobilizes an animal so that she cannot "protest" or writhe but does nothing to ease the unpleasant states caused by surgery.[3]

Errors such as these demonstrate the importance of studying animal minds. But reasons to do so are not limited to an ulterior ethical interest in appropriate treatment of animals. Animal minds are fascinating in their own right. Such questions as which animals are conscious, what kinds of feelings they have, and whether and to what extent they can communicate are of tremendous intrinsic interest. And the public's hunger for answers to these sorts of questions is growing rapidly.

Thus, in my view, taking animals seriously means taking their minds seriously—both in order to know how we should treat them and just to know what they are like. Doing so naturally requires attending to evidence. But what sorts of evidence should count? The discussion of method that follows addresses this question.

METHOD

Seeking reflective equilibrium using several approaches

We need a method for collecting and assessing evidence regarding animal mentation. The method I favor involves striving to attain reflective equilibrium among four ways of finding out about mental phenomena: (1) human phenomenology; (2) the study of animal behavior; (3) functional-evolutionary arguments; and (4) physiological evidence.[4]

---

[2] James Rachels, *Created from Animals: The Moral Implications of Darwinism* (Oxford: Oxford University Press, 1990), p. 132

[3] Bernard E. Rollin, *The Unheeded Cry: Animal Consciousness, Animal Pain, and Science* (Oxford: Oxford University Press, 1989), pp. 146–47. Extensive study of the practices and professional culture of animal researchers leads Rollin to conclude that they tend to be quite uninformed about many mental and physiological features of the animals they use. As an example, few researchers control for, or even think of, the effects of caretakers' behavior and attitudes on animal subjects (pp. 125–26). He also presents striking examples from American medicine of how a casual attitude about the mental lives of certain *humans*—such as women, minorities, the indigent, and infants—often accompanies a casual moral attitude about them (pp. 131–33).

[4] Much of the spirit of this method can be found in Owen Flanagan, *Consciousness Reconsidered* (Cambridge, MA: MIT Press, 1992), pp. 11–12. Flanagan has a different list of approaches to work into reflective equilibrium, no doubt because he is wrestling with a different problem—the nature of human consciousness in particular.

The idea is to treat with respect each kind of evidence—without prioritizing any of them—and work toward theses about animal mentation that do justice to all of the available evidence. The four (sub)methods approach mental phenomena in different ways, but they are compatible. Some philosophers and scientists disagree, and, as we will see, many prioritize one kind of evidence over others. Later I will argue against such prioritizing in reviewing their positions.

1. Human phenomenology: A familiar point of departure.[5] We want to study animals' minds and learn about their contents, but we have no direct experiential—that is, phenomenological—access to animals' minds. I assume, first, that human minds have contents and, second, that our study of human phenomenology (explained more fully later) helps us to understand these contents. Evidence of the kinds discussed in the next three sections provides good reason to believe (as we will see in Chapters 5, 6, and 7) that many animals have minds whose contents are not wholly dissimilar to the contents of human minds. Therefore, we need human phenomenology to study animal minds. Specifically, human phenomenology *sets an agenda of what kinds of mental states to look for* in animals and *provides a start in understanding the qualitative features* of animal mentation. Both of these functions merit elaboration in the context of a fuller discussion of human phenomenology.

Human phenomenology is the study of the subjective experiences of human beings—how things seem or feel to them. In the absence of human phenomenology, we could describe animals' behavior in certain ways, argue that certain behaviors seem to have been favored by natural selection, and describe animal brains. But in studying animals' *mental* lives, we need a clearer sense of what to look for—namely, certain *mental states*. Thus, we need to have some referents. We can use the same referents as we use in human phenomenology—such as *pain, fear,* and *desires*—and attribute the mental states to which they refer to animals, as long as the available evidence justifies the attributions.

Underlying both the assumption that we can profitably employ the referents used in human phenomenology and the assumption (mentioned earlier) that human phenomenology helps us to understand our mental contents is a more basic assumption: that folk psychology is more or less in order. *Folk psychology—or common-sense psychology—*makes use of everyday mental vocabulary in talking and theorizing about human mental life and behavior. It speaks of beliefs, desires, intentions, fears, memories, and the like. Phenomenology is assumed to give us information about such states (even if not infallibly). I assume

[5] The structuring of this section owes much to Steve Fleishman's criticisms of an earlier draft.

without argument that normal human beings have the mental states countenanced in folk psychology.[6]

In addition to its agenda-setting function, phenomenology also explores the more qualitative features of mental states, such as pleasantness and unpleasantness. Human phenomenology, which gives us a great deal of information about the qualitative features of human mental life, also (in combination with other forms of evidence) helps us begin to understand the more qualitative features of animal mentation. For moral purposes, we must explore how animals (qualitatively) experience the world because part of their world is the effects of our actions on them, and that is our major moral concern.

By *phenomenology,* philosophers sometimes seem to refer specifically to the study of how things seem to oneself, the subject herself, and no one else. But presumably even Descartes' *Meditations,* although composed in the first-person singular, was written so that readers could introspect in parallel with Descartes and reach similar results.[7] In speaking of *human* phenomenology, I mean the way things seem or feel to humans, plural; the method has both first- and third-person components and is neutral between them. The basic idea is to take, more or less at face value, the apparently sincere testimony of apparently normal human beings about how things seem to them. The testimony is neither challenged without special cause nor accepted as infallible; it is taken seriously as a source of data about human beings' mental lives. We might question—not reject out of hand—testimony that we have trouble understanding, as when someone claims she feels great pain but doesn't mind it at all (since we might wonder whether what she feels is really pain). We might question someone's testimony when we doubt its sincerity, like that of a drug dealer who checks into a psychiatric hospital every time he gets into legal trouble, with no physiological symptoms to corroborate his complaints. But in ordinary cases, we do not doubt someone's testimony about her subjective states.[8]

---

[6] For philosophical defenses of folk psychology, see, e.g., Patricia Kitcher, "In Defense of Intentional Psychology," *Journal of Philosophy* 81 (1984): 89–106; and Jerry A. Fodor, "Banish DisContent," in J. Butterfield (ed.), *Language, Mind and Logic* (Cambridge: Cambridge University Press, 1986).

[7] René Descartes, *Meditations on First Philosophy* (Paris: Michel Soly, 1641). The observation about Descartes is made in Daniel C. Dennett, *Consciousness Explained* (Boston, MA: Little, Brown and Company, 1991), p. 66.

[8] Some may argue that acceptance of other people's testimony begs a major philosophical question—*the problem of other minds.* Since I can experience only my own consciousness, how do I know other persons are conscious (let alone, have particular mental states, such as fears and memories)? My assumption that folk psychology is more or less in order already assumes that other people have minds. I am content to beg that question. (Fortunately, you, reader, agree that other people have mental states and that you often have reasonable beliefs about what they are.)

Appeals to human phenomenology allow us to argue by analogy, using the other three methods (described later), to claims about the mental states of animals. How so? First, let us assume something that all scientists and good metaphysicians assume—the principle of parsimony. This principle states that if two explanations of some phenomenon have equal explanatory power (and are otherwise equally coherent), we should accept the simpler of them. As we will learn in Chapters 5, 6, and 7, the simplest explanation of similarities between human and animal behavior, selective pressures, and nervous systems will often be a specific similarity in mental life. Note that the sort of analogy constructed here is not from the case of a single individual, the subject, but from the case of human beings generally. There is nothing inherently irresponsible about this sort of generalization. Indeed, given the principle of parsimony, it would be irresponsible—irrational—to abstain from such inferences when the relevant sorts of evidence support them.

2. Animal behavior: Labs and fields, controls and anecdotes. Do animals experience pleasure and pain? Do they fear, remember, and anticipate? Well, for starters, do they act as if they do? Some people believe that they can answer many questions about the mental lives of animals on the basis of casual observation of animal behavior. At best, this armchair view depends on highly contentious philosophical theses. Part of my strategy in this chapter is to avoid such contentious theses— at any rate unnecessary ones—so I reject the armchair view. There are more reliable ways of observing animal behavior.

But, first, why believe that behavior has any role in understanding the mental lives of animals? The short answer is that there are obviously important connections between mental life and behavior. So animal behavior is an important source of evidence. How should it be studied?

Most of the scientific study of animals in recent decades has been in laboratories. Laboratory studies permit considerable rigor; observations are repeatable, typically measurable, and relatively well controlled in the scientific sense of weeding out irrelevant factors that might otherwise influence data. Part of mainstream science, laboratory studies enjoy the reputation of both a history of success and grounding in sound scientific principles.

But laboratory studies also have some disadvantages, which until recently have been largely ignored by scientists and funding bodies. (Ignoring these disadvantages is probably due in part to ideological commitments mistaken for objective scientific thinking.[9]) One disadvantage of such studies is that they require animals to be examined in

[9]See Rollin, *The Unheeded Cry*, pp. 39–42.

conditions that are extremely unnatural to them. These unnatural conditions can influence animals' behavior—and even physiology—in ways that invalidate results. Another disadvantage with laboratory studies is that use of multiple trials, which allows for statistical validity, can make it difficult to test animals in truly novel settings. Yet the capacity for reasoning, for example, is probably best studied in the context of novelty. Laboratory studies also tend to be extremely expensive, so there are financial constraints to how much we can learn from laboratories. (There are, of course, also ethical issues concerning the use of animals in laboratory studies, which usually harm the animal subjects.)

For these and other reasons, some scientists prefer to observe the behavior of animals in their natural habitats. But field studies pose special methodological problems. Reports of animals' responses to truly novel settings are anecdotal; they are not subject to repetition and are usually unquantifiable. It used to be the case that saying that certain data were anecdotal was tantamount to saying that they were scientifically invalid. Today, there is a lively debate about whether anecdotes have any scientific value. So here is our question: In observing animal behavior, should we favor lab studies or field studies, carefully controlled experiments or anecdotes?

Let us take each type of study seriously but also critically. Despite some difficulties, controlled laboratory studies of animal behavior undeniably provide useful information. But developments in ethology (see the next major section) make field studies and even some use of anecdotes scientifically respectable. Not only do field studies have the advantages associated with observing animals in their natural habitat; they also admit of controls, if researchers are sufficiently imaginative. And, as Dawkins points out, there are such things as disciplined anecdotes—case histories of specific incidents that have been collated and critically scrutinized with a view toward finding out whether a species of animal has a particular capacity, such as the ability to deceive.[10] At the very least, anecdotal data are appropriately used to guide further data collection and to suggest new experimental designs.[11] Thus, each type of study has limitations but clearly provides data worth considering, and there is no reason to think that the different kinds of data are incompatible.

3. Functional-evolutionary arguments: Mind in Darwinian context.
One type of evidence about the mental life of animals has, until recently, been largely neglected. Dorothy Cheney and Robert Seyfarth, who are

[10] Marian Stamp Dawkins, *Through Our Eyes Only?: The Search for Animal Consciousness* (Oxford: Freeman, 1993), p. 129
[11] Marc Bekoff (personal communication)

renowned for their research on vervet monkeys, introduce the approach as follows:

> [W]e have adopted a functional, evolutionary approach to the study of primate intelligence. If representations of certain aspects of the world exist in the minds of monkeys, we assume that they do so because they confer a selective advantage on those who make use of them. We also assume that what is represented, as well as the structure of information contained within a representation, will be determined by the relative utility of one sort of mental operation as opposed to another.[12]

That Cheney and Seyfarth focus on intelligence here might be taken to exclude certain mental states (e.g., sensations, emotions), but we will not restrict our inquiry in that way. We might recast their statement, more cautiously, as follows: *In the absence of a reason to think otherwise in a particular case,* we should assume that if an animal has a type of mental state, the type of mental state confers a selective advantage on its possessor. Not every trait that survives natural selection increases reproductive fitness. Like genes, traits are inherited in bundles, and some are free-riders on others that confer advantages. Male nipples and blushing may be free-riders, whereas female nipples, clearly, and shame, probably, have functions.[13] Maybe some types of mental states are free-riders.

Colin Allen and Marc D. Hauser elaborate on the theoretical role played by mental concepts in cognitive ethology (a discipline to be discussed more fully in the next major section):

---

[12] D. L. Cheney and R. M. Seyfarth, "The Representation of Social Relations by Monkeys," in C. R. Gallistel (ed.), *Animal Cognition* (Cambridge, MA: MIT Press, 1992), p. 186. As Hugh LaFollette pointed out to me, some philosophers might question the authors' assumption that animal mentality must involve *representations;* indeed, some philosophers apparently believe that there are no such things. While I am not sure exactly what theoretical baggage they put into their conception of a representation, I think that there is a conception innocent enough to obviate serious criticism. Dennett puts it better than I can:

> Some of the variability in a brain is required simply to provide a medium for the moment-to-moment transient patterns of brain activity that somehow *register* or at any rate *track* the importantly variable features of the environment. Something in the brain needs to change so that it can keep track of the bird that flies by, or the drop in air temperature, or one of the organism's own states—the drop in blood sugar, the increase of carbon dioxide in the lungs. Moreover . . . these transient internal patterns come to be able to continue to "track" (in an extended sense) the features they refer to when they are temporarily cut off from causal commerce with their referents. (*Consciousness Explained*, p. 191)

[13] For some plausible speculations about the adaptiveness of shame for a social species, see Allan Gibbard, *Wise Choices, Apt Feelings* (Cambridge, MA: Harvard University Press, 1990), pp. 136–40, 295–98.

Questions about the function of a particular behavior are commonly answered by explaining how the behavior in question contributes to the fitness of the organism. Mentalistic terms provide a level of description that is appropriate to the functional level of description that is the concern of evolutionary hypotheses. Mental states relate organisms to their environments through the notion of content. A mental state will be adaptive insofar as its content provides for appropriate links between environment and behavior. Mentalistic terms thus provide a natural vocabulary for cognitive ethologists to frame their hypotheses.[14]

While animals' behaviors and physical traits have long been studied in terms of evolutionary function, scientific confidence about applying cognitive or mentalistic vocabulary to animals is a recent development. The attribution of a type of mental state to an animal receives support from a functional-evolutionary argument if that type of mental state would appear to be advantageous for the animal—in terms of reproductive fitness—given the animal's environment, characteristic behaviors and physical traits, and other known facts about it.

It is not claimed that such arguments *by themselves* justify attributions of particular mental states to animals, just that they furnish one form of evidence supporting such attributions. Could anyone claim that functional-evolutionary arguments are irrelevant here? Not reasonably. Some persons, of course, deny the "theory" of evolution, yanking the foundational rug from under the present sort of argument. I simply note that I assume this theory to be true at least in rough outline.

4. Physiology: Looking at the hardware. A fourth type of evidence for the existence of mental states in animals comes from physiology, especially neurophysiology, the study of the brain and central nervous system. Even with different philosophies of mind, on the basis of available evidence, we can agree that mental states in humans are closely related to brain structure and activity. This is so whether mental states in general are identical with, caused by, emergent properties of, or just correlated with, brain states.

Although it may seem obvious to say, respectable scientific theories hold that humans cannot have certain mental states without certain parts of the brain functioning. The existence of very similar neurological structures in other animals constitutes *some* evidence that they can have the sorts of mental states correlated with those parts of the human brain. The evidence can be strengthened by (1) evidence that the animal brain part *functions similarly* to the way the corresponding human brain part functions (say, if the animal becomes incapable of certain behaviors

[14] "Concept Attribution in Nonhuman Animals: Theoretical and Methodological Problems in Ascribing Complex Mental Processes," *Philosophy of Science* 58 (1991), p. 224

in the event that the brain part in question is badly damaged), or (2) the observation of certain *structural neurophysiological connections* (e.g., connections, in humans and animals, from the occipital lobes to what is already known to be the visual sensory apparatus). A promising sort of evidence of type (1) comes from brain-scanning techniques, such as positron emission tomography (PET) scans. PET scans allow a viewer to observe, via a special camera, the activity of specific brain parts. For example, if subjects listen to speech in a language that they understand, certain association areas in the cortex light up; but if they hear speech in a language they do not understand, these same areas do not light up.[15] Creative use of this technology may help greatly in understanding the function of animal brain parts that are anatomically similar to human brain parts.

As long as we are duly cautious in using neurophysiological evidence, there seems no good reason to deny its legitimacy. To be sure, similar mental states may be realized in different ways. Thus, we cannot assume that animals must have brain part B in order to have mental state M just because B is associated with M in our case; animals might lack B but have C, which functions similarly in producing M. But, in principle, we can detect when alternative anatomical routes have been taken in different species, again by examining the function and structural connections of animal brain parts. Now we also cannot assume that if animals have brain part B, which in us is associated with mental state M, they must also have M. The animals' environmental niche may have led to different sensory specializations, such that B in those animals is associated with a different mental state N. But, again, independent evidence can help in sorting out such matters. Thus, the presence of brain part B is itself neither necessary nor sufficient for having mental state M, but additional empirical data can establish that link.

That neurological analogy between humans and animals provides evidence about the mental states of animals is implied by the principle of parsimony and what we know about evolution. For the most part, what worked well in our ancestors will be found in us *Homo sapiens,* unless there was selective pressure to get rid of it (or, possibly, just lack of pressure to keep it).

The role of cognitive ethology and "the intentional stance"

What is cognitive ethology, and how does it fit into the methodology described here? Cognitive ethologists sometimes say that they take "the intentional stance." What does that involve?

---

[15] Derek Denton, *The Pinnacle of Life: Consciousness and Self-Awareness in Humans and Animals* (Sidney: Allyn & Unwin, 1993), pp. 166–68

Ethology is the study of animal behavior in the context of evolutionary theory. A behavior is studied in light of its function and its evolution.[16] *Cognitive ethology*, more specifically (at least as I use the term), is ethology that incorporates these rough tenets of cognitive psychology: (1) The explanation of behavior must posit inner states and episodes (as long as these are construed as physical); and (2) humans and other psychological organisms are best viewed as, in some sense, information-processing systems.[17] Cognitive ethology posits distinctively cognitive states and processes, such as desires and beliefs, as intermediaries between an animal's environment and behavior (as described previously by Allen and Hauser); many ethologists also posit more affective states such as pain, distress, and fear.[18] A little history will situate this approach in the vicinity of some of its competitors.

Like present-day cognitive ethologists, Charles Darwin argued for mental continuity between humans and animals, attributing cognitive states to animals. But he did so on the basis of observation of particular cases rather than controlled experiments. His approach might therefore be characterized as *anecdotal cognitivism*. *Behaviorism* arose partly in response to the anecdotal approach, hoping to bring rigor into the study of behavior. Controlled experiments in laboratories became the standard, and unobserved entities were taboo. Thus, animal consciousness and intentionality came to be seen as mysterious and scientifically inaccessible; confidence grew that all animal behavior could be described in stimulus–response terms. (Especially influential behaviorists were J. B. Watson in the 1920s and B. F. Skinner for several decades thereafter.) *Classical ethology* developed with the work of such pioneers as Konrad Lorenz and Niko Tinbergen, who emphasized such putative internal states as *instincts, drives,* and *motivational impulses*. But even as they received the Nobel Prize in 1973, many thought their "grand theory" of the instincts was already in shambles. No similarly comprehensive theory of instinct has arisen to replace the Lorenz-Tinbergen model. Some have turned to *neuroethology*, which examines animal behavior through the lens of neurology. While neuroethology has enjoyed great advances, many people believe that much of what we know about animal behavior cannot be explained in neurological terms (now or in the foreseeable future, perhaps even in principle). In any case, the publication in 1976 of Donald Griffin's *The Question of Animal Awareness*, which

[16]Colin Allen and Marc D. Hauser, "Concept Attribution in Nonhuman Animals," p. 224
[17]This characterization of cognitive psychology is found in William G. Lycan, "Ontology from Behaviorism to Functionalism: Introduction," in Lycan (ed.), *Mind and Cognition* (Cambridge, MA: Blackwell, 1990), p. 8.
[18]Dale Jamieson and Marc Bekoff, "On Aims and Methods of Cognitive Ethology," *Philosophy of Science Association* 2 (1993), p. 116

focused on thinking and feelings in animals, can serve to mark the rise of cognitive ethology.[19]

An explanation of *the intentional stance* will help to illuminate cognitive ethology. The intentional stance is a strategy for interpreting behavior in which an organism is regarded as having beliefs, desires, and other intentional states and as behaving for the most part rationally.[20] Thus, a dog who, upon the sounding of a dinner chime, rushes into the kitchen and in the direction of a dogfood dish is interpreted in this way: She desires food, believes that rushing toward the dish will get her food, and (quite rationally, given the desire and belief) intentionally rushes toward the dish. It would *not* be an interpretation taken from the intentional stance to interpret the dog as responding automatically and unwittingly to certain auditory and olfactory stimuli, or to regard her behavior as completely reducible to the activity of elementary particles dancing to the laws of physics. The intentional stance is to be preferred if it works better in explaining and predicting animals' behavior—in context and given what is known about their evolution—than any other interpretive perspective.

Note that our use of human phenomenology incorporates the intentional stance. In taking people more or less at their word as they describe their mental life, we treat them as agents with intentional states. As Dennett puts it,

> we must treat the noise-emitter as an agent, indeed a rational agent, who harbors beliefs and desires and other mental states that exhibit *intentionality* or "aboutness," and whose actions can be explained (or predicted) on the basis of the content of these states. Thus the uttered noises are to be interpreted as things the subjects *wanted to say,* of *propositions* they meant to *assert,* for instance, for various *reasons.*[21]

Now in interpreting animal behavior, we are (with very rare possible exceptions) deprived of such speech-acts. But, again, we can adopt the intentional stance toward animals. Indeed, taking the intentional stance toward animals, under proper evidentiary and theoretical constraints, is tantamount to cognitive ethology.

Increasingly, many scientists and philosophers of mind are coming to the conclusion that, for many "higher" animals, the intentional stance works better than any presently known alternative—most notably, be-

---

[19] *The Question of Animal Awareness* (New York: Rockefeller University Press, 1976). This paragraph owes much to the historical story presented in Jamieson and Bekoff, "On Aims and Methods of Cognitive Ethology," pp. 2–4.
[20] See Daniel C. Dennett, *The Intentional Stance* (Cambridge, MA: MIT Press, 1987).
[21] *Consciousness Explained*, p. 76

haviorism, which developed a "physical stance."[22] Of course, "higher" animals include humans. Accordingly, human sciences, such as economics, that have employed intentional concepts have seemed more successful at explaining and predicting behavior than sciences that have not, such as behavioristic psychology.

With this understanding of cognitive ethology and the intentional stance, how should we understand their relation to our overall methodology? Answering that question requires explaining the distinction between *weak cognitive ethology* (WCE) and *strong cognitive ethology* (SCE). In this section, I have spoken of the intentional stance as an approach that many people believe to be relatively successful in explaining and predicting animal behavior. WCE countenances the use of cognitive terms for these purposes but not for the additional purpose of describing animal behavior. To describe what a dog does in terms of desires, beliefs, and the like is to suggest that the dog really has such mental states. But WCE wants to assert only that treating the dog as if she had such mental states is useful in explaining and predicting her behavior. (Assuming that intentional idioms are to be used in describing human behavior, WCE holds a noteworthy double standard with respect to human and animal behavior.) SCE more boldly uses such vocabulary for explaining, predicting, and describing—some would prefer to say "interpreting"—the behavior of some animals.[23]

SCE risks begging many of the questions to be addressed in Chapters 5, 6, and 7, by regarding animals as *having* desires, beliefs, and other intentional states. Thus, we should not, in any given case, accept the intentional description of an animal's behavior (say, that a fox intends to avoid a predator) unless such a description really appears superior—all things considered—to alternatives (such as a description in terms of bodily movements). Among "all things considered" are general arguments for and against attributing intentional states to animals, which will be considered at length in Chapter 6.

Of course, our methodology takes the behavior of animals to furnish evidence about their mental lives, including whether or not they have intentional states. So how should we describe the evidence-furnishing behavior if we want to avoid begging questions in the way just

---

[22] John Dupré, "The Mental Lives of Nonhuman Animals," in Marc Bekoff and Dale Jamieson (eds.), *Interpretation and Explanation in the Study of Animal Behavior*, vol. I (Boulder, CO: Westview, 1990), pp. 441–42. For several reasons that I will not review here, the modifiers *higher* and *lower*, as applied to animals, are problematic. For a sensible discussion of why they are problematic but also helpful if construed rightly, see Roger Crisp, "Evolution and Psychological Unity," ibid, pp. 401–3.

[23] This characterization of WCE and SCE draws from Jamieson and Bekoff, "On Aims and Methods of Cognitive Ethology," pp. 115–18. Their discussion summarizes very good reasons to prefer SCE.

described? If we remain mindful of the conceptual loadedness of descriptions of behavior, I suspect that we can avoid circularity or keep it to a manageable minimum. Earlier I described a dog as rushing into the kitchen in the direction of a dogfood dish upon the sounding of a dinner chime. That description seems sufficiently neutral to permit an investigation of how the dog's behavior should be interpreted. Disputants could share a rough picture of what the dog did while disagreeing about whether she really had a desire for food and intentionally ran toward it.

Some who do not use this method

We have sketched a method for investigating the mental life of animals that seeks to bring into reflective equilibrium four specific methods: (1) human phenomenology; (2) the study of animal behavior; (3) functional-evolutionary arguments; and (4) appeals to physiology. I am hardly the first to employ more than one kind of evidence in arguing about animals' mental states.[24] In fact, once it is spelled out, the method I have described may seem so natural and obvious as to be trivial.

I do think the method is natural, and I am pleased if it seems obvious after being defended. Is it trivial and unworthy of explicit defense? No, because numerous highly regarded thinkers don't use it.

Some philosophers prioritize phenomenology as a method for finding out about the mind. According to Descartes and other *substance dualists* (who hold that mind and matter are mutually irreducible substances), mental states are states of mind and in *no* respect physical states. It follows, for them, that no investigation of the physical world— whether of brains, behavior, or evolution—puts us into contact with mind. Even if certain physical states and mental states are correlated, the former is merely evidence for the latter. Thus, direct contact with mental states—that is, phenomenology—must take priority in any apparent conflicts with physical evidence.

Substance dualists are very rare among philosophers today. There are more *property dualists,* who hold that mental and physical properties are mutually irreducible, even if, as *physicalism* holds, all substances (as opposed to their properties) are ultimately physical. Property dualists might prioritize phenomenology, which from their view involves direct access to those properties that interest us: the mental ones. Even if mental states are at some level brain states, our interest in the mental life

---

[24]See, e.g., Peter Singer, *Animal Liberation,* 2nd ed. (New York: New York Review, 1990), pp. 10–15.

is an interest in its mentality, subjectivity, or intentionality. So it would seem that physical data can't compete with phenomenological data.

A general reason not to prioritize phenomenology is that we are not perfectly authoritative about what happens in our mental worlds.[25] One is *at most* authoritative about what it is like to have a certain experience, how it seems to one. But the event of, say, seeing red, if physicalism is true, includes more than what it is like; it includes certain processes in the brain, which are beyond the reach of phenomenology. But even regarding what it's like to experience something, there are limits to one's authority, surprising as that may sound. For starters, memory is fallible, and so is one's use of the language with which one expresses one's experiences. So even first-person phenomenology regarding what an experience is like does not deserve absolute priority in conflicts with other kinds of evidence.

Some philosophers and scientists have granted excessive methodological priority to behavior. An easy example is that of the behaviorists, who went so far as to claim that behavior was the *only* relevant form of evidence. To be precise, that view is *methodological* behaviorism. *Metaphysical* behaviorism, in philosophy, argues that mental states themselves can be reduced to actions and behavioral dispositions. Enough has been said in defense of our pluralistic approach to justify setting aside methodological behaviorism. On a historical note, this view was put out of business in psychology largely by cognitive psychology, while metaphysical behaviorism (whose many problems we need not review) was superseded in philosophy by *identity theory*. (Identity theory argues, against behaviorism, that mental states are genuinely internal; against substance dualism, it identifies mental states with neurological states and processes.) Despite the demise of behaviorism, many thinkers prioritize behavior as evidence about the mental.

Wittgenstein, whose influence in the philosophy of mind remains strong, argued that nothing in a person's head is relevant to whether she is reading, doing arithmetic, or engaging in any other conscious activity.[26] Our linguistic practices are such that mental states are ascribed to others on the basis of behavior in context. Now these linguistic practices, the argument continues, establish the very *meanings* of mental terms (in their third-person usage). Thus, it is conceivable that someone doing arithmetic, as demonstrated by mastery of math problems, has a

---

[25] Anyone who doubts this claim is urged to read Dennett, *Consciousness Explained*, especially chs. 3–5.

[26] Ludwig Wittgenstein, *Philosophical Investigations*, 2nd ed., trans. G. E. M. Anscombe (New York: Macmillan, 1958)

head full of straw. Strikingly, this position apparently implies that nothing nonbehavioral has a role *even as evidence* for the existence of these mental activities.

The argument supporting this conclusion fails. Empirical evidence concerns the contingent empirical world, not logically necessary connections between words and their application. Maybe, as a matter of *logic,* one's head could be full of straw when one does math. As a matter of empirical *fact,* it could not. Thus, Wittgenstein's points about the meaning of mental terms are irrelevant to our methodological concerns. (Also, he may be wrong about the meaning of mental terms.)

Today many functionalists, some fans of Artificial Intelligence (A.I.), and others appear to overemphasize behavior as a form of evidence for mental states. As explained by Lycan, *functionalism* arose in reaction to perceived weaknesses in identity theory (as this theory is normally conceived):

> In the mid-1960s [Putnam and Fodor] pointed out a presumptuous implication of the Identity Theory understood as a theory of "types" or *kinds* of mental items: that a mental state such as pain has *always and everywhere* the neurophysiological characterization initially assigned to it. [I]f the Identity Theorist identified pain itself with the firings of c-fibers, it followed that a creature of any species (earthly or science-fiction) could be in pain only if that creature *had* c-fibers and they were firing. . . . The Identity Theorist had . . . fallen into species chauvinism.
>
> Fodor and Putnam advocated the obvious correction: What was important was not its being c-fibers (*per se*) that were firing, but what the c-fiber firings were doing, what their firing contributed to the operation of the organism as a whole. . . . Thus, to be in pain is . . . merely to be in some state or other, of whatever biochemical description, that plays the same causal role as did the firings of c-fibers in [human beings]. We may continue to maintain that pain "tokens," individual instances of pain occurring in particular subjects at particular times, are strictly identical with particular neurophysiological states of those subjects at those times. . . . Mental state-types are identified not with neurophysiological types but with more abstract functional roles, as specified by state-tokens' causal relations to the organism's sensory inputs, motor outputs, and other psychological states.[27]

In attempting to overcome species chauvinism, then, functionalists have understood types of mental states, such as pain or suffering, in terms of their causal relations to the rest of whatever system they occur in; no specific neurological or even material realization is essential.

But, then, there would seem no reason *in principle* to think that computers, which are information-processing systems, could not have men-

[27] Lycan, "Ontology from Behaviorism to Functionalism," p. 7

tal states—hence one motivation for the burgeoning field of A.I. The functionalists and A.I. enthusiasts whom I criticize here are those who take "species (or system) liberality" so far that they think a system's behavior is the *only* evidence relevant to ascribing mental states to the system. For them, neurology and evolutionary considerations are per se irrelevant.

I maintain that just as identity theorists overreacted to the problems of behaviorism, the functionalists and A.I. people in question have overreacted to the weaknesses of identity theory. True, it is logically possible that any physical stuff could underlie mental states. But, again, our world is a contingent world with empirically discovered laws. While I will not speculate on the possibilities for computers, certainly neurology and evolution are very relevant in making intelligent conjectures about the mental lives of actual animals.

Suppose that we are very impressed by the behavior of certain insects, such as ants or bees, or even worms (as Darwin was). We believe that the behavior is suggestive of consciousness or practical reasoning. Since behavior is but one kind of evidence, this should be the beginning of our researches, not the end. Do these organisms have nervous systems organized in such a way that, even if very different from our own, might subserve consciousness or practical reasoning? Would consciousness or practical reasoning afford such organisms an edge, given their life expectancy, body type, behavioral repertoire, environmental niche, and so on? Surely the pluralistic approach is more reasonable than placing behavior on an evidentiary pedestal.

Finally, notice that sometimes we can attribute mental states in the absence of any behavioral evidence. For example, no human has observed the behavior of dinosaurs. But knowing a fair amount about the nervous systems and evolution of various dinosaur species, we can infer a good deal about their mental lives.

Some philosophers and scientists give priority to physiology, in particular, neurology. This appears to be true of identity theorists, who identify not just tokens (individual instances) but also general types of mental states with certain neurological states. From this view, behavior is relevant as evidence for mental states only if there is a well-established empirical connection between the behavior type and particular neurological states. Again, many have thought this approach chauvinistic in foreclosing the possibility that nature has other ways to produce the mental states that interest us. To do justice to this possibility, the best strategy is not to ignore neurology but to regard behavior and evolutionary function as rounding out the neurological data.

The alleged "looseness" of the social sciences—which countenance such flabby theoretical entities as behaviors—and of evolutionary biology has prevented some scientists from taking these disciplines seriously. For these tough-minded types, the closer a science is to physics, the more rigorous and respectable it is. Thus, in their eyes, there is good reason to favor neurology as a form of evidence. But how could such scientists believe that a strictly neurological approach is adequate? Are they unaware of the cognitive revolution (the emergence of cognitive psychology and other cognitive sciences)?

Whatever such scientists actually think, they could join theoretical hands with eliminative materialists, *eliminativists,* in the philosophy of mind. Eliminativists believe that the major concepts of folk (or common-sense) psychology, such as beliefs and desires, do not correspond to anything in reality. Thus, they reject the cognitive revolution. Paul Feyerabend was the first to argue this thesis openly. He was followed notably by Patricia and Paul Churchland. The latter summarizes the position in a way that explains why this school of thought would prioritize neurology:

> Eliminative materialism is the thesis that our common-sense conception of psychological phenomena constitutes a radically false theory, a theory so fundamentally defective that both the principles and ontology of that theory will eventually be displaced, rather than smoothly reduced, by completed neuroscience.[28]

Eliminativists would argue that my pluralistic approach incorporates (sub)methods that are not just unrigorous but based on false premises. Earlier in this chapter, I noted my assumption that folk psychology was more or less in order. If you, reader, *believe* that there are beliefs and desires, don't leave me for the eliminativists.

In conclusion, while the pluralistic model that I have described may seem natural, many individuals in the disciplines that study mental phenomena do not use it. As we have seen, there are various philosophical and scientific motivations for prioritizing one kind of evidence over all others. I have argued that the soundest approach in exploring animal mentation is one that takes seriously each of the four (sub)methods I have described, without assigning priority to any one of them.[29]

---

[28] Paul M. Churchland, "Eliminative Materialism and the Propositional Attitudes," *Journal of Philosophy* 78 (1981), p. 67

[29] It might be thought that my method prioritizes human phenomenology. In fact, my method in a sense *begins with* human phenomenology and argues by analogy using the other three kinds of evidence, but it does not *prioritize* human phenomenology. For example, it will be argued in Chapter 5 that many animals experience anxiety. But, in part because of neurological differences between humans and these animals, no strong claims are made about the qualitative features of animal anxiety (what it feels like). The earlier discussion of dualism shows that human phenomenology is not prioritized even in exploring humans' mental lives.

WHY CONCEPTUAL CLARITY IS WORTH LABORING OVER

Philosophers often invest a lot of time and energy in clarifying concepts that are central to their area of inquiry. To laypersons and other professionals, this nonempirical work may seem odd. What is its purpose? Is conceptual clarity really worth troubling over? Let me say, first, that I do not aspire for authoritative classical definitions—final sets of necessary and sufficient conditions—for our mental vocabulary. Many mental terms are used in a variety of ways; mental phenomena are, as we have seen, studied in different ways at different levels of analysis. It should not be surprising, then, that even such a seemingly simple concept as pain may defy efforts to pin down its meaning with a single, authoritative definition.

Nevertheless, in studying the mental lives of animals we need a certain degree of conceptual clarity. Sloppy conceptualizations can lead to significant errors. Let me offer a few examples. Two concepts that scientists and laypersons often conflate are (1) responsiveness to noxious stimuli, and (2) unpleasant experiences caused by such stimuli. I cannot count the number of times I have been asked why I don't think plants have moral status, since they too are "obviously" sentient. I ask the questioners why they think plants are sentient. It usually turns out that they have conflated some plants' capacity to respond to certain stimuli with the capacity to have pain. For someone who (like me) believes that sentience is sufficient for moral status, whereas responsiveness to stimuli is not, it is essential to avoid this error.

Conceptual confusions can have disastrous consequences:

> [A] veterinary student . . . was shocked to learn that some members of the department were routinely doing Caesarean sections on moose [who had been given an injection of succinyl-choline chloride,] which paralyses all muscles by blocking neuro-transmission across the neuro-muscular junction, but has no anaesthetic or analgesic properties. [R]eports from humans on whom it has been used indicate that it heightens pain response, given the extraordinary panic which accompanies total paralysis . . . , even when one understands *exactly* what is happening and why. [The student was told that if the moose were in pain, they would be making noise]—no mean feat when totally paralysed.[30]

Sometimes conceptual confusions spoil otherwise fine work by invalidating conclusions drawn from valuable empirical data. Gordon Gallup provides an illuminating example. Gallup conducted a fascinating study on the differing abilities of primates to use mirrors, which

[30] Rollin, *The Unheeded Cry*, p. 146

were needed to detect paint that had been applied (while the primates were unconscious) on their heads where they could not directly see it.[31] Such empirical work might be very useful in determining whether certain primates are self-aware in certain ways. In a later, more speculative article, Gallup draws from this work, and other empirical data, to support various theses about animal mentation.[32] Unfortunately, a plethora of conceptual confusions and non sequiturs invalidate the author's speculations.

A few examples follow. Gallup states that, as "a working definition, mind can be defined as the ability to monitor your own mental states, and the corresponding capacity to use your experience to infer the experience of others."[33] That mind is the ability to monitor your own mental states is debatable, requiring argument, at best. I suspect it is incorrect. One can have mental states, such as discomfort, without monitoring them, and it is natural to think that the existence of *mental* states implies a mind (since it is plausible to construe a mind as something that can have mental states). That having a mind requires the capacity to infer the experience of others is almost certainly false—and at best contentious. To infer the experience of others is a very complex mental operation, possibly limited to a small number of species. But, as we will see, many mental states—pain, distress, suffering, desires, and many others—do not require this capacity. As mental states, though, they would seem to imply the presence of a mind.

Gallup goes on to make this assertion:

> [I]f self-awareness is defined as the ability to become the object of your own attention, consciousness as being aware of your own existence, and mind as the capacity to be aware of your own mental states, then it should be obvious these are not mutually exclusive cognitive categories.[34]

Why would anyone even be tempted to think self-awareness, consciousness, and mind are mutually exclusive? Clearly, one who is self-aware has consciousness, and the latter—being a mental state—would seem to imply mind. But neither mind nor consciousness clearly implies self-awareness. Why, then, does Gallup understand consciousness as awareness of one's own existence? One can be conscious of simpler things than oneself, such as an object ahead. Thus, the claim that all consciousness requires awareness of *self* is a substantive, unobvious philosophical thesis requiring argument. Certainly, one can't stipulate

[31] Gordon G. Gallup, Jr., "Self-Recognition in Primates: A Comparative Approach to the Bidirectional Properties of Consciousness," *American Psychologist* (1977): 330–38
[32] Gordon G. Gallup, Jr., "Do Minds Exist in Species Other Than Our Own?," *Neuroscience & Biobehavioral Reviews* 9 (1985): 631–41
[33] ibid, p. 633
[34] ibid

away philosophical issues with a definition. Finally, once again, why is mind the capacity of being aware of your own mental states, rather than simply the having of mental states?

Two more examples from Gallup's article will suffice. Here is one: "Either you are aware of being aware or you are unaware of being aware, and the latter is tantamount to being unconscious."[35] Whether birds and mice are aware of being aware is an open question; it seems very possible that they are not capable of such a reflexive mental act. But to think that a bird or mouse who is neither sleeping nor under anesthesia is unconscious seems extraordinary in this post-behaviorist day. As we will see, the evidence that they are (usually) conscious is massive—and it is not the same evidence as that for attributing self-consciousness. The second example displays a non sequitur that may be at the root of some of Gallup's muddledness: "If you grant that *it is we who experience pain and not the pain centers,* then that is the same as saying that awareness presupposes self-awareness."[36] That is simply false. That it is we who are in pain when pain occurs entails that we—certain selves (in an ordinary sense of the term)—must exist when pain occurs; it implies nothing whatsoever about awareness of such selves.[37]

The examples of this section illustrate the importance of conceptual clarity in studies of mental phenomena.

OUR MODEST AND IMMODEST AIMS

Taking animals seriously requires taking their minds seriously. To do so requires availing ourselves of relevant empirical data. I have argued for a method that involves treating with respect four kinds of empirical evidence. If I am right, then, philosophers interested in animal mentation cannot seriously expect to accomplish their work by conceptual analysis and a priori argumentation alone. To make well-grounded assertions about the extent and limits of the mental lives of animals, we must work across disciplines.

To aspire to well-grounded yet interesting assertions about animal minds is clearly ambitious. But I think we must limit our ambitions to allow some hope of success. We cannot hope to achieve full closure on many issues. When we *can* claim to know about some aspect of an

[35] ibid, p. 638
[36] ibid, p. 639
[37] In their overview of evidence for animal pain and suffering, Margaret Rose and David Adams note that there are conflicting definitions of *mind, consciousness,* and *awareness* ("Evidence for Pain and Suffering in Other Animals," in Gill Langley, *Animal Experimentation: The Consensus Changes* [New York: Chapman and Hall, 1989], p. 59), supporting the thesis that attention to conceptual issues is warranted in this area. Cf. John H. Crook, "On Attributing Consciousness to Animals," *Nature* 303 (May 5, 1983): 11–14.

animal's mental life, we cannot, of course, claim to know everything about its mental life. While I do not believe there are a priori limits to what we can learn about animals, the practical challenges are great, and no one has an infinity of time, energy, insight, or other resources. We must aspire for intelligent, reasonably well-grounded assertions—not for absolute certainty or full penetration of animal minds.

By honoring several kinds of evidence, our method allows the possibility of fairly robust confirmation of certain theses. We are, most fundamentally, seeking to explain data of different sorts, and our investigations take this form: Are the currently available data best explained by taking the animal or animals to have mental state M? The answer is *no* if there are simpler (and otherwise equally coherent) explanations of the data.

With that much clear on our modest and not-so-modest aims, there remains the question of which possible mental states in animals to explore. An exhaustive study is out of the question. With an eye to both moral relevance and general interest, in Chapters 5, 6, and 7, I will explore the following mental states (and closely related phenomena and characteristics of interest): nociception, consciousness, pain, distress, fear, anxiety, suffering, pleasure, enjoyments, happiness, desires (and conation generally), concepts, beliefs, thinking, expectations, memory, intentional action, self-awareness, language, moral agency, and autonomy.

Chapter 5

Feelings

In investigating the mental states of animals, we will start with what seem to be simpler states and work our way to more complex ones. This chapter treats a cluster of mental states of interest to hedonistic utilitarians—mental states that are typically pleasant or unpleasant—as well as consciousness in general (and one nonmental state). We might, roughly, refer to this cluster of mental states as *feelings*. (As in Chapter 4, I will often use the term *mental states* as a shorthand for mental states, events, or processes.)

A PRELIMINARY MATTER

Thus far we have spoken of mental states without saying exactly what they are. Relying on an intuitive understanding of this concept is fine for most purposes, because people usually agree on which states are mental. But confusion is possible.

Dominating modern philosophy and still influential today, the Cartesian tradition takes *consciousness* to be the defining feature of the mental.[1] From this view, there can be no unconscious mental states, by definition. (For convenience, I will use the term *unconscious* to modify all things that are not conscious, even never-conscious beings and their states.) Freudian psychology and other developments made a good case for reconstructing the concept of the mental such that consciousness was not strictly essential. One could have unconscious desires, for example, which might become conscious if certain causes of repression were removed.[2] Freud aside, we now know that a great deal of information processing occurs outside of awareness. For example, our brains note (without our awareness) the relative times at which a sound

[1] René Descartes, *Meditations on First Philosophy* (Paris: Michel Soly, 1641)
[2] See Sigmund Freud, *Introductory Lectures on Psychoanalysis* (New York: Horton, 1917).

reaches our ears, indicating the direction of the source. And you may be unaware of intentionally patting your pocket to check for keys unless, to your surprise, they are missing. Today, many philosophers and scientists think of *information processing* as essential to the mental.[3] But it would be highly counterintuitive to grant minds to small calculators, although they process information. Information processing seems necessary but not sufficient for mentation. Consciousness seems sufficient but not necessary.

An adequate definition of *mental state* would avoid the mistakes of (1) reducing the mental to the conscious, (2) defining the term too liberally by insufficiently restricting the kinds of information processing that count, and (3) being chauvinistic by requiring central nervous systems like ours, when it is conceivable that functionally similar systems might subserve mentation. It is extremely difficult to provide an adequate definition, and I will not attempt to do so. However, under the umbrella of mental states I include all conscious states, events, and processes as well as all states, events, and processes that are of a type whose tokens, typically, are at least potentially conscious. For example, one might not be conscious of some of one's desires and beliefs, but one can generally become conscious of them through reflection and other means (more on this later).

It is tempting to define *mental states* as states that involve information processing and are of a type whose tokens, typically, are at least potentially conscious. This definition would avoid mistakes (1) and (2) but would exclude two classes of states that arguably should count as mental states. First, it would exclude complex forms of information processing that subserve mental states in humans but are not themselves consciously accessible, such as the aforementioned auditory decoding that lets us know the direction of a sound source. (It might be tempting to count all brain states as mental states. If human brains are meant, error (3) is committed; if any brains count, that is arguably too liberal since, as we will see, some apparently never-conscious animals have brains. Also, the human lower brain regulates heartbeat, but it is counterintuitive to count this brain process as a mental process.) The proposed definition would, secondly, exclude the most complex information processing of imaginary beings who outperform humans on everyday intellectual tasks but cannot become aware of their information processing: They respond to environmental circumstances and intellectual challenges as automatically as we "make" our hearts pump. I do not know whether these two classes of states or processes should count as

[3] For an effort to link some recent developments in cognitive science with Freudian psychology, see Dan Lloyd, "Connectionist Hysteria: Reducing a Freudian Case Study to a Network Model," *Philosophy, Psychiatry, & Psychology* 1 (June 1994): 69–88.

mental. In any case, as we will see in later chapters, the mental states of moral concern are (typically) at least potentially conscious. The ones that we investigate in depth share this property.

A SOURCE OF SOME CONFUSION: NOCICEPTION

Let us begin by examining a physical event that is often mistakenly taken to be a mental state: *nociception*. Nociception, the first event in a sequence that often includes pain, is the detection of potentially tissue-damaging (noxious) stimuli by specialized neural end organs, nociceptors, which fire nervous impulses along axons.[4] Such stimuli include pricking, cutting, cold, heat, pressure, inflamation of tissues, muscle spasms, and the like. If stimuli are insufficiently strong, nociceptors do not respond; a threshold of intensity must be met. Nociception is not per se a conscious event, although the detection of noxious stimuli is often accompanied by conscious states, typically painful ones. A paraplegic whose foot touches a hot iron will not feel anything in her foot, because of her spinal cord's being severed, yet will withdraw her foot from the iron. Withdrawal of the foot follows nociception without pain (at least, as I will propose that we understand pain).

Rather than enter into the scientific details of nociception, let us consider its relevance to animals. First, it is important to distinguish nociception from pain and other mental states. Conflation of these concepts often leads to the conclusion that because an organism has responded to a stimulus, it is therefore sentient. *Sentient* is defined in slightly different ways, but I will use it to mean *capable of having feelings* (mental states, such as sensations or emotional states, that are typically pleasant or unpleasant). Some take insects' and even plants' responsiveness to touch and other stimuli to show that they are sentient. Intuitively believing that such responsiveness is of no great moral importance, they unsoundly conclude that sentience is morally insignificant. The responsiveness cited is likely nociception (or an analogous event in organisms that lack nociceptors but are capable of responding to certain stimuli), not pain or any other mental state.

It is worthwhile to distinguish nociception—the activity of nociceptors—from other types of responsiveness to stimuli, such as a plant's movement of leaves toward a light source. While nociception is not itself a mental state, in humans it is closely tied to pain. (Rollin helpfully characterizes nociception as "the machinery or plumbing of

---

[4] Margaret Rose and David Adams, "Evidence for Pain and Suffering in Other Animals," in Gill Langley (ed.), *Animal Experimentation: The Consensus Changes* (New York: Chapman and Hall, 1989), p. 47

pain."[5]) Its evolutionary function is apparently to signal the presence of stimuli that could endanger the organism, since the detected stimuli are potentially noxious or tissue-damaging. In humans, nociception typically, but not always, leads to pain. We will discuss pain in detail later. For now, it is worth noting which animals have nociceptors, because their presence constitutes some evidence that the animals in question can have pain (though, of course, other forms of evidence would be required to make the attribution confidently).

In their review article on evidence for pain and suffering in animals, Rose and Adams report that

> nociceptors exist in all mammals (Wall and Melzack 1984) and birds (Breward and Gentle 1985). There may, however, be differences in the neurotransmitters involved (Pierau et al. 1985). How can nociception be identified in other taxa? The primary criterion may be the presence of clearly aversive behaviours in response to those stimuli associated with nociception in mammals. . . . [T]he withdrawal reflex stimulated by squeezing the claw of pithed toads is evidence that nociceptive pathways exist in this amphibian. The responses of *Octopus* and *Sepia* species to electric shock (Boycott 1965, Messenger 1977) indicate that nociception occurs in these cephalopods. Embryological and anatomical evidence in fish, amphibians and reptiles indicates that in these species, neural reflexes are modulated by internuncial fibres such that behaviour is not simply a reflex but becomes "variable, unique and creative" (Whiting 1955). . . . Evidence supports the existence of nociception in all vertebrates, and possibly in some invertebrates such as cephalopods.[6]

We will consider later whether types of evidence other than the presence of nociceptors support the attribution of pain to vertebrates and possibly other species.[7]

[5] Bernard E. Rollin, *The Unheeded Cry: Animal Consciousness, Animal Pain and Science* (Oxford: Oxford University Press, 1989), p. 124
[6] Rose and Adams, "Evidence for Pain and Suffering," pp. 48–49. The studies cited are Patrick D. Wall and Ronald Melzack (eds.), *Textbook of Pain* (Edinburgh: Churchill Livingstone, 1984); J. Breward and M. J. Gentle, "Neuroma Formation and Abnormal Afferent Nerve Discharges After Partial Beak Amputation (Beak Trimming) in Poultry," *Experientia* 41 (1985): 1132–34; Fr.-K. Pierau, G. Harti, and D. C. M. Taylor, "Local Administration of Capsaicin Does Not Deplete Substance P in Primary Sensory Neurones of the Pigeon," *Pflugers Archiv: European Journal of Physiology* 403 (1985), supplement R60; Brian B. Boycott, "Learning in the Octopus," *Scientific American* 212 (March 1965): 42–50; John B. Messenger, "Prey Capture and Learning in the Cuttle Fish, *Sepia*," in Marion Nixon and John B. Messenger (eds.), *The Biology of Cephalopods* (London: Academic, 1977), pp. 347–76; and H. P. Whiting, "Functional Development in the Nervous System," in Heinrich Waelsch (ed.), *Biochemistry of the Developing Nervous System* (New York: Academic, 1955), pp. 85–103.
[7] For a discussion of nociception and its relation to pain in animals, see David DeGrazia and Andrew Rowan, "Pain, Suffering, and Anxiety in Animals and Humans," *Theoretical Medicine* 12 (1991), pp. 194–99.

CONSCIOUSNESS

What is *consciousness*? I do not think the term can be given a (noncircular) classical definition, because it seems to be a basic, irreducible concept within our conceptual scheme. But, as argued in Chapter 4, airtight sets of necessary and sufficient conditions may be an impossible ideal in the study of the mind and are unnecessary anyway; sufficient clarity can be achieved with elucidations or characterizations of key concepts.

John Searle offers one characterization: "By 'consciousness' I mean those subjective states of sentience and awareness that we have during our waking life (and at a lower level of intensity in our dreams)."[8] This characterization is arguably circular because it appeals to the concepts of subjectivity, sentience, and awareness, which may be in no less need of definition than is consciousness. In any case, it rightly directs our attention to the character of our waking and dreaming life. Owen Flanagan characterizes conscious experience as "the class of mental states or events that involve awareness."[9] These working definitions suggest that there is a tight circle of interlinked concepts, none of which is strictly reducible to the others: consciousness, awareness, experience, subjectivity, and perhaps others. The following elucidation may be a useful primer for the conceptual imagination: "A conscious experience is a state such that there is something that it is like to be in it."[10] These elucidations will suffice for our purposes.

Note that the *concept* of consciousness does not include that of self-consciousness (or self-awareness). The latter concept is more specific and complex, involving the concept of a self. And on the face of it, there is no obvious reason why, as a factual matter, all consciousness must involve awareness of a self. Seeing a yellow flower involves consciousness, and some subject must do the seeing, but the experience itself does not seem to necessitate any conscious noting of who is doing the seeing.

All of the specific mental states we will examine are at least potentially conscious; they are conscious, or they are of a type tokens of which, typically, can be made conscious. For example, one may have a belief or desire without consciously manifesting it at a given time. Beliefs and desires can be *dispositional* in the sense that one can have them over long periods of time during which one is not usually consciously attending to or manifesting them. My belief that iron is an element is like this. A belief or desire is *occurrent* if it takes the form of a transient event, such as my desire to stretch my legs. Dispositional states can

---

[8] John R. Searle, "Animal Minds" (unpublished manuscript)
[9] *Consciousness Reconsidered* (Cambridge, MA: MIT Press, 1992), p. 31
[10] ibid. A more formal statement of this idea appeared in Thomas Nagel, "What is it Like to be a Bat?," *Philosophical Review* 83 (1974): 435–50.

generally be made occurrent and conscious by bringing attention to them, as in response to the question "Do you think iron is an element?" However, perhaps some dispositional (or even occurrent) states cannot be brought into consciousness due to repression or other factors. In any case, the mental states we explore are, typically, at least potentially conscious. Because evidence that animals have these mental states will, a fortiori, be evidence that they are conscious beings (beings who sometimes have conscious states), there is no need for a separate presentation of evidence for consciousness. Still, a number of general points about the scientific study of consciousness are worth making here.

I believe that consciousness is part of the natural or physical world, not a supernatural phenomenon. But, in keeping with my strategy of avoiding controversial philosophical theses where possible, I will insist only that mental states and natural phenomena are in some way closely correlated, so that empirical evidence of the kinds described in Chapter 4 are relevant to the study of the mental. Emphasizing this point helps with the worthy goal of demystifying consciousness. Consciousness is, without a doubt, one of the most baffling, amazing, wonderful phenomena in the universe. But we seek understanding. And understanding is generally obstructed by imbuing phenomena with untouchable majesty. "It's a mystery" has rich aesthetic power, but, epistemologically, it's a cop-out.[11]

[11] Many recent bits of theorizing about the science of consciousness intrigue me. Let me mention a few. Using conservative estimation techniques, Paul M. Churchland has estimated that you have about as many neurons in your brain as there are stars in our galaxy and that—given connections between synapses—the total number of distinct neural states in your brain is 10-to-the-100-trillionth-power. To write that nonexponentially would require writing 10 and adding 100 trillion zeros! To put that into perspective, Churchland points out that the total number of elementary particles in the universe is estimated to be around 10-to-the-87th! (See *A Neurocomputational Perspective* [Cambridge, MA: MIT Press, 1989], p. 132. For a lively discussion of these computations, see Flanagan, *Consciousness Reconsidered*, pp. 35–37.) Contemplating this sort of power may make it easier to fathom that matter could produce something as wondrous as consciousness.

Francis Crick and Christof Koch hypothesize that neuronal oscillations at around 40 hertz are correlated with different types of conscious states, raising the possibility that all consciousness (at least in humans) is correlated with oscillations of roughly this frequency ("Towards a Neurobiological Theory of Consciousness," *Seminars in the Neurosciences* 2 [1990]: 263–75). Other research suggests a range from 35 to 65 hertz. See John Kulli and Christof Koch, "Does Anesthesia Cause Loss of Consciousness?", *Trends in Neurosciences* 14 (1991): 6–10; and I. Keller, C. Madler, D. Schwender, and E. Poeppel, "Analysis of Oscillatory Components in Perioperative AEP-Recordings: A Nonparametric Procedure for Frequency Measurement," *Clinical Electroencephalography* 21 (1990): 88–92.

Finally, while I cannot summarize his theorizing here, Daniel C. Dennett provides a fascinating, admittedly speculative story of how consciousness might have

Our earlier characterization of mental states did not, in principle, exclude the possibility that some beings might have kinds of mental states that are not potentially conscious—hence, the thesis of *conscious inessentialism:* For some specified kind of mental state or process (say, thinking), even if in humans it usually occurs consciously, it could, in principle, occur in some being without ever being conscious.[12] On this thesis, a computer's incapacity for consciousness would be irrelevant to whether it could think.

It is a well-established fact that our informational sensitivity far exceeds what we consciously experience. Massive amounts of the parallel information processing that occurs in our brains occurs without our awareness. Drawing from such facts, Flanagan provocatively asserts that, conceivably,

> there might have evolved creatures as capable as us and more or less behaviorally indistinguishable from us who can [sic] get by on pure informational sensitivity and unconscious higher-level problem solving (for example, the way a computer plays chess) without ever experiencing a thing.[13]

Consciousness *may* not be essential to higher-order mental phenomena such as reasoning and complex pattern recognition per se. But, given the neural hardware that we happen to have inherited in our evolution, consciousness may be necessary for some of *our* mental tasks, a fact that would give it a functional role. We would like to think that consciousness has some function or use, that it is not just an evolutionary free-rider on other traits. The *epiphenomenal suspicion* is that conscious states are mere epiphenomena, states that are caused by physical states but are themselves causally inert with respect to physical states (including those of our brain and motor system).[14]

Although I suspect that the epiphenomenalist suspicion is false, I can offer only a few suggestive arguments. Moreover, our investigations are not crucially affected by whether consciousness itself has a functional-evolutionary role. We know that we humans are conscious and that

emerged in evolution (*Consciousness Explained* [Boston, MA: Little, Brown and Co., 1991], ch. 7.

[12] Flanagan states the thesis in roughly this way (*Consciousness Reconsidered,* p. 5).

[13] *Consciousness Reconsidered,* p. 45. Some would disagree, denying that consciousness is so separable from cognitive performance. See, e.g., Richard Rorty, *Philosophy and the Mirror of Nature* (Princeton: Princeton University Press, 1979), ch. 2.

[14] A thought that might motivate this suspicion is that our consciousness, which we experience as flowing serially or in successive states, is inefficiently implemented on hardware (our brains) that was selected for its parallel-processing capacities. But Dennett suggests that precisely because of such inefficiency, awareness of our own perceptual systems might have been necessary (*Consciousness Explained,* pp. 218–25).

some of our mental states are typically potentially conscious. Given evolutionary continuity, neurological and behavioral analogues between humans and animals can ground attributions of similar mental states to them. Even if conscious aspects of our thinking, for example, turned out to have no function, evidence that animals could think would be prima facie evidence that their thinking was (at least potentially) conscious.

Here are a few briefly stated reasons to believe that our consciousness has some function and is not just a delightful free-rider. First, consider mental processes that, in humans, can occur either consciously or unconsciously. These processes work better unconsciously with familiar situations and demands but work better consciously in the presence of novelty, unpredictability, or situations in which one needs to be "one jump ahead."[15] This suggests that, with respect to these mental processes, consciousness increases our capacity to manage complexity. For example, in playing a guitar song that you have thoroughly mastered, you might play the G string at all the right times without ever consciously intending to hit it in particular. If someone teaches you a new song, the first time you play it, you will make conscious decisions about particular strings and notes ("Hit G . . . now A sharp . . . now. . . .").

Second, consider which kinds of information processing are consciously accessible to us and which are not. Processes *underlying* recognition of faces, discrimination of flavors, and ordinary remembering exemplify those that are not consciously accessible. Generally, we have conscious access to data that inform us of what we seem to have the most need to know about (e.g., the state of our sensory environment, important facts about our past), suggesting that conscious capacities were selected on the basis of their adaptive value.[16]

Furthermore, many experiments suggest that knowledge acquired unconsciously is accessed and deployed less well than knowledge acquired consciously.[17] Consciousness involves attention, which may secure better treatment by memory gatekeepers.[18] Also suggestive are blind-sighted persons, whose behavior shows that they register visual information, yet they report not consciously seeing anything (providing a good example of unconscious information processing): They have *less*

[15] Marian Stamp Dawkins, *Through Our Eyes Only?: The Search for Animal Consciousness* (Oxford: Freeman, 1993), pp. 171–72.
[16] Flanagan, *Consciousness Reconsidered*, p. 134
[17] See L. Weiskrantz, "Some Contributions of Neuropsychology of Vision and Memory to the Problem of Consciousness," in A. J. Marcel and E. Bisiach (eds.), *Consciousness in Contemporary Science* (New York: Oxford University Press, 1988), pp. 183–99.
[18] Flanagan, *Consciousness Reconsidered*, p. 140 (citing several studies)

informational sensitivity than those with normal sight.[19] (Blind-sight
and similar phenomena have prompted one theorist to posit a neural
monitoring system that creates conscious awareness by monitoring
other neural networks.[20]) Myriad other interesting neurological cases
provide further data.[21]

Most of the evidence for consciousness in animals will come in later
sections, when we explore more specific mental phenomena. But it is
worth noting, summarily, that available evidence suggests that consciousness is associated with complex central nervous systems (CNSs).
A vertebrate's CNS consists of a comparatively complex brain and a
spinal cord. Lacking spinal cords, octopi, squid, and cuttlefish—the
cephalopods—have CNSs of a different sort. For example, much of an
octopus' movement is controlled by nerve cords in the arms, which
contain nearly three times as many neurons (nerve cells) as does the
brain—a highly diffuse CNS by vertebrate standards![22] In contrast,
while some insect behavior is very impressive, insects have extremely
primitive CNSs, consisting of a nerve cord, ganglia (bundles of nerve
cells found at intervals along the nerve cord), and a "brain" at one end
composed of several fused ganglia. The extreme simplicity of their
CNSs makes it unlikely that insects are conscious (but more details and
evidence are presented later).

PAIN

What is pain?

In this post-behaviorist day, it is so widely believed and so well established that animals experience pain, that this section might seem gratuitous. But even today, a behaviorist residue obscures the vision of
many scientists and some laypersons. And unclarity about the concept
of pain can lead to errors. Moreover, even if it is obvious that *some*
animals have pain, for ethical purposes, it is important to try to determine *which ones* do.

What is pain? This is a surprisingly difficult question. Let's start by

---

[19] ibid, p. 141; Drakon Nikolinakos, "General Anesthesia, Consciousness, and the
Skeptical Challenge," *Journal of Philosophy* 91 (1994), p. 100
[20] L. Weiskrantz, "Neuropsychology and the Nature of Consciousness," in Colin
Blakemore and Susan Greenfield (eds.), *Mindwaves: Thoughts on Intelligence, Identity,
and Consciousness* (Cambridge: Blackwell, 1987), pp. 307–20; discussed in
Nikolinakos, "General Anesthesia," p. 100. See also Dennett, *Consciousness Explained*,
pp. 218–25; and Derek Denton, *The Pinnacle of Life: Consciousness and Self-Awareness
in Humans and Animals* (Sydney: Allyn & Unwin, 1993), pp. 176–77.
[21] For a summary, see Flanagan, *Consciousness Reconsidered*, pp. 142–45.
[22] Martin J. Wells, *Octopus* (London: Chapman and Hall, 1978)

getting some examples of pain in view: headaches, sunburns, finger pricks, cramps, and back pains. First, pains—painful experiences—are, or at least involve, *sensations*. (I take *mental pain* and *emotional pain* to be metaphorical extensions of the literal use under investigation; often *suffering* is an accurate alternative for these terms.) Phenomenologically, we can identify sensory properties of a given pain: its location, duration, intensity, and features that permit classifying it as a particular kind of pain, such as an ache, twinge, or sting.

In addition to these sensory properties, a pain also has an *affective* aspect—how much we mind it. It sometimes seems that pains that are comparable in their sensory aspects are experienced very differently. Puzzling cases include lobotomized persons, who often report that they feel pain but don't mind it,[23] and wounded soldiers removed from battle who endure, with little apparent distress, what would normally be excruciating pain. Less pathological cases include the enjoyment that one can get from painfully probing a loose tooth with one's tongue, the welcomed soreness following one's first marathon, and the stoicism that some women display in the face of the pain of childbirth.[24]

The apparent separability of sensory and affective aspects of pain makes it difficult to define *pain*. If pain is merely a kind of sensation, with no intrinsic affective dimension—as in *the sensation model*—we are left with the arguably paradoxical implication that the most intense pains could be liked just for the way the feel (could be pleasant, in one sense of the term, as explained later). Indeed, from this view, there could be a planet whose inhabitants found all pains to be likable for the way they feel! One wonders what *pain* means, then: What kind of sensation, exactly, is it? Another approach, *the attitude model,* identifies pain with our aversive response, so that pain is any sensation we dislike for its own felt qualities.[25] This model has difficulty handling at least some of the cases mentioned previously, in which pain does not seem to be minded. Also, we dislike certain sensations other than pain, such as nausea, irritating itches and tickling sensations, and the discomfort that comes from sitting too long.[26]

---

[23] Frederick W. L. Kerr, *The Pain Book* (Englewood Cliffs, NJ: Prentice Hall, 1981), pp. 146–49

[24] These three examples appear in L. W. Sumner, "Welfare, Happiness, and Pleasure," *Utilitas* 4 (1992), p. 209.

[25] These two approaches are lucidly distinguished ibid, pp. 209–10. But Sumner takes the attitude model to identify pain with any feeling or mental state that we dislike or find intrinsically disagreeable.

[26] I believe that a defining property of pain is that it is unpleasant or intrinsically disagreeable, so that the attitude model is on the right track. Admittedly, the model has to deal with the problem of distinguishing pains from other unpleasant sensations. Doing so would require revising the model such that pains are not *any* unpleasant sensations but perhaps unpleasant sensations within some phenomeno-

We can sidestep the philosophical issue of the precise nature of pain. First, clearly the vast majority of pains are unpleasant or aversive. Second, our ethical concern about animal pain surely concerns pain that is unpleasant; we need hardly worry about animal pain that is enjoyed, welcomed, or not minded by animals (if such a notion makes sense). Indeed, the ethical importance of aversive mental states motivates defining *pain*—perhaps reconstructively—partly in terms of unpleasantness. Some such concept is needed for practical purposes. I suggest that we understand pain, for our purposes, as *an unpleasant or aversive sensory experience typically associated with actual or potential tissue damage.*[27] Unpacking *pain* in terms of its connection with tissue damage takes advantage of the tie between pain and nociception (and may succeed in distinguishing pain from other unpleasant sensations).

A few basic facts about human pain will help in our study of animal pain. We have seen that sensory and affective aspects of pain can be distinguished. Sensory aspects seem to be concerned with locating and understanding the source of pain (e.g., a thorn in one's foot), the stimulus' intensity, and the danger with which it is associated; affective aspects appear to be concerned with escaping the painful stimulus or taking some other adaptive action.[28] Pains themselves may be importantly divided into two kinds: rapid and slow. Rapid pain is acute and transient, usually not outlasting the painful stimulus; slow pain typically results from actual tissue damage. As Rose and Adams point out, the adaptive significance of the two kinds of pain may differ: "[R]apid pain may serve as a response to the threat of tissue damage, by leading

logical range. But I think handling cases in which pain may seem not to be unpleasant is relatively easy. In such cases, either the subjects (1) experience pain, which is unpleasant but also associated with things that are valued or bring pleasure, so that the pain is gladly tolerated, or (2) experience no pain because their brains—using a *gate-control system*—have extinguished pain (or nociceptive) signals before they reach the CNS. Surely such a gate-control system would have an evolutionary value: "[T]he chances of an organism's survival are increased if, in the midst of violent battle, it is not distracted from what it is doing by *pain*. The beneficial behavior that pain normally produces is, after all, not likely to be possible in desperate situations anyway!" (George Pitcher, "The Awfulness of Pain," *Journal of Philosophy* 68 [1970], p. 489) Pitcher attributes the idea of a gate-control system to Ronald Melzack and Patrick D. Wall ("Pain Mechanisms: A New Theory," *Science* 150 [1965]: 971–79). See also Dana H. Murphy, "The Problem of Pain: What Do Animals Really Feel?," *International Journal of the Study of Animal Problems* 3 (1982), pp. 278–79; and, for an interpretation of such cases that preserves the idea that pain is intrinsically unpleasant, DeGrazia and Rowan, "Pain, Suffering, and Anxiety in Animals and Humans," pp. 194–96.

[27] A similar definition occurs in Hyram Kitchen, Arthur L. Aronson, et al., "Panel Report on the Colloquium on Recognition and Alleviation of Animal Pain and Distress," *Journal of the American Veterinary Medical Association* 191 (1987), p. 1187.

[28] Rollin, *The Unheeded Cry*, p. 144

to rapid limb movement away from a noxious stimulus. [Slow] pain leads to tonic contraction of muscle, causing immobilisation and allowing healing and repair. This is seen in 'favouring' of a limb. . . . "[29]

Evidence for pain in animals

Let us consider evidence for pain in animals. That animals often *behave* as if in pain is well known, but the data must be considered critically. In humans, the affective component of pain motivates actions that seek to (1) avoid or escape the noxious stimulus (e.g., by withdrawing a hand from a hot object), (2) get assistance (e.g., by crying out), or (3) limit the use of an injured or overworked body part to allow rest and healing (e.g., by immobilizing a pulled muscle and favoring another limb).[30] Many animals, including insects, demonstrate actions of type (1), raising the question of whether these actions are sometimes merely reflexive or nociceptive.[31] The human *pain detection threshold*—the smallest stimulus that humans experience as painful 50% of the time—appears to correspond to a similar threshold in (at least) vertebrates, as indicated by avoidance or escape behavior.[32] Among invertebrates, such behavior is also found in cephalopods.[33] Vertebrates and perhaps some invertebrates also demonstrate behavior of type (3). [Type (2) is common among mammals and probably birds but may be relevant only to comparatively social animals.]

Highly suggestive evidence that actions of types (1) or (3) are responses to pain (and not simply automatic and unconscious) is evidence of either (a) adaptation and learning or (b) behavior modification by pharmacological inhibition or stimulation.[34] Regarding (a), it seems logically possible that even the most nuanced behavior is entirely unconscious. But given evolutionary continuity, and the fact that adaptation to novelty is associated with consciousness in humans, the fact that an animal's response to a novel situation is adaptive constitutes some evidence that it is conscious. (Pharmacological evidence will be discussed later.) Drawing from several studies, Rose and Adams con-

---

[29] "Evidence for Pain and Suffering," p. 47

[30] Such quiet inactivity is described by Robert C. Bolles and Michael S. Fanselow in their perceptual-defensive-recuperative model of pain and fear ("A Perceptual Defensive Recuperative Model of Fear and Pain," *Behavioral and Brain Research* 3 [1980]: 291–323).

[31] See Peter Harrison, "Do Animals Feel Pain?", *Philosophy* 66 (1991), p. 26.

[32] See DeGrazia and Rowan, "Pain, Suffering, and Anxiety," p. 197; and Jane A. Smith and Kenneth M. Boyd, *Lives in the Balance: The Ethics of Using Animals in Biomedical Research* (New York: Oxford University Press, 1991), p. 65.

[33] Smith and Boyd, *Lives in the Balance*, p. 64

[34] Rose and Adams, "Evidence for Pain and Suffering," p. 61

clude that at least vertebrates and cephalopods seem to meet the behavioral criteria:

> All vertebrates demonstrate a capacity for learning and discrimination, and behavioural evidence of pain (Zimmerman 1986) which has been the basis for successful detection and alleviation of pain in these species (Vierck and Cooper 1984, Wright *et al.* 1985, Morton and Griffiths 1985, Sanford *et al.* 1986). Other species such as cephalopods have also demonstrated the capacity for learning and discrimination (Young 1961).[35]

There is also considerable *physiological* data relevant to the issue of pain in animals. In the brains of vertebrates, the neural mechanisms implicated in what is apparently pain behavior are very similar across vertebrate species (including humans).[36] Anesthesia and analgesia control what is apparently pain in all vertebrates and some invertebrates; in all vertebrates, the biological feedback mechanisms for controlling what seems to be pain—involving serotonin, endorphins, and what is known as *substance P*—are remarkably similar.[37]

That's a summary story. Let us look at some details.[38] The basic neurophysiology of nociception is similar across species, although there is wide variation in the details of nociceptive pathways. These ascending pathways (which carry peripheral stimuli to the CNS) are being intensively studied, and the differences and similarities between humans and animals are gradually being elucidated. Beginning with the discovery of the body's natural opiates—the endorphins—consid-

[35] "Evidence for Pain and Suffering," p. 61. The sources cited are M. Zimmerman, "Behavioural Investigations of Pain in Animals," in I. J. H. Duncan and V. Molony (eds.), *Assessing Pain in Farm Animals* (Luxembourg: Office for Official Publications of the European Communities, 1986), pp. 16–27; C. J. Vierck and B. Y. Cooper, "Guidelines for Assessing Pain Reactions and Pain Modulation in Laboratory Animal Subjects," *Advances in Pain Research and Therapy* 6 (1984): 305–22; E. M. Wright, K. L. Marcella, and J. F. Woodson, "Animal Pain: Evaluation and Control," *Lab Animal* 9 (1985): 20–36; David B. Morton and P. H. M. Griffiths, "Guidelines on the Recognition of Pain, Distress and Discomfort in Experimental Animals and an Hypothesis for Assessment," *Veterinary Record* 116 (1985): 431–36; J. Sanford, R. Ewbank, et al., "Guidelines for the Recognition and Assessment of Pain in Animals," *Veterinary Record* 118 (1986): 334–38; and J. Z. Young, "Learning and Discrimination in the Octopus," *Biological Reviews* 36 (1961): 32–96.
[36] See, e.g., Smith and Boyd, *Lives in the Balance*, pp. 63–65; and Rollin, *The Unheeded Cry*, pp. 153–54. Patrick Bateson reports that pain fibers identical to those in humans exist in mammal species ("Assessment of Pain in Animals," *Animal Behavior* 42 [1991]: 872–89). E. H. Chudler and W. K. Dong report that the pattern of electrical activity in the somatosensory cortex of monkeys, dogs, and cats in response to electric stimulation is very similar to that evoked in the human somatosensory cortex ("The Assessment of Pain by Cerebral-Evoked Potentials," *Pain* 16 [1983]: 221–44).
[37] Rollin, *The Unheeded Cry*, p. 154
[38] I borrow heavily in this and the next paragraph from DeGrazia and Rowan, "Pain, Suffering, and Anxiety," p. 198.

erable research has been undertaken on the descending nerve pathways (which carry stimuli from the CNS) that appear to be involved in human pain control. Under some circumstances, the endorphins are involved in the alleviation of pain in humans; matters are complicated by the fact that endorphins also have other functions, including effects on mood. It is speculated that these opiates are involved in a survival mechanism that allows an injured animal to function normally until it has escaped immediate danger. There are other pathways in the nervous system, not involving the opiates, that may also mediate analgesia. These pathways are observed in animals, but the precise mechanism is not well understood.

The naturally occurring opiates have been found in a wide variety of species, including some invertebrates.[39] Opiates and their receptors have been discovered in insects;[40] endorphins have even been reported in earthworms.[41] (It does not immediately follow, of course, that insects and earthworms feel pain, only that their nociceptive pathways might be inhibited by opiates.) Moreover, the biological role of the endorphins is very complicated. At least four different receptors for the endorphins have been detected, and each has different properties. One is closely associated with pain modulation, while the others are associated with mood changes and other biological effects. It is not yet known what role endorphins play in insect and earthworm neurophysiology. But several other chemicals are also associated with pain, including substance P, which has been found in mammals, birds, frogs, and fish.

Insects are an especially interesting case. While they are very primitive, their behavior in response to noxious stimuli can appear to be pain behavior. We will take up behavioral, physiological, and evolutionary evidence regarding insects after reviewing evolutionary arguments for animal pain more generally.

It is a truism that evolution tends to preserve successful biological systems. We know that in humans the ability to feel pain is important for functioning and, ultimately, for survival. Persons with an inability to feel pain or with diseases such as leprosy, which affects the capacity to feel pain, are at risk of not surviving without extraordinary attention.[42] The fact that neural machinery similar to that which subserves our

---

[39] Rose and Adams report that opiate-like activity is found in vertebrates and several invertebrates, and that opiate peptides modulate responses to stimuli that are nociceptive and elicit self-preserving behavior ("Evidence for Pain and Suffering," p. 61). For a summary of relevant evidence, see Smith and Boyd, *Lives in the Balance*, pp. 63–65.

[40] Smith and Boyd, *Lives in the Balance*, p. 64

[41] J. Alumets, R. Hakanson, et al., "Neuronal Localisation of Immunoreactive Enkephalin and B-endorphin in the Earthworm," *Nature* 279 (1979): 805–6

[42] Rollin, *The Unheeded Cry*, pp. 154–55

consciousness is found in vertebrates—in conjunction with their pain behavior—suggests that pain has a similar function for them.

Pain seems to be a product of the development of consciousness in creatures endowed with that highly developed response system known as *nociception*. Consciousness may have developed as a free-rider on certain inherited gene groups that included genes allowing relatively complex information processing; or it may have evolved as a way of focusing an organism's attention to those areas of information processing that are most vital at a given time. Either way, pain was apparently the new conscious companion of responses to potentially harmful stimuli (in these creatures, nociception) in the animals in which consciousness emerged.

To conclude, given the convergence of various kinds of evidence, it is parsimonious to attribute pain, and consciousness generally, to most or all vertebrate species and probably at least some invertebrates such as cephalopods.

It is doubtful that the same can be said for insects. Their behavior, while sometimes impressive (as in the case of bees and ants), seems explicable in terms of stimulus–response mechanisms without consciousness; when studied carefully, it often reveals a stereotyped, as opposed to innovative or flexible, quality.[43] Consider the behavior of caterpillars when, right after hatching, they climb to the tops of trees to eat the leaves there. They can do this because, when more light enters one of their two eyes, the legs on that side of the body move more slowly so that caterpillars move toward light. When trees are artificially lit at the bottom, caterpillars descend the trees and remain until starving; blinding one eye causes them to move in a circle until they starve.[44] In addition to being rigid, insect behavior is notable for the lack of known examples of insects protecting injured body parts, say, by taking weight off a damaged limb.[45] They continue normal behavior even after severe injury or loss of body parts. Thus, a locust keeps eating while being devoured by a mantis.[46] Finally, insects lack the extensive CNS processing mechanisms that appear to be necessary to feel pain.[47]

[43]See, e.g., Dawkins' careful discussion of bee dances (*Through Our Eyes Only?*, pp. 88–99).

[44]This example is developed in Peter Carruthers, *The Animals Issue: Moral Theory in Practice* (Cambridge: Cambridge University Press, 1992), pp. 56–57. Carruthers cites H. Rachlin, *Behaviour and Learning* (Oxford: Freeman, 1976), pp. 125–26.

[45]Andrew N. Rowan, Franklin M. Loew, and Joan C. Weer, *The Animal Research Controversy* (North Grafton, MA: Tufts Center for Animals and Public Policy, 1994), p. 74

[46]Bateson, "Assessment of Pain in Animals," p. 6. Bateson cites C. H. Eisemann, W. K. Jorgensen, et al., "Do Insects Feel Pain?—A Biological View," *Experientia* 40 (1984): 164–67.

[47]See Eisemann, Jorgensen, et al., "Do Insects Feel Pain?"

How can insects not feel pain yet achieve most of the survival advantage of pain (generally getting out of danger's way)? Well, while acute pain can protect an animal from noxious stimuli capable of producing immediate tissue (or bodily) damage, a startle reflex would also confer this advantage. By contrast, chronic pain promotes adaptive recuperative behavior. Animals with short life spans and modest learning needs, such as insects, would derive little advantage from this kind of pain.[48] So there would seem to be little or no selective pressure for its occurrence in such creatures.[49]

Might all animal pain—or animal mentation generally—be unconscious?

If the preceding arguments are sound, we have very good reason to believe that many animals have pain. Our working definition of *pain* defines it as unpleasant and, by implication, consciously experienced, in which case, animals susceptible to pain must be conscious creatures. But some may prefer to define *pain* (I think, wrongly) purely in terms of its functional role—roughly, as a mental event that provides information about stimuli that tend to threaten tissue damage. That would make it meaningful to speak of unconscious pain. Recently, there has been some interest in the idea that all animal mentation may be entirely unconscious. Since Peter Carruthers' work has been prominent in this recent skeptical wave, I will respond to it in particular.[50]

Carruthers makes essentially the following case for the thesis that all animal mentation is unconscious. First, he notes that it can make sense to speak of "unconscious experiences." A common example is driving while distracted, steering in such a way that shows that you see a double-parked car (since you deftly steer around it), although minutes later you cannot recall the obstacle. This suggests that your visual experience of that car (unlike your reflection on whatever occupied your mind) was unconscious. Carruthers puts it this way:

[48]Cf. Rowan, Loew, and Weer, p. 74
[49]Also concluding that insects are unlikely to experience pain are Eisemann, Jorgensen, et al., "Do Insects Feel Pain?"; G. Fiorito, "Is There Pain in Invertebrates?", *Behavioral Processes* 12 (1986): 383–86; and V. Wigglesworth, "Do Insects Feel Pain?", *Antenna* 4 (1980): 8–9. For a good overview of evidence for pain in animals, see Smith and Boyd, *Lives in the Balance*, pp. 58–67.
[50]Equally skeptical but less developed is the view in Harrison, "Do Animals Feel Pain?" A rather obscure (and, I believe, unsuccessful) set of arguments is presented by Michael P. T. Leahy in defense of what seems to be a semi-skeptical view about animal mentation (*Against Liberation: Putting Animals in Perspective* [London: Routledge, 1991], ch. 6).

Only conscious experiences have a distinctive phenomenology, a distinctive feel. Non-conscious experiences are ones that may help to control behavior without being felt by the conscious subject. . . . It is an open question whether there is anything that it feels like to be a bat, or a dog, or a monkey.[51]

He takes blind-sight to motivate this question further:

Human subjects who have suffered lesions in the striate cortex (the visual centre in the higher part of the brain) may lose all conscious experience in an area of their visual field. They insist that they can see nothing at all within that region. Nevertheless, if asked to guess, they prove remarkably good at describing features of objects presented to them in that area. . . . Subjects can reach out and grasp objects of varying shapes and sizes, at various distances, with about 80–90 per cent of normal accuracy. . . . It may be that in the case of everyday non-conscious experience the striate cortex is indeed active, but that its information is not made available to whatever structures in the human brain underlie consciousness. And it may be that even animals with a striate cortex do not possess those structures at all.[52]

Carruthers goes on to define *conscious* in a way that appears to exclude most or all animals: "I propose that a conscious experience is a state whose existence and content are available to be consciously thought about (that is, available for description in acts of thinking that are themselves made available to further acts of thinking).[53]

I believe Carruthers' skepticism about animal consciousness is entirely mistaken. The first of my four rejoinders appeals to common sense: It is extremely hard to believe that all mental states of all nonhuman animals—including dogs and dolphins, elephants and monkeys—are unconscious. Even Carruthers seems to have trouble swallowing the thesis, which he says "may well turn out to be mistaken" and is "too highly speculative to serve as a secure basis for moral practice."[54] That a thesis is strongly counterintuitive is, of course, not a fatal flaw, but it places a burden of theoretical motivation on its defender. We will see that Carruthers does not sufficiently motivate his view.

Second, it was argued earlier that consciousness probably has a functional role (though the matter is far from settled). In fact, blind-sight supports this claim, since blind-sighted persons perform less well on visual tasks than do normal-sighted persons. But even if consciousness

[51] *The Animals Issue*, p. 171
[52] ibid, pp. 172–73
[53] ibid, p. 181
[54] ibid, pp. 192, 194

has no functional role, there is excellent reason to think that many animals are conscious creatures. Again, we know that we humans are conscious. Given evolutionary continuity, behavioral and neurological analogues between humans and many animals support the common-sense claim that animals too have conscious mental states.

Carruthers may question any argument based on neurological analogues, since he wonders whether even animals possessing a striate cortex have "whatever structures in the human brain underlie consciousness." My third rejoinder is that his doubts here are very poorly motivated. The idea that some specific part of the human brain—unshared by any other animal—"underlies consciousness" is quite implausible. One would think that by now we would have identified a few good candidates for this brain part, if it existed. Dennett has powerfully argued that current neurological data simply do not support the view that there is a crucial place in the brain where information "comes together" to produce consciousness.[55] On the other hand, if we wish to speak of a "brain part" that underlies consciousness, we might speak of a very gross one—maybe the entire cerebrum—which would hardly exclude animals. At the very least, Carruthers owes us some reason to think that there is a specific, exclusively human brain part underlying consciousness.

My final rebuttal is to reject Carruthers' analysis of consciousness: "[A] conscious experience is a state whose existence and content are available to be consciously thought about (that is, available for description in acts of thinking that are themselves made available to further acts of thinking)." The nonparenthetical part of the definition is circular, since it appeals to the notion of consciousness, which he is trying to define. If we let the parenthetical phrase do its work, we avoid circularity and get this: A conscious experience is a state whose existence and content are available for description in acts of thinking that are themselves made available to further acts of thinking. A conscious visual experience, then, is one that is available to be thought about in ways that, in turn, can be thought about.

Carruthers' acknowledgment that experiences can be unconscious leads to a problem with this analysis. For if a conscious visual experience is one that is available to be thought about in a certain way, what if it is available to be thought about only unconsciously? Carruthers is in no position to rule out unconscious thought. He may allow that the experience in question might be thought about unconsciously but stress his additional requirement that this thinking must, in turn, be available

---

[55] *Consciousness Explained*, ch. 5

to be thought about. But the higher-order thinking could also be unconscious.

Imagine a twenty-first-century robot equipped with sophisticated light-pattern sensors, which function as eyes, and other sensors. It can move around in response to environmental conditions and process information about its sensory data in ways that account for its own perspective (its location, condition, etc.). All of this seems compatible with an unconscious robot. Yet this robot, by hypothesis, has experiences that are available to be thought about (unconsciously)—and we could stipulate that it could think about its own thinking (unconsciously). Carruthers has not captured what it is to be conscious, having missed some necessary condition.

Moreover, he is probably wrong that an experience must be available to be *thought about* in order to count as conscious. I suspect that this condition overintellectualizes consciousness, as may be more clear in this elaboration: "There will only be something that my experiences *are like*, for me, if I am capable of drawing distinctions and making comparisons between them."[56] This is a dubious claim at face value. The capacity to make distinctions and comparisons among conscious experiences would seem to be something beyond the capacity to have them; if not, Carruthers needs some further argument to make the claim stick.

Carruthers gives the impression of conflating basic consciousness with something more intellectual, either thinking or self-consciousness. He asserts that to produce consciousness, "all that would need to be grafted on to a cognitive structure with the capacity for thought would be a sort of feedback loop, giving [the beings] the further capacity to think about their own process of thinking."[57] But feedback loops are irrelevant if all of the beings' thoughts—like those of our robot—are unconscious. Conflating consciousness with thinking is problematic because the latter is not sufficient for consciousness. Conflating consciousness with self-consciousness is mistaken because the latter is not necessary for consciousness.

Returning to the common-sense understanding of consciousness presented earlier in this chapter, a conscious experience is one such that there is something that it is like to be in it. If an experience feels like something, it is conscious. We have excellent reasons, based on several kinds of evidence, to believe that many animals have such experiences. What goes for pain goes for other mental states. Carruthers' arguments do not cast doubt on the conscious status of the other mental states to be explored.

[56] *The Animals Issue,* p. 182
[57] ibid, p. 186

SOME BADS: DISTRESS, FEAR, ANXIETY, AND SUFFERING

The concepts

Some discussions treat pain as if it were merely a sensation, contrasting other mental states such as distress and suffering by tying them to affect or emotion. Yet pain, understood as an *unpleasant* state, is affective to some degree, making the contrast artificial. But the states to be considered in this section are not sensory, and they implicate emotions in a more obvious way. Thus, they bring their bearers somewhat closer to the mental life of humans.

Let us begin with *suffering,* which in some sense has an umbrella relationship to the other states. Suffering is not the same as pain. Pain without suffering can be caused by an ordinary hand pinch, for example. Nor is suffering the same as distress; the mild distress of a professor who is late to her own class need not involve suffering. I believe that the following analysis, which will be suitable for our investigations, is roughly correct: *Suffering is a highly unpleasant emotional state associated with more-than-minimal pain or distress.*[58]

The words "associated with" bypass the difficult conceptual and scientific issue of whether more-than-minimal pain and distress *cause* or *are forms of* suffering. It seems natural to me to regard great distress as a form of suffering. And, given the affective dimension of pain, why not regard intense pain as a form of suffering (or, better, regard the affective component of intense pain as suffering, since sensory properties, such as bodily location, do not seem ascribable to suffering)? One who accepts the sensory model of pain (see the previous section) must hold that pain can cause but not be (or conceptually overlap with) suffering. Perhaps some will argue that even intense distress is not a form of suffering but rather causes it. My definition remains neutral on these questions. Note that because suffering is defined in terms of pain and distress, there is no need for a separate discussion of the empirical correlates of suffering. Reviewing the evidence for pain (given earlier) and for distress will suffice. So let us turn to *distress.*

Consider a characterization from a panel report by veterinarians: "Distress is a state in which the animal is unable to adapt to an altered environment or to altered internal stimuli."[59] Now, clearly, distress is an *emotional* state. It also tends to be unpleasant; I leave open the possibility that mild distress can sometimes be pleasant (a plausible example of which appears later). And what seems crucial is not than an animal is

[58]Cf. Kitchen, Aronson, et al., "Panel Report," p. 1188; and DeGrazia and Rowan, "Pain, Suffering, and Anxiety," p. 201.
[59]Kitchen, Aronson, et al., "Panel Report," p. 1188

actually unable to adapt but that the animal has difficulty in adapting, believes she cannot adapt, or just has certain emotional experiences in the face of perceived challenges. Here is a working analysis: *Distress is a typically unpleasant emotional response to the perception of environmental challenges or to equilibrium-disrupting internal stimuli.*

Distress includes a very broad range of psychological phenomena. It can be caused by the sight of charging elephants, the belief that one will fail, or diarrhea. Distress, I take it, can be caused by, or take the form of, various more specific mental states, including fear, anxiety, discomfort, and perhaps others. I think *discomfort* is reasonably well understood conceptually; it bears a close relationship to pain. Anyway, few who accept the evidence for animal pain presented earlier will doubt that animals can be uncomfortable. So let us move on to the more complex and disputable states of fear and anxiety.

Fear and *anxiety* are closely related. Intuitively, fear seems cognitively simpler and perhaps more primitive (evolutionarily old); it seems less controversial to ascribe fear to animals than to ascribe anxiety to them. Yet fear and anxiety appear to work hand in hand, as we will see. The intuition that fear is more primitive may be due to a tendency in ordinary language to use *anxiety* in reference to cognitively complex mental states in humans. But the evidence may not support this intuition. Nevertheless, I will discuss anxiety in greater detail than I discuss fear. If the evidence for anxiety in animals is compelling, we should not be skeptical about animal fear. Even if every animal capable of experiencing fear can also experience anxiety, there is no reason to think that some animals who can experience anxiety cannot be afraid.

Before moving on to specifics, it is worth noting that fear and anxiety—along with anger, sexual arousal, and several other states— are associated with the sympathetic autonomic nervous system. The latter is designed for action (or preparation for action, which may include temporary inhibition) in what we might broadly call *emergency* situations. Fibers in the sympathetic system increase heart rate, sweating, and general arousal while decreasing digestion and other processes associated with rest. Also implicated is the closely related limbic system, a relatively old group of neurological structures that appear to be essential to motivation, emotion, and, in "higher" animals, personality. For example, removing the amygdala—a small organ in the limbic system—can turn a wild animal into a tame one.[60]

A passage from the aforementioned panel report provides a very helpful beginning in understanding how anxiety and fear can serve common protective goals:

[60] D. O. Hebb, *Textbook of Psychology*, 3rd ed. (Philadelphia: W. B. Saunders Company, 1972), pp. 182–83

Anxiety and fear may have the same evolutionary benefit as pain. Anxiety is activated by novel stimuli to increase the state of the animal's awareness. When placed in an unfamiliar environment, a rat initially will become motionless before cautiously beginning to explore its new surroundings. Anxiety can be defined as an emotional state involving increased arousal and alertness prompted by an unknown danger that may be present in the immediate environment. Fear can be defined similarly, except that fear would refer to an experienced or known danger in the immediate environment. Thus, anxiety appears to be a generalized, unfocused response to the unknown, and fear is a focused response to a known object or previous experience. A dog may tremble in a veterinarian's examination room during the first visit because of anxiety about what will happen. On the second visit, the dog may whine or try to escape from fear of a remembered event.[61]

Bolles and Fanselow offer a plausible account of the functional-evolutionary role of fear in relation to pain:

Fear, produced by stimuli that are associated with painful events, results in defensive behavior and the inhibition of pain and pain-related behaviors. . . . The fear motivation system activates defensive behavior, such as freezing and flight from a frightening situation, and its function is to defend the animal against natural dangers, such as predation. A further effect of fear motivation is to organize the perception of environmental events so as to facilitate the perception of danger and safety.[62]

Fear clearly has adaptive value for animals unable to get by on relatively simple, unconscious stimulus–response routines. It motivates appropriate, focused responses to perceived dangers and preparation for future focused responses to such dangers. The need for focused attention is served by the capacity of fear to *inhibit* pain; better not to attend to one's stubbed toe if one has to outrun a predator. I would add, however, that fear can also sometimes *intensify* pain—especially, when defensive actions such as fleeing are precluded. A beaten-up prisoner of war might suffer more from pain or have more pain (depending on one's model of pain) due to being terrified.

At this point, a few conceptual points are in order. First, fear, generally, is no fun; it is typically unpleasant. (I say "typically" to leave open the possibility of mild fear that is pleasant, such as that associated with

---

[61] Kitchen, Aronson, et al., "Panel Report," p. 1187
[62] A Perceptual Defensive Recuperative Model," p. 291

skiing.[63]) What about the idea that fear concerns a present or known object, unlike anxiety, which concerns an unknown object or danger? That gets us close to the truth, but the fears of schizophrenics, for example, do not always concern present or known objects. It is also sometimes said that fear concerns the present (in the temporal sense), requiring no sense of the future, whereas anxiety concerns future objects.[64] This is oversimplified. My fear of failure, and of death, concern the future. But perhaps I could be convinced that these states are really anxieties. Setting aside such examples, how could *any* fear not require some sense of the future, since what is feared is feared for what it might do to one (or perhaps to others)—in the future? Even fear caused by a charging elephant would seem to require some sense of the near future. Finally, fear typically seems to be triggered by sense perception of (1) what is taken to be danger, or (2) conditions associated, via memory, with what is taken to be danger. The dog may fear the vet when she sees him, or before seeing him when she remembers his office. I propose the following working analysis: *Fear is an emotional response to what is taken to be danger—a response that is typically unpleasant, is typically prompted by a known object in the immediate environment, and typically focuses attention to facilitate protective action.*[65] We will consider the plausibility of ascribing fear to animals after we have seen the evidence for animal anxiety.

Some writers have asserted that anxiety is an exclusively human state.[66] Let us begin, then, with human anxiety. Anxiety often intensifies pain;[67] one has a more unpleasant experience in the dentist's chair if one is anxious. Anxiety is also a direct cause, or form, of suffering; a person having an anxiety attack clearly suffers. In humans, anxiety involves a generalized, as opposed to focused, state of heightened

---

[63] Arguably, however, all fear is unpleasant. The skier may have *excitement* rather than fear. Or perhaps she experiences fear (which is unpleasant) but also something valued, such as excitement or thrill over the mastery of fear. On this model, take away the excitement or thrill over mastery, and give the skier just raw fear, and she won't like it! Similarly with horror movies.

[64] See, e.g., G. B. Cassano, "What is Pathological Anxiety and What is Not," in Erminio Costa (ed.), *The Benzodiazepines* (New York: Raven Press, 1983), p. 289.

[65] Perhaps nonparadigm cases like fear of failure could be accommodated by stretching the meaning of *danger* to include threats to one's psychological health or sense of self. And *object* need not always refer to something tangible.

[66] See, e.g., USDA, "Animals and Animal Products," *Code of Federal Regulations*, Title 9. USDA, ch. 1, sec. 113 99 (C) 4 (1979); and Cassano, "What is Pathological Anxiety and What is Not," p. 288.

[67] See, e.g., Richard A. Sternbach, *Pain Patients* (New York: Academic, 1974); and Ruth Schumacher and Manfred Velden, "Anxiety, Pain Experience and Pain Report: A Signal Detection Study," *Perceptual and Motor Skills* 58 (1984): 339–49. Not surprisingly, a reduction in anxiety typically ameliorates the painful experience (K. D. Craig, "Emotional Aspects of Pain," in Wall and Melzack, *Textbook of Pain*, pp. 153–61).

arousal and attentiveness to the environment. It often succeeds in mobilizing our mental resources to attend to our environment until we can determine how to respond to challenges. Such attention typically requires the temporary inhibition of action.[68] When dysfunctional, anxiety can overwhelm other mental functions, paralyzing us or otherwise rendering us ineffective.

Anxiety is closely related to fear and probably even overlaps with it in the sense that some states could equally well be described as fear or anxiety. But anxiety appears to serve especially well in relatively unfamiliar situations, explaining why it would tend to be less focused than fear. But it does not follow that anxiety always or even usually takes something unfamiliar as its object. Anxiety is often stimulated by impending but quite familiar settings, such as presenting a paper or running in a race. Even very concrete objects can provoke anxiety. A certain person might consistently make you anxious (even someone you do not fear).

As a working analysis, I propose the following: *Anxiety is an emotional response—typically unpleasant, typically involving heightened arousal and attentiveness to the environment, and typically inhibiting action—to what is taken to be a threat to one's physical or psychological well-being.* Instead of simply speaking of danger, as in the analysis of fear, I speak of threat to physical or psychological well-being because anxious humans quite often experience their egos as what is at risk (as suggested by some of the foregoing examples). This definition, then, covers cases of human anxiety without begging the question of whether animals can be anxious.

The evidence

Let us turn to evidence for animal anxiety. The arguments are, of course, analogical, starting with the human case. First, typical behavioral and physiological details of human anxiety are also found in animals in circumstances that seem likely to make animals anxious, if any would: (1) motor tension, as seen in shakiness and jumpiness; (2) autonomic hyperactivity (sweating, pounding heart, increased pulse rate and respiration, frequent urination, diarrhea); (3) inhibition of behavioral repertoire in novel situations; and (4) hyperattentiveness, as seen in vigilence and scanning.[69]

---

[68] Jeffrey A. Gray argues that anxiety is a result of the operation of a behavioral inhibition system that creates heightened arousal and attentiveness in novel situations (*The Neuropsychology of Anxiety* [New York: Oxford University Press, 1982], pp. 11–14).

[69] P. T. Ninan, T. M. Insel, et al. state that "the endocrine, somatic and behavioral effects of B-CCE [a chemical of the carboline class that has been found to cause

The evidence just mentioned is fairly well known. Less widely known is some fascinating recent evidence concerning anxiety-mediating drugs. The crux of the argument is that human anxiety and certain mental states in animals are mediated in similar ways by certain drugs, which produce very similar neurophysiological and neurochemical changes. The inference is that these mental states in animals are anxious ones.[70]

In the late 1970s, it was shown that there were high affinity, saturable, and specific receptors for benzodiazepines in the mammalian CNS. (Benzodiazepine receptors in humans are the apparent substrate for the action of nearly all anxiety-mediating agents identified to date.) A flurry of research has demonstrated that this receptor is part of a large, multifunctional complex that includes a barbiturate and ethanol binding site, a chloride ion channel, and a neurotransmitting binding site.[71] Thus, the known anti-anxiety properties of alcohol, the barbiturates, and the benzodiazepines (e.g., valium, xanax) can be tied to a single neurochemical substrate.

There are currently two main classes of animal tests for anxiety-reducing agents. One class involves conflict or conditioned fear, as caused by punishing drinking by a thirsty rat. An apparently anxious state is caused by punishing the drinking on a random basis. But an anti-anxiety drug will increase the amount of drinking. The other class of tests concerns apparent anxiety generated by novel environments such as a brightly lit open space.

Research using these texts has not only identified new anti-anxiety agents for human use but has also turned up substances that cause anxiety, such as beta-carboline compounds that bind to the benzodiazepine receptor. When given to humans, these compounds cause intense inner strain and excitation, increased blood pressure and pulse, restlessness, increased cortisol and catecholamine release, and stereotyped rocking motions.[72] The administration of anxiety-producing beta-carbolines to primates caused piloerection (hair raising) and struggling in the restraint chair, increased blood pressure and pulse, in-

anxiety when given to humans] are reminiscent of changes observed in anxious patients and in animals and humans exposed to anxiety-provoking or stressful situations" ("Benzodiazepine Receptor-Mediated Experimental Anxiety in Primates," *Science* 218 [1983], p. 1334).

[70] In the following paragraphs, which describe this evidence, I borrow heavily from DeGrazia and Rowan, "Pain, Suffering, and Anxiety," pp. 204–5.

[71] J. G. Richards and H. Mohler, "Benzodiazepine Receptors," *Neuropharmacology* 23 (1984), p. 240

[72] R. Dorow, R. Horowshi, et al., "Severe Anxiety Induced by FG7142: A Beta-Carboline Ligand for Benzodiazepine Receptors," *Lancet* (vol. II for 1983), p. 99

creased cortisol and catecholamine release, and increased vocalization and urination.[73]

It would seem, then, that the physiological and behavioral results from drug studies (along with a plausible evolutionary story about how anxiety can be generally adaptive) strongly indicate that at least mammals experience anxiety. Shortly after the discovery of the high-affinity benzodiazepine receptors, an analysis of the distribution of such receptors throughout the animal kingdom reported that none of the five invertebrate species tested (earthworm, locust, woodlouse, lobster, and squid), nor the one representative of cartilaginous fishes, had these receptors. (Cartilaginous fishes could be classified among invertebrates about as well as among vertebrates; their primitive skeletons are composed mainly of cartilage.) All the other seventeen species, however— all vertebrates including three species of birds, a lizard, turtle, and frog, and three species of bony fishes—proved to have such receptors.[74] (Interestingly, the invertebrates investigated for benzodiazepine receptors did not include the octopus, but some behavioral data suggest that members of this species may experience anxiety.[75])[76]

None of this evidence, of course, suggests that different animals and humans have *qualitatively similar* anxious states. There is evidence that the frontal lobes play an important role in mediating anxiety and play a greater role in humans than in animals. Language appears to play a considerable part in the mediation of human anxiety. Interestingly, neurophysiological correlates of anxiety appear in humans in response to

[73] Ninan, Insel, et al., "Benzodiazepine Receptor-Mediated Experimental Anxiety in Primates," p. 1333

[74] M. Nielsen, C. Braestrup, and R. F. Squires, "Evidence for a Late Evolutionary Appearance of a Brain-Specific Benzodiazepine Receptor," *Brain Research* 141 (1978): 342–46. A lucid summary of data concerning the benzodiazepine receptors and anxiety is presented in Murphy, "The Problem of Pain," pp. 279–80. A more detailed discussion is contained in Richards and Mohler, "Benzodiazepine Receptors."

[75] See A. Packard and G. D. Sanders, "What the Octopus Shows to the World," *Endeavour* 28 (1969): 92–99; and J. A. Mather, "Ethical Treatment of Invertebrates: How Do We Define an Animal?", in J. W. Driscoll (ed.), *Animal Care and Use in Behavioral Research* (Animal Welfare Information Center, National Agricultural Library, 1989), pp. 52–59. For a summary of such behavioral evidence, see Smith and Boyd, *Lives in the Balance*, pp. 71–72.

[76] Andrew Rowan pointed out to me that the benzodiazepine-receptor story has grown somewhat more complicated in the 1990s (though not in a way that affects my basic assertions). First, in addition to the benzodiazepine receptors found in the CNS, more recently peripheral benzodiazepine receptors have been found (e.g., in toes and fingers). These peripheral receptors, which seem to have a different function from the CNS receptors (though their function is not yet well understood), are found more widely throughout the animal kingdom. Also, several anti-anxiety drugs have been developed that act not by way of benzodiazepine receptors but by way of other receptors.

potentially stressful verbal instructions, but these physiological responses are absent in patients with prefrontal lobe damage affecting the language systems of the temporal and frontal cortex.[77]

Of course, the brains of different species of animals differ greatly in terms of size and structure. All vertebrates have a cerebrum, the presumed anatomical seat of consciousness. But, even among mammals, the surface area of the cerebral cortex—where the highest-order processing is believed to occur—varies greatly. This finding tends to support the idea of significant qualitative differences in the anxious states of different species.[78]

The available evidence, taken together, suggests that many species of animal—indeed, there is some reason to think, most or all vertebrates, and possibly a few invertebrates—can experience anxious states of mind, although there are probably great qualitative differences among the states experienced by different species.[79] Additionally, given the close—probably overlapping—relationship between fear and anxiety, it is reasonable to conclude that these animals can also experience fear. Supporting this proposition is the fact that all vertebrates have autonomic-nervous and limbic systems, which contain the basic substates of anxiety and fear.

What about suffering? Given the conceptual relationships just mapped out, animals capable of having anxiety and fear are probably capable of suffering. That would admittedly not be the case, however, if some animals could experience only mild fear or anxiety. But we have also seen evidence that all vertebrates, and maybe some invertebrates such as cephalopods, experience pain. That is a good case for asserting that these species are also capable of suffering—unless some of them can experience only mild pain. *In conclusion, the available evidence suggests that most or all vertebrates, and perhaps some invertebrates, can suffer.*

SOME GOODS: PLEASURE, ENJOYMENT, AND HAPPINESS

The concepts

In this section, we will examine certain states that are normally liked or experienced as pleasant or agreeable. Our examination will be brief, because evidence for unpleasant or aversive states (as presented in the previous section) is more fundamental to our investigations. That is

[77] Gray, *The Neuropsychology of Anxiety*, pp. 409–23
[78] Smith and Boyd, *Lives in the Balance*, p. 72
[79] In their study of the evidence, Smith and Boyd confidently conclude that mammals experience anxiety, while inclining slightly toward the conclusion that non-mammalian vertebrates (and possibly octopi) do as well (*Lives in the Balance*, p. 72).

because, first, demonstrating that animals have aversive mental states will suffice to show that they have interests (as we will see in Chapter 8). Second, the aversive states we have attributed to animals—pain, distress, fear, anxiety, and suffering—seem unlikely to exist without certain corresponding positive states, such as pleasure, calm, comfort, and contentment. Indeed, in us, sometimes the mere reduction or removal of aversive mental states causes positive ones. Evolutionary continuity plus the adaptive value of feeling good at the demise of bad feelings (whose functions we have discussed) strongly suggest a similar phenomenological network for animals. Finally, there just isn't as much empirical evidence about the positive mental states—beyond the sort of behavioral evidence with which we are all familiar, and well-known evolutionary considerations (which are discussed later).

Let us begin with *pleasure*. What is pleasure? Or, better, what are pleasures? One might think that pleasures, like pains, are sensations. But the pleasures of contemplation, of admiring beauty, and of reading are not sensory. They are feelings of some sort. What do pleasurable feelings all have in common? In answer to this, there is both a feeling model and an attitude model.[80]

According to the *feeling model* (defended by Bentham), pleasures have nothing more in common than being feelings with an intrinsic quality called *pleasantness* that cannot be further analyzed. On this model, then, it is a contingent matter whether one likes or desires pleasures. Those who believe pleasures are necessarily liked or desired at some level have reason to adopt the *attitude model*. Another motivation for the latter is the great phenomenological diversity among pleasures, which casts doubt on the claim that they all share some intrinsic quality. Henry Sidgwick puts it this way:

> Let, then, pleasure be defined as feeling which the sentient individual at the time of feeling it implicitly or explicitly apprehends to be desirable;— desirable, that is, when considered merely as feeling, and not in respect of its objective conditions or consequences, or of any facts that come directly within the cognisance and judgment of others besides the sentient individual.[81]

I think the attitude model, as stated by Sidgwick, is correct. The only serious objection to it seems to be that we sometimes do not want or

---

[80] For an insightful discussion of these models (though the second model is described somewhat differently), see Sumner, "Welfare, Happiness, and Pleasure," pp. 203–6.

[81] *Methods of Ethics*, 7th ed. (London: Macmillan, 1907), p. 131. Robert Nozick gives an equivalent definition (*The Examined Life* [New York: Simon & Schuster, 1989], pp. 103–4).

enjoy pleasures. Think of the monk who renounces worldly pleasures, the self-loather who feels he doesn't deserve pleasures, the student who is worried that available pleasures will distract him when he should be studying for finals. But these objections miss the model's claim that pleasures are desired *for their own felt qualities*. The monk is averse to pleasures' worldliness, not to the way they feel; he would welcome the pleasures of heaven. The self-loather does not dislike pleasures per se but only when they are perceived as undeserved treats. And the student would gladly feast on pleasures if you convinced him that they would not interfere with necessary studying.

At the same time, the possibility of rejecting pleasures in some circumstances, all things considered, motivates a distinction between pleasure and some other state of mind. Clearly, we care about and desire things other than pleasures, such as spiritual purity, moral desert, and good grades. We might even say that some people cannot enjoy certain pleasures in certain circumstances, such as those described previously. Let me use *enjoyment,* then—somewhat stipulatively—to designate an all-things-considered endorsement of, or preference for, an experience. The monk cannot deny that sexual pleasure feels good—that the associated feelings just in themselves are desirable—but he might not enjoy them due to attitudes about their source.[82]

Let us turn briefly to happiness, before asking whether animals can have these states. To some ears, *happiness* has a profound ring; many people view it as the major aim in human life. We cannot explore this concept or its opposite—unhappiness or misery—in depth here. But a few points are worth making.

First, it is helpful to distinguish two main senses of the term. Take the sentence, "The happy man was miserable playing tennis." (Assume "miserable" describes him and not the quality of his play.) In one sense of *happiness,* this sentence is quite intelligible; in another sense of the term, it is contradictory. If *happy* describes how the man feels while playing tennis, the sentence is contradictory because one cannot feel, at a particular time, both happy and miserable. But if *happy* describes some general state of the man over a long period of time, the sentence is fine: The man's bad feeling while playing is compatible with his long-term condition.

[82]I got the idea of distinguishing pleasure and enjoyment from Sumner ("Welfare, Happiness, and Pleasure," p. 214), but he and I understand their relationship differently due to our different understandings of pleasure. Sumner makes the interesting point that not only do we often respond positively to (enjoy) an experience because it is pleasant; we often find an experience pleasant because we value (enjoy) it, as might be the case when walking with a companion (ibid).

Let us distinguish *feeling happy* and *being happy*. Feeling happy is an occurrent mental state of an individual over some stretch of time. It seems roughly the same as enjoyment. (But enjoyment, as defined previously, takes an object—it is always enjoyment *of* something— whereas one can simply feel happy or be in a happy mood.[83]) The man having a bad time playing tennis is not happy in this sense. But he might *be* generally happy, happy over the long haul. This is the sense of *happiness* that gives the word its profound ring. For Aristotle and the classical utilitarians, the word can sum up a person's well-being over a lifetime.

I think of being happy as *feeling satisfied or fulfilled by the basic circumstances of one's life, such that one is disposed to endorse or affirm them in terms of one's own priorities.*[84] For our purposes, the precise analysis of this concept is not so important. What *is* important is that one who is happy in this sense (1) is disposed to make an overall positive judgment about the way his or her life is going (a judgmental element), and (2) feels good about it (an affective element).[85]

Can animals have these mental states?

Given all the evidence for unpleasant mental states discussed previously, there is good reason to believe that many animals—most or all vertebrates and maybe some invertebrates—can have pleasure. If they can have unpleasant or aversive mental states, they are, by definition, conscious. Such mental states in these creatures are motivational; pain, discomfort, distress, fear, anxiety, and suffering motivate doing things that tend to make the unpleasant experiences stop. It is difficult to see how evolution might have conferred consciousness on these animals, provided them aversive states, provided human beings both aversive states and pleasurable ones, yet not provided nonhuman animals any capacity for pleasure. For pleasure, too, is motivating; we seek it, other things being equal. And neural pathways apparently associated with pleasure have been located in the brains of mammals, birds, and fish.[86] In addition, animals certainly act as if they experience pleasure, although their apparent pleasure behavior becomes vastly more convincing as one moves up the phylogenetic scale. (I doubt that controlled

---

[83] At the same time, maybe it is always true that someone who is feeling happy is enjoying herself. These points about feeling happy are made in L. W. Sumner, *Welfare and Welfarism* (book in progress), ch. 6. Cf. Wayne Davis, "Pleasure and Happiness," *Philosophical Studies* 39 (1981): 305–17.

[84] See Sumner, "Welfare, Happiness, and Pleasure," p. 220.

[85] I got the idea of distinguishing the judgmental and affective elements from Sumner, *Welfare and Welfarism*, ch. 6.

[86] Rollin, *The Unheeded Cry*, p. 153

laboratory studies would convince us more than common observation.) Given the function of pleasure—to attract one to what is generally beneficial—in addition to the physiological and common-sense behavioral observations, it would be unparsimonious to deny that many animals can have this mental state.

But if certain animals can experience pleasure, they can also have enjoyments. Recalling our analysis of enjoyment, saying that an animal *endorses* a pleasurable experience may sound strained, but saying that the animal *prefers*—or, better, desires or likes—it sounds natural. Indeed, assuming that animals generally lack the sorts of judgmental hang-ups of the monk, self-loather, and anxious student, there may be no experiential distance between pleasures and enjoyments for animals (with, at most, a few exceptions). The dog who finds eating pleasurable enjoys the activity. The horse who gets pleasure from scratching against a post enjoys doing so.

Some may object to saying that any nonhuman animal *desires* an experience. But our analysis of pleasure implicates the notions of liking or desiring certain experiences based on how they feel—just as pain, being unpleasant, implicates disliking. One might reply that an animal could like or dislike certain things without having any desires. But it is difficult to see how one could dislike X without desiring (other things being equal) that X discontinue or stay away, or like X without desiring (other things being equal) to have X. Anyway, the relations between feelings and desires will be spelled out in more detail in Chapter 6.

What about the idea of animal happiness? If the foregoing arguments are sound, animals can certainly feel happy—because they can enjoy themselves (which comes to roughly the same thing). If anyone finds it odd to speak of happy animals, that may be due to connotations of the other sense of happiness: being happy. Animals cannot be happy, as we defined this term, unless they can make evaluative judgments about their lives as wholes (something one might reasonably doubt).

On the other hand, we could say that the sense in which beings who cannot make judgments of the relevant sort *are* happy is simply that they *feel* happy at that time. In this case, we could speak of their having *happy lives* if they mostly feel happy during their lifetimes.

As an aside, we can also correctly say that animals are happy by invoking a third major sense of *happy,* one that clearly does not refer to a feeling. One is a happy individual in this sense if one has a *happy disposition or personality,* a tendency toward feeling happy. Such individuals are thought of as upbeat and cheerful.[87] Most of us have known dogs and human babies who are like that.

---

[87] This idea comes from Sumner, *Welfare and Welfarism,* ch. 6.

CONCLUSION

To sum up our investigations, many animals—most or all of the vertebrates and possibly some others, such as the cephalopods—can experience a wide variety of feelings. These animals can have pleasures and enjoyments (and, therefore, feel happy). They can experience pain and distress. And there is good reason to think that most, if not all, of them can experience fear and anxiety and, we may assert even more confidently, suffering.

These propositions are asserted as very reasonable and presumptive given currently available evidence, not as absolutely certain. The simpler the mental state, and the more neurologically and behaviorally complex the animal, the closer we come to certainty.[88] We can be about as certain that chimpanzees experience pain as we are that humans do. That fish can have anxious states is much less firmly established; perhaps further evidence about the neurochemistry of anxiety and an improved theory of anxiety will overturn this thesis. And it is conceivable that some animals, maybe fish, can experience pain and distress, yet not suffer, because their pain and distress never gets very intense. We must have due modesty, but we must also avoid the anthropocentric temptation to be skeptical without cause.

Have we really demonstrated that all of these animals are capable of having desires, as suggested by our analyses of pain and pleasure? Desires sound more mentally heavyweight than feelings. As we will see, desires may even require beliefs, which sound really heavyweight. Are we prepared to ascribe all this to nonhuman animals, especially such apparent simpletons as reptiles, amphibians, and fish?

I have, of course, *argued* that pleasures and pains involve liking and disliking and that these entail desires. If I am right here, then solid evidence for pain and pleasure in certain animals is solid evidence that they have desires. But I will take the case made thus far for desires as presumptive, not conclusive. Special challenges to ascribing this class of mental states to animals must be confronted. Let us turn, then, to those challenges.

---

[88] Admittedly, complexity proves to be a tricky concept. See John Tyler Bonner, *The Evolution of Complexity by Means of Natural Selection* (Princeton: Princeton University Press, 1988).

Chapter 6

Desires and beliefs

A circle of conative concepts

In the last chapter, we learned that many animals have certain kinds of feelings. Can animals have *desires*? What are desires? One's first attempt to clarify this concept is likely to be in terms of other concepts equally in need of clarification: *wants* or *preferences*, perhaps. Desires, wants, and preferences all suggest being disposed to "go for" something; they all suggest action tendencies. But not just that. These terms, in their paradigmatic senses anyway, also suggest *caring* about what you're going for—there is an affective component to them. We do not say the wind-up toy desires the object toward which it ambulates, because, lacking consciousness, it doesn't care about this object (or anything else). But to care about something is to be *concerned about* getting it; it *matters* to one whether one gets it. Often, of course, what we desire and care about are not physical objects to be hunted down but changes in our situation; we might want rest, for example. And what we want and care about are things we *like;* we also care, in a negative way, about things we *dislike,* and they too matter to us.

What we have, then, is a tight circle of what I will call *conative* concepts: desires, wants, preferences, caring, concerns, mattering, liking and disliking, and perhaps others. Sometimes the concept of conation is closely tied to action tendencies (going for it) and distinguished from affect and cognition.[1] But since desires are paradigmatically con-

---

[1] For example, this is the first definition of *conation* in *Webster's Third International Dictionary:*

> the conscious drive to perform apparently volitional acts with or without knowledge of the origin of the drive—distinguished from *affection* and *cognition.* (unabridged [Springfield, MA: Merriam-Webster, 1981], p. 468)

scious (at least potentially), and conscious desires involve caring about what is desired, any conation–affect division is artificial. So in my perhaps reconstructive use of the term, conation involves "going for it" *and* "caring about it."

It is difficult to find a completely satisfactory representative of this circle. *Desire* is often used, but sometimes one has a conative attitude about the lesser of perceived evils, and it sounds odd to speak of desiring that alternative. *Preference* deals well with such circumstances but may connote having alternatives in mind—one presumably prefers X to some Y. But what if an animal is mentally very simple and has a minimal pro-attitude or con-attitude toward something, say, eating or getting kicked. Isn't it possible that this creature has no alternative Y in mind? One might say that the animal prefers food to not-food, or prefers not-being-kicked to (not-not-) being kicked—but this may feel artificial. In that case, maybe *liking* and *disliking* are better for the job. But, for fancier desires, such as the desire to get tenured, what exactly is liked? Getting tenured? But I haven't yet. The idea of getting tenured? That's not what I want! We could speak of what one *would* like. But that will not help in cases of the lesser of perceived evils. *Concern, caring,* and *mattering* are general terms that cover the terrain fairly well, I think. But these terms have, for some, connotations of intellectual sophistication beyond what we are after here. For me, it is natural to say that, if a mouse is suffering from electric shocks, she wants the shocks (or perhaps the suffering) to stop and therefore cares (is concerned) about her predicament (which matters to her). But some who grant the suffering and the want will hesitate at the other attributions.[2]

An appropriate lesson to draw from these linguistic data is that these words have differing connotations such that no word within the cluster is a perfectly apt representative. That does not vitiate the claim that these words refer to the same class of mental states, however. I will usually speak of *desires* but will sometimes employ other words from the cluster.

In preparation for considering further evidence for desires in animals, it will be helpful to enumerate some necessary conditions for a desire: *A desires X only if (1) A is disposed to go for X (or bring X about), (2) this disposition is at least potentially conscious, and (3) A is disposed to have some pleasant feelings upon attaining X and some unpleasant feelings at prolonged failure to attain X.* (These conditions are not claimed to be jointly sufficient, because we have not confronted the issue of whether beliefs are required.)

A few comments are needed here. Condition (1) is not sufficient because even an undesiring wind-up toy can meet this condition. But

---

[2] This observation is based on conversations with several philosophers.

the toy will not meet (2) or (3). As for (2), one might object to requiring potential consciousness of a desire (strictly speaking, of a behavioral disposition), claiming that some desires (say, for one's mother or father) are so deeply repressed that no amount of analytic work can make one aware of them. I do not want to plunge deep into psychoanalytic theory here. My reason for requiring only *potential* consciousness is that desires (e.g., to be a good parent) can exist over stretches of time when one does not have the object of desire consciously in mind (see Chapter 5). Some desires, apparently, are also repressed. I leave open the possibility of thoroughly repressed desires. The inclusion of a potential-consciousness condition for desires means that each desire is of a type (desires) tokens of which *typically* can be made conscious. Is condition (3) needed? In the real world, maybe not. The selective pressures that produced consciousness (either as an advantage or as a free-rider) also seem to have produced affect in animals. But we can conceive of a being that is mechanically driven to attain X, is conscious of its action tendency, but couldn't care less about X or anything else. Since this being would not seem to desire X, I explicitly tie desires to pleasant and unpleasant feelings. This brings together at least some feelings and the phenomena of going for it.

Presumptive evidence for animal desires

Given the previous necessary conditions (1)–(3), what would count as *evidence* for animal desires? The most natural evidence for the disposition to go for something is actually going for it, so behaving as if one desires something counts as evidence that one does. But behavioral evidence is insufficient. The action tendencies must be potentially conscious, and the animal must be capable of experiencing pleasant feelings upon getting what she wants and unpleasant feelings when her efforts are thwarted. Thus, we want evidence that the animal is *sentient*, that she has at least some feelings. Physiological evidence is especially helpful here: Does the animal appear to have a nervous system capable of producing conscious and, more specifically, pleasant and unpleasant states? Finally, evolutionary-functional arguments to the effect that conation would be adaptive for the animal, given its evolutionary niche, would be a further form of evidence.

That many animals behave as if they have desires may hardly seem to require argument. Dogs chase balls, elephants reach for peanuts, rats run for cover, and fish flee predators. But we must be certain to distinguish apparently desiring behaviors from undesiring movements. Only the latter are adequately explained in stimulus–response terms. Much animal behavior seems inexplicable in these terms. (Stimulus–response interpretations might also be refuted on physiological and evolutionary grounds, but let us set that point aside for now.) As Searle summarily puts it (addressing beliefs as well as desires),

> the behavior is unintelligible without the assumption of beliefs and desires; because the animal, e.g., barks up the tree even when he can no longer see or smell the cat, thus manifesting a belief that the cat is up the tree even when he cannot see or smell that the cat is up the tree. And similarly he behaves in ways that manifest a desire for food even when he is neither seeing, smelling, nor eating food.[3]

Everyday observation tends to bear out Searle's common-sense claim about desires. But more rigorous evidence is available.

Before turning to that evidence, we need to consider an objection. It might be argued that the fact that animals behave *as if* they have desires is not evidence that they *really do* have desires. Proponents of WCE (weak cognitive ethology—see Chapter 5) grant the "as if" claim but stop short of the "really do" claim. They are mistaken. If an animal's behavior is unintelligible—or even significantly less intelligible—without positing desires or other intentional states, how could that fail to constitute evidence for the existence of such states? The *best explanation* of their behavior is that they have those states, by hypothesis. Fodor puts it well:

> The predictive and explanatory success of commonsense belief/desire psychology [is remarkable]. . . . And, by all reasonable empirical criteria, this theory . . . appears to be *true:* its predictive adequacy is not susceptible to serious doubt, and it has repeatedly proven superior to such rival theories as have sought to replace it (e.g., behavioristic theories and pie-in-the-sky neuroscience . . .).[4]

Moreover, the conditions for A's desiring X include A's being disposed to go for X. So how could actually going for X not count as evidence of desiring X? Some proponents of WCE may hold that there are no such things as desires—even in the human case—although the concept is helpful given the immature state of neurophysiology. For the purposes of this book, however, I am assuming that humans have desires, beliefs, and other folk-psychological states (see Chapter 5).

Certain behaviors count as evidence for desires. Some of the evidence has established more than what we need: behaviors that appear to manifest not just desires but the testing of hypotheses (about how to obtain desired food). M. E. Bitterman studied "progressive adjustment"

[3] Searle, "Animal Minds" (unpublished manuscript)
[4] Jerry A. Fodor, *A Theory of Content and Other Essays* (Cambridge, MA: MIT Press, 1990), p. 174

in "multiple reversal trials" by representatives of different animal taxa. He devised simple ways to test how rapidly various animals could adapt to the reversal of learned reward patterns. Herpetofauna (reptiles and amphibians), birds, and mammals demonstrated progressively faster adaptations as reversal trials were continued. But fish did not. Bitterman's study suggests that animals of taxa "higher" than fish can *learn* from their experience (beyond the classical-conditioning sense of *learning* as acquiring habits based on brute repetition of associated events). On the basis of multiple trials, they apparently *form hypotheses* of what they must do to obtain rewards and *test* these hypotheses by behaving accordingly (thereby "leapfrogging" the many repetitions that would be required to establish a new habit, as in classical conditioning).[5]

Bitterman's study was designed to reveal certain cognitive capacities, or their lack, as revealed by the reward-seeking behavior of various animals. Herpetofauna—let us call them *herps*—as well as birds and mammals obviously displayed desire *behavior* in this study. They obviously pursued various rewards. And so did fish, even if their behavior did not amount to hypothesis testing and intelligent learning. Fish certainly *behave* as if they desire certain things, such as food, a gulp of air, or escape from a predator. Indeed, arguably, so do many invertebrates, including insects. But, as we have seen, we must also examine physiological and evolutionary evidence before attributing desires.

Marian Stamp Dawkins provides extensive up-to-date evidence not only for the existence of animal conation but also for *what*, specifically, animals want and even *how much* they want it. Some of the reasoning behind the design of her preference tests is explained here:

> [Are particular animals] prepared to make an effort, spend time, give up an opportunity to feed, etc. to get what they want? An animal prepared to "do anything" to escape from a small cage or to cross an electrified grid to get at a female is showing what matters to it. . . . In theory, then, we can "ask" animals what matters to them, using actions not words. The clearest answers so far have come from experiments done by psychologists training animals to perform actions for various sorts of reward. . . . Now, by turning our attention to the value the animal places on the reward itself, particularly in relation to the effort it has to make to get it, we can learn not just what, but also how much, something matters to it. For instance, when a pigeon has learnt to peck a key for food, will it still keep pecking

[5] "The Evolution of Intelligence," *Scientific American* 212 (January 1965): 92–100. Writing in the 1960s, Bitterman did not himself attribute hypothesis formation and testing to the animals, more modestly speaking of the emergence of dramatically more "flexible" behaviors. The attribution of hypothesis formation and testing are a reasonable inference drawn from Bitterman's data by Gary Varner, in his *In Nature's Interests?: Interests, Animal Rights, and Environmental Ethics* (book in progress), ch. 2.

when instead of having to give just one or two pecks per item of food, it has to peck four, eight or even 50 times? . . . Animals with hands like those of rats or racoons are easy to work with because they can be given levers or little handles to press and large birds can be given keys to peck. Smaller birds or animals less able to manipulate things can be trained to hop onto a special perch or sit on a panel built into the floor. [Fish] can be trained to swim through hoops or tunnels. . . . If an animal will repeatedly go to considerable lengths to make something appear [or disappear], then it is telling us by its behaviour that it values that commodity (or its absence). It is telling us something about what it wants or finds desirable.[6]

I think Dawkins has captured very nicely the relation between conation and behavior. There have been, of course, countless studies measuring animals' responses to choice situations. Thus, there is not only everyday observation to support the claim that many animals behave as if they have desires; there are a plethora of rigorous scientific studies as well.[7]

Many, perhaps most, animals behave as if conative. What about the physiological evidence? Let us take our start from Searle, who is very confident in the case of at least some mammals:

Given what we know about the brains of the higher animals, especially the primates, any such speculation [that animals lack intentional states] must seem breathtakingly irresponsible. Anatomically the similarities are too great for such a speculation to seem even remotely plausible, and physiologically we know that the mechanisms that produce intentionality and thought in humans have close parallels in other beasts. Humans, dogs and chimpanzees all take in perceptual stimuli through visual, tactile, auditory, olfactory and other sensory receptors, they all send the signals produced by these stimuli to the brain where they are processed, and eventually the resultant brain processes cause motor outputs in the forms of intentional actions such as socializing with other conspecific beasts, eating, playing, fighting, reproducing, raising their young, and trying to stay alive. It seems out of the question, given the neurobiological continuity, to suppose that only humans have intentionality and thoughts.[8]

Intentionality, of course, includes desires. No doubt Searle is right that the physiological evidence supports attributing desires to "higher" animals such as dogs, pigs, elephants, monkeys, chimps, and dolphins. But what about rodents, birds, herps, fish, and invertebrates?

[6] *Through Our Eyes Only?: The Search for Animal Consciousness* (Oxford: Freeman, 1993), pp. 147–49
[7] I assume that it would be pointless and arbitrary to cite examples, since there are thousands of them.
[8] "Animal Minds"

Remember that, in addition to having certain behavioral dispositions, an animal must be *sentient* to have desires. Evidence about animal
sentience was given in Chapter 5, which counted most or all vertebrates
among sentient creatures. Still, it will be useful to examine some specifics of animal physiology.[9]

The brains of vertebrates, and some invertebrates, divide into the
parts of hindbrain, midbrain, and forebrain. Vertebrates have more
developed forebrains than do invertebrates; they are distinguished,
specifically, by the presence of a *cerebrum*. But a *cerebral cortex* clearly
emerges only in the herps; fish have a cerebrum but apparently no
cortex.[10] Birds and mammals, who evolved from reptiles, are
distinguished from lower vertebrates by their more developed cerebra.
But the avian and mammalian cerebra have specialized in importantly
different ways:

> In birds, the base of the cerebrum, the stratium, is highly developed and
> the cap of the cerebrum, the cerebral cortex, is vestigial. In mammals the
> situation is reversed: the cortex has expanded, overgrowing and covering
> the stratium, and the most highly developed portion of the avian strat-
> ium, the hyperstratium, is entirely absent. Today, ethologists generally
> take development of the cerebral cortex to be the best measure of relative
> intelligence among mammalian species, and development of the hyper-
> stratium to be the best measure of relative intelligence among avian
> species.[11]

Birds, then, are distinguished from lower animals by the presence of a
hyperstratium, while mammals are distinguished from lower animals by
the development of their cerebral cortex—specifically, by a stucture
known as the *prefrontal cortex* (or lobe).

These fascinating distinctions among vertebrate taxa may help us in
attributing various mental states to different animals. But in Chapter 5,
we reviewed extensive evidence that most or all vertebrate species can
experience pleasure as well as pain, distress, and other unpleasant
states. On the basis of that evidence, we might conclude that having a

---

[9] In the discussion of animal physiology that follows, I have benefited extensively
from Varner, *In Nature's Interests?*, ch. 2.
[10] But what exactly should count as a cortex? Reptile brains have a conspicuous sheet
of grey matter—uncontroversially a cortex—on the posterior surfaces of the
cerebrum. Jane A. Smith and Kenneth M. Boyd, however, separate reptile and amphibian brains, grouping the latter with fish brains. They note that only small
patches of neurons are found on the surfaces of fish and amphibian cerebra, suggesting the ambiguity of their status as cortexes (*Lives in the Balance: The Ethics of Using
Animals in Biomedical Research* [Oxford: Oxford University Press, 1991], p. 48).
[11] Varner, *In Nature's Interests?*, ch. 2. To support the last sentence, Varner cites Laurence Jay Stettner and Kenneth A. Matyniak, "The Brain of Birds," *Scientific American*
(June 1968).

functioning cerebrum (or a functionally equivalent part of a nervous system) is sufficient for sentience. And, given the behavioral evidence discussed previously, we seem to be in a position to say that there is presumptive evidence that vertebrates have desires.

Some readers might feel I've pulled a fast one. They might still be uncomfortable with the thesis that sentient animals necessarily have desires. Some philosophers apparently think that desires demand more sophisticated neural machinery than does sentience. But I did argue— as opposed to simply assume—that feelings were closely connected with desires (in Chapter 5). Moreover, I have added behavioral evidence for desires in this section.[12] And our whole argument so far has only been about *presumptive* evidence for animal desires; two tough challenges are around the corner. But let me add one more piece of evidence to the presumption.

For the sake of argument, assume that sentience does not *logically* entail the existence of any desires. Nevertheless, in evolutionary terms, sentience does not make sense in the absence of conative states, as argued by Sapontzis: "[T]here would be no evolutionary point to their being sentient if they could not recognize, desire, and pursue those things that give them pleasure and recognize, desire, and seek to avoid those things that give them pain."[13] If sentience were only the capacity to detect certain stimuli that threatened harm (as in nociception), responses to those stimuli could be automatic and unconscious. But sentient creatures have pleasant and unpleasant feelings, which would have no advantage absent an ability *to do something in response to those feelings*. Now surely goal-directed behavior in response to pleasant and unpleasant feelings involves desires (say, to escape the source of pain).[14]

We have presumptive evidence that most or all vertebrates have desires. Maybe some invertebrates, such as cephalopods, do as well. But we are not entitled to conclude that animals have desires unless we can handle two challenges: (1) the difficulty of making sense of the *content* of putative animal desires; and (2) the possibility that desires require *beliefs*, which perhaps animals lack.

---

[12] That evidence may seem coextensive with the evidence for feelings reviewed in Chapter 5. That would not be surprising if pain, distress, and related feelings implied desires and vice versa. But, in considering what evidence would count for animal desires, we did so on the basis of what desire seems to be (that is, on an analysis of the concept of desire).

[13] S. F. Sapontzis, *Morals, Reason, and Animals* (Philadelphia: Temple University Press, 1987), p. 186

[14] Frederik Kaufman misses this point in arguing that sentience does not entail preferences ("Machines, Sentience, and the Scope of Morality," *Environmental Ethics* 16 [Spring 1994], pp. 67–69).

What about the content of animals' desires?

Our first challenge really has two aspects. First, in light of the apparent impossibility of precisely specifying the content of putative animal desires, perhaps these states therefore lack content and (since desires have content) are therefore not desires. Second, even if we surmount this difficulty, what can we say about the content of animals' desires?

1. What if animals' putative desires lack specific content? Desires are generally categorized, in the philosophy of mind, as *propositional attitudes*. These are, roughly, mental states that take propositions as their objects (or can be stated that way). Thus, I believe that "It is going to rain." I suspect that "The Redskins will get swept by the Giants." I want a drink. Where is the proposition here? Well, stated more fully (and awkwardly), I want that "I have a drink" (or something like that). Now some philosophers debate whether the objects of these attitudes are really propositions or sentences, but I cannot take on the issue here.[15] For our purposes, we may think of desires, beliefs, hopes, and the like as either propositional attitudes or *sentential* attitudes.

Now here's the problem. We see a wolf chasing a rabbit and we think the wolf wants to catch the rabbit. More fully, the wolf desires that "The wolf catches the rabbit." But is this *the* correct translation of the wolf's mental representations into our vocabulary? Does the wolf have our concept of wolf? Or, if she desires that "I catch the rabbit," does she have the concept of selfhood? There are grounds for skepticism even if we limit our question to "rabbit." Our concept of rabbit is the concept of a certain species of rodent. Does the wolf have the concepts of species and rodent? Very doubtfully. Maybe the wolf does not want to catch the rabbit but rather the "furry, white, quick thing." But some rabbits are not white. Does the wolf think of this rabbit, which is white, as being of the same kind of thing as brown rabbits? And so on.

These concerns motivate the first premise of this skeptical argument: (1) There is no fact of the matter as to the precise content of the animal's mental state; therefore (2) The animal's mental state lacks content; (3) Desires have content; therefore (4) The animal's mental state is not a desire.[16]

This argument is invalid because premise (2) does not follow from (1): A mental state does not require precise content in order to have content. What is required, then, for content? To have content, a mental

---

[15] For a scholarly discussion of the issues involved, see Daniel C. Dennett, *The Intentional Stance* (Cambridge, MA: MIT Press, 1987), ch. 5.

[16] My formulation of this argument is influenced by a similar formulation in Searle, "Animal Minds."

state must be *intentional;* that is, it must be *about* something. (Notice that all propositional attitudes are intentional states.) How do we know whether a state is intentional? Here I follow Searle: "[H]aving an intentional state requires the capacity to discriminate conditions which satisfy from those that do not satisfy the intentional state."[17] The wolf can discriminate conditions in which her desire is frustrated (those in which the rabbit gets away) from conditions in which her desire is satisfied (those in which she catches the rabbit). Without this capacity to discriminate these conditions, the wolf and like animals would not display signs of displeasure at prolonged frustration of their desires, and signs of pleasure when their desires are gratified. But they do display such signs.

Furthermore, even human desires probably do not usually—or at least not always—have precise, determinate content, despite our linguistic abilities. I, for one, do not know the precise content of my own concept of rabbit. Indeed, I doubt it has a precise content. Or suppose you want breakfast, surely a desire in good standing. You go to the diner and order eggs, hashbrowns, toast, and coffee. Does that mean you wanted precisely these four foods? Maybe some elements of this initial, vague desire were optional or substitutable: You would have settled for grits rather than browns, or a muffin instead of toast. Others, perhaps, were nonoptional and specific: Coffee was a must. That some parts of your desire were substitutable and unspecified suggests that the desire's content was vague. But it was a desire all the same.[18]

We can be somewhat rough about the content of desires and other propositional attitudes. Slippery as their content may be, desires work remarkably well in explaining and predicting the behavior of humans and "higher" animals.

2. What can we say about the content of animals' desires? Having removed an argumentative roadblock in the path of assigning content to animals' desires, can we reach our goal? Animals can't tell us what they want, not in words anyway. And their forms of life are so different from ours. How do we go about assigning content? I will have much to say later about content in discussing animal beliefs. For now it will be enough to motivate moderate optimism about the prospects for assigning rough content to animals' desires in many circumstances.

To begin, let us pick up Searle's commonsensical point that animals often display the capacity to discriminate conditions that satisfy and frustrate their desires. This suggests a rough tool for determining what

---

[17] ibid
[18] Gary Varner gave me this example.

an animal wants. Let us assume that a given animal shows a tendency or disposition to go after something, and that we are well positioned to say the animal is conscious.

Suppose an apparently normal African elephant (who we assume has a functioning cerebrum) *seems* to go for water. After a long trudge in the hot sun, he hunts around in places likely to have water (not in the air, for example) and, upon seeing water, drinks it heartily until apparently sated. Is it water the animal wants? Maybe it's any liquid. Well, watch how he reacts to nonwater liquids in similar circumstances. Gather data on what conditions appear to satisfy him and which ones frustrate him. The elephant would probably either not drink from a pool of black oil, or, if he did, he would probably recoil and stop drinking. Such behavior would tell us that what he wants is not just any old liquid. We could go on to try out—again, in similar circumstances, where we can presume he's thirsty—nonwater liquids less likely to be noxious, such as orange juice. Even if we cannot specify *precisely* what the elephant wants, we can considerably narrow down possible satisfaction conditions, increasing the specificity of our attribution. Once we have suitably specified the content of the desire, it figures into the best explanation of the elephant's behavior.

Admittedly, that is too simple. Suppose that the elephant has drunk nothing but water in his life. We offer him orange juice when he's thirsty, and there's no water around, and he happens to like it. Maybe he wanted water but appeared satisfied when drinking orange juice because it tasted good and quenched his thirst. We should generally restrict the content of desires to what an animal has already experienced, although we may have to guess what that is.[19]

Our case for moderate optimism about assigning content has appealed to hypothetical examples in which informal, if persistent, observation allows reasonable conjectures about what animals want. But recall that in reviewing evidence for the existence of animal conation, we learned of Dawkins' leading work on animal preferences. Studies like hers are far more rigorous than the sorts of observations just described, admitting of controls and readily quantifiable data.[20]

[19] See Fred Dretske, *Explaining Behavior: Reasons in a World of Causes* (Cambridge, MA: MIT Press, 1988), pp. 128–29. More complex animals warrant exceptions where we have good reason—based on extensive knowledge of an animal's behavior and social life—to think the animal has a goal that has not yet been gratified. Think of social-climbing chimpanzees who want to become *alpha* (top chimp) and human virgins who want sex.

[20] For a fascinating running commentary on numerous studies of animal preferences, see Dawkins, *Through Our Eyes Only?*, pp. 143–64.

Do desires require beliefs and practical reasoning?

Having seen reasons for optimism regarding the challenge of content, let us turn to a second major worry. Having desires may require having beliefs—perhaps even practical reasoning—and it is far from obvious that animals are so sophisticated.

As noted in Chapter 1, R. G. Frey attempts to demonstrate, mostly on a priori grounds, that animals lack desires. We should be highly suspicious of a priori arguments about what animals can and cannot do, but let us consider this one on its merits. The structure is as follows: (1) One cannot have a desire (e.g., to own a book) without a corresponding belief (e.g., that one lacks a book); (2) A belief always amounts to a belief that a certain sentence (e.g., "I lack a book") is true; (3) It is impossible to have beliefs about sentences without language; (4) Animals lack language; therefore (5) Animals cannot have beliefs about sentences and, therefore, (6) cannot have beliefs and, therefore, (7) cannot have desires.[21] Premise (4) may be debated in some cases; we will confront the issue in Chapter 7. I believe premise (2) is false. I will address several more substantial arguments that have clearly influenced Frey's. Our immediate concern is premise (1)—that desires require beliefs.[22]

Let us consider a simple case in which desires might plausibly be thought to occur *without* beliefs. A hungry fish wants food. Note, first, that if the fish desires food, she must have an action tendency or disposition—to go for food. (The other necessary conditions stated earlier need not concern us now.) The hungry fish might look for food constantly. Or perhaps she only goes for food when she sees food. In either case, the fish has to deal with perceptions of the environment. If she is looking for food and goes around a rock and toward the water's surface to check, she perceives the rock and the surface. If she swims quickly to food that has appeared, she perceives the food. I contend that the fish's perceptual awareness of her environment implicates beliefs—assuming that the fish is credited with desires. The beliefs would, no doubt, be very simple. Any attempt to formulate them in English is likely to sound funny (since a fish's concepts would be very different from ours). But I do not think the fish's behavior—on the well-supported assumption that the fish is sentient and the present hypothesis that she desires food—can be explained without positing beliefs about her environment (e.g., something like "There is something edible

---

[21] See R. G. Frey, *Interests and Rights: The Case Against Animals* (Oxford: Clarendon, 1980), pp. 86–100.

[22] For efforts to refute Frey's argument at several points (in ways that differ from my approach), see Tom Regan, *The Case for Animal Rights* (Berkeley: University of California Press, 1983), pp. 39–49; and Sapontzis, *Morals, Reason, and Animals*, pp. 120–28.

ahead"). So I am prepared to grant that *desires entail beliefs.* That means we need to formulate another necessary condition for having desires.

But, first, let us see if even more is required. It is commonly thought in the philosophy of mind that beliefs and desires work together in a familiar way that explains intentional action; this is part of "folk (common-sense) psychology."[23] For example, I open the refrigerator because I want some carrots and I believe there are some in my fridge. If I did not believe that there were carrots in the fridge, I wouldn't look there, as long as it was carrots I wanted. We can construe my intentional activity as involving a piece of *practical reasoning:* (1) I desire carrots; (2) I believe opening the fridge is a means to getting carrots; therefore (3) I should (other things being equal) open the fridge. (Some, following Aristotle, would say that the conclusion is not that I should do something but rather the action itself.)

Intuitively, it may seem odd to attribute practical reasoning, which has such a heady ring, to a fish. Gary Varner provides an analysis of desire that includes a rather elaborate condition of practical reasoning. A desires X, he states, if and only if:

> 1) A is disposed to pursue X,
> 2) A pursues X in the way he, she, or it does because A previously engaged or concurrently engages in practical reasoning about how to achieve X or objects like X, where engaging in practical reasoning included both drawing inferences from beliefs of the form "Y is a means to X," and the hypothesis formation and testing by which such beliefs are acquired and revised; and
> 3) this practical reasoning is at least potentially conscious.[24]

Condition 1) is essentially the same as our first condition. In 2), Varner requires practical reasoning of a sort that involves hypothesis formation and testing, and drawing inferences about the means to get what one desires. Can fish do that? It sounds like a lot. But notice that, in 3), Varner requires that this reasoning be at least potentially conscious. I seriously doubt that fish can consciously reason in the robust way required by Varner. In fact, Varner interprets experimental data from Bitterman as showing that such reasoning is beyond the capacities of fish.[25]

I reject Varner's analysis of desire, which is too stringent. There is no obvious reason to require that a desiring creature be able to reason *consciously* about how to get what she wants. (The creature must have the capacity for consciousness, as we have seen, but that is a more

[23] See Donald Davidson's classic *Essays on Actions and Events* (Oxford: Clarendon, 1980).
[24] *In Nature's Interests?*, ch. 2
[25] ibid

modest condition.) And while it might not be strictly incorrect to require "hypothesis formation and testing" and "drawing inferences" (depending on how they are unpacked), these words have very intellectual associations and may seem to require more than is necessary for beliefs and desires to interact in action-explaining ways. Varner apparently reads his condition (2) such that a desiring creature must be able to learn on the basis of experience—in a way transcending pure repetition-based habit formation—as demonstrated in repeated testing in problem situations.[26] But why can't a desiring creature be a dunce who "learns" only in a slow, habit-based way? I believe Varner has packed more into the notion of desire than it actually contains.

Two apparent implications of Varner's analysis cast further doubt on it. First, while Varner cites evidence suggesting that fish do not meet his conditions for having desires, he acknowledges that fish *have pain* and apparently even allows that they *suffer*.[27] But any being who suffers also desires (other things being equal) an end to the suffering. Suppose that we take his position to be that fish can have pain but not suffer. As we saw in Chapter 5, even pain seems to implicate a desire (other things being equal) that the experience end. While Varner and many others try to separate sentience and conation, I maintain that neither makes sense without the other.

Another implication of Varner's analysis concerns those "frontal patients"—persons who have had lobotomies or have incurred major injuries to the prefrontal cortex—who have such difficulty forming and testing hypotheses that they do not learn from their mistakes in the required way: They have no desires! Yet even such (admittedly very rare) patients would presumably engage in many activities that give the appearance of involving intentional actions, such as talking and actively taking part in experiments, even if they couldn't plan ahead effectively.[28] There seems no good reason to doubt that they regularly do things they want to do.

While Varner's practical-reasoning conditions may require too much for desires, we do need to add to the necessary conditions stated earlier. I propose this additional condition: *(4) A has one or more beliefs that are part of the explanation of A's pursuit of X (when A does pursue X).* Now my fourth condition does not mention practical reasoning. But the sort of belief-desire interaction that explains behavior in the human case *is* practical reasoning (even if very simple, automatic, or unconscious). Practical reasoning in humans is presumably at least potentially con-

---

[26] ibid
[27] ibid
[28] See Alexsander Luria, *Higher Cortical Functions in Man*, trans. Basil Haigh (New York: Basic Books, 1966), pp. 294–306.

scious. But such conscious ratiocination seems inessential to desire. We could regard action-explaining belief-desire interactions as practical reasoning even if they are always unconscious (as may be the case with fish).[29] But "practical reasoning" has a learned flavor that we might wish to avoid in describing such cases.

That leaves us with one problem: Can animals have beliefs? If not, they lack desires. Stay tuned.

MORE HEADY STUFF

Some prominent arguments against attributing beliefs to animals

Can animals have beliefs? We have seen ample evidence that animals have desires, and we have conceded that desires require beliefs, implying that animals do have beliefs. Strong cognitive ethology (SCE) asserts the same. But many philosophers, scientists, and laypersons will balk at this conclusion. Beliefs—and the related phenomenon of thinking—are surely too heady for the brutes, they will say. Then let us examine the most prominent arguments against animal belief.[30] Later, we will confront some conceptual challenges, examine further evidence regarding animal belief, and investigate animal thinking.

1. Can animals discriminate among types of intentional states? One argument goes as follows. To attribute beliefs to a being, we must be able to distinguish cases in which it believes that p (some proposition) from cases in which the being merely surmises that p, has a hunch that p, hypothesizes that p, is darned sure that p, and so on. Now we cannot make these distinctions for a being that cannot make them for itself. Lacking the relevant (or any similar) vocabulary, animals cannot make these distinctions for themselves. Thus, we cannot say which of these intentional states a given animal has, barring us from attributing beliefs to the animal.[31]

I believe Searle's reply to this argument suffices to refute it. Searle attacks the premise that we must be able to make fine-grained discriminations among intentional states in order to attribute any intentional states to a being:

[29] I am not suggesting that the fish's beliefs and desires might always be unconscious, just that their crucial interactions might be.
[30] Previously we outlined Frey's argument against animal desires, which includes a case against animal belief. Because Frey's skeptical argument appears to be based on some of those discussed later, I do not take it up here.
[31] This argument is presented by Searle, who states that it was popular at Oxford in the 1950s ("Animal Minds").

Very general psychological verbs like "believe" and "desire" are often used in such a way as to allow for a slack, an indeterminacy, as to which of the subsidiary forms of the general attitude are exemplifed by the agent. Thus I may believe that it is going to rain, without it being the case that I myself could say without reflection whether it is a strong or weak belief, a hunch, a conviction, or a supposition. And even if I can answer these questions on reflection, the reflection itself may fix the relevant attitude. Before I thought about it there simply may not have been any fact of the matter about which kind of belief it was, I just believed it was going to rain. So I conclude that the fact that fine grained discriminations cannot be made for animal beliefs and desires does not show that animals do not have beliefs and desires.[32]

Lassie can believe there is food ahead even if we cannot determine— and even if there is no fact of the matter—whether she is certain, or merely supposes, that there is food ahead.

2. Stich's problem of attributing content. Stephen Stich has argued that some mental states of "higher" animals have one major feature of beliefs while lacking another, making it unclear (given the imprecision of the concept of belief) whether we should call these states *beliefs*.[33] Specifically, Stich asserts that (1) "we take beliefs to be functional or psychological states [that] interact with desires, with perception and with each other," while (2) beliefs are also "states with content; they are propositional attitudes."[34] Assertion (1) places beliefs within belief-desire psychology, as discussed in the previous section. Stich grants that many animals have states that work this way, interacting with desires and other states in ways that make the animals' behavior intelligible. But he denies that these animal states have feature (2). Why?

Stich's answer is summarized in this passage:

> *We are comfortable in attributing to a subject a belief with a specific content only if we can assume the subject to have a broad network of related beliefs that is largely isomorphic with our own.* When a subject does not share a very substantial part of our network of beliefs in a given area we are no longer capable of attributing content to his beliefs in the area. The greater the disparity between a subject's beliefs and our own, the clearer it becomes that, as Armstrong puts it, "he lacks our concepts."[35]

Charity requires taking the first three words of this passage as simply bad writing; obviously, no one's comfort level is relevant to whether

---

[32] ibid
[33] Stephen P. Stich, "Do Animals Have Beliefs?," *Australasian Journal of Philosophy* 57 (1979): 15–28
[34] ibid, p. 25
[35] ibid, p. 22

animals have beliefs. Keeping in mind Stich's statement that "beliefs are states with content," I think we can reconstruct the argument as follows: (1) For a state to have content, the content must be expressible; (2) For a state's content to be expressible, we human language users must be able to express it; (3) For us human language users to be able to express a state's content, the subject of the state must have a broad network of beliefs that are largely isomorphic with our beliefs; (4) Animals do not have a broad network of beliefs largely isomorphic with ours; therefore (5) we cannot express the content of their putative beliefs; therefore (6) their putative beliefs lack expressible content and therefore (7) lack content.[36]

Unlike some philosophers, I am inclined to grant premise (1). (An ineffable state lacks content.) I have doubts about (2). Why must the mental state of a Martian be expressible *by us*, for it to have content? What if Martians express it very aptly to each other—and to Jupiterians to boot? We might not be able to express it because it involves a sensory mode very unlike any of ours and because we do not know enough about the beings who have it. But perhaps (2) should be read this way: For a state's content to be expressible, we human language users must—*in principle, given all relevant information about the state and the beings who have it*—be able to express it (at least roughly). Philosophers such as Nagel and Jackson would deny even this claim, but I will follow the likes of Dennett and accept it.[37]

Let us concentrate on claims (3) and (4). It is unclear how much isomorphism Stich would require between our beliefs and an animal's to enable us to express the content of—that is, interpret—the animal's beliefs. Therefore, it is difficult to answer the question of whether animals meet the standard. But we can ask, independently of Stich, what standard of belief overlap would be reasonable for attributing inten-

---

[36]Some might interpret Stich to be arguing not that these states lack content but that they lack *specifiable* or *expressible* content. Indeed, Stich often uses these qualifiers in the article. But, again, he explains the second central feature of beliefs as being "states with content" (no qualifier). He drops the qualifiers elsewhere as well (see, e.g., ibid, pp. 26–27). I think that Stich sometimes uses a qualifier and sometimes does not because he thinks of expressible content and content as pretty much interchangeable—a sensible attitude for someone who thinks lack of expressible content entails no content.

[37]Thomas Nagel ("What Is It Like to Be a Bat?", *Philosophical Review* 83 [1974]: 435–50) and Frank Jackson ("Epiphenomenal Qualia," *Philosophical Quarterly* 32 [1982]: 127–36) argue for a special kind of fact, the fact of "what it is like" to have a certain experience—which is irreducible, in principle, to facts expressible in physical terms. Against this position, see, e.g., Laurence Nemirow, "Physicalism and the Cognitive Role of Acquaintance," in William G. Lycan (ed.), *Mind and Cognition* (Oxford: Blackwell, 1990), pp. 490–99; and Daniel C. Dennett, *Consciousness Explained* (Boston: Little, Brown & Co., 1991), ch. 12.

tional states to an animal. As a preliminary, it will be helpful to consider Davidson's arguments against attributing intentional states to animals, because the belief-overlap requirement comes from him (as Stich notes).

3. Davidson's progression of arguments against animal beliefs.
Donald Davidson has developed a number of arguments against ascribing intentional states to animals. His position is important both because of its influence on others (such as Stich and Frey) and because of Davidson's standing as a great philosopher of language and mind. The relevant texts are dense and difficult. But, if I have read Davidson correctly, his case against animal "thought"—by which he means all propositional attitudes—may be understood as containing a progression of related arguments.[38]

The first may be called the *indeterminacy-of-content argument*. Suppose we watch a dog chase a cat, who runs up an oak tree. The dog remains, barking, at the foot of the tree and looks upward. We might feel justified in saying that the dog believes that the cat ran up the tree (and that the dog wanted to catch the cat). But Davidson wonders what he can say about the content of the putative belief:

> That oak tree, as it happens, is the oldest tree in sight. Does the dog think that the cat went up the oldest tree in sight? Or that the cat went up the same tree it went up the last time the dog chased it? It is hard to make sense of the questions. But then it does not seem possible to distinguish between quite different things the dog might be said to believe.[39]

My rebuttal has two parts. First, regarding the claim that it is hard to make sense of the questions asked, I simply disagree. The dog almost certainly does not believe the cat went up the oldest tree in sight, because the dog almost certainly does not know, or believe, that the tree in question is the oldest in sight. And whether the dog believes that the cat went up the same tree as last time depends on whether the dog remembers the last time and recognizes this tree as the same one—a difficult question to answer, surely, but not to make sense of.

Moreover, even if we allow that the content of the dog's mental state is indeterminate, as we saw earlier, indeterminacy of content does not entail lack of content. Even in the human case, the content of our mental states is probably not perfectly determinate. And, again, we may understand the content of an animal's intentional state, however roughly, on

---

[38] Commentators frequently cite his "Thought and Talk," in Samuel Guttenplan (ed.), *Mind and Language* (Oxford: Clarendon, 1975), pp. 7–23. But I find a more recent book chapter to be clearer and more developed: "Rational Animals," in Ernest LePore and Brian P. McLaughlin (eds.), *Actions and Events: Perspectives on the Philosophy of Donald Davidson* (Oxford: Blackwell, 1985), pp. 473–80.

[39] "Rational Animals," p. 474

the basis of the animal's history, her present circumstances, and the satisfaction conditions for the state as revealed by the animal's behavior. (More on that later.)

This brings us to Davidson's second argument, which I call the *unshared-dense-network argument*. (The assumptions in Stich's argument that we left open have their roots here.) We can imagine Davidson saying, "Surely, if the dog believes the cat went up the tree, the dog must have the concept of tree." But

> can the dog believe of an object that it is a tree? This would seem impossible unless we suppose the dog has many general beliefs about trees: that they are growing things, that they need soil and water, that they have leaves or needles, that they burn. There is no fixed list of things someone with the concept of a tree must believe, but without many general beliefs there would be no reason to identify a belief as a belief about a tree. . . .
>
> We identify thoughts, distinguish between them, describe them for what they are, only as they can be located within a dense network of related beliefs. If we really can intelligibly ascribe single beliefs to a dog, we must be able to imagine how we would decide whether the dog has many other beliefs of the kind necessary for making sense of the first.[40]

Davidson doubts that animals share enough of our beliefs to justify attributing any particular beliefs to them, such as the belief that the cat ran up the tree. Why?

Here is the *very-complex-behavior argument:*

> From what has been said about the dependence of beliefs on other beliefs . . . , it is clear that a very complex pattern of behavior must be observed to justify the attribution of a single thought. Or, more accurately, there has to be good reason to believe there is such a complex pattern of behavior. . . . I think there is such a pattern only if the agent has language.[41]

But remember that Davidson assumes that we must make all sorts of discriminations of content to assign *any* content. We have argued that such a rigorous standard is inappropriate. With no need to make all of the fine discriminations that Davidson calls for, our standards for behavioral evidence may be correspondingly more relaxed. So maybe a being can demonstrate sufficiently complex behavior short of language.

Interestingly, Davidson acknowledges that we succeed in explaining and sometimes in predicting the behavior of animals by adopting what we called *the intentional stance* in Chapter 5: attributing beliefs, desires, and similar states to animals. He even admits that we have no other successful framework for doing so. (Note that this counts as excellent

[40] ibid, p. 475
[41] ibid, p. 476

behavioral evidence for asserting that animals do, in fact, have beliefs and desires. But, like defenders of WCE, Davidson resists this conclusion.) He argues that taking the model's success as evidence for actual beliefs and desires would imply that an uninformed observer should ascribe these states to a heat-seeking missile. But such an observer would be wrong, so the general pattern of inference is wrong.[42]

This is a puzzling argument. The problem with the uninformed observer of the missile is that she is uninformed. Sufficiently informed, she would *not* be better enabled to explain and predict the movements of the missile by using the intentional stance than by understanding the program guiding the missile. Furthermore, the behavior of "higher" animals such as mammals is immensely more subtle than that of a heat-seeking missile; to take, say, the genetic stance (or some other physical stance) with bears or foxes would work much less well than taking the intentional stance.

Davidson acknowledges that the missile analogy does not suffice to show that animals lack intentional states[43]—presumably, he thinks that it only casts doubt on animal intentionality. Davidson states that, to complete the argument, he must show that only language can supply something required of propositional attitudes. Since the latter require a background of beliefs, we know beliefs are essential to the possession of any propositional attitude. What's needed now, according to Davidson, is what I call the *belief-requires-the-concept-of-belief* argument:

> First, I argue that in order to have a belief, it is necessary to have the concept of belief.
> Second, I argue that in order to have the concept of belief one must have language.[44]

Then, since animals lack language, they must also lack beliefs.

Davidson defends the first thesis in this way. Having a belief requires the possibility of *surprise,* say, upon learning that one's belief is untrue. Surprise requires an awareness of the contrast between what one did believe and what one came to believe. Now, such awareness is a belief about a belief—for example, that my first belief is false. One must therefore have the *concept* of belief. Regarding the second thesis, the concept of belief is connected with those of truth and falsity and of the subjective–objective contrast; to have the concept of belief, one must have some sense of an objective (or intersubjective) world, which one can, with particular beliefs, get right or get wrong. Without language,

---

[42] ibid, p. 477
[43] ibid
[44] ibid, p. 478

Davidson assumes, one could not demonstrate that one has the requisite concepts.[45]

For the sake of argument, I will grant that language is required for having the concept of belief. I nevertheless reject the first thesis—that one can have a belief only if one has the concept of belief. Let us grant that having beliefs requires the possibility of some surprises. The problem, I think, is that Davidson has overintellectualized what is required for surprise (on any reading of *surprise* that lets us plausibly say that belief requires it).

Surprise requires only an expectation of something and then an awareness (perhaps with a sudden, alert feeling) that the expectation was not met. But, once again, many animals seem to be aware that certain conditions satisfy their beliefs and desires whereas other conditions do not. Searle is right to insist that

> animals distinguish true from false beliefs, satisfied from unsatisfied
> desires, without having the concepts of truth, falsity, satisfaction, or even
> belief and desire. And why should that be surprising to anyone? After all,
> in vision animals distinguish between red colored from green colored
> objects without having the concepts vision, color, red or green.[46]

After several rounds of throwing a tennis ball in the yard and letting his dog retrieve it, a boy pretends to throw the ball, keeping it in his hand. The dog, expecting to see the ball fly somewhere in the yard in front of the boy, begins in that direction, stops abruptly, looks around, looks back at the boy. The dog is surprised at the unprecedented situation, having believed that the ball would appear immediately. Surprise, but no belief about a belief—unless we want to count the dog's awareness that something is amiss as a belief about his belief that the ball would appear. Either way, the dog makes the grade. And we could multiply realistic examples indefinitely.[47]

I conclude that Davidson's cumulative case against animal beliefs (and other intentional states) is unsuccessful.[48] Nevertheless, Davidson has raised legitimate concerns about the difficulties involved in at-

[45] ibid, pp. 479–80
[46] "Animal Minds"
[47] For surprise in monkeys deprived of expected food, see O. L. Tinklepaugh, "An Experimental Study of Representative Factors in Monkeys," *Journal of Comparative Psychology* 8 (1928): 197–236. Surprise, like fear and various other emotions, implicates the sympathetic autonomic nervous system (see Chapter 5, this volume, and Jenefer Robinson, "Startle," *Journal of Philosophy* 92 [1995], pp. 56–57).
[48] For somewhat different sets of arguments against Davidsonian scepticism, see Richard Jeffrey, "Animal Interpretation," in LePore and McLaughlin, *Actions and Events*, pp. 481–87; and John Dupré, "The Mental Lives of Nonhuman Animals," in Marc Bekoff and Dale Jamieson (eds.), *Interpretation and Explanation in the Study of Animal Behavior*, vol. I (Boulder, CO: Westview, 1990), pp. 440–43.

tributing content to animal beliefs. If he is right about the need for networks of beliefs, we cannot just *assume* that animals have what it takes (even if he failed to show that they do not). These two issues—let us call them *the concern about content* and *the concern about holism*—will be treated later.[49]

Problems with the very concepts of concept and belief

Before plunging deeper into our investigation of animal beliefs, we need to manage a conceptual problem. The problem arises from the enormously varying ways in which the word *concept* is used.[50] Since concepts are generally taken to be constituents of beliefs, we had better not get tripped up by the many meanings of *concept*, because its ambiguity might infect *belief* with similar ambiguity. And excessive ambiguity in our notion of belief could muddle our meaning when we say animals have beliefs.

What is a concept? What is required for us to say that a creature has one? One rather undemanding criterion is that a being has a concept if that being can "discriminate what falls under it from what does not."[51] Thus, one has the concept of food if one can discriminate food from

---

[49] One might wonder why I have not included a section discussing Wittgenstein's challenge to animal beliefs. The reason is that contrary to popular academic lore, Wittgenstein was not skeptical about animal belief, as I argue in "Wittgenstein and the Mental Life of Animals," *History of Philosophy Quarterly* 11 (1994): 121–36. Other discussions that recognize that Wittgenstein was not skeptical about animal intentionality are Dupré, "The Mental Life of Nonhuman Animals," and David Pears, "Have They Anything to Say?: Wittgenstein's Views on Animals' Capacity for Thought" (unpublished manuscript).

[50] One likely source of ambiguity is that different explorers of mental phenomena have different ways of arranging them according to what they consider important. Traditional philosophers of mind have apparently taken concepts to be constituents of *thought* (or beliefs) and, following Descartes, taken thought to be *conscious*. Since the Freudian revolution allowing unconscious thought, an updated branch of this tradition, as I understand it, continues to link concepts to thought and to regard thought as at least potentially conscious. Thus, consciousness is importantly linked to concepts. Cognitive scientists, however, tend to deemphasize consciousness; some apparently even consider it irrelevant. They generally emphasize *representations,* which are something like units of information within the information processing that is the mind. (See, e.g., C. R. Gallistel, "Representations in Animal Cognition: An Introduction," in C. R. Gallistel [ed.], *Animal Cognition* [Cambridge, MA: MIT Press, 1992], pp. 1–2; cf. Dennett, *Consciousness Explained,* p. 191.) In one way or another, concepts are understood in terms of representations. Since *information processing* is considered most important, some representations may be conscious, while others are not (even potentially), but consciousness plays no crucial role in classifying types of representation and, therefore, concepts.

[51] Dupré, "The Mental Lives of Nonhuman Animals," p. 440

things other than food. Is successful discrimination really enough? Do insects so clearly have concepts?

Many thinkers have stressed a distinction between the conceptual and the (merely) *perceptual*. Colin McGinn, for example, holds that "perceptual content is pre- or nonconceptual: it feeds information into the conceptual system without itself being conceptual. (We need this level of content if we are to attribute perceptual content to creatures without beliefs. . . .)"[52] On this view, certain creatures (perhaps all conscious, nonlinguistic ones) have perceptions but not concepts and, therefore, no beliefs. Perceptions allow disciminations—frogs, for example, recognize flies—but more is required of *conceptualizing*.

What more is needed, then? Allen and Hauser take this approach:

> The distinction to be made is between recognizing an X, and recognizing something *as* an X or recognizing it to be an X. The first of these can be thought of as [involving] discriminatory ability. . . . [But] to have a concept of X where the specification of X is not exhausted by a perceptual characterization [as with the concept of *death* but not that of *red*], it is not enough just to have the ability to discriminate X's from non-X's. One must have a representation of X that abstracts away from the perceptual features that enable one to identify X's.[53]

Ants, for example, recognize their dead conspecifics—an ability that allows them, adaptively, to remove them. But they appear to do so purely on the basis of a perceptual stimulus, oleic acid. Given their normal environment, a mechanism that moves them to remove objects emitting oleic acid gets them to remove their dead fellows. Observations that they remove other objects artificially covered with oleic acid, or that they do not remove ant corpses that have been manipulated so as not to produce the usual odor, would suggest that ants lack the concept of death.[54] In general, possessors of a particular concept should be able to "generalize information obtained from a variety of perceptual inputs and use that information in a range of behavioral situations [and] alter what they take as evidence for an instance of that concept."[55]

So various authors distinguish mere discrimination, which depends on perceptual cues, and conceptualization, which abstracts from and is therefore relatively independent of perceptual cues. But further distinctions may be made. R. J. Herrnstein proposes the following schemata: (1) *discrimination;* (2) *categorization by rote* (memorizing a list of items);

[52] *Mental Content* (Oxford: Blackwell, 1989), p. 62
[53] Colin Allen and Marc D. Hauser, "Concept Attribution in Nonhuman Animals: Theoretical and Methodological Problems in Ascribing Complex Mental Processes," *Philosophy of Science* 58 (1991), p. 227
[54] ibid, pp. 230–31
[55] ibid, p. 232

(3) *open-ended categories* (grouping by perceptual similarity, an ability that would seem adaptive in the face of certain environmental contingencies); (4) *concepts* (representations more inclusive than already-encountered exemplars and their perceptual-similarity domains—whose flexibility allows more efficient adaptation to changing circumstances and is especially useful for animals who learn); and (5) *abstract relations* (relations among different concepts, e.g., "acorns on stumps," "color chips in stacks of the same colors"—which increase efficiency by obviating the learning of many individual concepts that are related in the same way).[56]

McGinn, Allen and Hauser, and Herrnstein seem to converge significantly in what they require of a concept. But remember that *concepts are generally taken to be constituents of beliefs.* Could Herrnstein's open-ended categories, for example, not be such constituents? If they could, maybe they are better described as concepts. One might argue that open-ended categories and, a fortiori, categorizations by rote and discriminations, are dependent on perceptual cues—and that we need to preserve a clear distinction between perception and belief, à la McGinn. But this separation of the two is artificial. While perception and belief are distinct concepts, our perceptions generally determine our beliefs. Searle is on the right track with this comment:

> Typically, for animals as well as humans, perception fixes belief, and belief together with desire determines courses of action. Consider real life examples: Why is my dog barking up that tree? Because he *believes* that the cat is up the tree, and he wants to catch up to the cat. Why does he believe the cat is up the tree? Because he *saw* the cat run up the tree. Why does he now stop barking up the tree and start running toward the neighbors' yard? Because he no longer believes that the cat is up the tree, but in the neighbors' yard. And why did he correct his belief? Because he just saw (and no doubt smelled) the cat run into the neighbors' yard; and *Seeing and Smelling is believing.* [A]nimals correct their beliefs all the time on the basis of their perceptions. In order to make these corrections they have to be able to distinguish the state of affairs in which their belief is satisfied from the state of affairs in which it is not satisfied. And what goes for belief also goes for desires.[57]

This position suggests that the perception-belief and, therefore, perception-concept distinctions are overplayed. To be sure, seeing is not literally believing; the concepts are not *identical,* and some perceivers (such as humans) can do a lot of critical thinking about their perceptions. But, generally, we believe what we see and otherwise sense, and

[56] "Levels of Stimulus Control: A Functional Approach," in Gallistel, *Animal Cognition,* pp. 135–38
[57] "Animal Minds"

we use updated sensory data to change our beliefs; there is no clear reason to think that matters should be otherwise with animals.[58]

I recommend a moratorium on philosophical worrying about the nature of a concept. There are various categorizing feats that form a continuum. Identifying one of these as capturing the essential properties of a concept may therefore be arbitrary. I am prepared to count as a concept any constituent of a belief, redirecting our focus to the latter notion. (In practice, evidence for the possession of concepts and evidence for beliefs can be difficult to distinguish. As we will see, what is considered evidence for concept possession—say, that a pigeon has the concept of tree—is also evidence for a belief: the pigeon's belief that what is in front of him is a tree.) Now for the inevitable question: *What is a belief?*

For starters, beliefs are propositional attitudes. So they have *propositional content*.[59] Second, they *interact with desires to produce action*. (Of course, this statement is circular in the sense of invoking another notion—desire—equally in need of definition. Conversely, the analysis of *desire* mentioned belief. The concepts of desire and belief may be too interdependent to elucidate either adequately without mentioning the other.) A third feature of beliefs—explaining their unique contribution to the belief-desire system—is that, in some very general sense, they *represent*. That's not to deny that they often misrepresent (when we are wrong). Nor is it to take a realist position on the nature of truth (that truth is an accurate representation, by our beliefs, of a mind-

---

[58] Aristotle emphasized the distinction between perception and belief, attributing perception but not belief to animals. For an impressive historical analysis, see Richard Sorabji, *Animal Minds and Human Morals* (Ithaca, NY: Cornell University Press, 1993), Part I. I cannot find arguments in this analysis that make a compelling case for attributing perception, but not belief, to animals. The best argument seems to be that we can fail to believe what appears to us—that is, what we perceive (see, e.g., pp. 31, 35). But it hardly follows that animals cannot both perceive and believe. And the denial of belief removes the best way of explaining much animal behavior, as we have seen. Another Aristotelian argument is that all beliefs are incorporated into reason (which animals lack), because belief involves a rational process of being persuaded by oneself or others (p. 68). But, as we will see, reason is not the exclusive property of humans; and the idea of belief as necessarily involving persuasion by oneself or others is hardly plausible. If belief requires persuasion of some sort, perception should often serve to do the job. The sense one gets from Sorabji's scholarly analysis is that Aristotle's denial of reason and belief to animals was more an organizing conceptual decision—causing a reanalysis of other psychological capacities such as perception and memory—than a result of open-minded empirical argument.

[59] So do desires, by the way. But in defining *desire,* it seemed more natural to cover the content aspect, implicitly, by addressing the action-tendency aspect. The content of a desire is determined by what the action tendencies aim at—that is, by satisfaction conditions.

independent reality). The point is simply that beliefs purport to say something about the way things are (our garden, your mood, the origin of the universe).

Beliefs, then, are representational states (with propositional content) that interact with desires in the production of intelligible behavior. Are these conditions jointly sufficient? According to Davidson and his followers, beliefs cannot be isolated states; they come in "dense networks." Some in this tradition, such as Stich, think that for animals to have beliefs, they not only need a dense network of beliefs; they need one largely overlapping with ours! We found that the Stich-Davidson case for such conceptual anthropomorphism fails. But many philosophers believe that at least this much is right about the holism requirement: Beliefs come in dense networks.

The challenges before us, then, are these: (1) Can we establish that animals have such dense networks of beliefs (and desires)?; and (2) If so, assuming that their networks are very different from ours, can we reasonably attribute content to their beliefs?

The challenges of holism and content: some suggestions

Can we establish that animals have dense networks of beliefs, and other intentional states, a requirement imposed by the holistic approach to beliefs? I think the answer is a confident *yes*.

Let's return to an earlier example. The thirsty elephant has an enormous variety of beliefs and desires, although at any one time most of them are dispositional or "in the background." This claim rests on a combination of neurological data (the fact that mammals have frontal lobes and comparatively developed cerebral cortexes), evolutionary data (the fact that elephants live very long lives characterized by social relations and changing environmental circumstances), and, most crucially, behavioral data. All three suggest a relatively intelligent animal. When this relatively intelligent animal lumbers toward a pool on a hot day following a long march, she wants to drink and believes that there is something ahead to drink. But more, the elephant must believe (at least dispositionally), very roughly, the following: that she can reach the pool by walking, that she is in the company of her fellows (assuming she is), that she has been with these fellows before (they are, after all, highly social creatures), that certain things are good to eat, that certain other things are not good to eat, that certain animals pose threats, that certain other animals do not pose threats, that danger is right ahead when a potentially threatening animal rushes toward the group, that the smallest members of the group need protection, that spraying water on the back when it's hot feels good, and countless other things. We could similarly enumerate many beliefs of the animals starring in our other examples, taking care not to attribute more than the animal's behavior, evolutionary niche, and physiology warrant.

This brings us directly to our remaining worry concerning content. In the elephant example, I tried to invoke relatively modest concepts (e.g., *fellows*, not *elephants* or *conspecifics*) so as not to overattribute, and to cover myself with the qualifier "very roughly." Still, I invoked such concepts as *fellow, walking,* and *animal.* Since our concepts are essentially connected to many beliefs, some of which animals surely lack, maybe we cannot attribute these concepts to animals. But, then, what concepts *can* we attribute to them? Any concept or belief we try to identify will be described in *our* language, which invokes *our* concepts. For example, our concept of animal is connected with a mass of biological ideas that nonlinguistic beings seemingly lack. Even if no *one* of those beliefs is necessary to the (our) concept of animal, *having many of them* is. Well, then, if elephants cannot have beliefs about other *animals* exactly, what is the belief that we are trying to describe? We seem mute in the face of this problem. How can we attribute content to animals' beliefs? How can we attribute beliefs at all—if we can't say anything about their content? We have returned to a worry from the Davidson-Stich tradition.

To help remove this worry, remember that (1) a mental state does not require *perfectly determinate* content in order to *have* content, and (2) our basic question is whether animals *have* concepts (and beliefs), not whether they have *ours.* Let us add a third reasonable assumption, which makes sense in light of (2): (3) In order to assert *something meaningful* about the content of animal beliefs, it is sufficient to make a *very rough* attribution. There is no need to establish *exactly* what animals believe (to the extent that the content is determinate) in order to show *that* they believe something and approximately *what* that is.[60]

Recall Davidson's skepticism about a dog's having the concept of tree. For the sake of argument, assume that the dog lacks *our* concept of tree.[61] It seems most reasonable to suppose that the dog has some

---

[60] Regan also confronts Stich's concerns (*The Case for Animal Rights,* pp. 53–61). But his discussion does not, in my opinion, penetrate the basic issues in sufficient depth. In addition, after arguing that concepts can be shared "more-or-less," Regan contents himself with the assertion that an animal's sharing of a single concept-relevant belief with humans is enough to share that concept "more-or-less." This claim is debatable, and the strategy of trying to show that animals share our concepts is, I think, not optimal.

[61] Some philosophers of language, following Kripke, would assert that *tree* refers to a *natural kind*—trees—and functions somewhat analogously to a name. (See Saul A. Kripke, *Naming and Necessity* [Cambridge, MA: Harvard University Press, 1972].) On that view, dogs may very well have *our* concept of a tree. But this approach is decidedly unholistic about concepts and meanings. I have been assuming holism both for the sake of argument and because I am somewhat inclined to accept it.

concept that picks out the tree, a concept that picks out the cat, and one that picks out what the cat did. If the dog's concepts pick out not just these individual items in this case but trees generally, cats generally, and acts of climbing or running generally, then these canine concepts would seem to overlap with our corresponding concepts to an impressive degree. And canine evolution may well have supplied dogs with concepts that pick out such objects. But we need not assume as much.

The dog sees the cat run up the tree and—we have very good reason to suppose—believes (putting it in our words) that the cat ran up the tree. It does not matter, for our purposes, whether the dog concept that picks out this tree comes closest to our concept of *tree, tall, thin thing, thing one can go up,* or even *that thing.* We do not know what a human one-year-old believes, exactly, when she believes (in our words) that her mother has come into the room. The baby lacks *our* concept of mother, for example. But that does not block our attributing some beliefs to her about this woman who is so important to her. In the case of the dog, attributing to her, very roughly, the belief that the cat went up the tree, along with the desire to get the cat, explains her behavior in a way that no other kind of description seems able to do so adequately.

As another example, what might we say about a dog's concept of food? Should we be skeptical that dogs have such a concept, since they presumably have no understanding of nutrition? Well, presumably there was a time when humans had a concept of things that are good to eat, without any grasp of nutritional value; maybe there are such humans today. Of such humans, Stich and Davidson would probably say that they lack the concept of food. But even if the word *food* does not denote what these humans, or the dog, have in mind, that hardly means that they have no concept of what they eat. Understanding their concept requires trying to understand their perspective and needs.[62] Regarding the dog's concept, we might begin by saying that the dog has a concept similar to our concept of food in that it covers things that are part of a normal canine diet, but dissimilar in that the concept is not connected to beliefs about nutritional value. We could go on to note further presumable similarities and dissimilarities, thereby constructing a clumsy description that we could tag with a new name (say, *dood*) to avoid giving the impression that the dog has precisely our concept of food. One more example: A dog might have not exactly our concept of ice but a concept, roughly, of cold, hard, shiny, brittle stuff.[63]

[62] Daisie Radner, "Heterophenomenology: Learning about the Birds and the Bees," *Journal of Philosophy* 91 (1994): 389–403.
[63] In this paragraph, I borrow several points from Colin Allen, "Mental Content," *British Journal of the Philosophy of Science* 43 (1992), pp. 545, 552.

Let us approach the issue from another angle. Suppose our worries about content prevented us from attributing any content to animals' mental states. As stressed previously, we would lose much explanatory and predictive power regarding animal behavior. But we would also lose much in understanding *natural selection*. Other things being equal, natural selection operates on the *functional* aspects of a system. For example, eyes are adaptive because of what they do—their function— not because of their specific physiological design. (Octopi and most vertebrates both have the advantage of sight, although they have no common ancestor with eyes.) Now, *content-bearing terms,* which allow functional descriptions of cognitive abilities, permit generalizations across species that implement the cognitive abilities differently. For example, possession of the concept of (very roughly) *one's kin* is adaptive, other things being equal, for highly social species—regardless of the specifics of a given species' physiology. This point could not be made if we denied that animals' mental states had content.[64]

Fair enough. But are there certain concepts, and beliefs invoking them, that are such that animals presumably *cannot* have them? I think so. For the moment, let us assume that all nonhuman animals lack language, so that we can consider what sorts of concepts and beliefs require language. (If we decide in Chapter 7 that some animals are linguistic, we can revise our present conclusions.) Language is a conceptual rocket. Linguistic beings are capable of a system of beliefs that is enormously richer than the conceptual worlds of nonlinguistic beings—due to the symbolic, indefinitely combinable nature of language. Let me elaborate.

Among the forms of evidence on the basis of which we can attribute beliefs, behavior is the sharpest instrument for cutting out content. Evolutionary biology is a very rough science that produces broad generalizations. Neurophysiology is in its scientific childhood and cannot now tell us much about the specific content of animal beliefs. Behavior is situation-specific and nuanced and, in context, tells us about satisfaction conditions. We might adopt this general rule: *We may attribute particular beliefs (particular contents) to animals only to the extent that the attribution is (1) supportable on the basis of the animals' behavior in context, within limits imposed by our knowledge of evolution and physiology, or (2) inferrable, in the present context, on the basis of knowledge obtained in accordance with (1).* I include (2) to cover cases in which present behavior is largely unrevealing, but in which beliefs can be reasonably attributed on the basis of past observations. If for the fourth time a dog is given curare and totally paralyzed (but kept awake and unanesthetized),

---

[64] Colin Allen, "Mental Content and Evolutionary Explanation," *Biology and Philosophy* 7 (1992), p. 8

when the familiar surgeon approaches, we can suppose that the dog believes that (in our words) bad times are ahead.

Now consider language. If behavior provides different kinds of knives for cutting out content, language gives us a scalpel. (Charades challenges us by making us cut without our finest tool.) Searle lists five types of intentional states that nonlinguistic beings would seem to lack: (1) those about language; (2) those concerning facts of which language is partly constitutive (e.g., beliefs about a twenty-dollar bill, since money involves human institutions that essentially involve language); (3) those representing facts so remote in space and time from the animals' experience as to be unrepresentable without language (e.g., beliefs about one's distant ancestors); (4) those representing facts so complex as to be unrepresentable without language (e.g., beliefs about the law of gravity); and (5) those about facts where the mode of presenting the fact locates it relative to some linguistic system (e.g., the belief that 8/17/95 is a humid day). Searle notes that these types of intentional state fall into broader groups: Either the state in question has satisfaction conditions that are essentially linguistic, or the mode of representing these satisfaction conditions is essentially linguistic.[65]

This is only a start, of course. But it is a good start, one that may inspire confidence that we can avoid *both* unwarranted skepticism about the content of animal beliefs *and* excessive liberality in our ascriptions. Moreover, we can do so in a semi-principled way.

Examples of kinds of animal beliefs (concepts, learning)

The empirical evidence suggestive of animal beliefs is enormous. Most or all of the studies of animal *learning*, for example, are suggestive (since learning by conscious creatures at least typically involves acquiring new beliefs). Here I present just a few samples of evidence that indicate something about the range of animals who have beliefs, as well as the range of beliefs that animals have. Some of the studies were designed to demonstrate an animal's possession of a particular *concept,* but we will see that such studies (if valid) demonstrate beliefs as well. Other studies purport to show that certain animals engage in *thinking* or *reasoning.* But, in fact, each of the examples provides evidence of some animal's beliefs, concepts, and thinking.

Bowman and Sutherland trained *goldfish* to distinguish perfect squares from squares with bumps on their tops. In one variation, goldfish who were trained to swim in the direction of a square having a small triangle on its top also selected a circle with a semicircular indentation in its upper edge, over an ordinary circle. They apparently

[65] "Animal Minds"

learned to distinguish simple shapes such as squares and circles from similar shapes with the irregularities of either bulges or indentations.[66]

The goldfish presumably used concepts separating the two types of shapes (simple ones and irregular ones). There is no need to attribute any human concepts to them, but *some* representations guided their better-than-chance responses. Moreover, because the goldfish were trained with the customary food rewards, they presumably believed that they could get food by swimming toward certain targets. It is difficult to avoid the conclusion that, when presented with novel stimuli, such as the irregular circle, the fish thought, however simply, about where to swim in order to get a reward. (We will say more about thinking in the following section.) These attributions are made awkwardly, being expressed in English, although there is no presumption that the fish employed concepts reflected in English. (The same goes for the other examples to be given.)

Birds have a reputation for astonishing memories for where they have hidden food.[67] Marsh tits and chickadees, for example, may hide hundreds of food items in a single day, each in a separate place, and find them days later. Sherry, Shettleworth, and Krebs endeavored to rule out simpler explanations for the birds' feats than the hypothesis that the birds had great visual memories.

First, the researchers eliminated the possibilities that the birds were simply (1) smelling the food, (2) getting into the right area and spotting a subtle cue such as disturbed bark, or (3) just looking everywhere. They presented captive tits and chickadees with artificial trees—tree trunks with holes drilled into them—and fitted each hole with a velcro door that the birds could easily operate. Because the birds had to pull aside a door to see whether any food was present, their doing so clearly indicated where they thought food was stored, even when they could not see it.

In one experiment, birds were given sunflower seeds, which they then stored, before being chased away. The holes where seeds were stored were carefully noted. Twenty-four hours later, the birds were let back in to the aviary, after (unbeknownst to the birds) all of the seeds

[66]Rosemary S. Bowman and N. S. Sutherland, "Shape Discrimination by Goldfish: Coding of Irregularities," *Journal of Comparative and Physiological Psychology* 72 (1970): 90–97. This study is discussed in Donald R. Griffin, *Animal Minds* (Chicago: University of Chicago Press, 1992), p. 124.
[67]Recent data suggest that at least some birds, including chickadees, may experience enormous neuronal growth (new neurons replacing dead ones) each fall before hiding seeds for the winter—when insect food sources are unavailable, increasing reliance on seeds. Neuronal growth apparently occurs in the hippocampus, a region of the brain thought to be crucial for memory and spatial learning (Natalie Angier, "To Remember Seed Caches, Bird Grows New Brain Cells," *New York Times* [November 15, 1994]: C1, C14).

were removed from the holes, so that the holes all looked and smelled the same. The birds—who had been given 15 seeds each (there were 72 holes)—systematically searched the holes into which they had put seeds. (A similarly careful study revealed that the birds did not, after a 24-hour period, revisit a hole from which they had already taken food.)[68]

The most parsimonious explanation for the birds' feats is that they remembered where they stored food. But I submit that *remembering is believing!* More precisely, one believes what one remembers. These birds believed that food was where they remembered storing it. They used avian concepts to pick out the food items that they sought and the places to look for them. At some level, they even reasoned their way to their destinations (since, wanting food, they had to figure out how to get it).

In several experiments, Herrnstein and his colleagues demonstrated that *pigeons* had, or could learn, a concept that served to pick out human beings on the basis of visual stimuli. He showed pigeons numerous photographic slides, which contained pictures of human beings with many variations: both genders, all races, various ages, different bodily positions, some clothed and some not. Pigeons, who were rewarded only if they pecked when shown slides containing a picture of a human being, performed very well on this task despite its abstractness. In later experiments, Herrnstein and colleagues showed that pigeons could recognize individual persons, water, fish under water, trees, and other objects or kinds of object.[69]

Since pigeons presumably desire rewards, their accurate sorting of very different photographic images into various categories may be taken to indicate that they believed that certain images belonged together—or at least that they, the pigeons, could get rewards by responding only to certain kinds of pictures. Thus, we have evidence of concepts or representations (fairly abstract ones), beliefs, learning (through trials), and elementary reasoning about how to get rewards.

One of the most important recent events in the scientific study of animals is an extraordinary series of controlled ethological studies by

[68] David F. Sherry, "Food Storage, Memory and Marsh Tits," *Animal Behaviour* 30 (1982): 631–63; David Sherry, "Food Storage by Black-Capped Chickadees: Memory for the Location and Content of Caches," *Animal Behaviour* 32 (1984): 451–64; and Sara J. Shettleworth and John R. Krebs, "Stored and Encountered Seeds: A Comparison of Two Spatial Memory Tasks," *Journal of Experimental Psychology: Animal Behavior Processes* 12 (1986): 248–56. These studies are discussed in Dawkins, *Through Our Eyes Only?*, pp. 41–43.

[69] R. J. Herrnstein and D. H. Loveland, "Complex Visual Concept in the Pigeon," *Science* 146 (1964): 549–51; R. J. Herrnstein, Donald H. Loveland, and Cynthia Cable, "Natural Concepts in Pigeons," *Journal of Experimental Psychology: Animal Behavior Processes* 2 (1976): 285–311

Cheney and Seyfarth, culminating in their highly acclaimed book *How Monkeys See the World*.[70] The details of their studies of the highly social *vervet monkey* are too extensive to summarize here. With some regret for not providing their evidence, I present a summary of their findings, taken from an abstract to an overview that they published subsequent to their book. Their methods have been widely lauded and their conclusions generally found reasonable in light of their data. But the reader is encouraged to check up on their work.

Cheney and Seyfarth write the following:

> Monkeys recognize the social relations that exist among others in their group. They know who associates with whom, for example, and other animals' relative dominance ranks. In addition, monkeys appear to compare types of social relations and make same/different judgments about them. In captivity, long-tailed macaques (*Macaca fascicularis*) trained to recognize the relation between one adult female and her offspring can identify the same relation among other mother–offspring pairs, and distinguish this relation from bonds between individuals who are related in a different way. In the wild, if a vervet monkey (*Cercopithecus aethiops*) has seen a fight between a member of its own family and a member of Family X, this increases the likelihood that it will act aggressively toward another member of Family X. Vervets act as if they recognize some similarity between their own close associates and the close associates of others. To make such comparisons the monkeys must have some way of representing the properties of social relationships. We discuss the adaptive value of such representations, the information they contain, their structure, and their limitations.[71]

Monkeys have rich social worlds and considerable knowledge about social relations. (Such knowledge implicates innumerable beliefs about social relations within a monkey's group.) They learn about the particulars of their relations on the basis of mutual observation.

On the other hand, the authors' book asserts that monkeys do not have introspective awareness (beliefs about their own mental states) or awareness of the intentionality of others (beliefs about others' mental states). A result, they argue, is a severely limited capacity to transmit information, feel empathy for others, or deceive.[72] But let us examine some evidence that may suggest that monkeys *can* deceive.

---

[70] Dorothy L. Cheney and Robert M. Seyfarth, *How Monkeys See the World: Inside the Mind of Another Species* (Chicago: University of Chicago Press, 1990). This volume brings together findings published by the authors throughout the 1980s in such journals as *Animal Behavior, American Zoology, Behavioral Ecology and Sociobiology,* and *Behavior.*

[71] "The Representation of Social Relations by Monkeys," in Gallistel, *Animal Cognition,* p. 167

[72] *How Monkeys See the World,* p. 312

As observational criteria for attributing deceit, Byrne and Whiten suggest that (1) the behavior be part of an animal's normal repertoire, (2) it rarely be used in the putatively deceitful way (allowing a background of trust), (3) it be used in such a way that makes others misconstrue it, and (4) the agent gain from her behavior. Applying these criteria, they present two anecdotal cases that they believe involve deceit.

Baboons make clear gestures of "looking" when they see another troupe of baboons or predators. Other baboons spontaneously follow the gaze (a reaction with clear adaptive value, given the need to respond quickly to danger). In the first case, a male attacked a younger baboon, who screamed, provoking several adults to run toward them. The running adults were giving aggressive "pant grunt" calls, presumably preparing to attack the offending male, who—seeing their approach—suddenly "looked" into the distance, despite the absence of predators or baboons in that direction. The adults stopped and followed his gaze, at which time the male escaped to safety. On another occasion, a juvenile, after watching a female feed for some time, screamed. Normally, juveniles scream only when attacked, summoning adults who typically chase off the attacker. This scream prompted an adult male to chase away the feeding female, whereupon the juvenile took over her food.[73]

Kummer provides another anecdote arguably portraying deception. A troupe of baboons were resting when, over a period of about twenty minutes, a female gradually moved about two meters, ending up behind a rock where she groomed a male. Had the dominant male observed the grooming, he would have attacked both baboons. But from where he sat, he could see only the female's back and tail and the top of her head. He could not see the male being groomed, who had bent down behind the rock, presumably so the dominant male could not observe what the female was doing.[74]

The major disadvantage of these data is that they are anecdotal and therefore unrepeatable. As discussed in Chapter 5, this fact does not mean the data are inadmissible into the court of serious investigation. Assuming the descriptions of the animals' behaviors are accurate, the primates in question appear to have met the criteria listed above for deceit.

---

[73] Richard W. Byrne and Andrew Whiten, *Machiavellian Intelligence* (Oxford: Clarendon, 1988), chs. 15, 16.

[74] H. Kummer, "Social Knowledge in Free-Ranging Primates," in Donald R. Griffin (ed.), *Animal Mind—Human Mind* (Berlin and New York: Springer-Verlag, 1982), pp. 113–20. In reconstructing both the proposed criteria for deceit and the three anecdotes, I have borrowed from Dawkins, *Through Our Eyes Only?*, pp. 132–33.

Can we safely infer that baboons have beliefs about the mental states of others? Maybe not. The innovative behaviors might have been calculated to affect, not other baboons' minds, but their actions. And some—maybe including Cheney and Seyfarth—require the capacity to think about others' mental states as a condition for deception (suggesting the insufficiency of the previous observational criteria). The baboon's surreptitious movement to behind a rock, however, is impressive in the degree to which the dominant baboon's (merely spatial?) perspective was taken into account. We should perhaps hold open the possibility of baboons' attributing mentality to others. Rather than pursue this issue here, I leave these anecdotes as evidence of at least impressive *manipulative* behaviors, demonstrating sophisticated problem solving (and the plethora of beliefs, desires, and intentions that go with it).

Some thoughts on thought, thoughts, and thinking

We have devoted much attention to beliefs. Related notions, which we have not examined closely, are those of *thought, thoughts,* and *thinking.* What are these phenomena? Which animals think and have thoughts?

These terms are ambiguous. I will unpack a few worthwhile conceptions. One very broad conception comes from Davidson, who speaks of all *propositional attitudes* as thoughts.[75] But it is unusual to classify some of the propositional attitudes, such as desires, as thoughts. Thoughts seem more explicitly cognitive than desires. Dennett takes folk psychology to equate thoughts with *occurrent beliefs:*

> [I]t distinguishes *beliefs,* which are the underlying dispositional states, from *thoughts,* which are occurrent or episodic states—transient events. Your *belief that dogs are animals* has persisted continuously as a state of your mind for years, but my drawing attention to it just now has spawned a *thought* in you—[viz.,] that dogs are animals.[76]

Both conceptions treat what *a* thought is.

In contrast, *thought* (without an article) seems more or less interchangeable with the noun *thinking.* Sometimes these terms seem to refer to the set of all thoughts (however defined). But often they refer to something suggested by the present participle *thinking*—namely, certain mental processes known as *thought processes.* What is thinking in this sense? In one extremely broad use of the term, influenced by Descartes, it refers to all *conscious phenomena.*

In philosophy, this usage is uncommon today due to the conviction that some processes worthy of the term *thought* or *thinking* occur uncon-

---

[75] "Rational Animals," p. 475
[76] *Consciousness Explained,* p. 307

sciously.[77] I have noticed a post-Freudian usage, influenced by cognitive science, that is also very broad: Thinking is all *information processing* (or perhaps information processing of a certain degree of complexity). This not only allows for unconscious thinking; it seems to allow for thinking by never-conscious entities.

A somewhat narrower and commoner usage is reflected by Searle. He understands thought processes as "those temporal sequences of intentional states that are systematically related to each other, where the relationship is constrained by some rational principles."[78] This definition invokes intentionality and rationality. Remember that in folk psychology, intentional agents are understood to have beliefs and desires *that interact in ways that make the agent's behavior intelligible.* In at least this minimal sense, the agent is thought to be acting *rationally* or according to a *reason.* One wants some X, believes doing Y will be a means to X, and so does Y.

But such rationality-based conceptions of *thinking*—commonly equated with *reasoning* in this usage—reveal an ambiguity. Sometimes any mental means-ends fitting counts as thinking (reasoning), whereas in a more restricted usage, some degree of *innovation* or *flexibility* is required. This ambiguity is reflected by Rachels, who says that we behave rationally

> when we make choices that are appropriately motivated by our beliefs and attitudes. If we want X, and realize that by doing Y we can get X, and act accordingly, then our behaviour is rational. We act "for a reason." If, in addition, we are able to improvise, by responding to previously unexperienced environmental conditions, manipulating them to get what we want, the case for attributing rationality is strengthened.[79]

Dawkins, who construes thinking in terms of manipulations of internal representations, inclines in the direction of the flexibility requirement for thinking:

> The first [basic attribute of thinking] is that the thinker should have some sort of internal representation of the world in his, her, or its head. This means that it does not just respond to the stimuli immediately surrounding it but carries a memory of things that were there in the past but are now gone or out of sight. The second is that something is done to that representation to enable the true thinker to work out what would happen

[77] Does this run counter to Dennett's claim that folk psychology takes thoughts to be occurrent or episodic? I think Dennett mischaracterizes folk psychology only if he means to suggest that occurrent thoughts must be *conscious.*
[78] "Animal Minds"
[79] James Rachels, *Created by Animals: The Moral Implications of Darwinism* (Oxford: Oxford University Press, 1990), p. 140

under new circumstances. . . . The classic case is of a rat being taught to run a maze and then finding that part of its usual route has been blocked off. Can the animal work out in its head which alternative route it should now take . . . ?[80]

The rat facing a new challenge has to think in order to reach her goal.

But notice that even a rat running down a familiar path with no new challenges has to do some simulating (or manipulating of representations), which we might express, roughly, thus: "To get the grub, gotta go this way!" And, in some sense, every situation is a new one. There may not be a bright line between situations that we typically regard as familiar and those that demand flexibility. Part of the motivation for a flexibility requirement may stem from the fact that much of our means–ends processing automatically becomes conscious when we do not "know our way around"—plus the fact that, historically, we have tended to connect thinking with consciousness. So we are tempted to count only our innovative problem solving, which tends to be conscious, as thinking.

There is no pressing need to adjudicate among these usages, as long as we are clear about what we mean. In the minimal means–ends sense of *thinking* that is basic to belief-desire psychology, it would appear that all animals who have beliefs and desires—probably most or all vertebrates and some invertebrates—can think. If some standard of innovation is required, presumably only some smaller set would pass.

Let us conclude by briefly taking stock, combining the insights of Chapter 5 and this chapter. *If our reasoning has been sound, feelings, desires, and beliefs—despite having increasingly cognitive associations— seem to go together in nature.* Sentient or affective beings (who have feelings), conative beings (who have desires), and cognitive beings (who have beliefs) seem to be coextensive on our planet: the vertebrates, give or take a few species. While some vertebrates might not qualify, this possibility strikes me as somewhat unlikely. What evolutionary explanation would there be for a scenario in which the vast majority of organisms endowed with a complex (vertebrate) CNS have feelings, desires, and beliefs, while some minority with similar CNSs lack these phenomena? In any event, probably at least a few invertebrates also have this cluster of mental states; there is good reason to think that cephalopods are such animals. Whatever the precise range of animals partaking of the mental states that we have examined, their mentality will prove important when their moral status is further examined. But before turning to value theory (Chapter 8) and returning to ethics (Chapter 9), we will consider further mental characteristics of special interest (Chapter 7).

[80] *Through Our Eyes Only?*, p. 105

Chapter 7

Self-awareness, language, moral agency, and autonomy

In Chapters 5 and 6, we found that animal feelings, desires, and beliefs were interconnected in nature. Animals possessing one of them (say, feelings) possessed the others (desires and beliefs) as well, even if the terms designating them sound unequally cognitive. Feelings, desires, and beliefs have something else in common: Many persons would attribute all of them to "higher" animals, such as mammals, with little hesitation.

In this chapter, we examine some mental phenomena and capacities that seem to be of a different order. These phenomena and capacities may be grouped into the categories of *self-awareness* (self-consciousness), *language, moral agency,* and *autonomy.* If any of these is entailed by mental phenomena studied in Chapters 5 and 6, this fact is not obvious and would have to be argued carefully. Nor are we, prereflectively, as likely to attribute such phenomena and capacities to animals. But no thorough exploration of animals' mental life—much less a well worked-out animal ethics—can avoid confronting some of the issues that we tackle in this chapter.

THE WORLD AND SELF OVER SPACE AND TIME — SELF-AWARENESS

Distinguishing one's own body from the rest of the environment

Are any nonhuman animals *self-aware?* We will approach this question gradually, by considering various capacities each of which may suggest a degree of self-awareness. The first and perhaps most basic capacity of this sort is *the ability to distinguish one's own body from the rest of the environment.*

This sounds like a rather primitive capacity. It may be even more primitive than it sounds. Dennett provides a reason to think that it

166

might extend to the entire animal kingdom: "As soon as something gets into the business of self-preservation, boundaries become important, for if you are setting out to preserve yourself, you don't want to squander effort trying to preserve the whole world; you draw the line."[1] Fair enough. There would be terrific selective pressure favoring organisms that functioned in ways that were self-protecting rather than world-protecting. This principle would seem to extend all the way to single-cell organisms, in the animal kingdom, maybe even to plants.

To discriminate in this rudimentary functional sense implies nothing about *awareness* of a distinction between self and world. There need only be an informational sensitivity (about what is "within" and what is "without") that, by itself, implies no consciousness at all. An organism's responsiveness to sensory stimuli must be such that it does not devour itself, but such sensitivity does not require conscious experience.

So evolutionary-functional arguments suggest the capacity to *function* in accordance with a self-world discrimination. The most basic behavioral evidence does as well. Animals generally behave in ways that tend to be self-preserving but not rest-of-the-world-preserving. But which animals can be *conscious* of the difference between their own bodies and the rest of the world? Clearly, only those who can be conscious—and maybe only some subset of these, since consciousness does not logically entail self-awareness. Nor does consciousness plus informational sensitivity to the self–world distinction logically entail self-awareness; a being might be conscious of some things but not this distinction, which is dealt with unconsciously. (It will be argued later, however, that real-world conscious animals must have some degree of bodily self-awareness, which involves conscious self–world discrimination.)

A sense of time—Memory and anticipation

Another capacity potentially relevant to self-awareness is *a sense of time*—most basically, *memory* (a sense of the past) and *anticipation* (a sense of the future). First, let's eliminate some ambiguities. We are not asking whether animals have a highly abstract sense of time, according to which time is infinite or began with the origin of the universe; nor are we asking whether they have a conventional sense of time, including the concepts of weeks, months, and New Years. Both would presumably require language (see Chapter 6). On the other hand, we are not—at least I am not—asking whether animals can, in some way or another, represent the past or future. The temporal capacity most germane to

---

[1] Daniel C. Dennett, *Consciousness Explained* (Boston: Little, Brown and Company, 1991), p. 174

animal self-awareness is the capacity to have temporal thoughts or representations that are actually or potentially *conscious*. So only conscious animals can make this grade.

Some persons are skeptical about animal temporality. They say that animals "are stuck in the moment" or "live moment-to-moment." Although these assertions are usually undefended, I suspect that they are motivated by a sense that time is a highly abstract notion and a hunch that animals are incapable of such abstraction. While the people I have in mind here are mostly laypersons, they will find support from certain philosophers.

Typically, these philosophers offer no empirical arguments and seem to think empirical evidence is irrelevant to the issue. Kant contributed greatly to the tradition of a priori skepticism about animal temporality. Kant argued that (1) to move mentally beyond the particulars of sensation one must have thought, and (2) to have thought one must have concepts.[2] Others have added that (3) to have concepts, one must have language, and, of course, (4) animals lack language. They confidently conclude that animals lack concepts and, therefore, thought and, therefore, any sense of time.

Given our work in Chapter 6 to refute the a priori arguments by Davidson and others against animal beliefs, the reader might find this case against animal temporality highly dubious. In any event, let us grant premises (1) and (2). Premise (4) may prove to be true; we have not yet considered the evidence. However, in Chapter 6 we refuted (3). Thus, the argument is unsound.

But some philosophers would still be inclined to buy an argument like the one just outlined. In his 1987 Presidential Address for the American Philosophical Association, Jonathan Bennett argues that animals are rooted in the present.[3] After arguing that behavior is the only evidence that could decide the issue (a rather one-sided methodological claim), he states that his "hunch is that only through language can one show that one has thoughts that are not about what is present and particular."[4] He considers the celebrated chimpanzee language experiments, but comments that "[chimps'] imperatives always call for *immediate* action, and their indicatives always describe the *immediate* environment."[5] Bennett must have been so influenced by the a priori tradition that he felt little need to do empirical homework—because, as we will later learn, both claims in that last quotation are simply false.

[2] Immanuel Kant, *Critique of Pure Reason,* trans. Norman Kemp Smith (London: Macmillan, 1963; originally published 1787)
[3] "Thoughtful Brutes," *Proceedings and Addresses of the American Philosophical Association* 62 (1988), p. 199
[4] ibid, p. 204
[5] ibid

What reason is there to think that conscious animals have a sense of time? Let us begin with evolutionary considerations. First, memory would be adaptive in allowing an animal to acquire new information (that is, beyond what is hard-wired or instinctual) about which sorts of things and circumstances are pleasant and which unpleasant (which will generally be survival-enhancing and dangerous, respectively)— the subject of the most rudimentary *learning*. Memory is useful for learning, which is adaptive for animals living long enough to benefit from learning. Anticipation is useful for "getting a jump on" predictable events and selecting actions accordingly. And memory and anticipation work together. Whales who remember which sea vessels harass them can anticipate what will happen if they again approach such craft, what will happen if they avoid them, and then make the prudent choice.[6]

Midgley presents an evolutionary argument concerning animals with highly variable environments:

> Consider migrations, pregnancies, seasons, brief harvests and the constant need to anticipate the movements of prey and predators. Many animals move continually from one food source to another, often with their young to provision, and sometimes with responsibility for a whole pack or herd. They have to be able to think how long this or that will last, or when it will recur. If they had not enough memory and anticipation of order to fit their plans into the probable train of events, with alterations for altered circumstances, they often could not survive.[7]

Clearly, some sense of past and future would be highly adaptive.

It might be argued, however, that what is adaptive is the capacity to *encode* information gained from experience and to *use* that information in modifying future behavior. There is no additional adaptive value to representing that information *consciously,* as in remembering (in any sense potentially relevant to self-awareness) or to projecting future possibilities *consciously,* as in full-blown anticipation. Indeed, according to this objection, animal behavior is more parsimoniously explained without positing such conscious temporal awareness.

This argument can be rebutted. First, we are talking about animals whose consciousness is no longer in question (see the reply to Carruthers in Chapter 5). Second, there probably is additional adaptive value to being able to remember and anticipate consciously. In humans, the ability to manage complexity and novelty, to improvise in un-

---

[6] Dolphins apparently do this (Kenneth S. Norris and Thomas P. Dohl, "The Structure and Function of Cetacean Schools," in Louis M. Herman (ed.), *Cetacean Behavior: Mechanisms and Functions* [New York: John Wiley & Sons, 1980], p. 244).

[7] Mary Midgley, *Animals and Why They Matter* (Athens, GA: University of Georgia Press, 1983), p. 58

familiar situations, is associated with conscious mental states, whereas unconscious information processing often suffices in familiar terrain (see Chapter 5). Again, animals have to deal with variable environments: moving predators or prey, changing weather and food supplies, and—in social species—evolving social dynamics between oneself and others. So conscious anticipation and remembering would seem advantageous in novel situations. It is unclear what reason there is to suppose that animals capable of consciously perceiving their present environment could never recall similar images to represent the past or project similar images to represent the future. We seem to have good reason to believe that conscious animals can consciously remember and anticipate. Of course, if there are any exceptions, they are likely to be on the "lower" end of the conscious-life scale, at which animals have less sophisticated mental lives.

That much said, what specific empirical data can be brought to bear? We saw data in Chapter 6 that showed that some animals, such as pigeons, have excellent recall. And as we just saw, learning by any conscious creature may suggest memory, prompting the question of which animals can learn. Even goldfish can learn certain tasks and would therefore seem to qualify for the class of animals with a sense of time. But, again, with "lower" conscious creatures, such as fish, inferring memory is less certain (a consideration we can keep in mind, without repeating it, as we review other kinds of evidence).

As discussed in Chapter 6, the emotion of fear, which most or all vertebrates can have, implies some sense of the future, since one is afraid of what might happen (as when a lion is racing toward one). These animals also have desires. But desire is future-oriented, so desiring animals would seem to have some grasp of the future. We also reasoned, on the basis of everyday observation, that animals commonly have expectations (which concern the near future), allowing the possibility of surprise.

Some anecdotal evidence is also impressive. For example, feral cats who were fed weekly learned to show up early on the day feedings were due.[8] Even more striking is an account of the chimpanzee Washoe's reaction to a surprise visit by his former teachers, the Gardners. Washoe (whose training in sign language is discussed later) had not seen them *for eleven years,* since he was seven. When the Gardners entered the house where Washoe now lived, Washoe signed their names! Washoe then signed "COME MRS. G" to Beatrice Gardner, led her into a room, and initiated a game that Washoe had not been seen playing since she was five. (Three other chimps, who had not seen the

---

[8] For a discussion of this and other anecdotal evidence, see Midgley, *Animals and Why They Matter,* pp. 57–58.

Gardners for several years, also behaved as if they clearly remembered them.)[9]

For those inclined to doubt anecdotal evidence, more rigorous evidence is available. For example, Louis Herman and his associates have conducted numerous controlled studies demonstrating various memory capabilities of dolphins.[10] But carefully controlled studies have amply demonstrated that mammals and birds generally, not just such mental giants as dolphins, represent temporal intervals.[11]

Drawing from all of these considerations, it seems reasonable to conclude that animals who are sentient, experience fear, have desires and beliefs, and learn, also remember and anticipate and therefore have some conscious sense of time (a conclusion to be reinforced in the next section). These animals are not, after all, stuck in the present. Although it is possible that there are exceptions among the "lower" vertebrates, I believe the evidence suggests that they, too, have some conscious sense of time.

Intentional action

In action theory (the area of philosophy that studies the nature and conditions of action), a distinction is usually drawn between those things we do unintentionally, such as trip and spill a cup of coffee, and

[9] Roger S. Fouts and Deborah H. Fouts, "Chimpanzees' Use of Sign Language," in Paola Cavalieri and Peter Singer (eds.), *The Great Ape Project: Equality Beyond Humanity* (New York: St. Martin's Press, 1993), pp. 37–38. The authors provide other impressive anecdotal data about chimpanzee temporality (ibid). For a summary of anecdotal and other evidence of chimpanzee memory and expectations for the future, see Jane Goodall, *The Chimpanzees of Gombe* (Cambridge, MA: Harvard University Press, 1986), pp. 29–33. Goodall stresses chimpanzees' ability to remember individuals who have been important in their lives and to anticipate the social consequences of their own behavior.

[10] See, e.g., Louis M. Herman, "Interference and Auditory Short-Term Memory in the Bottlenosed Dolphin," *Animal Learning and Behavior* 3 (1975): 43–48; Roger K. R. Thompson and Louis M. Herman, "Memory for Lists of Sounds by the Bottle-Nosed Dolphin: Convergence of Memory Processes with Humans?", *Science* 195 (1977): 501–3; and Louis M. Herman, "Cognitive Characteristics of Dolphins," in Herman, *Cetacean Behavior*, pp. 367–90.

[11] See, e.g., P. Killeen, "On the Temporal Control of Behavior," *Psychological Review* 82 (1975): 89–115; John Gibbon, "Scalar Expectancy Theory and Weber's Law in Animal Timing," *Psychological Review* 84 (1977): 279–335; John Gibbon and Lorraine Allan, *Timing and Time Perception* (New York: New York Academy of Sciences, 1984); F. B. Gill, "Trapline Foraging by Hermit Hummingbirds: Competition for an Undefended Renewable Resource," *Ecology* 69 (1988): 1933–42; C. R. Gallistel, *The Organization of Learning* (Cambridge, MA: MIT Press, 1990); and John Gibbon and Russell M. Church, "Representation of Time," in C. R. Gallistel (ed.), *Animal Cognition* (Cambridge, MA: 1992), pp. 23–54.

intentional actions, such as drinking a cup of coffee.[12] Those who perform intentional actions are known as *agents*. On an influential model that systematizes folk psychology (see Chapter 6), one always performs an intentional action for a reason, which consists of some appropriately related desire and belief. So, for example, I drink my cup of coffee because, say, I want to become more alert (desire) and I think drinking a cup of coffee will make me more alert (belief). In the case of tripping and spilling a cup of coffee, assuming it was accidental, I do not have a reason that explains why I did so. What I did was caused, no doubt, but it is not the case that some related desire and belief caused it. Now, if I wanted to ruin someone's rug, and saw spilling coffee as a nifty way of doing that, then my intentionally tripping and spilling would be explained, and caused, by my desire and belief.

We have already seen that many animals have desires and beliefs that explain their actions. It follows that *these animals are agents.* This conclusion may seem counterintuitive. "How can rats, bluejays, lizards, and tuna be agents?," some might ask. Assuming they grant that vertebrates have appropriately related desires and beliefs, they may be thinking of agency in more robust terms than those basic to intentional action, picking up associations with moral agency, autonomous action, or the like. But the thesis that vertebrates are agents does not mean that they are moral agents or autonomous beings. Those controversial theses will be considered later.

Do these capacities imply self-awareness?

Do the capacities described in the last three subsections imply self-awareness? The ability to distinguish one's own body from the rest of the environment does not, by itself, imply self-awareness, for a never-conscious creature might have the requisite informational sensitivity. Does the ability of actual conscious animals to make the discrimination implicate self-awareness?

Donald Griffin argues that self-awareness is a natural consequence of various perceptual abilities—including awareness of one's own body—that are clearly possessed by some animals:

> If we grant that some animals are capable of perceptual consciousness, we need next to consider what range of objects and events they can consciously perceive. . . . [T]here is no part of the universe that is closer and more important to an animal than its own body. But those who hold that self-awareness is a unique human attribute often fall back to an insistence that although animals may be perceptually conscious of their

[12] For a leading set of essays, see Donald Davidson, *Essays on Actions and Events* (Oxford: Clarendon Press, 1980), Part I.

own bodies, they nevertheless cannot think such thoughts as "It is I who am running, or climbing this tree, or chasing that moth."

Yet when an animal consciously perceives the running, climbing, or moth chasing of another animal, it must also be aware of who is doing these things. And if the animal is perceptually conscious of its own body, it is difficult to rule out similar recognition that it, itself, is doing the running, climbing, or chasing.[13]

In some sense, Griffin must be right: There is no reason to think that conscious animals have some perceptual hole when it comes to themselves. When a hyena is running after a zebra, she is aware not only of the zebra's running but also of her own, at least at some level. But, as Griffin notes, some might hold out for a more sophisticated mental feat, such as *having an "I"-thought*. Then, again, it is not obvious what having such a thought amounts to. More generally, it is difficult to know what criteria to use in deciding whether a being is self-aware.

In Chapter 4, we alluded to Gallup's study of the use of mirrors by primates. While Gallup's philosophical inferences proved reckless, his data are fascinating. Primates who had become familiar with mirrors were anesthetized and painted with odorless markers on parts of their heads that were visually inaccessible without the use of mirrors. After awakening, the primates quickly used mirrors to pick at the marks (something they did not do without mirrors). Interestingly, only chimpanzees and orangutans exhibited the ability to use mirrors to examine themselves. Only they (and humans), it seemed, had the ability to see their reflections *as* reflections of their own bodies, an ability that requires displacing one's self-image away from one's body.

Flaws in experimental design, however, may have caused certain primates to fail the mirror test despite having the ability to pass it. The behavior of gorillas, for example, is greatly inhibited by the presence of strangers, such as unknown testers. In more suitable experimental conditions, the gorilla Koko has apparently demonstrated the capacity to examine herself in mirrors.[14]

---

[13] Donald R. Griffin, *Animal Minds* (Chicago: University of Chicago Press, 1992), pp. 248–49

[14] Francine Patterson and Wendy Gordon, "The Case for the Personhood of Gorillas," in Cavalieri and Singer, *The Great Ape Project*, p. 71. Another ingenious test had a chimp try to reach an object by hand, while the hand was visible only via a TV monitor (E. W. Menzel, Jr., E. Sue Savage-Rumbaugh, and Janet Lawson, "Chimpanzee (*Pan troglodyte*) Spatial Problem-Solving with the Use of Mirrors and Televised Equivalents of Mirrors," *Journal of Comparative Psychology* 99 (1985): 211–17). For a discussion of exploratory actions by chimps using a video screen, such as looking down their throats with the help of a flashlight, see E. Sue Savage-Rumbaugh, *Ape Language: From Conditioned Response to Symbol* (New York: Columbia University Press, 1986), ch. 13.

Should we require this ability for self-awareness? It seems more complex than the general perceptual awareness of one's own body invoked by Griffin. On the other hand, it might be less involved than the ability to have an "I"-thought (which, some would argue, requires language). How much is enough for self-awareness?

Interestingly, chimps who were raised in complete social isolation were not able to recognize their reflections in mirrors, regardless of how familiar they were with mirrors. Apparently, raising other social animals such as dogs in complete isolation stunts the learning necessary for appropriate action toward their own bodies. Scottish terrier puppies raised this way were unresponsive to contact with hot radiator pipes that a normal dog would avoid.[15] These data concerning primates and dogs together lead me to a *social relations thesis:* If our criteria for self-awareness exclude some conscious animals, *self-awareness is more likely to develop in highly social animals (reared normally) than in solitary animals.* Social animals need to be perceptive about the behaviors of conspecifics. But one is more likely to develop self-awareness if one is highly aware of others, because the self–world boundary is likely to be that much clearer and more important to one. Moreover, a social animal would be advantaged by being able to take the perspective of group members toward herself, an ability clearly involving self-awareness. (We will return to this thesis shortly.)

Let us turn to the next capacity discussed. Do memory and anticipation, by themselves, imply self-awareness? It would seem not. An alligator might see the big rock and remember it; it looks the same as last time. Obviously the alligator must have been around the last time to perceive it, in order to remember it now. But remembering does not entail an awareness of oneself as perceiver (either the last time or now). For an example of anticipation, recall the dog who expected to see the tennis ball after his owner made a throwing motion (Chapter 6). The expectation of a certain sight does not necessitate a sense of oneself as the one expected to do the seeing. It may be true that the alligator and the dog are self-aware (by some standard), but the fact that they have memories and anticipations does not entail self-awareness.

A stronger case can be made that intentional action implies self-awareness. Tom Regan makes the case: "For an individual, A, to act now in order to bring about the satisfaction of his desires at some future time is possible only if we assume that A is self-aware at least to the extent that A believes that it will be his desires that will be

---

[15] The points about the effects of social isolation on animals come from Rosemary Rodd, *Biology, Ethics and Animals* (Oxford: Clarendon, 1990), p. 65. For the data regarding the dogs, Rodd cites John Paul Scott, *Animal Behavior*, 2nd ed. (Chicago: University of Chicago Press, 1972), p. 170.

satisfied. . . ."[16] If a hungry rabbit sees a carrot, forms a desire for it, and hops in order to get the carrot, the rabbit must have some awareness, however dim, of herself doing the hopping and, assuming things go as planned, eating the carrot. The belief that hopping will get her the carrot makes sense only if she expects herself to be around long enough to eat it. And we have seen that attributing such desires and beliefs to animals like our rabbit is justified by available evidence.

Regan also argues that, given the continuity of evolution, which implies that more complex forms of mental life evolved from less complex forms, we should expect that there are some conscious animals who are not self-conscious.[17] Because Regan cautiously attributes agency only to mammals, he might regard other vertebrates as conscious but not self-conscious. But this won't do on my view. I have argued that we have good reason to suppose that all conscious animals can experience pleasant and unpleasant feelings, that such feelings implicate desires, and that desires work with beliefs in intentional action. (Again, what function does sentience have if one cannot act in ways that get one away from painful stimuli and toward pleasant ones?) If we combine my "conscious animals are agents" thesis with Regan's "agency implies self-consciousness" thesis, we get the perhaps surprising thesis that all conscious animals are self-conscious. But in Chapter 4, in discussing Gallup's confusions, I was at pains to argue that consciousness does not imply self-consciousness. Have I not contradicted myself?

I have not. First, consciousness does not *logically entail* self-awareness. It may be, however, that what we know about evolutionary pressures (as well as animal behavior and physiology) suggests that actually existing conscious animals are probably self-aware. Also, we have not yet decided on appropriate criteria for self-awareness.

Further reflections and data

Further reflections on the adaptive value of self-awareness, and additional empirical findings, should move us forward. Recall the social relations thesis: *Self-awareness is more likely to develop in highly social animals than in solitary animals.* That is, again, because self-awareness would appear to have greater adaptive value for social animals. We have also found that the ability to discriminate one's own body from the rest of the environment is crucial for survival. Then it might reasonably be conjectured that, other things being equal, *the greater one's bodily awareness, the better.* But note that the kind of self-awareness that may be

[16] *The Case for Animal Rights* (Berkeley: University of California Press, 1983), p. 75
[17] ibid, pp. 76–77

tied to normal perceptual abilities à la Griffin, or to intentional action à la Regan, might be bodily self-awareness and nothing more. In contrast, some philosophers and scientists take self-awareness in an *introspective sense*—as awareness of one's own mental states. It has been argued that self-awareness (of this type) functions to allow monitoring and improvement of one's own thought processes.[18] This sort of self-awareness is relatively complex because it involves beliefs (or other propositional attitudes) about certain mental states, such as beliefs. Colin McGinn elaborates on the benefits:

> [Introspection] enables one to control one's behaviour more effectively than if one did not have such beliefs [about beliefs]. Suppose, then, that the introspective beliefs did not exist though the perceptual experiences did; what benefit would thereby be sacrificed? Presumably the experiences would then have to shape and control world-directed beliefs directly. . . . [Introspection], acting as an intermediary between perception and world-directed beliefs, can, as it were, put an experience in neutral—it can decline to be guided by it in the formation of beliefs about the world. The subject can judge, of a perceptual experience, that it is not to be trusted, and hence not to be acted upon.[19]

In examining animal self-awareness, we should mind the distinction between bodily self-awareness and introspective awareness.

Let us turn now to further examples of animal behavior that may suggest self-awareness of one form or another. Various authors have described the tactics of grizzly bears in locating positions from which they can observe hunters or other intrusive humans without being seen; grizzlies have also been reported to make efforts to avoid leaving tracks.[20] These data suggest an impressive degree of bodily self-awareness. The bears' behaviors may also manifest a capacity to imagine the mental perspective of others, but this attribution is much less safe. The bears may have learned to position their bodies in particular ways (in relation to certain objects, humans) and not to leave tracks, simply because in the past less harm followed when they behaved this way.

Returning to an example explored in Chapter 6, vervet monkeys have extensive knowledge about the particularities of social relations

---

[18] See, e.g., R. H. Kluwe, "Cognitive Knowledge and Executive Control: Metacognition," in Donald R. Griffin (ed.), *Animal Mind—Human Mind* (Berlin and New York: Springer Verlag, 1982), pp. 201–24.

[19] *Mental Content* (Oxford: Blackwell, 1989), p. 90

[20] Griffin, *Animal Minds*, p. 249. Griffin cites Bessie D. Haynes and Edgar Haynes (eds.), *The Grizzly Bear: Portraits from Life* (Norman, OK: University of Oklahoma Press, 1966); E. A. Mills, *The Grizzly* (Boston: Houghton Mifflin, 1919); and William H. Wright, *The Grizzly Bear* (New York: Scribner's, 1909).

within their group. (Note that such knowledge depends on remembering many details about individuals within the group in order to anticipate their reactions—further illuminating the adaptive value of temporality for social animals.) This knowledge includes considerable understanding of how they themselves fit into the social structures of the group. They have *social self-awareness*. According to Cheney and Seyfarth, however, the vervets appear not to have awareness of their own (or others') mental states. In any event, there is abundant evidence that many other higher mammals—including other monkey species, Great Apes, the lesser apes (gibbons and siamangs), elephants, and dolphins—are socially self-aware.[21]

Dolphins, as aquatic creatures, may be the least well known among these animals, so a word about them is in order. (In my use of *dolphin*, I do not distinguish members of the family Delphinidae from porpoises—members of the family Phocoenidae.) Like the other animals just mentioned, dolphins are highly social creatures. Most spend their entire lives in moving schools, within which there are dominance hierarchies and long-term relationships.[22] Because each dolphin appears to have a unique "signature whistle," there is some reason to conjecture that they relate to each other as distinct individuals.[23] Indeed, close observation apparently supports the claim that they have distinct personalities.[24]

Another example from Chapter 6 combines social self-awareness with a high degree of bodily self-awareness: that of the baboon who slowly moved to a position from which she could groom a male without the dominant male being able to see what she was doing. She apparently grasped her social status in relation to the dominant's, the rule against doing what she wanted to do, and the usual consequence for

---

[21] See, e.g., Goodall, *The Chimpanzees of Gombe*, chs. 7–8, 19; Holger Preuschoft, David J. Chivers, Warren Y. Brockelman, and Norman Creel (eds.), *The Lesser Apes: Evolutionary and Behavioural Biology* (Edinburgh: Edinburgh University Press, 1984), Part IV; Iain and Oria Douglas-Hamilton, *Among the Elephants* (New York: Viking, 1975), ch. 4; and Norris and Dohl, "The Structure and Function of Cetacean Schools."
[22] Norris and Dohl, "The Structure and Function of Cetacean Schools"; Lisa T. Ballance, "Residence Patterns, Group Organization, and Surfacing Associations of Bottlenose Dolphins in Kino Bay, Gulf of California, Mexico," in Stephen Leatherwood and Randall R. Reeves (eds.), *The Bottlenose Dolphin* (San Diego, CA: Academic Press, 1990), pp. 267–83
[23] Melba C. Caldwell and David K. Caldwell, "Statistical Evidence for Individual Signature Whistles in Pacific Whitesided Dolphins, *Lagenorhynchus obliquidens*," *Cetology* (1971): 1–9; Melba C. Caldwell, David K. Caldwell, and Peter L. Tyack, "Review of the Signature Whistle Hypothesis for the Bottlenosed Dolphin," in Leatherwood and Reaves, *The Bottlenose Dolphin*, pp. 199–234
[24] Christina Lockyer, "Review of Incidents Involving Wild, Sociable Dolphins, Worldwide," in Leatherwood and Reeves, *The Bottlenose Dolphin*, p. 340

breaking the rule. Her bodily self-awareness, and her ability to take the dominant's spatial perspective into account, permitted her to crouch in such a way that she would still be visible (giving no cause for special concern to anyone watching) although her actions were not.

Similar behavior has been frequently noted in apes. As examples, each of the following chimpanzee behaviors has been observed on several occasions. A young male leads a female out of the view of higher-ranking males in order to copulate. A subordinate courting a female covers his erection when a superior male suddenly appears. While fighting a rival, a male apparently hides signs of fear (which might embolden the rival) by suppressing instinctive facial expressions and vocalizations or by manually covering his mouth. A chimp avoids looking at food that only she knows about until other chimps have departed, thereby securing sole access to the prize.[25] In addition to suggesting bodily and social self-awareness, these actions reveal impressive self-control.

Various species of Cetacea (members of the order of whales, which includes dolphins) have been observed apparently attempting to assist distressed animals of other species, such as humans and sharks, struggling in the water. While this behavior does not directly suggest self-awareness, it may display an extraordinary degree of social awareness (which is likely correlated with self-awareness). As Rodd puts it, humankind "is the only other wild animal known to do this, and it is possible that the common factor is an ability to recognize what distress is (rather than simply reacting to species-specific signals)."[26] The ability to recognize species-independent signs of distress would also indicate a significant capacity for abstraction. On the other hand, at least some cetacean species have a natural habit of pushing unusual objects to the surface.[27] So until the apparent rescuing behavior is described in greater detail, interpretations of that behavior will be somewhat speculative.

Imitative behavior also suggests a nontrivial degree of self-awareness. To be sure, one must be mindful of the possibility that a particular piece of imitative behavior is purely instinctual and automatic, as when someone's yawning causes everyone else nearby to yawn. But the more nuanced and context-sensitive an act of imitation, the more likely the imitator is thinking in terms of doing what another

---

[25]Goodall, *The Chimpanzees of Gombe*, pp. 570, 577–80

[26]*Biology, Ethics and Animals*, pp. 68–69 (emphasis added). Rodd cites Norris and Dohl, "The Structure and Function of Cetacean Schools," p. 238.

[27]Lockyer, "Review of Incidents Involving Wild, Sociable Dolphins, Worldwide," p. 344

does. No doubt at least some of the following examples reveal a considerable degree of self-awareness.

The chimpanzee Washoe "adopted" a young chimp who eventually mastered thirty-nine signs, without human instruction, by imitating Washoe. Chimps raised in homes have been found to imitate a plethora of actions performed by caretakers.[28] The same is true of Chantek, a language-trained orangutan, who imitated many signs and actions by the time he was two. Often his imitations were in response to trainers' signing "DO SAME." Sometimes he imitated with a twist, as when he moved his eyelid up and down with his finger in order to wink.[29] He even imitated a photograph of a gorilla pointing to her nose.[30] A study of feline behavior reports an orphaned kitten who had been reared with dogs and picked up the habit of lifting his leg at trees, just as male dogs do.[31]

Imitation has not been confined to land animals. Dolphins have proved to be very impressive imitators of others' behaviors and postures (including those of seals, penguins, humans, and other dolphins).[32] There have also been reports of dolphins' spontaneously learning complex acts by observing others.[33] Octopi have apparently learned relatively simple tasks by observing the training of other octopi and then behaving similarly.[34]

There are even examples of animals imitating in the context of apparent make-believe, suggesting the additional power of a fertile imagination. For example, Washoe bathed and oiled a doll the same way her

[28] Goodall, *The Chimpanzees of Gombe*, pp. 23–24. On Washoe's pupil, Goodall cites R. S. Fouts, D. H. Fouts, and D. J. Schoenfeld, "Sign Language Conversational Interactions Between Chimpanzees," *Sign Language Studies* 34 (1984): 1–12.

[29] H. Lyn White Miles, "Language and the Orang-utan: The Old 'Person' of the Forest," in Cavalieri and Singer, *The Great Ape Project*, p. 49

[30] H. Lyn White Miles, "The Cognitive Foundations for Reference in a Signing Orangutan," in Sue T. Parker and Kathleen R. Gibson (eds.), *"Language" and Intelligence in Monkeys and Apes* (Cambridge: Cambridge University Press, 1990), p. 535

[31] Bonnie Beaver, *Veterinary Aspects of Feline Behavior* (St. Louis, MO: Mosby, 1980), pp. 34–35. In this and the foregoing paragraph (except for the examples involving Chantek), I borrow from Rodd, *Biology, Ethics and Animals*, p. 71.

[32] See, e.g., C. K. Taylor and G. S. Saayman, "Imitative Behavior of Indian Ocean Bottlenosed Dolphins (*Tursiops aduncus*) in Captivity," *Behaviour* 44 (1973): 286–98; Herman, "Cognitive Characteristics of Dolphins," pp. 401–3; and P. Tyack, "Whistle Repertoires of Two Bottlenosed Dolphins, *Turiops truncatus*," *Behavioral Ecology and Sociobiology* 18 (1989): 251–57.

[33] These are reviewed in Herman, "Cognitive Characteristics of Dolphins," pp. 406–7.

[34] Derek Denton, *The Pinnacle of Life: Consciousness and Self-Awareness in Humans and Animals* (Sydney: Allyn & Unwin, 1993), pp. 163–64

human companions bathed and oiled her.[35] A rhesus monkey is reported to have imitated the way a rhesus mother carried and repositioned an infant by carrying and repositioning a coconut shell.[36]

Among the most impressive forms of evidence for animal self-awareness are self-statements and self-descriptions by language-trained apes. The first may have come from Washoe. Asked "WHO THAT?" as she gazed in the mirror at herself, she replied "ME WASHOE."[37] When the gorilla Koko was asked "WHAT'S A SMART GORILLA?", she answered "ME." Now one must always bear in mind the possibility that the animal is repeating what others have previously said. It is not unlikely that trainers had described Koko as a smart gorilla in her presence. Still, whether or not Koko grasped what the attribution meant, she clearly grasped whom the attribution was about! Interestingly, when described in ways that she clearly did not understand—for example, as a "goofball," "juvenile," or "genius"—Koko corrected her interlocuter with "NO, GORILLA."[38] Some of her self-descriptions may even indicate *introspective awareness*. When angered, Koko once described herself as a "RED MAD GORILLA." Another time, she repeatedly asked a companion for juice, without success. Resorting to drinking water through a thick rubber straw from a pan on the floor, she called herself a "SAD ELEPHANT."[39] It is *very* doubtful that in these last two instances Koko was repeating others' descriptions.

One very abstract application of self-awareness is a grasp of what happens (or doesn't happen) to one at death. Some remarkable data about Koko—suggesting a grasp of death, both hers and others', and perhaps also introspective awareness—merit quoting a somewhat lengthy passage:

> When Koko was seven, one of her teachers asked, "When do gorillas die?" and she signed, "TROUBLE, OLD." The teacher also asked, "Where do gorillas go when they die?" and Koko replied, "COMFORTABLE HOLE BYE." When asked "How do gorillas feel when they die—happy, sad, afraid?" she signed, "SLEEP." Koko's reference to holes in the context of death has been consistent and is puzzling since no one has ever talked to her about burial, nor demonstrated the activity. [T]here may be an instinctive basis for this. . . .

[35] R. Allen Gardner and Beatrice T. Gardner, "Teaching Sign Language to a Chimpanzee," *Science* 165 (1969), p. 666
[36] J. A. Breuggeman, "Parental Care in a Group of Free-Ranging Rhesus Monkeys (*Macaca mulatta*)," *Folia Primatologica* 20 (1973), p. 196
[37] Goodall, *The Chimpanzees of Gombe*, p. 35. Goodall cites Gardner and Gardner, "Teaching Sign Language to a Chimpanzee."
[38] Patterson and Gordon, "The Case for the Personhood of Gorillas," p. 64
[39] ibid, p. 65

[A] tragic accident indicated the extent to which gorillas may grieve over the death of their loved ones. Koko's favourite kitten, All Ball, . . . was killed by a speeding car. Koko cried shortly after she was told of his death. Three days later, when asked, "Do you want to talk about your kitty?" Koko answered, "SLEEP CAT". When she saw a picture of a cat who looked very much like All Ball, Koko pointed to the picture and signed, "CRY, SAD, FROWN".[40]

An animal less closely related to humans, the elephant, has also exhibited remarkable behavior at times of death. There have been observations of apparent grieving, of burial in our sense of covering up corpses, and of an odd, ritualistic sort of "burial" involving the removal, smelling, and dispersion of a corpse's tusks and bones.[41] Considering the extensive social self-awareness of elephants, perhaps they have some grasp of their own deaths.

Koko has shown signs of embarrassment, an emotion requiring self-awareness. She has sometimes appeared embarrassed when found signing to herself, especially when playing with dolls. Once she was observed constructing what looked like an imaginary social scene involving two gorilla dolls. Looking at one doll, she signed "BAD, BAD"; looking at the other, "KISS." Then she signed "CHASE, TICKLE," pushed the dolls together, and wrestled with them, signing "GOOD GORILLA, GOOD GOOD." Upon noticing that she was being observed, she abruptly put the dolls down.[42] (Koko has been noted to engage in such imaginary play on several occasions.[43])

Types and degrees of self-awareness

By now it is clear that there are different sorts of self-awareness: (1) *bodily self-awareness,* awareness of one's own body as distinct from other things—sometimes including awareness of one's position from another's spatial perspective, or of how to do what another is doing (imitation); (2) *social self-awareness,* which involves understanding one's social relations to others in one's group, the expectations that follow

---

[40] ibid, p. 67

[41] Douglas-Hamilton and Douglas-Hamilton, *Among the Elephants,* ch. 16

[42] Patterson and Gordon, "The Case for the Personhood of Gorillas," p. 74. The authors' chapter contains further data that strengthen the case that Koko is self-aware to a high degree.

[43] Using a remote videorecorder, Mary Lee Abshire has demonstrated numerous cases in which chimpanzees engaged in similar imaginative play ("Imagination in Chimpanzees," *Friends of Washoe Newsletter* 9 [1989]: 2–10). An extraordinary, early set of anecdotal data suggesting a fertile imagination in a chimpanzee, Viki, is described in Keith Hayes and Cathy Hayes, "The Intellectual Development of a Home-Raised Chimpanzee," *Proceedings of the American Philosophical Society* 95 (1951): 105–9.

from these, and how to work within these expectations toward desired goals; and (3) *introspective awareness,* awareness of some of one's own mental states.[44] (I do not claim that these are the only types of self-awareness.)

Each of these types of self-awareness admits of degrees. For example, the rabbit's bodily self-awareness as she goes for a carrot may be slight compared to that of the secretly grooming baboon. The three types of self-awareness themselves may fall on a continuum of complexity. Introspective awareness, which requires abstraction from one's perceptual states, seems more complex than the other two types of self-awareness. And to have some minimal social self-awareness seems a more complex mental capacity than having a minimal degree of bodily awareness; that comparison is supported by the intuition that cognizing social relations is generally more abstract than grasping physical relations.

Our inevitable conclusion is that *self-awareness is not all-or-nothing but comes in degrees and in different forms.* This conclusion is important because it opposes a long tradition of speaking and theorizing about self-awareness as if it were all-or-nothing. Often this thesis was used in the service of defending a thick ontological line between humans and other animals. One might, of course, insist that only one sort of self-awareness—say, introspection—is morally important and that only humans have it. But, first, one would have to explain why just this form of self-awareness is so important. Second, one would have to admit that whether any animals are introspectively aware is an empirical question. Then one would have to look at the evidence. (Some additional evidence relevant to introspection, suggesting that certain apes may have this capacity, will be noted later.)

Note that the possibility (however arbitrary) of singling out one type of self-awareness as morally important does not change the fact that, as a *descriptive* matter, self-awareness comes in different forms and degrees. The phenomena we have discussed clearly involve types of self-awareness. Here is a confirming passage from Rodd, who comments further on the adaptive value of self-awareness:

> Self-consciousness might initially take a fairly simple form. It is possible to be aware that what one sees is not what another sees, without possessing elaborate theories of knowledge. It appears that evolutionary pressure for reliable prediction of the behaviour of others would give an important selective advantage to self-conscious animals within a group

[44] John H. Crook distinguishes several types of awareness, some of which seem to implicate types of self-awareness, but his discussion is not very clear on the conceptual connections between awareness and self-awareness ("On Attributing Consciousness to Animals," *Nature* 303 [May 5, 1983]: 11–14).

who were already conscious. Self-consciousness seems to be something which could be expected to evolve gradually (and which probably develops gradually as we grow up), starting from very simple beginnings, like the ability of rats to use knowledge of what they are at present doing as cues to decide the correct response to an unvarying signal, and going on to much more complex calculations about what one would feel in certain circumstances (and hence what the other chap is likely to feel if you manoeuvre him into the same situation).[45]

LANGUAGE

Introduction

One of the most passionately debated issues involving animals in recent decades is whether any animals have, or can learn, *language*. We saw in Chapter 6 that language is not as important as many have traditionally thought. Belief does not require language, contra Davidson; much less does consciousness or mentality itself depend on language, contra Descartes. It is not immediately obvious that language has any moral importance. On the other hand, language does seem to enhance enormously the conceptual powers of a mind. Thus, an interesting part of understanding animals is understanding to what extent, if any, the mentality of some animals is boosted by language. Depending on the details of our value theory, degree of mental complexity beyond sentience may prove to have moral significance. (Also possibly relevant, of course, are self-awareness, moral agency, and autonomy.)

Still, our discussion of the question of animal language will be compressed. There are several valuable discussions of this topic already in the literature.[46] Moreover, to do justice to all of the complex issues involved would require much more space than we can afford here.

It is worth noting from the outset the distinction between communication and language. As I use the term, *communication* occurs when one animal deliberately, and successfully, transmits information to another animal; when that happens, let us count both animals as having communicated.[47] A communicator might only want to affect another's behavior (as opposed to mind) in transmitting information.

---

[45] *Ethics, Biology and Animals*, p. 72. Cf. Goodall, *The Chimpanzees of Gombe*, p. 589.
[46] See, e.g., Savage-Rumbaugh, *Ape Language*; Rodd, *Biology, Ethics and Animals*, ch. 4; Marc Bekoff and Dale Jamieson (eds.), *Interpretation and Explanation in the Study of Animal Behavior*, vol. I (Boulder, CO: Westview, 1990), Part III; and Cavalieri and Singer, *The Great Ape Project*, Part II.
[47] Cf. Michael Philips and Steven N. Austad, "Animal Communication and Social Evolution," in Bekoff and Jamieson, *Interpretation and Explanation in the Study of Animal Behavior*, vol. I, p. 258. Some may prefer a definition that does not require *deliberate* transmission of information, allowing that certain kinds of instinctual, automatic signaling count as communication.

Perhaps this is the case when a dog scratches at the front door, informing her owner of her presence. We will see later that language is a subset of communication.

There can be little question that many animals communicate, to each other and sometimes to humans. One research team documented the use of precopulation gestures by pygmy chimpanzees who had never been trained by humans. The team noted twenty-one gestures that could be placed into three categories: (1) positioning motions, whereby one chimp gently pushes the other in the direction desired; (2) touch plus iconic hand motions, in which one chimp touches the limb to be moved and gestures the desired direction of movement; and (3) iconic hand movements, which involve gesturing without touching. The gesturing presumably functions to allow pygmy chimps to convey their desires regarding copulatory positions.[48]

Cheney and Seyfarth's extensive study of vervet monkeys revealed that they had three different alarm calls warning about predators. One call warns other vervets of the presence of a leopard. Since leopards can climb, this call sends vervets to the smallest branches of a tree. Such a sanctuary does not work in the presence of an eagle, the sight of which evokes a different call, which sends vervets into thick vegetation near a tree trunk or at ground level (a bad hiding place if a leopard is nearby). When they hear a third call, the snake alarm call, vervets stand on their hind legs and look around at the ground; they can run away from a snake if they see it first. Since different predators demand different, incompatible responses, accurate information of what kind of predator is threatening is essential.[49]

There is a great deal of communication in the animal kingdom and some of the forms it takes are rather impressive.[50] Why do these forms of communication not count as *language*? The literature on the question

[48] E. Sue Savage-Rumbaugh, G. J. Wilkerson, and R. Bakeman, "Spontaneous Gestural Communication among Conspecifics in the Pygmy Chimpanzee (*Pan paniscus*)," in Geoffrey Bourne (ed.), *Progress in Ape Research* (London: Academic, 1977), pp. 97–116. For a discussion of this and other examples of animal communication short of language, see Rodd, *Biology, Ethics and Animals*, pp. 79–86.

[49] Dorothy L. Cheney and Robert M. Seyfarth, *How Monkeys See the World: Inside the Mind of Another Species* (Chicago: University of Chicago Press, 1990), ch. 4. For a helpful discussion of the vervets' alarm calls, see Griffin, *Animal Minds*, pp. 156–60.

[50] David Bright's *Animal Language* (Ithaca, NY: Cornell University Press, 1984) is informative. For specifics on wild dolphin communication, see Caldwell, Caldwell, and Tyack, "Review of the Signature-Whistle Hypothesis for the Atlantic Bottlenose Dolphin"; and Louis M. Herman and William N. Tavolga, "The Communication Systems of Cetaceans," in Herman, *Cetacean Behavior*, pp. 149–209. For specifics on natural ape communication, see, e.g., Robert M. Yerkes and Ada W. Yerkes, *The Great Apes* (New Haven: Yale University Press, 1929); Frans B. M. de Waal, *Chimpanzee Politics: Power and Sex Among Apes* (New York: Harper and Row, 1982); and Goodall, *The Chimpanzees of Gombe*, ch. 6.

of animal language, as I understand it, typically sets two major conditions for language. Wading through a plethora of distinct usages and considerable technical details, these conditions can be expressed by saying that *language requires of an act of communication both content (sometimes spoken of as* meaning *or* reference *in this context) and syntax*. Both conditions are taken up later.

Early disappointments

In the 1970s, some dramatic claims were made about the linguistic abilities of chimpanzees who were trained to communicate in sign language (used by deaf persons) or by manipulating symbols in certain ways. Allen and Beatrix Gardner claimed that the young chimpanzee they had raised and trained, Washoe, learned 132 signs of American Sign Language (ASL) and combined them in meaningful, sometimes novel, ways. Washoe apparently used signs in appropriate contexts, including signs designating quite general categories (such as "DOG" whether seeing a real dog, seeing a picture of one, or hearing one bark, and regardless of breed). An example of her novelty was combining signs for "WATER" and "BIRD" upon seeing a duck.[51]

David Premack took a somewhat different approach with a chimp named Sarah, teaching her to manipulate plastic, magnetized symbols that could be moved around on a board (and bore no resemblance to what they denoted). Some of the strings of symbols that Sarah created appeared to demonstrate a mastery of syntax. When, for example, a human trainer arranged the symbols for "Sarah insert banana pail apple dish," Sarah placed each fruit into the proper container. Premack claimed that such responses demonstrated, for instance, that Sarah grasped that the verb *insert* applied both to the banana and to the apple—requiring her to transcend mere word order, which would have *insert* apply only to the word immediately following it.[52]

Such studies seemed to provide a strong case for animal language. Chimps used symbols in combinations, even novel ones, mastered verbs and not just nouns, sometimes referred to things not immediately present, and so on. But then a wave of skeptical interpretations drowned the initially confident claims. Marian Stamp Dawkins enumerates three kinds of simpler explanations that, given the principle of

[51] See, e.g., Gardner and Gardner, "Teaching Sign Language to a Chimpanzee"; Beatrix T. Gardner and R. Allen Gardner, "Two-Way Communication with an Infant Chimpanzee," in Allan M. Schrier and Fred Stollnitz (eds.), *Behavior of Nonhuman Primates* (New York: Academic, 1971); and B. T. Gardner and R. A. Gardner, "Early Signs of Language in Child and Chimpanzee," *Science* 187 (1975): 752–53.
[52] See David Premack, "Language in a Chimpanzee," *Science* 171 (1971): 808–22; and *Intelligence in Ape and Man* (Hillsdale, NJ: Lawrence Erlbaum, 1976).

parsimony, appeared to undermine the assertions of chimpanzee language: (1) the Clever Hans effect (unwitting cueing of animals by humans, as in the famed case of the horse Clever Hans, whose apparent counting proved to be no more than responses to trainers' subtle cues); (2) a subjective sense that results are significant that stems from a failure to specify in advance what results will count as significant; and (3) an animal's adherence to "rules of thumb" (simple, unimpressive rules, the following of which might appear sophisticated to hopeful testers).[53]

Clever Hans phenomena were likely in the cases of Washoe and Sarah, who developed intimate relationships with the very persons who tested their abilities. Herb Terrace reared a young chimp, Nim, and taught him sign language, before concluding that cueing was probably occurring almost all the time. Terrace gained objectivity by using a videotape during training and testing. He learned that Nim's appropriate responses depended heavily on the immediately preceding behavior by the trainer (such as unwittingly giving a partial signing of the sign expected from Nim). Terrace concluded that only 10 percent of Nim's responses were truly his own and that a full 40 percent were imitations of the sort just described. Moreover, Nim's "sentences" may have resulted from relatively uncomprehending use of rules of thumb. "GIVE DRINK" looks like a sentence, an imperative. But Nim, having apparently learned that "give" tended to get him things he liked, often just added whatever word the trainer signed last. So if Terrace signed "NIM WANT DRINK?," Nim signed "GIVE DRINK." (Studying unedited tapes of the Gardners and Washoe, Terrace argued that Washoe engaged in similarly unexceptional exchanges.)[54]

When Premack attempted to control for Clever Hans phenomena by using a tester who was unfamiliar with the plastic symbols' meanings, Sarah performed considerably less well. She placed symbols in an apparently random order and mixed them around, very possibly waiting for cues (which now did not come) to tell her when to stop mixing the symbols. As with the Gardners, Premack regrouped and tried to devise better controls. In general, however, the more carefully experiments were controlled, the less impressive the performance by chimp symbol users.

Regarding Dawkins' second kind of simpler explanation, we often

[53] *Through Our Eyes Only?: The Search for Animal Consciousness* (Oxford: Freeman, 1993), pp. 74–75
[54] See Herbert S. Terrace, *Nim* (New York: Knopf, 1979); and "Animal Cognition," in H. L. Roitblat, Thomas G. Bever, and Herbert S. Terrace (eds.), *Animal Cognition* (Hillsdale, NJ: Lawrence Erlbaum, 1984). The apparent use of rules of thumb as opposed to language, as well as other interpretative issues, are discussed in Mark S. Seidenberg and Laura A. Petito, "Signing Behavior in Apes: A Critical Review," *Cognition* 7 (1979): 177–215.

"see" connections that we want to see, imputing more significance to data than a cold statistical analysis would warrant. For example, Premack

> claimed that because Sarah could act appropriately when instructed to "insert banana pail apple dish", she understood the hierarchical or grammatical structure of the sentence. Sarah was provided with a choice of fruit and a choice of containers but . . . she was only required to do one sort of action (put a piece of fruit into some sort of container for the whole of one test session). So obviously, the word "insert" referred to both the banana/bucket problem and the apple/dish instruction—it couldn't refer to anything else. In other words, the number of possible outcomes of this experiment was actually quite limited and so the possibility of getting the observed result by chance alone was correspondingly high.[55]

The inconclusiveness of Sarah's actions is representative. The *content, meaning,* or *reference* of her symbol use was unclear. Indeed, these symbols might not have referred to anything for Sarah; perhaps she was just moving them around to get rewards from trainers. Even less did Sarah's manipulations demonstrate a grasp of *syntax*—some set of rules that determines a word's function by its position among other words, while allowing for indefinitely many novel combinations. Such conclusions about the performances of Sarah and other chimps disappointed many who hoped to credit animals with language.

Some problems with the critique

The pioneering chimpanzee language studies have been subjected to a considerable body of criticisms, which we may collectively refer to as "the critique." If the critique inspires pessimism about animals' linguistic capacities, this reaction might be tempered by the realization that the critique itself is subject to significant challenges. Several such challenges follow.

Louis Herman and his associates have criticized both the early studies and the critique for *excessive attention to language production as opposed to comprehension.* Herman and Palmer Morrel-Samuels note that in children learning their first language and in adults learning foreign languages, comprehension of others' language use exceeds productive capabilities at any given time.[56] They credit Premack as the only early researcher to give much attention to comprehension. More recently,

---

[55] Dawkins, *Through Our Eyes Only?*, pp. 81–82. My discussion of the chimp language studies has profited considerably from Dawkins' discussion (pp. 71–82).
[56] "Knowledge Acquisition and Asymmetry Between Language Comprehension and Production," in Bekoff and Jamieson, *Interpretation and Explanation in the Study of Animal Behavior*, vol. I, p. 287

Savage-Rumbaugh's study of pygmy chimpanzees took an interesting turn when Kanzi, a young chimp, learned—by observation without explicit training—to use the keyboard on which his mother was being tutored, quickly becoming more proficient than the intended pupil. Spoken English was used both in Kanzi's presence, among trainers, and to Kanzi—who demonstrated facility in understanding spoken English imperatives.[57] Although "common chimpanzees" were the subjects of the pioneering studies, it has been speculated that pygmy chimpanzees—a distinct but lesser-known species also known as *bonobos*—may have greater native linguistic capacities.[58]

Herman and his associates trained two bottlenosed dolphins, one in a language in which words were represented by computer-generated sounds, the other in a language featuring signing with a trainer's hands and arms. Words referred to objects, actions, properties, and relationships; "sentences" were constructed according to a set of word-order rules allowing for more than 2,000 combinations with different meanings. Notably, different

> sequences of the same words created different instructions as in the semantic contrasts requesting the dolphin to take the surfboard to the person (PERSON SURFBOARD FETCH) versus the person to the surfboard (SURFBOARD PERSON FETCH). Comprehension of these sequences required that the dolphin take account not only of the meanings of the individual words but of their sequences. Comprehension of the language was measured by the accuracy of response to the instructions. Comprehension was in general good and understanding of new instructions was in most cases not significantly different from the understanding of familiar instructions. . . .[59]

The authors assert that the comprehension studies revealed both semantic (content) and syntactic processing by dolphins. The claim about syntax was bolstered, in part, by the dolphins' ability "to relate nonadjacent words in an anomalous string and to delete extraneous words from the string in order to construct a semantically and syntactically correct sequence."[60] Moreover, after learning (through exemplars) syntactic rules governing two- and three-word strings, the dolphins under-

[57] Savage-Rumbaugh, *Ape Language*, pp. 385–97
[58] Sue Savage-Rumbaugh, Mary Ann Romski, William D. Hopkins, and Rose A. Sevcik, "Symbol Acquisition and Use by *Pan Troglodytes, Pan Paniscus, Homo Sapiens*," in Paul G. Heltne and Linda A. Marquardt (eds.), *Understanding Chimpanzees* (Cambridge, MA: Harvard University Press, 1989), pp. 266–95. For an excellent introduction to bonobos, see Heltne and Marquardt, *Understanding Chimpanzees*, Part II.
[59] Herman and Morrel-Samuels, "Knowledge Acquisition and Asymmetry Between Language Comprehension and Production," p. 296
[60] ibid, p. 297

stood four-word strings the first time they were given, suggesting a grasp of the rules (since rules for the longer strings were logically related to those for shorter strings). They also rejected sentences with unknown action words.

To what extent were the dolphins' performances dependent on the presence of their trainers? The dolphins demonstrated their ability to interpret televised images of signers, images that in subsequent trials became increasingly degraded, down to images of only hands and arms—and finally simply two white spots tracing out paths of the gesture. Despite being untrained with such degraded images, dolphins demonstrated high comprehension.[61]

Savage-Rumbaugh and Brakke argue that the early studies played into the hands of the critique by incorporating certain invalid methodological practices and assumptions (typically shared by proponents of the critique). For example, unlike human children—our paradigm language learners—Premack's Sarah was never given an opportunity to go beyond what she was trained to do and share new information. *Without an opportunity for spontaneity, an animal's language capabilities cannot be properly assessed.* Herman et al.'s studies of the receptive capabilities of dolphins, and Schusterman and his colleagues' similar study of sea lions (described later), are somewhat closer to the natural setting in which human children learn language. But, like the chimp studies, these encourage "successful" performances only by offering rewards (in the case of sea mammals, fish). In the routines of daily life, human children learn to perform actions for many different sorts of ends. Reward-driven trials are artificial and provide an ulterior motive for correct responses. The animals cannot be presumed to have any intrinsic interest in the activity under study:

> [A] young child, upon hearing his friend say "would you like to play 'tagerm'" and then being shown the game, might find he would like to play again. He could initiate the game by asking to play "tagerm" even if he had never heard the word before. The dolphin, however, has little reason to learn in this way, since it a) cannot make the signs the experimenter makes, and b) probably does not particularly want to "take the frisbee to the hoop" in any case. It is more interested in reinstating the "effect" of receiving a fish. . . .[62]

One major problem with the critique is a common attitude about syntax. According to the authors, the influential Terrace assumed that

---

[61] ibid, pp. 298–301
[62] Sue Savage-Rumbaugh and Karen E. Brakke, "Animal Language: Methodological and Interpretive Issues," in Bekoff and Jamieson, *Interpretation and Explanation in the Study of Animal Behavior,* vol. I, p. 320

syntax is necessary for generating novel meanings, whereas word combinations themselves can create new meanings. Kanzi, they claim, often created such combinations. For example, his string "car trailer," made when he was in a car, indicated that he wanted the car to go to the trailer rather than having to walk there; he followed with a gesture to the trailer. When asked if he wanted the car to be driven to the trailer, he gave a positive vocal response and gestured again to the trailer.[63] Griffin makes a similar claim about syntax:

> Terrace (1979) and Terrace, Petitto, and Bever (1979) report that one of the longer series of signs used by Nim was "Give, orange, me, give, eat, orange, give, me, eat, orange, give, me, you." And one of the longest utterances reported by Patterson and Linden (1981) from the gorilla Koko was "Please milk, please, me, like, drink, apple, bottle." Terrace and others have concluded that signing apes are not using anything that deserves to be called a language, because of the almost total lack of rule-governed combinations of signs. But however ungrammatical and repetitious these strings of signs may have been, they leave no doubt what Koko and Nim wanted.[64]

Koko and Nim communicated with their utterances. One might want to go further and argue that their strings represented language (a claim that would return us to the issue of what is required for language). Griffin also observes that the great emphasis on syntax has come from scholars whose native language is English, a language that has the unusual feature that word order, as opposed to inflection, provides most of the syntax. *Perhaps inflection is an easier way to express syntax than word order is.* There is even some evidence that signing chimps may have been inflecting signs.[65]

According to Savage-Rumbaugh and Brakke, *the critique has also gone overboard in its reaction to cueing and to close relationships between trainers and animal subjects.* They note, first of all, that parents cue children all the time in teaching them language (or anything else). Cueing is perfectly appropriate in training, although it must be withheld in testing. And there are many ways to control for cueing; animal language studies are not doomed to succumb to the Clever Hans effect. One important

---

[63] ibid, p. 329

[64] *Animal Minds,* p. 223. The works he cites are Terrace, *Nim;* H. S. Terrace, L. A. Petitto, and T. G. Bever, "Can an Ape Create a Sentence?," *Science* 206 (1979): 891–902; and Francine G. Patterson and Eugene Linden, *The Education of Koko* (New York: Holt, Rinehart & Winston, 1981).

[65] See Deborah H. Fouts, "Signing Interactions Between Mother and Infant Chimpanzees," in Heltne and Marquardt, *Understanding Chimpanzees,* pp. 249–50; and Beatrix T. Gardner and R. Allen Gardner, "Cross-Fostered Chimpanzees II: Modulation of Meaning," in Heltne and Marquardt, *Understanding Chimpanzees,* pp. 234–41.

way to avoid cueing is not to have a preset correct answer but to foster conditions in which spontaneous language use can occur and simply observe what happens.[66] As for close relationships between the trainers and animals, it is difficult to see how language competence could develop in the absence of such rapport.[67] Indeed, in higher primates, merely disrupting the mother–child bond can result in behavioral abnormalities and retardation.[68] Rodd notes that chimps who performed worst as language users seem to have been the ones treated as intellectual problems rather than as social beings with feelings; they were "worked on" by a changing population of graduate students with no opportunity to establish stable relationships.[69]

A final rejoinder responds not to the claim that animals lack language but to the perhaps tempting inference that animals are therefore not very intelligent. Such an inference would be unwarranted. *There might be crucial differences between species, unrelated to intelligence, that make certain nonhumans unlikely to perform well by linguistic criteria.* Humans may have an innate disposition to learn structured symbol systems, in which case humans may find language use intrinsically rewarding while apes value it only instrumentally. If so, humans will need less intelligence to master language than will a similarly competent ape. Young children enjoy repeating pleasant-sounding words and playing with words and sounds. There may be a human urge to imitate sounds and rearrange them creatively. One reason why parrots do surprisingly well in language experiments[70] might be that they find it amusing to play with sounds; this innate tendency would make them more likely to cooperate and concentrate in language studies. Descrip-

---

[66] The way Kanzi's comprehension of spoken English is tested provides another good example of how to control for cueing. Kanzi wears headphones so only she can hear the target word. The tester does not know what Kanzi hears or what lexigrams Kanzi can choose from in responding. Target words and alternatives are selected randomly for each trial. Also, Kanzi is given food for participating, but only upon request as opposed to being rewarded for correct responses. As Savage-Rumbaugh and Brakke put it, if an animal "has nothing to gain by being correct and nothing to lose by being incorrect, it has no reason to search for cues, inadvertent or otherwise . . . ," ("Animal Language," p. 337). Such a research set-up certainly controls adequately for cueing. On the other hand, there may be a problem of *motivation*. Just as there is no incentive for cueing, maybe there is no motivation to try for correct answers—in which case limited capacity could not be inferred from poor performance! See the next section for a discussion of the ways in which various methodological concerns are not entirely compatible.

[67] ibid, p. 335–36

[68] Goodall, *The Chimpanzees of Gombe*, p. 379

[69] *Biology, Ethics and Animals*, p. 93

[70] See, e.g., Irene M. Pepperberg, "Cognition in the African Grey Parrot: Preliminary Evidence for Auditory/Vocal Comprehension of the Class Concept," *Animal Learning and Behavior* 11 (1983): 179–85.

tions of the ape studies suggest that the subjects often found repeated trials frustrating and boring.[71]

In conclusion, there seem to be as many problematic presuppositions underlying the critique as there are methodological and interpretive problems with the pioneering ape language studies themselves.

A balanced critical perspective

By now we have accumulated quite a bag of critical tools. On the side of the critique—as well as plain old good sense—we have the three kinds of concerns outlined by Dawkins. We must be sure to minimize or eliminate the risk of cueing by testers. We should specify in advance what responses by subjects are to count as evidence for language (and employ observational instruments, such as videotapes, that help make objective assessments of when such responses have been given, and statistics to guard against subjective estimates of significance). And we must not attribute language when subjects' behavior is explained more parsimoniously by assuming that they followed simple rules of thumb (such as "Sign "GIVE" plus the last sign the researcher made.").

On the other side, we have numerous criticisms of (1) assumptions underlying the critique, and (2) features of the early studies that may have inhibited subjects' ability to display linguistic capacities (thereby needlessly playing into the hands of the critique). Each criticism seems reasonable. Yet it is impossible to satisfy all of these critical concerns— those motivating and those countering, the critique—at the same time.

For instance, if Savage-Rumbaugh and Brakke are right, we should remove rewards as incentives for accurate responses. Then we can more safely assume the animals are not just performing uncomprehending tricks to get food. But what if nonhuman primates lack a natural disposition to enjoy manipulating sounds and other signs? How will we know when poor performance results from lack of capacity, as opposed to lack of interest? Or suppose that we maximally allow for spontaneous production of signs, not even determining in advance what counts as a favorable performance. How will we be able to prevent our interests and biases from infecting our interpretation of data? And if we focus on spontaneous production, have we not missed Herman's point about the importance of comprehension? Well, we can study that, too. But, in testing for comprehension, how can we test for creativity? Isn't creativity an important feature of language? An affirmative answer suggests the importance of syntax, which allows for indefinite recombinability of signs. Yet if we require syntax for language, will we not, in effect, brush aside some creative communications

[71] These points are developed in Rodd, *Biology, Ethics and Animals*, pp. 98–99.

deserving to be called *language*? On the other hand, if we drop the syntax requirement, can we be confident about distinguishing instances of genuine language use from more random, or relatively uncomprehending, play with signs?

The lesson I draw from all of these methodological and interpretive dilemmas is that we must return to the spirit of methodological pluralism. We should approach these questions from various angles, taking each to be potentially informative but not potentially conclusive. We should respect studies of productive abilities *and* studies of receptive abilities, studies emphasizing naturalness and opportunities for spontaneity *and* those with more rigorous criteria for success. We should look hard for evidence of syntax but not throw away apparently novel and meaningful productions that apparently lack syntax—yet we need to explore the possibilities of inflected syntax, too. And so on.

Some of the more promising studies—and conclusion

In this spirit, I think we may regard some of the animal langugage research as quite promising. Herman's work with dolphins seems very strong and may provide the most solid evidence to date of syntactical competence by animals. I believe that Griffin is fair in making the following assessment:

> The overall success of these two dolphins on 405 novel "sentences" was 66 percent correct. While 66 percent may not seem very close to perfection, it should be realized that the chance score was very low indeed, since there were a very large number of possible actions among which the dolphins had to choose. Thus these two dolphins had clearly learned not only the meanings of the individual commands but the sequence rules governing which was direct and which was indirect object, and which modifier applied to a given object name.[72]

The other marine mammal studied for receptive abilities, the sea lion, has also apparently demonstrated some significant capacities. Schusterman and Krieger trained two sea lions to respond accurately to 64 and to 190 gestural signs displayed by humans, respectively.[73] Schusterman and Gisiner trained sea lions to comprehend combinations of commands, demonstrating some capacity to master syntactical rules.[74]

---

[72] *Animal Minds*, p. 216
[73] Ronald L. Schusterman and Kathy Krieger, "California Sea Lions are Capable of Semantic Comprehension," *The Psychological Record* 34 (1984): 3–23
[74] R. I. Schusterman and R. Gisiner, "Artificial Language Comprehension in Dolphins and Sea Lions," *The Psychological Record* 38 (1988): 311–48; "Animal Language Research: Marine Mammals Re-Enter the Controversy," in Harry J. Jerison

Research conducted at the Language Research Center in Atlanta, where Savage-Rumbaugh pursues her studies, also holds much promise. These studies operationalize the principles motivating Savage-Rumbaugh and Brakke's criticisms of other studies. For example, the newer apes at the Center have been taught not to label things on demand but to ask for things that interest them. These communications were first made nonverbally and, later, verbally (by pressing keys on a keyboard). For example, if a chimp needed a tool to solve a problem, at first she might gesture toward the tool; later, a symbol was used as an alternative way to get it. A chimp's grasp of what tool she had asked for was tested by giving her the wrong tool, and observing the response, or by giving her the toolkit and letting her choose. This sort of verbal-behavioral concordance also allowed a chimp to announce an intention (e.g., to "go outdoors") and have the comprehension of the communication verified (e.g., by seeing whether she then goes outside). In these and other ways, chimp performances apparently indicated that they intended to communicate—not simply get rewards.

Kanzi's feats were discussed earlier. Kanzi's siblings also acquired large vocabularies. Simply by watching and listening to caretakers, they began to use symbols correctly, reinforcing the conclusion that *language learning can occur without training*.[75] This finding is important for those who believe that apes' language capacities are so poor that they have to be "trained to death" to make any progress, whereas human children learn effortlessly.

A crucial feature of the Center's research is its naturalization of the language acquisition process, permitting results that allow more meaningful comparisons with human language acquisition (and making chimp learning more likely in the first place). Learning at the Center follows the chimp's initiative:

> Unlike apes whose symbol vocabulary was assigned by the experimenter, the bonobos "selected" the symbols they were ready to acquire from the hundreds used around them each day. Like children, their first words were not all the same. . . . Also unlike other apes, the bonobos first learned to associate the spoken word with its real world referent, not the geometric symbol. Only after learning the relationship between a spoken word and its referent did they connect the word and the geometric symbol. Their initial acquisition was receptive.[76]

and Irene Jerison (eds.), *Intelligence and Evolutionary Biology* (New York: Springer, 1988); "Please Parse the Sentence: Animal Cognition in the Procrustean Bed of Linguistics," *Psychological Research* 39 (1989): 3–18
[75] Savage-Rumbaugh and Brakke, "Animal Language," p. 325
[76] ibid, p. 326. For more detail about the researchers' careful and sophisticated methodological considerations, see Savage-Rumbaugh, *Ape Language*. Interestingly, Herb

Research at the Language Research Center promises to continue to provide important data in our ongoing collective effort to study linguistic and other cognitive capacities of apes.[77]

Research by Roger and Deborah Fouts further undermines the claim that chimpanzees must be "trained to death" to use language. The Fouts' chimp subjects include Washoe, who had been raised by the Gardners. Loulis, an infant chimp "adopted" by Washoe, was spoken to in English but not taught sign language by humans. On her own initiative, Washoe taught Loulis signs—and Loulis eventually taught a new playmate signs.[78]

Their research also renders dubious the claim that, in signing, chimpanzees might be uncomprehendingly manipulating symbols just to receive rewards. In one study, the Fouts recorded 5,200 instances of chimpanzee-to-chimpanzee signings; interestingly, only 5 percent concerned food. Many of these—119—were private signings (signings to oneself), as when a chimp labeled pictures of things she saw in a magazine.[79] But this study may have been biased against private signings, because a videocamera was used only when two or more chimps were in the frame (since the study focused on dialogues). Another study, correcting for this possible bias, found private signings to increase threefold.[80] As for the common claim that chimpanzees never refer to things that are not immediately present—as Bennett asserted—the two

---

Terrace, whose criticisms of early language studies was a major force behind the critique, strongly endorses the present research project. See his "Foreword" to *Ape Language.*

[77] Considerations of space prevent me from discussing the impressive case of a parrot, Alex, who has acquired a sizable vocabulary and demonstrates surprising abilities to group items that form abstract categories. See, e.g., Pepperberg, "Cognition in the African Grey Parrot"; Irene M. Pepperberg, "Evidence for Conceptual Quantitative Abilities in the African Grey Parrot," *Ethology* (1987): 37–61; "Cognition in an African Grey Parrot (*Psittacus Erithacus*)," *Journal of Comparative Psychology* 104 (1990): 41–52; and "A Communicative Approach to Animal Cognition: A Study of Conceptual Abilities of an African Grey Parrot," in Carolyn A. Ristau (ed.), *Cognitive Ethology* (Hillsdale, NJ: Lawrence Erlbaum, 1991).

[78] Roger S. Fouts and Deborah H. Fouts, "Loulis in Conversation with Cross-Fostered Chimpanzees," in R. Allen Gardner, Beatrix T. Gardner, and Thomas E. Van Cantfort (eds.), *Teaching Sign Language to Chimpanzees* (Albany, NY: SUNY Press, 1989), pp. 293–307; Fouts, "Signing Interactions Between Mother and Infant Chimpanzees." Interestingly, B. F. Skinner in the late 1980s expressed his skepticism that chimpanzees had ever shown each other how to sign ("Signs and Countersigns," *Behavioral and Brain Sciences* 11 [1988]: 466–67).

[79] Fouts, Fouts, and Shoenfeld, "Sign Language Conversational Interactions Between Chimpanzees." Chimps apparently even grumble to themselves, as when Washoe used her favored bad word, "DIRTY," when Loulis stole the magazine she had been looking at (Fouts and Fouts, "Chimpanzees' Use of Sign Language," p. 36).

[80] Fouts and Fouts, "Chimpanzees' Use of Sign Language," p. 35

studies just mentioned found chimps to achieve such "displacement" in 12 to 14 percent of their signings.[81]

Chimpanzees' reputation as the most intelligent nonhuman primate may stem partly from the great, perhaps disproportionate, attention given to chimps in language studies. (This focus may reflect a prejudice rooted in the knowledge that chimps are our closest cousins, both genetically and physically.) It is worth noting results of language studies involving other Great Apes—the family that includes humans, common and pigmy chimps, gorillas, and orangutans. (The lesser apes are gibbons and siamangs.[82])

Koko and other *gorillas* have demonstrated a surprising range of linguistic capacities. For about two decades, Koko has been in a language environment that includes ASL and spoken English. According to her trainers, she combines her working vocabulary of more than 500 signs into strings averaging three to six signs in length. She has used about 1,000 signs correctly at least once. Her receptive vocabulary in English is several times as large. Michael, an eighteen-year-old gorilla who was not introduced to ASL until he was three and a half, has used over 400 signs. Both gorillas initiate most of their conversations with humans, sign to themselves and to each other, and have been seen signing slowly and repeating signs when working with humans who are less fluent in ASL than they are.[83]

Their specific feats include the following. They have apparently *inflected* signs to alter meanings. For example, Koko seemed to exaggerate by signing "THIRSTY" from the top of her head to her stomach, instead of down her throat. (These modifications are not claimed to function as syntax.) Gorillas may have insulted each other by signing "STINKER" and "ROTTEN."[84] They have demonstrated some creativity in offering novel definitions, such as these by Koko. "What's an insult?" "THINK DEVIL DIRTY." "What's a stove?" "COOK WITH." "What's an injury?" "THERE BITE" (pointing to a cut on her hand). "What is crazy?" "TROUBLE SURPRISE." "When do people say darn?" "WORK. OBNOXIOUS." "What can you think of that's hard?" "ROCK. WORK." "What's a smart gorilla?" "ME."[85]

An analysis of the 876 signs emitted by Koko during the first decade

---

[81] ibid. On interchimp communication, see also Savage-Rumbaugh, *Ape Language*, ch. 7.

[82] Although traditionally referred to as *gibbons* and *siamangs*, there is considerable controversy about how many species of lesser ape there are and how exactly to classify them. See Preuschoft, Chivers, et al., *The Lesser Apes*, Part V.

[83] Patterson and Gordon, "The Case for the Personhood of Gorillas," pp. 59–60

[84] ibid, p. 63

[85] ibid, pp. 63–64

of the language project showed that six percent were her own inventions; another two percent were compounded out of signs she had been taught. Examples of the latter by Koko are "BOTTLE MATCH" for cigarette lighter, "WHITE TIGER" for zebra, and "EYE HAT" for mask. Michael came up with "ORANGE FLOWER SAUCE" for nectarine yogurt and "BEAN BALL" for peas, among others. As we saw in discussing self-awareness, Koko even described herself as "RED MAD GORILLA" and "SAD ELEPHANT" in circumstances that made perfect sense of these appellations.[86] Koko allegedly even scored higher on a test for metaphorical capacity than average human seven-year-olds.[87] As with chimpanzees, gorillas have shown their capacity for referential displacement. For example, six days after Koko's birthday, she was asked "What happened on your birthday?" She responded "SLEEP EAT," leaving it unclear whether she really distinguished this day from other days. But asked "Didn't something special happen on your birthday?", Koko replied "OLD GORILLA."[88]

Among the Great Apes, *orangutans* are even less familiar to us than are gorillas. For several years, H. Lyn White Miles has been teaching sign language to an orangutan, Chantek, who has acquired a vocabulary of about 150 signs. Without being trained, Chantek learned to comprehend spoken English. At about two, he began to sign for things that were not present, for example, asking to go places in his yard to look for a cat and pet squirrel who served as playmates.[89]

Chantek has used language for manipulative purposes (some instances of which might count as deceit):

> He learned that he could sign DIRTY to get into the bathroom to play with the washing machine, dryer, soap, etc., instead of using the toilet. He also used his signs deceptively to gain social advantage in games, to divert attention in social interactions, and to avoid testing situations and coming home after walks on campus. On one occasion, Chantek stole food from my pocket while he simultaneously pulled my hand away in the opposite direction. On another occasion, he stole a pencil eraser, pretended to swallow it and "supported" his case by opening his mouth and signing "FOOD-EAT", as if to say that he had swallowed it. However, he really held the eraser in his cheek, and later it was found in his bedroom where he commonly hid objects.[90]

---

[86] ibid, p. 65. Drawing from several studies by other researchers, Goodall offers some wonderful examples of creative word combinations by chimpanzees (*The Chimpanzees of Gombe*, p. 34).

[87] F. G. Patterson, "Innovative Uses of Language by a Gorilla: A Case Study," in K. Nelson (ed.), *Children's Language*, vol. II (New York: Gardner, 1980), pp. 497–561

[88] Patterson and Gordon, "The Case for the Personhood of Gorillas," p. 74

[89] Miles, "Language and the Orang-utan," pp. 46–48

[90] ibid, p. 48

Some of these bits of chicanery demonstrated Chantek's creativity, a quality manifested in other ways as well. For example, he invented such signs as "NO-TEETH" (apparently to say that he would not use his teeth in rough play), "EYE-DRINK" (for contact lens solution), and "DAVE-MISSING-FINGER" (for someone with a hand injury). Chantek sometimes used objects other than hands for signing; once he gave the sign for biting using the blades of a scissors.[91]

At this point, is it worth taking a stab at the question of whether any nonhuman animals have language? We could get tripped up by scholars' differing standards for language possession. For example, it is debatable how important syntax is (as is how syntax is most likely to be revealed). Nevertheless, at the very least Herman and his associates appear to have demonstrated, rather clearly, syntactical—as well as semantic—capacities in dolphins. So even those who require syntax for language and maintain fairly tough evidentiary criteria are, I think, compelled to acknowledge (at least) the language comprehension capacities of some animals. Historically, it has served human narcissism to require language for high mental—or moral—honors and to set high standards for language. Sometimes we may learn more about the motivations of individuals who insist on some particular standard for language possession than we learn about language itself. I recommend abandoning the view that language has an "essence" (a specifiable set of necessary and sufficient conditions) such that beings either have it or don't have it (the all-or-nothing view). It seems more honest and profitable to understand language as both multidimensional and gradational. Two dimensions of language are (subsets of) *receptive* and *productive communicative feats,* which form continua or axes from a point of origin. Two more dimensions—forming a different plane, as it were—are *referential achievement* and *syntactical achievement,* which also form continua.

On the present view, no simple answer can be given to the question of whether animals have language. Because language has dimensions, there are different *kinds* of linguistic achievement. Because language is gradational, *there are no precise boundaries for language* along continua of communicative feats; any stipulated boundary would be arbitrary. But, allowing that there are different kinds of linguistic achievement, whose boundaries are imprecise, we can still agree that there are feats that clearly count as language and feats that clearly do not. In light of findings presented previously, it seems most reasonable to say that some apes and cetaceans have used, and many of their conspecifics can no doubt learn, certain forms of language.

---

[91] ibid, pp. 49–50. For more on orangutans, see Terry L. Maple, *Orang-utan Behavior* (New York: Van Nostrand Reinhold, 1980).

MORAL AGENCY

A modest sort of virtue?

Many contributors to animal ethics maintain that animals with interests have moral status, but few argue that any nonhuman animals are *moral agents*. That many animals have moral status while only normal humans are moral agents might even be considered an orthodoxy in the literature. But, as Sapontzis writes, "we commonly deal with actions as . . . expressions of character, and many of the flexible, responsive, purposive, intelligent actions of animals seem to express such character traits as responsibility, courage, and compassion."[92] To follow up on this claim, we need to make several distinctions and consider examples.

According to Sapontzis, actions that flow from traits that, in humans, we consider virtues *are* forms of moral agency even in cases in which the actions appear instinctual or conditioned:

> [A]n action can be instinctual, in the sense of being directed by something we have inherited, or conditioned, in the sense of being directed by something we have been taught, yet still be a response to [moral] goods and evils. For example, maternal instincts are responses to the needs of the young. A wolf's care for its young is not mechanical nor carried out inflexibly, without regard to the actual needs of the young in particular situations.[93]

And in morally educating children, we try to instill *habits* of responding to need with compassion and to danger with courage; that is, we try to inculcate *virtues*. If we are successful and these traits become habitual, or conditioned, that hardly means that one fails to manifest moral agency when one acts spontaneously from these virtues.[94]

Many animals reveal dispositions to respond to natural goods and evils in socially useful ways; they reveal what, in humans, are considered virtues. Mammals provide many examples. Mothers care tenderly for their babies. Orphans are adopted by other members of a group. Sometimes animals care for old or feeble companions (even though the adaptive value of doing so is not obvious).[95] After moving to a primate institute, Washoe is reported to have displayed both courage and con-

---

[92] S. F. Sapontzis, *Morals, Reason, and Animals* (Philadelphia: Temple University Press, 1987), p. 32. See also Stephen R. L. Clarke, "Good Dogs and Other Animals," in Peter Singer (ed.), *In Defense of Animals* (Oxford: Blackwell, 1985), pp. 41–51.
[93] *Morals, Reason, and Animals*, pp. 32–33
[94] ibid, p. 33
[95] James Rachels, *Created from Animals: The Moral Implications of Darwinism* (Oxford: Oxford University Press, 1990), p. 148

siderable altruism in saving a drowning chimp she hardly knew;
Washoe jumped an electric fence and risked drowning herself by slid-
ing into a moat to assist the young chimp.[96] Apparently, compassionate
acts toward conspecifics are frequently observed. It might seem far-
fetched to think that animals could evince a sense of reciprocity or
fairness, but intriguing anecdotal data exist. Frans de Waal contends
that chimpanzees take reciprocity seriously:

> The rules [of reciprocity and "an eye for an eye"] are not always obeyed
> and flagrant disobedience may be punished. This happened once after
> Puist had supported Luit in chasing Nikkie. When Nikkie later displayed
> at Puist she turned to Luit and held out her hand to him in search of
> support. Luit, however, did nothing to protect her against Nikkie's attack.
> Immediately Puist turned on Luit, barking furiously, chased him across
> the enclosure and even hit him.[97]

In a fascinating, detailed account, Marian Stamp Dawkins describes a
social system among vampire bats that is based on reciprocity for favors
given in the past and sanctions against those who do not comply with
this standard.[98]

One possible view is that we cannot deny that such animals have a
minimal form of moral agency without also excluding many humans
whom we would ordinarily consider moral agents. A mother who in-
stinctively rushes into a burning house to save a neighbor's child would
ordinarily qualify. This is true even if she is unreflective, of borderline
intelligence, and unable to say anything illuminating about why she did
what she did beyond "The child was still in there!"

On the other hand, we might insist that the mother manifests moral
agency in rushing for the child not simply based on her action in this
case, but because presumably she sometimes acts, for moral reasons, in
ways that override instincts or conditioning—showing that she can
exert her will against such influences. (If she never does, we should
judge that she is not a moral agent.) This position—with which I tend to
agree—implies that animals fail to manifest such agency if they never
override instincts and conditioning in this way. But perhaps some animals do, in which case even their instinctual or conditioned actions
might sometimes manifest moral agency.

---

[96] Fouts and Fouts, "Chimpanzees' Use of Sign Language," p. 29
[97] *Chimpanzee Politics* (London: Unwin, 1982), pp. 175–77. Goodall also reports at
length on both "reciprocal altruism" and acts of apparent compassion among wild
chimpanzees (*The Chimpanzees of Gombe*, pp. 376–86).
[98] *Through Our Eyes Only?*, pp. 57–61

Virtue that seems inexplicable by instincts or conditioning

It is possible that the actions of animals just described were all instinctual or conditioned (even if not unconscious and mechanical, like the behavior of some invertebrates). So let us turn to apparently virtuous animal behaviors that may be inexplicable in terms of instincts or conditioning. These should meet any reasonable standard of moral agency. The literature supplies many examples.

Sapontzis considers a well-known, striking form of cetacean behavior:

> [T]here are cases of porpoises helping drowning sailors. There is no reason to believe that porpoises have developed an instinct for saving humans, and these wild creatures certainly have not been conditioned to perform such acts through training or repetition. It has been suggested that these porpoises were merely playing cetacean volleyball with these sailors and only accidently deposited them safely on shore. But if that were so, there would be reports of porpoises kidnapping hapless, unendangered human swimmers to be their toys for the day. There are no such reports.[99]

As noted earlier in this chapter, dolphins apparently have a natural habit of pushing unusual objects to the surface, motivating the "cetacean volleyball" hypothesis that Sapontzis rejects. But Sapontzis is wrong that there are no reports of the kind that might support this hypothesis. One dolphin reportedly developed the habit of pushing swimmers and surfers out to sea and actively preventing them from swimming to shore; another pushed swimmers out to sea and disrupted surfboards while people were riding them.[100] On the other hand, reports like these appear to be exceptional. Based on the cognitive capacities and extensive social awareness of these animals (including the capacity to recognize and distinguish human individuals, on different encounters in the wild), and the fact that dolphins frequently initiate social contact with humans (in friendlier ways than by butting them),[101] I am inclined to accept the impressions of near-drowners that dolphins were trying to help them. But, without more evidence, the attribution remains uncertain.

Rodd argues that cetaceans who rescue members of other species must recognize distress for what it is, responding to species-independent signs (thereby revealing impressive ability for abstraction), and *decide* to respond to that distress. That suggests, Rodd argues, that

[99] *Morals, Reason, and Animals*, p. 34
[100] Lockyer, "Review of Incidents Involving Wild, Sociable Dolphins, Worldwide," pp. 341–42
[101] ibid

cetaceans are moral agents in the way we are.[102] (The last claim will prove to be oversimplified.)

Jane Goodall presents a touching account of the altruism of a chimpanzee, Old Man, toward a human. Marc Casano was employed to feed, at a safe distance, four chimpanzees who had been abused and were now living on an artificial island in Florida. Ignoring advice, Marc eventually went onto the island to feed the chimps rather than throw food from his boat. Old Man took food from his hand and even allowed Marc to groom him. They had apparently become friends. One day, Marc slipped and fell, scaring an infant chimp, whose scream caused the mother to leap forward and bite Marc's neck. Two other females quickly helped their friend by biting Marc's wrist and leg. When Old Man came running, Marc thought he was a goner. But Old Man pulled the females off Marc, hurled them away, and kept them at bay, allowing Marc to drag himself to safety.[103]

Stella Brewer relates what may have been acts of compassion by one of the captive chimpanzees she had rehabilitated, on a day when a younger chimp was thought to have been killed by a lion:

> I searched the ground for signs of blood. In my aching, empty head I heard again Pooh's voice screaming fear. . . . William touched my leg. He was holding out a dry leaf to me. When I didn't immediately accept it he tossed it to my feet. . . . William perhaps could sense but could not comprehend my uncontrollable sobbing. He handed me small stones, a twig, and finally patted my back as I had often patted his and Pooh's.[104]

Now consider these intriguing observations from de Waal:

> Tarzan is kidnapped by his "aunt" Puist. . . . When Puist is high up in the tree Tarzan panics and starts to scream, so that his mother, Tepel, comes rushing up. . . . When Puist has climbed down again and Tepel has Tarzan safely back, Tepel turns on the much larger and more dominant female and begins to fight with her. Yeroen [a dominant male in the group] rushes up to them, throws his arms around Puist's middle and flings her several metres away.
>
> This intervention was remarkable, because on other occasions Yeroen had always intervened in Puist's favour. This time, however, he agreed, so to speak, with the protest of the mother and waived his usual preference.[105]

---

[102] *Biology, Ethics and Animals*, pp. 68–69
[103] "Chimpanzees—Bridging the Gap," in Cavalieri and Singer, *The Great Ape Project*, p. 17
[104] *The Forest Dwellers* (Glasgow: Collins, 1978), pp. 157–58
[105] *Chimpanzee Politics*, pp. 171–72

Interestingly, Yeroen might have considered his usual preference to side with Puist and rejected it (that is, formed a preference not to abide by this preference) in light of the circumstances. If so, as we will see later, his action would qualify as autonomous. In any event, Yeroen gives the appearance of making some sort of moral choice, perhaps even manifesting a sense of fairness or desert.

These examples support the attribution of moral agency—specifically, actions manifesting virtues—in cases in which the actions are not plausibly interpreted as instinctive or conditioned. On any reasonable understanding of moral agency, some animals are moral agents. This conclusion, again, contradicts the assumption, common even among contributors to animal ethics, that nonhuman animals may be "moral patients" (bearers of moral status) but not moral agents.

Full-fledged moral agency: Moral deliberation and justification

There is a sense of moral agency according to which perhaps no, or at any rate very few, nonhumans are moral agents. In this sense, one is a moral agent only if one is capable of (1) deliberating on the basis of what one takes to be moral reasons, (2) acting on the basis of such deliberation, and (3) justifying one's decision with an explicit argument appealing to moral reasons.[106] Philosophers, who tend to place a lot of stock in rational decision making and justification, may regard this as the paradigm sense of moral agency. Moral agents of this type are indisputably subject to moral obligations.[107]

It is possible that no animal fully meets this standard. Perhaps animals who make certain tough choices—taking a chimp mother's side against one's usual social preference, or rescuing a human rather than allowing fellow chimps to maul him—actually deliberate and act for moral reasons. The same may be true of dolphins who rescue humans (even if no tough choice is involved). But the requirement of *moral*

[106] In making roughly the same point, Sapontzis emphasizes the third condition (*Morals, Reason, and Animals,* p. 35).

[107] Robert Mitchell argues that Great Apes cannot be held morally responsible for their actions due to their insufficiently complex mental lives ("Humans, Nonhumans and Personhood," in Cavalieri and Singer, *The Great Ape Project,* p. 244). I would argue, however, that *different beings can have moral responsibilities over different ranges of possible actions.* The range over which a given being is responsible is determined by the range of action possibilities for which the being can understand a rule of conduct, roughly what its point is, the consequences of breaking it, and so on. That is why it is not unfair to punish (proportionately) a four-year-old for gratuitously hitting his little sister, whereas it would be unfair to punish him for loudly calling attention to a handicapped person. Analogously, I would argue, language-trained apes can be morally responsible for not biting others (assuming they have been adequately instructed not to do so).

justification would seem to implicate language. Even if we allowed that what counts as moral justification could be made entirely to oneself, "internally," it is doubtful that the languageless could achieve this relatively complex form of reason giving, which involves giving an explicit argument. And although some animals have used language, moral justification is not, to my knowledge, within their repertoire.

Rather than further unpack different senses of moral agency, I will conclude with a simple point. The fact that there are several defensible ways of understanding moral agency—which involve different capacities that are not all-or-nothing—suggests that this trait, like self-awareness and language, admits of both kinds and degrees. But perhaps, in contrast to the case of language, the different kinds of moral agency fall on the same dimension or continuum. Virtuous action that is independent of conditioning and instinct arguably manifests a higher degree of moral agency than virtuous action that is conditioned or instinctual (perhaps even if the latter is performed by one who sometimes overrides conditioning and instincts for moral reasons). Arguably, actions stemming from moral deliberation and justification manifest the highest degree of moral agency known to terrestial beings. But we need not settle these questions. For our purposes, it is enough to note that there are different kinds and degrees of moral agency, and that the crude statement that no nonhuman animals are moral agents cannot be sustained.

AUTONOMY

Autonomous action, autonomous beings, and autonomous living[108]

What is *autonomy*? To begin, autonomy is not simply liberty—or freedom—of action (in at least one important sense of the latter terms). A patient may freely, or with liberty, sign a consent form to electroconvulsive therapy yet fail to sign it autonomously. This would be the case if she signed voluntarily but lacked even a rudimentary understanding of what she was consenting to. Or she might comprehendingly sign the consent form but only because she is terrified that she will otherwise be put out on the streets. Roughly, liberty or freedom of action is the absence of external constraints—such as prison walls or coercive measures—that impede one from doing what one wants. Autonomy is more involved.

On what is sometimes called the *multi-tier account of autonomy*, while freedom of action involves governing one's actions by one's desires (doing what one wants to do), autonomy involves governing one's first-

---

[108] This section borrows from my "Autonomous Action and Autonomy-Subverting Psychiatric Conditions," *Journal of Medicine and Philosophy* 19 (1994), esp. pp. 283–88.

order desires—desires to do certain things—by second-order desires (so that one wants what one wants to want).[109] Autonomy requires more than intentional action, so we cannot assume that all agents are autonomous beings. A person may smoke cigarettes because she wants to smoke but may also want not to have, and may even fight, the desire to smoke; if so, her smoking is not autonomous. On the other hand, a smoker who identifies with the desire to smoke, who is addicted but contentedly so, smokes autonomously; she has decided to be that sort of person. Thus, on this view, autonomy is, in Gerald Dworkin's words, "a second-order capacity to reflect critically upon one's first-order preferences and desires, and the ability either to identify with these or to change them in light of higher-order preferences and values."[110]

What about autonomous *action*? Dworkin once stated that one acts autonomously when one acts "for reasons [one] doesn't mind acting from."[111] Clearly that is insufficient, if a person *would* mind acting for the reasons that motivate her, if she gave them any thought. Autonomous action requires dispositional second-order approval of the motivation that moves one to act. *Dispositional* indicates that one might act autonomously without any conscious higher-order valuation yet be *disposed* to approve of one's first-order motivation if the issue is raised.

Hence a link between autonomous *action* and autonomous *beings:* While one may (and perhaps typically does) act autonomously without higher-order valuation, autonomous action requires the *capacity* for such reflection and the disposition to react in certain ways on the occasion of reflection. Autonomous beings are beings with that capacity. Thus, mice presumably do not act autonomously even if they don't mind acting from the reasons (say, desire for cheese plus the belief that cheese is ahead) that move them to act. At least, it is very difficult to imagine what mouse behavior (science-fiction aside) might convince us that mice could reflect critically on their desires, identify with them, or the like.

This multi-tier model of autonomy has been subjected to several challenges, to which I have elsewhere responded in detail.[112] In brief, I believe that two innovations are needed to make the account work. First, *autonomy* needs to be redefined: A autonomously does X if and

[109] Harry Frankfurt speaks of "freedom of the will," instead of "autonomy," defining it as the ability to will what one wants to will ("Freedom of the Will and the Concept of a Person," *Journal of Philosophy* 68 [1971]: 829–39).

[110] *The Theory and Practice of Autonomy* (Cambridge: Cambridge University Press, 1988), p. 108. See also "Acting Freely," *Nous* 4 (1970): 367–83; and "Autonomy and Behavior Control," *Hastings Center Report* 6 (February 1976): 23–28.

[111] "Acting Freely," p. 381

[112] "Autonomous Action and Autonomy-Subverting Psychiatric Conditions," pp. 284–88

only if (1) A does X because he or she prefers to do X, and (2) A has this preference and any higher-order preferences relevantly related to X because he or she (at least dispositionally) prefers to have them.[113] The second innovation helps with a threat of infinite regress. How can I have my preference to do X and all relevantly related higher-order preferences because I prefer them? My higher-order preferences must stop somewhere with preferences or values that are "given" to me, that come from "outside" me. Still, we must allow, if we are to have any notion of autonomy at all, that it is compatible with shaping by certain unchosen influences. We need an account of what influences are autonomy-subverting.

Here is a promising suggestion from John Christman: "[A]ny factor affecting some agent's acts of reflection and identification [subverts autonomy] if the agent would be moved to revise the desire so affected, were she aware of that factor's presence and influence."[114] Clear examples of factors that can subvert autonomy are obsessions, compulsions, addictions, coercive threats, certain powerful forms of mind control such as hypnosis, seduction, and the onset of dementia. But, like other capacities we have examined in this chapter, autonomy admits of degrees. Suppose a man buys the medication Rogaine because he wants to do anything possible to minimize his hair loss. His desire, let's say, is influenced by Rogaine commercials, the absence of bald men in *GQ* magazine, and teasing by friends—but not so much that he changes his mind about Rogaine upon becoming aware of these factors' influence on him. His purchase is a more-or-less autonomous action, although there seems to be some compromising of autonomy in the social-conditioning process; some actions are more autonomous than this one, no doubt. But, while autonomous actions are autonomous to different degrees, the threshold for what counts as an autonomous action is high by animal standards.

Is the present account defensible? Some may find it overly intellectualized. Why have different orders of preferences at all? As an alternative one might accept something like this analysis: A acts autonomously if and only if A acts (1) intentionally, (2) with understanding, and (3) without controlling influences that determine the action.[115] However, this alternative analysis apparently allows the actions of many animals—not just such brainy mammals as dolphins and apes—to count as autonomous. As far I can see, a cat stalking a bird ordinarily

[113] This is a paraphrase of an analysis defended by Keith Lehrer ("Autonomy," a March 20, 1992, lecture at Georgetown University).
[114] "Autonomy: A Defense of the Split-Level Self," *Southern Journal of Philosophy* 25 (1987), pp. 290–91
[115] Tom L. Beauchamp, "The Moral Standing of Animals in Medical Research," *Law, Medicine and Health Care* 20 (1992), p. 12

fulfills the foregoing three conditions. Indeed, it is not clear to me why the same could not be said of a bird feeding its young or even a goldfish going after food. This analysis appears to make autonomous action almost the same as intentional action, suggesting a failure to capture the degree of critical reflection and decision making embedded in the concept of autonomy. Returning to the charge of overintellectualization, our account does not imply that preferences divide naturally into a hierarchy of levels. The point is simply that *autonomous beings can question their action-regarding preferences, note their influences, and decide whether they still prefer them.*

What, then, is autonomous *living* (a concept picked up in Chapter 8)? To live autonomously is to a live a life largely characterized by autonomous actions. But let us define *actions* here broadly enough to include agents' doings generally and not only intentional bodily movements, or relatively short sequences of them, and their causal consequences. *Actions* in the present sense includes not only throwing a baseball, signaling for a turn, and turning on a light, but also settling down in California, becoming a lawyer, and living the life of a housewife. For when we think of living autonomously, we think of painting some very broad, as well as minute, strokes of one's own life portrait. We think of life plans and not just of isolated actions (in the more ordinary sense).

Are any nonhuman animals autonomous beings?

Do any nonhuman animals qualify as autonomous beings? Do any animals possess the capacity for critically evaluating the preferences that move them to act, and sometimes modifying them on the basis of such higher-order valuation? Note that the requisite mental complexity is very high. Considerable ability for *abstraction* is required, for the autonomous individual must be able to *step back* from her motivations and *evaluate* them on the basis of higher-order preferences or values. This clearly implicates *an advanced form of self-awareness* (including introspective awareness). Additionally, one must be *an agent of a special sort:* one who has enough self-control to modify some preferences in light of certain other preferences or values. (If anyone objects to requiring occasional success in modifying one's preferences, as opposed to being mastered by them, let us at least agree that self-mastery of this sort is an issue for the autonomous being.) An autonomous being is likely to be a *moral agent* of the deliberative sort. While one might have higher-order preferences or values that are prudential, esthetic, religious, or based on some other kind of nonmoral value, a being with such an evaluative capacity seems likely to be capable of being moved by moral considerations.

I am not aware of evidence directly addressing the issue of whether any animals have the capacities tied to autonomy. We have seen evidence of impressive abilities for abstraction and of a high degree of self-awareness. We have learned that there is a surprisingly strong case for attributing certain kinds of moral agency to some animals. The toughest part of the case that some animals are autonomous—one that has not been established, to my knowledge—is demonstrating the capacity for *higher-order* preferences or values.

Can animals have preferences about their very preferences, or evaluate some of their preferences in light of values? I do not think we know. The best candidates for this capacity are probably language-users, because of the great thought-extending powers of language. Now one sort of speech act that seems to have been documented in apes, and may suggest the capacity in question, is *apologizing*. Apologies—at least the paradigm case of sincere apologies by humans—express *regret*, and regret suggests the capacity for higher-order disapproval. Disapproval of what? Typically, we regret what we have done, but the capacity to do so may exist along with the capacity to regret the very motivations that move us to act.

The gorilla Koko apparently apologized for something she had done considerably earlier in time:

> [T]he day after Koko bit a companion, I asked her WHAT DID YOU DO YESTERDAY? She replied, WRONG, WRONG. WHAT WRONG? I queried. BITE. . . . The following conversation took place three days after the event discussed:
>
> P: WHAT DID YOU DO TO P?
> K: BITE.
> P: YOU ADMIT IT? (Previously, Koko had referred to the bite as a scratch.)
> K: SORRY BITE SCRATCH (P shows Koko the mark on her hand—it really does resemble a scratch.)
> K: WRONG BITE.
> P: WHY BITE?
> K: BECAUSE MAD. . . .
> P: WHY MAD?
> K: DON'T KNOW.[116]

The following is a transcript of a signed conversation with a chimpanzee, Lucy, who had defecated in the middle of a room while no one was watching:

[116] Francine Patterson, "Linguistic Capabilities of a Lowland Gorilla," in Fred C. C. Peng (ed.), *Sign Language and Language Acquisition in Man and Ape* (Boulder, CO: Westview, 1978), p. 197

Roger: WHAT'S THAT?
Lucy: LUCY NOT KNOW
Roger: YOU DO KNOW. WHAT'S THAT?
Lucy: DIRTY, DIRTY.
Roger: WHOSE DIRTY, DIRTY?
Lucy: SUE'S.
Roger: IT'S NOT SUE'S. WHOSE IS IT?
Lucy: ROGER'S.
Roger: NO! IT'S NOT ROGER'S. WHOSE IS IT?
Lucy: LUCY DIRTY, DIRTY. SORRY LUCY.[117]

As discussed earlier, the gorilla Koko has sometimes acted as if *embarrassed* upon discovering that someone had spied her signing by herself, for example, while playing with dolls. Often one is merely embarrassed about what one has done; one's critical attitudes concern one's actions, say, playing with dolls. But sometimes we are embarrassed about our desires. We might hold open the possibility that Koko held a critical attitude—an embarrassed or shaming one—about being the sort of gorilla who likes to play with dolls, or sign by herself. Such a critical attitude would suggest an autonomous being.

These examples are, at most, suggestive. That they come from signing apes motivates the question of whether autonomy is possible without language. Consider the following hypothetical case involving chimps who lack language. Chimp Weak is much lower in the social hierarchy than Strong, who dominates the group. Strong has recently been challenged by Upstart. Lately, Strong has been very demanding of Weak's allegiance, once threatening Weak for not assisting in punishing a young member of the group who stole some fruit from Strong. Upstart and Strong get into a fight, and Strong screeches at Weak for assistance. Out of fear of Strong, Weak participates in beating Upstart, who cannot withstand an attack from two opponents. It does not seem impossible to me that Weak could beat Upstart reluctantly and only because Strong presents a credible threat for not helping—and that Weak might feel remorse for beating the chimp who, let us say, had never troubled him. In this case, Weak would have a discrepancy between his all-things-considered preference to take part in the thrashing and his desire not to have to go along with it. This would represent the conflict of an autonomous being who was not possessed of language.

We should be open to the possibility of some instances of autonomy in the animal kingdom, even among those who clearly lack language. At the same time, it would seem that the mental complexities involved

[117]Maurice K. Temerlin, *Lucy: Growing Up Human* (Palo Alto, CA: Science and Behavior Books, 1975), p. 122

in autonomy are so great that probably very few—if any—nonhuman animals are autonomous.[116]

[118]It might be wondered why I have not included a section on personhood. The reason is that I do not believe that there is a conception of personhood that is clear, nonarbitrary, and morally useful in any context in which who counts as a person is disputable. That is partly related to the fact that most or all candidate criteria for personhood—such as rationality, self-awareness, and moral agency—come in degrees. Any definition that tries to employ such criteria, while acknowledging that they come in degrees (and that animals sometimes have more than certain humans do), will have to stipulate arbitrary cut-off points in order to be clear, or will have to allow that personhood itself comes in degrees in order not to be arbitrary. If personhood itself is held to come in degrees, it is doubtful that the concept will be morally useful. Why not just appeal to particular criteria for particular purposes, for example, to autonomy in discussions of respect for autonomy? Moreover, if there are several criteria for personhood, then claims of the form "A is more of a person than B" will be "averagings-out" or summaries of several comparisons and, in close cases, very contentious. Imagine, for example, a case in which A is more self-aware and sociable than B, but B is more rational than A. If, for the sake of clarity, only one criterion is picked, that too would seem arbitrary. An extreme case of a unicriterial view is the popular belief that all and only humans are persons. If this claim is accepted, then the concept of personhood may be redundant and will definitely prove useless in honest efforts to explore the moral status of nonhuman animals. (I also doubt the claim's accuracy: Spock of *Star Trek* and the fully linguistic apes of *The Planet of the Apes* seem to be persons.) In animal ethics and perhaps generally, there is nothing you can do with the concept of personhood that you cannot do better with clearer concepts such as those explored in this chapter. The first draft of this chapter included a section on personhood, but it was full of arbitrary stipulations and added little or nothing of value. I thank L. W. Sumner for convincing me to reconsider its inclusion.

Chapter 8

The basics of well-being across species

Having done our homework on animal minds in Chapters 4, 5, 6, and 7, we can use much of what we learned as we return in this chapter to questions of value—this time, to *interspecific value theory*. Our task involves prudential value theory (value theory, for short). This is the study of *well-being*, or *the good of individuals* in a familiar nonmoral sense, at the most general and ultimate level. In contrast to ethics, value theory examines value from the self-interested perspective of an individual. What constitutes her good or well-being? What, ultimately, makes her life go better or go worse? Rather than confining our investigation to humans, we will broaden it in an effort to understand well-being generally and therefore across species. As we will see, any serious effort to do so will draw significantly from what we know about animal minds.

WHY THIS CHAPTER?

Exploring well-being across species is necessary for understanding what *benefits*, and what *harms*, animals. If the matters of benefit and harm to animals appear straightforward, appearances are deceiving. Consider an undomesticated dog living in the wild during winter. Food is somewhat scarce. We domesticate the dog and feed him well but keep him inside except for brief walks. He is often bored but hardly suffers. Has he been benefited, on balance? In the wild, let us say, he would exercise his native capacities much more but would also suffer more. Is his well-being reducible to *experiential well-being*, the quality of feelings: pleasure, enjoyment, satisfaction, and the like versus pain, distress, suffering, and the like (see Chapter 5)? Or does the exercise of capacities—certain kinds of *functioning*—have independent value? Suppose we slightly increase the experiential well-being of a cat by giving her an operation or drug that cuts deeply into her mental functioning. Is she better off? Who is better off: a captive monkey whose dampened expectations leave her with modest, easily satisfied desires (see Chapter 6), or a semi-flourishing, free monkey with more robust desires that are less often met? What if an elephant stands to live ten or so years in the wild with somewhat more suffering than enjoyments. Would a painless death benefit her? Is death per se a harm to an elephant? To a turtle?

A somewhat vague principle of equal consideration—which requires giving equal moral weight to relevantly similar interests—was defended in Chapter 3. We cannot fully understand our ethical obligations to animals unless we can apply this principle to them. But to do so requires understanding what equal consideration amounts to. In all but exceptional circumstances, we should not kill human beings. Does equal consideration imply such a strong presumption against killing ducks? Not if killing (as opposed to hurting) them doesn't harm them. What if death usually harms them, but far less than it harms humans? We have work to do.

There is almost no well-developed work on interspecific value theory in the literature. Value theory covering humans has been highly refined—with some excellent contributions in recent years—but this work makes at most passing reference to animals. In the opening sentence of a recent book on value theory, one reads that "every normative theory must contain an account of value, and the link that is often forged between what is valuable and what . . . we ought to do is *human* welfare or well-being."[1] Such a link is of questionable use for animal ethics.

Leaders in animal ethics are aware that animal well-being raises philosophical issues, but their treatment has been highly superficial. For example, in *Animal Liberation,* Singer touches on issues of prudential value in just a few pages.[2] Regan's discussions in *The Case for Animal Rights* are just slightly more developed.[3] Neither philosopher defends his commitment to a particular value theory in any depth. As its title suggests, Frey's *Interests and Rights* treats issues of prudential value at greater length. But his analysis is damaged by mistaken inferences in the philosophy of mind, an outdated interpretation of animal behavior, and considerable conceptual confusion. He concludes that animals have no interests and cannot be harmed, but they have unpleasant

[1] R. G. Frey and Christopher W. Morris, "Value, Welfare, and Morality," in Frey and Morris (eds.), *Value, Welfare, and Morality* (Cambridge: Cambridge University Press, 1993), p. 1, my emphasis
[2] Peter Singer, *Animal Liberation,* 2nd ed. (New York: New York Review, 1990), pp. 7–8, 17–21
[3] Tom Regan, *The Case for Animal Rights* (Berkeley: University of California Press, 1983), pp. 87–88, 99–103, 324–25

sensations and can therefore be hurt.[4] This is not the product of a well-developed value theory. A notable exception to the rule of superficiality is Sapontzis' treatment of these issues.[5] As explained later, however, I think his contribution has some important shortcomings.

In recent years, utilitarians have given the most attention to value theory. They judge the rightness of an action against the standard of maximizing good consequences—that is, prudential value. Other consequentialists also understand rightness in terms of good consequences, which they take to be commensurable, but do not understand rightness in terms of impartial maximizing. Even some nonconsequentialists take the good to be morally more basic than right action, while denying that all good things are commensurable.[6] Clearly, all who take the good to be prior to the right need to be concerned with value theory. Less obviously, so do theories that take the right to be prior to the good. The justification of principles or rights in such theories must address the interests to be protected by those principles or rights: What are those interests, and how is their importance to be explained?[7] Moreover, most theories of this kind hold that as long as we work within appropriate moral constraints, we should pursue the good—requiring an understanding of its nature.

Value theory is inescapable to moral theorizing. Interspecific value theory is essential to animal ethics. To clarify our options, however, we should begin where options have been deeply explored: value theory as it applies to humans.

A MORE-OR-LESS STANDARD STORY OF VALUE THEORY FOR HUMANS

The story that follows represents, in a compressed way, a more-or-less standard display of options in value theory as it is understood today. The standard classification divides value theories into mental statism (mental state theories), desire-satisfaction theories, and objective theories.[8]

---

[4] R. G. Frey, *Interests and Rights: The Case Against Animals* (Oxford: Clarendon, 1980), p. 170

[5] S. F. Sapontzis, *Morals, Reason, and Animals* (Philadelphia: Temple, 1987), pp. 115–37, 159–75, 218–21

[6] See, e.g., John Finnis, *Natural Law and Natural Rights* (Oxford: Clarendon, 1980). In tracing out the relations of these types of ethical theory to value theory, I borrow at points from L. W. Sumner, "Two Theories of the Good," *Social Philosophy and Policy* 9 (Summer 1992), p. 2.

[7] Thomas Scanlon, "Value, Desire, and Quality of Life," in Martha C. Nussbaum and Amartya Sen (eds.), *The Quality of Life* (Oxford: Clarendon, 1993), p. 195

[8] This schema traces back to Derek Parfit, *Reasons and Persons* (Oxford: Clarendon, 1984), Appendix I, although Parfit uses slightly different terminology. For a detailed

Mental statism and the move to desire-satisfaction theories

Mental statism holds that an individual's well-being consists solely of her having certain kinds of mental states. *Hedonism*, the most familiar version of mental statism, identifies well-being with the presence of pleasure (and absence of pain).[9] (Sometimes *happiness* is used to denote the valuable mental state.) One problem facing hedonism is that it is doubtful that there is any one mental state designated by *pleasure*. Consider the good feelings associated with being with friends, eating, skiing, contemplating, relaxing, making love. There does not seem to be a single mental state, or even a phenomenological component, common to all of these. So what do various pleasures have in common?

A likely reply is that pleasant experiences are ones *desired just for the way they feel*. The qualification excludes cases of desiring experiences for instrumental reasons, as one might desire the agony of a triathalon to see if one can endure it. I argued in Chapter 5 that *pleasure* was an apt word for experiences desired for the way they feel, but some might prefer Sidgwick's *desirable consciousness*. In any case, the resulting value theory has been called *preference mental statism* and *preference hedonism*.[10]

But now preference or desire seems to be what matters. If so, why limit the objects of desires that count to mental states? We clearly care about how things go in the world, and not just how things feel "from the inside."[11] Often we even care more about the former. I might prefer that money I could spend on medicine that would give me more desirable mental states, overall, instead be invested in my children's flourishing.

In this spirit, we might decide that satisfying our desires enhances our well-being, regardless of their objects. This is an unrestricted *desire-satisfaction theory*. (Here *satisfaction* means that what one wants to happen, happens; one need not have feelings of satisfaction.) But perhaps to push this far is to push too far. Suppose I meet a stranger on a train, form the desire that he succeed, and later forget about him entirely. If, years later, he succeeds (unbeknownst to me), my desire has been satisfied, increasing my well-being on the present account. Because this is

exploration of these options, see James Griffin, *Well-Being: Its Meaning, Measurement, and Moral Importance* (Oxford: Clarendon, 1986), Part I.
[9]See Jeremy Bentham, *An Introduction to the Principles of Morals and Legislation* (1789).
[10]See Shelly Kagan, "The Limits of Well-Being," *Social Philosophy & Policy* 9 (Summer 1992), p. 170; and Scanlon, "Value, Desire, and Quality of Life," p. 186. Henry Sidgwick first proposed this view (*The Methods of Ethics,* 7th ed. [London: Macmillan, 1907]).
[11]This point is classically argued in Robert Nozick's Experience Machine thought-experiment (*Anarchy, State, and Utopia* [New York: Basic Books, 1974], pp. 42–45). In a different way, David Gauthier argues that preference is a more basic concept than pleasure (*Morals By Agreement* [Oxford: Clarendon, 1986], pp. 35–6).

implausible, it is tempting to impose a *Success Requirement:* The only desires that affect my well-being are those whose fulfillment or frustration affect my life in some way.[12]

Another difficulty with the present theory is that it concerns *actual* desires, which may be uninformed, irrational, or otherwise distorted. If the desires of an addict are driven by addiction and distorted by systematically false beliefs, her well-being might not be maximized by maximizing her desire satisfaction. And long-term deprivation can water down expectations and, consequently, desires.[13] A political prisoner might eventually lose hope for freedom and stop desiring it, replacing his old robust desires with modest ones that are easily satisfied. Can we really assume that his well-being consists of maximizing the satisfaction of these modest desires? Perhaps we need to qualify further the desires that count.

The refinements offered by informed-desire theories

Informed-desire (or rational-desire) theories begin with the idea that actual desires can be faulty, from the standpoint of well-being. The fulfillment of Romeo's desire for death did not benefit him, for it was based on the misinformed belief that Juliet had perished. Some desires reveal faults of logic, as in the case of mutually inconsistent desires. More subtly, desires might be based on confused thinking or irrelevant considerations. One such mistake is overgeneralization.[14] A child may wish to avoid all grown men because his own father is so mean.

Can desires be corrected by appealing to considerations beyond facts and logic? Here matters become controversial. Arguably, there could be psychological corrections, such as drying out the political prisoner's dampened desires. One might argue for still subtler corrections. We might discount desires that show a lack of "insight" or "proportion"; perhaps an *informed* desire in this expanded sense is "one formed by appreciation of the nature of its object. . . . "[15] Thus, an extreme recluse may fail to appreciate what meaningful human relationships have to offer.

Informed-desire theories must specify and defend the sorts of corrections they permit. And there remains the problem of the enormous breadth of things we desire; whether the Success Requirement sets the right limit is disputable. There is also the problem of conflicting desires.

[12]Parfit, *Reasons and Persons,* Appendix I
[13]Amartya Sen, "Well-Being, Agency and Freedom," *Journal of Philosophy* 82 (1985), p. 191
[14]R. B. Brandt, *A Theory of the Good and the Right* (Oxford: Clarendon, 1979), pp. 120–22
[15]Griffin, *Well-Being,* p. 14

Sometimes what we want now (say, a tranquil mid-life) is not what we will want when the time comes (say, when we have a mid-life crisis).[16] Sometimes what we don't want now (say, to insulate our house for winter) we will later wish we had cared more about.[17] Which desire in each pair counts? An informed-desire theory must manage these and other challenges.[18]

The reemergence of objective theories

Probably most value theorists today favor some form of informed-desire theory.[19] Is there any good reason to subscribe to an objective theory? As I will use the term, an *objective* theory defines an individual's good (at least partly) by reference to conditions or factors that are independent of, and may diverge from, the individual's own desires, values, or authority. (A *subjective* theory, then, defines one's good entirely in terms that depend on one's desires, values, or authority.) Writing in the late 1970s, Brandt was dismissive of objective theories:

> Various philosophers have thought that some things, different from happiness and possibly not desired by anyone or everyone, are worthwhile in themselves and worthy of being produced for no further reason, for instance: knowledge and virtue. This view, however, seems to be obsolescent, and I propose to ignore it.[20]

But objective theories made a comeback in the 1980s and cannot be dismissed.[21] One reason to take them seriously is the possibility that some legitimate corrections of desires, at bottom, really appeal to what one *should* desire—to some particular content—rather than simply tidying up what one *actually* desires. If the recluse's not wanting company is thought to reflect a failure to appreciate the way in which

[16]Cf. Brandt, *A Theory of the Good and the Right*, pp. 249–51.
[17]Gauthier, *Morality By Agreement*, pp. 36–38
[18]One strategy is to conceive of a person's desires as forming a structure, a global ordering, and to appeal to this structure in resolving conflicts. Maybe you do not want to insulate now, but you also have a more global desire to be the sort of person who can delay gratification and plan prudently. Life-structuring desires generally carry more weight than transient whims. See Griffin, *Well-Being*, pp. 11–17.
[19]Two prominent representatives not already cited are John Rawls (*A Theory of Justice* [Cambridge, MA: Harvard University Press, 1971], ch. 7) and R. M. Hare (*Moral Thinking: Its Levels, Method and Point* [Oxford: Clarendon, 1981], ch. 5).
[20]*A Theory of the Good and the Right*, p. 246
[21]The comeback remains strong in the 1990s. In addition to works cited later, see, e.g., Richard Kraut's Presidential Address to the American Philosophical Association, in which he rejects desire theories in favor of an objective view ("Desire and the Human Good," *Proceedings and Addresses of the American Philosophical Association* 68 [November 1994]: 39–54).

meaningful relationships add substance or weight to a life, this judgment suggests the thesis that meaningful relationships have objective value.

At the same time, I will argue from the outset that what I call *perfectionistic theories* are not serious contenders today. These theories include a conception of *the good life for humans,* a particular ideal; one's well-being is then assessed in terms of how close one's life gets to that ideal.[22] Aristotle, for example, argued that there was a human function or *telos*—namely, rational activity (which he divided into two components)—and that humans flourished to the extent that they actualized their function. But it is very doubtful that there is a human telos and, consequently, a single good life for humans—much less, that it is rational activity. There may be, as flexible objective theories hold, various sorts of activities or conditions that are valuable for anyone, with no one of them supreme (as discussed later). If so, presumably no one mix of them would be authoritatively best.[23] To be plausible, a value theory needs to make more room for individual differences than seems possible within perfectionism.

Some objective theories are flexible enough to be contenders. Rather than arguing that there is an ideal life for humans, or that some mix of objective goods is best, they argue, more modestly, that some things in themselves make human life go better. It has been argued, for example, that such goods include enjoyments, autonomy, accomplishment, and deep personal relationships.[24] These are good in any life, even if individual differences ground very different proportions and realizations in different lives; for certain unusual persons, one such good might not be worth pursuing, on balance, due to conflicts with another good (say, if accomplishment makes one so anxious that one cannot enjoy anything). Note that including autonomy (autonomous living or pursuit of one's own life plan) and enjoyments (whose objects vary interpersonally) also makes this account sensitive to individual differences.

Some objective theories are explicitly mixed, granting a place to cer-

---

[22] Here I follow Griffin, *Well-Being,* p. 56. Sumner contends that the radical objectivity of perfectionistic theories prevents their *being* theories of prudential value; they don't address what is good *for the individual* ("Two Theories of the Good," pp. 4–5). I disagree. Again, such theories can hold that one's well-being is determined by how close one gets to the ideal.

[23] See Scanlon, "Value, Desire, and Quality of Life," p. 191; and Griffin, *Well-Being,* pp. 58–60.

[24] See James Griffin, *Well-Being,* pp. 26–34; "On the Winding Road from Good to Right," in Frey and Morris, *Value, Welfare, and Morality,* p. 158; "Dan Brock: Quality of Life Measures in Health Care and Medical Ethics," in Nussbaum and Sen, *The Quality of Life,* p. 135. While Griffin may appear to straddle the divide between informed-desire and flexible objective accounts, his movement to the latter territory is most apparent in recent writings such as the second and third above.

tain (desirable or agreeable) mental states, to desire satisfaction generally, or the like, while also including objective components of well-being. They often take *functioning* in various ways to have prudential value irreducible to the agreeable mental states or desire satisfaction that it allows. It has been argued, for example, that while a handicapped person might adjust well to his predicament, and be cheerful enough, his well-being would be enhanced per se by greater capabilities for functioning.[25]

Perhaps the greatest challenge to flexible objective accounts is the charge that they are not flexible enough. Suppose someone is not interested in a supposed object of prudential value, say, accomplishment. Clear in her mind about what genuine accompishment is, she even tries to accomplish and succeeds, but is not impressed. (Assume there is no violent conflict here between accomplishment and another good.) What we might call the *Satisfaction Requirement* has not been fulfilled. How can it be said that accomplishment is part of her well-being? Would she be better off if, other things staying equal, she were to accomplish a good deal more but become a little less happy? Many would think not.

Rather than pursue further details of this dialectic, let me conclude this more-or-less standard story with the claim that it appears to leave us with a tough choice between informed-desire and flexible objective theories. As noted earlier, desires can be corrected in numerous ways. Arguably, some forms of correction really appeal to objective conditions rather than tidying up actual desires; then again, maybe when we've gone this far, we've gone too far away from an individual's authority about his or her own good.

---

[25] Amartya Sen, "Well-Being, Agency and Freedom," p. 197; see also Dan W. Brock, "Quality of Life Measures in Health Care and Medical Ethics," in Nussbaum and Sen, *The Quality of Life*, p. 40. For an up-to-date statement of this approach, see Sen, "Capability and Well-Being," in Nussbaum and Sen, *The Quality of Life*, pp. 30–53. For a mixed theory whose objective element concerns biological needs, see Joseph Raz, *The Morality of Freedom* (Oxford: Clarendon, 1986). See also the discussion of Scanlon's view in the next section.

Some accounts leave it unclear whether what is claimed to have objective prudential value is regarded as *instrumentally* or *intrinsically* valuable; the search in value theory is for objects of ultimate or intrinsic prudential value. David Copp's theory incorporates a notion of basic needs—things needed in human life, given the laws of nature, facts about the human constitution, and the like ("Reason and Needs," in Frey and Morris, *Value, Welfare, and Morality*, pp. 112–37). Bernard Gert argues for a list of objective evils—death, pain, disability, loss of freedom, and loss of pleasure—the opposites of which, he claims, are objective goods (*Morality: A New Justification of the Moral Rules* [New York: Oxford University Press, 1988]). Copp appears to derive the value of basic needs from that of a rational and autonomous life (which is perhaps the ultimate value), whereas Gert is unclear about whether goods on his list are meant to be ultimate.

CHALLENGES TO THIS MAPPING OF OPTIONS

Scanlon: Well-being cannot consist of desire satisfaction

Thomas Scanlon has recently argued that well-being cannot ultimately consist of desire satisfaction. According to Scanlon, any plausible desire theory collapses into *hedonism* (which he uses to represent mental statism) or, more likely, a *substantive good theory* (his term for an objective theory), which can include agreeable mental states among the things that make a life go better. A summary of Scanlon's major arguments follows.[26]

What is essential to substantive good theories is that the assessment of well-being involves a substantive judgment about what makes a life go better, one that can conflict with the judgment of the individual whose well-being is in question. In contrast, desire theories defer questions about a person's well-being to her own judgment; the latter, at least, is the touchstone of desire theories, even if most depart from this standard in certain cases. At their core, then, desire theories are subjective accounts. Interestingly, classical hedonism—which takes certain mental states to be the only things of ultimate value—counts as a substantive good theory, since a given individual might have a different understanding of her own well-being. (Later we will see that Scanlon's classification of hedonism is oversimplified.)

In this light, *informed* desire is a major qualification, according to Scanlon. Such desires are ones that are responsive to the salient features of their objects. Asserting the importance of these features in correcting desires marks a radical shift from an unrestricted actual-desire theory, which takes the *satisfaction of actual desire* to enhance well-being. Now we can see why desire theories misplace ultimate value. If a desire theory were adequate, then one's desiring X would provide a basic reason for wanting X to occur. But when this is the case, the reason is either a reason of the sort described by a mental state view or a reason based on some other notion of substantive good—not a reason based simply on the fact of desire.

In many cases, the presence of my desire (say, for fish over tortellini, or to wear a particular necktie) indicates that I expect the outcome to be enjoyable or pleasant; here, the end is the expected experience. In other cases, my desires reflect conclusions based on other kinds of reasons, such as the judgment that something would be in my overall interest. These points help to explain Brandt's plausible thesis that past desires do not provide reasons for action. That as a child I wanted intensely to

---

[26] I draw from Scanlon, "Value, Desire, and Quality of Life," pp. 188–93.

celebrate my fiftieth birthday by going on a roller coaster ride provides no reason at all to do so if, as I approach that birthday, I no longer enjoy roller coasters and have no desire to ride them. There is no reason to think that satisfying that desire will make my life go better. How about future desires? If you agree with the judgment of desirability that a future desire will express, you have reason to promote the satisfaction of that desire now. If, as a young person, you care nothing about old family photographs, but think that in thirty years you will feel differently, you have reason to hold onto them in order to bring yourself pleasure, and avoid sadness, later.

I find some of Scanlon's points compelling. First, corrections of desires *can* represent a major departure from the spirit of subjectivity animating the desire approach in its purest form. When deprivation dampens expectations, creating more modest desires (as with the political prisoner), we tend to think that desire satisfaction does not adequately capture the person's good. If the desire theorist talks of "drying out" these wet desires, we might sense the tug of objective values, such as freedom.

One could reply as follows. The right account speaks to what one *would* desire *in certain ideal conditions,* preserving the authority of one's own desires (even if they have to be cleaned up). Sometimes what we would want (say, if not misinformed) better represents what we "really" want—or better expresses our values—than do our actual desires; our authority or autonomy might be best honored by certain corrections of our actual desires. But this reasonable reply might not be able to handle deeply entrenched desires that would not change in response to cognitive psychotherapy or whatever graces the ideal conditions.

Some theorists might simply allow that a slave with deeply entrenched desires based on lowered expectations would be best off if his actual desires were satisfied. But, if this judgment is to be at all plausible, we must assume that satisfying his actual desires would make the slave *happier* than if we satisfied idealized desires he does not have. It would be very odd to suppose that this person would be happier if we satisfied idealized desires, yet we should make him less happy by honoring his actual, oppression-based desires. Here we feel the pull of mental statism. Increasing this pull is the fact that we usually do feel pleasure or satisfaction when our desires are satisfied (see the analysis of desire in Chapter 6). When desire satisfaction and agreeable experiences part ways, is there any reason to think that the former is a better indicator of well-being—without its also being true that some objective standard of well-being underlies the judgment? This question challenges desire theorists who want to stay in business.

Sumner: Against desire theories and for updated mental statism

L. W. Sumner challenges common views about value-theory options by disputing both the good standing of desire theories and the dismissal of mental statism. In criticizing desire theories, he stresses two difficulties that he believes to be insuperable.[27] First, as *intentional* states, desires can take as their objects states of the world that are remote from the agent. That means one's desire can be satisfied without one's being aware of it. In contrast, one cannot be *enjoying* something without being aware of it. Sumner argues that a desire theory can be a contender only if it adopts the *Experience Requirement*: A state of affairs can make one better or worse off only if it in some way enters one's experience.

Second, desires are (again, unlike enjoyment) *prospective* or directed toward the future. Due to the very nature of desire, there is a temporal gap between desire and fulfillment. Thus, desire satisfaction can disappoint us. I might want to learn the intricacies of chess but then find that it bores me terribly. My desire might have been fully informed and free of mistakes—except for thinking that I would *enjoy* chess. But not only is desire satisfaction not sufficient for improvements in well-being. It is not necessary either:

> Having never heard of bluegrass, I chance on a band playing in the park and find that I like it. Having nursed a longstanding suspicion of the Mediterranean, I am persuaded against my better judgment to holiday there and have a wonderful time.[28]

Sumner recommends dropping desire accounts for an up-dated mental statism.[29] Unlike pain (on his analysis), *suffering* is something one cannot enjoy or be indifferent about, making it a good candidate for an intrinsic evil. And, while pleasure is something whose feeling tone we like, for various reasons (such as guilt, asceticism, or a desire to concentrate on something else) we might not welcome or enjoy it in certain contexts. Let us take *enjoyment* to be our response to a whole situation, to which we bring our values and concerns; its sources extend well beyond pleasure and (as explained later) can be taken to include the objective conditions of our lives. That makes enjoyment a plausible candidate for something that, in itself, makes our lives go better. But all

---

[27] My summary of Sumner's critique is based on arguments presented in his "Welfare, Preference, and Rationality," in Frey and Morris, *Value, Welfare, and Morality*, pp. 78–84.
[28] ibid, pp. 83–84
[29] My summary of Sumner's suggestions for such a theory are based on arguments in "Welfare, Happiness, and Pleasure," *Utilitas* 4 (1992): 199–223.

of this is consistent with Sidgwick's view that the good is desirable consciousness. Yet Nozick's fantasy—in which we can spend our lives in a machine preprogrammed to give us all the mental states that we would like—reminds us that we care about more than our states of mind, suggesting that any *pure* mental statism will be problematic.

Now *happiness*, the condition of being fulfilled or satisfied by the circumstances of one's life, seems a plausible candidate for the good. Maybe it should not be interpreted entirely in terms of mental states. Sumner presents an intriguing possibility: that we take enjoyment (whose presence, and absence of suffering, tend to make us happy) not as something separable from the activities causing the relevant mental states, but as a complex whole that includes those activities plus our subjective response to them.[30] Enjoyment, in this sense, is enjoyment *of* something in the world. You are enjoying playing tennis only if you are playing tennis. Analogously, to suffer *from* losing a job, I must have lost one. This reading of enjoyment and suffering allows us to keep the Experience Requirement without getting stuck in Nozick's machine.

These suggestions for renewing mental statism are very impressive but not free from difficulties. I find compelling Sumner's case that desire satisfaction is neither necessary nor sufficient for enhancing well-being. I agree that we should adopt the Experience Requirement. Now the possibility noted earlier for unpacking enjoyment and suffering also apparently introduces a *Reality Requirement*. In some cases, however, this requirement seems too strict. If a psychotic suffers horribly from imagined demons, his suffering counts negatively although it is not really suffering from demons (since there aren't any). And even if having a wonderful dream about playing tennis isn't as good as enjoying the actual playing of tennis, isn't it still pretty good?[31]

How did the Reality Requirement make its way into this version of mental statism? Again, we care about things other than mental states. But doesn't this mean that we *desire* such things? I suspect that desire has crept back, justifying a requirement whose fulfillment, by definition, cannot affect the quality of our mental states. Also, the phenomenological sides of enjoyment and suffering seem to involve *desirable and undesirable consciousness*, respectively—so that desire apparently creeps back in a second way. We will return to the possible roles of desire in a plausible value theory in the next section.

---

[30] Sumner told me that he does not, ultimately, endorse this move.
[31] Sumner's remarks about the strengths of classical hedonism suggest that he would accept my argument ("Welfare, Happiness, and Pleasure," p. 221), an impression confirmed in correspondence. He has since developed his theory of well-being in *Welfare and Welfarism* (book in progress), ch. 6, but I cannot enter into the details here.

Kagan: Hedonism not basic; better distinctions needed

Shelly Kagan has recently argued that mental statism collapses into either a desire theory or an objective theory, but that a better classification scheme is needed.[32] Kagan begins with hedonism, the familiar version of mental statism, which needs an account of pleasure or pleasantness. Pleasure does not seem to be a *kind* of mental state, or in any ordinary sense a *component* shared by all pleasant experiences. Perhaps it is a *dimension* along which experiences vary—just as loudness is not a kind of sound, or a component of sounds, but a dimension along which sounds vary. If so, what more can be said about the pleasure dimension?

Kagan proposes this analysis: *An experience E occurring at time t to a particular person P is pleasant if and only if (1) P has a desire at t that E occur at t, and (2) P's desire is an immediate response to E's occurrent phenomenal qualities.* (We have noted that desires are future-oriented. *Future,* of course, includes the immediate future. So let us assume a slight revision of (1): P has a desire at t that E continue to occur.) On this analysis, a mental state is pleasant if it is the object of such an immediate desire. The stronger the desire, the more pleasant the mental state—thus varies the pleasure dimension.

But two importantly different interpretations are possible. On a reductivist interpretation, pleasantness *is* strength of the immediate desire. On a nonreductivist interpretation, the desire dimension *helps to identify* pleasantness, but the latter is a psychological reality distinct from the immediate desire. On the reductivist option, I am well off to the extent that I have mental states for which I have the right sort of immediate desire, collapsing hedonism into a type of desire theory: *preference mental statism.* But the nonreductivist can argue that pleasantness, a distinct psychological reality, is objectively good; we might call this *objective mental statism.* Thus, hedonism collapses into a desire theory or an objective theory.

For each option, there is pressure to expand the objects of value. If the hedonist follows the desire route, why should only desires (preferences) *about mental states* matter? The restriction seems arbitrary, revealing pressure to expand in the direction of more traditional desire theories. The objective route also has difficulty justifying its restrictions. If pleasure is a distinct dimension of experiences that is objectively good to have, and not good in virtue of being desired, why think it is the only objective good? Maybe other mental states, on reflection, will seem to be objective goods, transforming the view from hedonism to a more

---

[32] The following summary is based on arguments appearing in "The Limits of Well-Being," pp. 172–89.

general mental statism. And why stop with mental states? Why not a broader objective theory?

Kagan goes on to argue that there are better ways to distinguish value theories than dividing them into mental statism, desire theories, and objective theories. Recall the stranger-on-the-train example. It is implausible to hold that the stranger's success, which you neither know nor even wonder about, enhances your well-being. Any desire theory must be restricted. Here is a possible restriction: Any change in someone's well-being must involve some change in the person. More specifically, one's *mental or bodily properties* must be affected; changes in merely relational properties do not count.

Admittedly, this thesis can be challenged by certain supposed counterexamples. For example, some would insist that if a person has been duped into believing she is loved, then she is less well-off than she would be if really loved (even if all else is equal). Kagan is inclined to think that such examples are mistaken. For how can something really benefit someone if it never "touches" her at all?

The proposed restriction does not imply mental statism unless purely bodily changes are not counted as affecting well-being. If that further restriction is rejected, then certain physical abilities or other bodily properties will count as partly constituting well-being. In any event, the traditional tripartite classification of value theories is misleading. It places mental statism in a separate category, wrongly suggesting its independence from the other options. A more illuminating division, Kagan argues, is between subjective theories (most saliently, desire theories) and objective theories. The subjective–objective choice arises within mental statism and within a cluster of theories drawing the limits of well-being more broadly, beyond facts involving mental states. The tripartite division also misses the fundamental distinction between theories restricting well-being to facts *internal* to the person (as in the foregoing proposed requirement) and theories allowing the relevance of facts *external* to the person (such as whether one is really loved, or facts about one's posthumous reputation). Because the subjective–objective and internal–external distinctions cut across each other, there are four basic types of value theory.

Suppose, as Kagan thinks, that *internalism* is correct: Your well-being is affected only if your body or mind is. This still allows the possibility that external goods matter morally, even if they do not benefit the person to whom they are external. We might be obliged to promote external goods out of *respect* for someone, suggesting that considerations of well-being do not exhaust what is morally important. Maybe not all wrongs are harms. (Several examples appear later.)

I find most of Kagan's arguments compelling. Our work in Chapters

5 and 6 suggested that pleasure and desire are intimately intertwined; as a rough analysis, Kagan's proposal (with our minor revision) is plausible. Seeing pleasure in this way sets up the choices discussed by Kagan. I favor the view that pleasantness—a dimension along which experiences vary—is, roughly, strength of desire for experiences desired for the way they feel, because this interpretation is in accord with the analysis of pleasure in Chapter 5.

If hedonism is updated with this analysis of pleasure, we get preference mental statism. But, again, it is far from clear that only mental states should count. We could honor desires for extra-mental objects, like writing a book (not just having the associated experiences). This move invites the Reality Requirement, which enjoys some intuitive plausibility.

Regarding another issue, I endorse internalism. It makes sense that a person's well-being is affected only if *she* is affected. Internalism makes even more sense in the case of animal well-being, since animals presumably do not care about states of affairs not affecting them. Internalism is easier to accept in the company of Kagan's idea about respect: External goods might be required out of respect, and internal goods, which concern well-being, are not all that matters. Desecrating a corpse, for example, does not harm the corpse or harm the person who died, who no longer exists (at least, not in that body). Desecration shows disrespect for the former person, the wrongness of which *may* be understandable in terms of virtue. And if you maliciously slander a living person, but neither your slander nor its repercussions affect him, he is not worse off. But you have shown disrespect in an objectionable way. (I would say the same about leering or laughing at zoo-confined apes as if they were mere objects of amusement.)

What about the role of desire? Scanlon and Sumner try to put desire theories out of business, but Kagan understands subjective theories in terms of desire. I believe that the good ideas behind traditional mental statism and desire theories depend on one another. Critics of desire theories are right that *mere* desire satisfaction is neither necessary nor sufficient for improved well-being; desire satisfaction is not basic to well-being in the way these theories have held. *Felt* satisfaction (which usually accompanies getting what we want) is often more to the point. But what is satisfaction if not an agreeable mental state? And what is it for something to be agreeable except to be the object of a kind of desire? Now if desires are important, why should only those for mental states count? We do care about other things. To see such a restriction as arbitrary is to move away from preference mental statism toward a view with an extramental component. On the other hand, the restriction isn't totally arbitrary. After all, when your well-being is affected, generally so are your mental states. And anything that does not affect your mental life at all, you don't even know about. Maybe "what you don't know can't hurt you"!

Thus, I think preference mental statism remains a contender. So does a subjectivism—essentially, a mental statism—that adopts a Reality Requirement (probably softening it so that dreams, delusions, and so on can have some value or disvalue). Earlier I accepted the Experience Requirement: What affects our well-being has to affect our experience (though it need not be reducible to our experience). Now internalism, which I also accept, is looser than the Experience Requirement, allowing that merely bodily effects count. Let us stipulate that the contending *reality-grounded subjectivism* adopt the Experience Requirement, which is intuitively plausible and more in keeping with the mental-statist flavor of the account.

Flexible objective theories are consistent with internalism but not the Experience Requirement. Autonomous living and the quality of one's mental life will count, since the view is flexible. So will certain experience-independent conditions of the individual, perhaps including bodily functioning, relationships with others, and accomplishments. Now any plausible item on an objective theory's list will be something we *tend* to find satisfying. This brings flexible objective theories a step closer to the reality-grounded subjectivism.

According to this critique of value-theory offerings, then, we are left with these options: (1) preference mental statism; (2) a subjective view adopting the Experience Requirement and a qualified Reality Requirement; and (3) a flexible objective theory adopting internalism. In practice, there are probably only modest differences between (1) and (2), since we are normally pretty aware of our circumstances (unlike someone in Nozick's machine). Thus, hereafter, I will simply place (1) and (2) together under the rubric of plausible subjective theories. But we have been considering only humans. Let us turn now to animals.

INTERSPECIFIC VALUE

Why only sentient beings have interests

Prudential value theory applies to beings who can be better or worse off, beings who have a welfare, "sake," or good (in some sense relevant to morality). In other words, value theory applies to beings with interests. Which beings have interests? Following numerous theorists, I maintain that only beings who are actually, potentially, or formerly sentient—*sentient beings* for short—have interests. (Maybe not all of this group has interests; I am not sure that potentially sentient and formerly sentient beings do. What is important for present purposes is the basic link to sentience.[33]) Work in earlier chapters made it clear that sentient animals have interests, such as avoiding aversive feelings (see Chapter 5). But why *only* sentient animals? It is most reasonable to believe that only they have interests because this thesis coheres far better with other beliefs in reflective equilibrium than does the thesis that nonsentient beings have interests.

That only sentient animals have interests is enormously common-sensical. Such animals can experience aversive states such as pain, discomfort, distress, fear, anxiety, and suffering, although some sentient animals might not be able to experience all of these. That these states are aversive means that they are not liked, preferred, or enjoyed—just the opposite, they motivate animals to escape conditions causing them. Now nonsentient animals, by definition, cannot feel anything, so they cannot have aversive states. Nor can they have any other experience. Nothing matters to them; they care about nothing. They have no concerns or desires.

On the other hand, common parlance does not unambiguously support the sentience requirement. Sumner puts the matter well:

> Much of our welfare vocabulary does apply to all living things with no evident strain; thus we speak easily of what is good or bad, harmful or beneficial, for bees and bacteria, trees and toadstools. There is no reason to think that these categories apply meaningfully only to creatures who are conscious or sentient. On the other hand, some of our categories do not generalize so easily, among them the central notions of welfare, well-being, and interest. (There are animal welfare groups but no plant welfare groups.)[34]

It sounds fairly natural to speak of harm to a plant, but not to speak of its welfare. If the sentience requirement is right, while it might not be incorrect to speak of what is good or bad, beneficial or harmful, to plants and nonsentient animals, these terms are not correctly applied to these beings *in any sense relevant to morality*. But this claim needs further arguing.

Many of our ethical intuitions are nicely accounted for by the sentience requirement. Kicking dogs, whipping horses, and otherwise hurting sentient animals is clearly prima facie wrong. To justify any such action would require a special explanation—say, the need to pre-

---

[33] See, e.g., Leonard Nelson, *A System of Ethics* (New Haven: Yale University Press, 1956), pp. 136–44; Joel Feinberg, "Human Duties and Animal Rights," in his *Rights, Justice, and the Bounds of Liberty* (Princeton: Princeton University Press, 1980), p. 194; Singer, *Animal Liberation*, pp. 7–8; Sumner, "Two Theories of the Good," pp. 7–12; and Sapontzis, *Morals, Reason, and Animals*, pp. 73–87.

[34] *Welfare and Welfarism*, ch. 3

vent the crazed dog from killing a child. But pulling weeds, tearing up the grass playing football, breaking stones for fun, and killing animals that are indisputably insentient (say, amoebas in a petri dish) generally do not seem even prima facie wrong, unless the actions affect the interests of sentient beings. It would be neurotic to worry about whether running through the park harmed the blades of grass underfoot.

Admittedly, the sentience requirement does not tidily account for *all* of our ethical intuitions in this area. We tend to think that there would be something wrong with gratuitously cutting down a magnificent oak, even if no sentient animals (including humans) were negatively affected. We tend to think that one should not destroy a great natural wonder, like the Grand Canyon, even if one were the last sentient being on earth and had a good-sized bomb. It is interesting to note how many such intuitions concern beauty and magnificence. Do we project the value of *appreciating* beauty onto *objects* of beauty? Well, many persons feel some compunction about killing ugly cockroaches, even persons who (like me) believe they lack sentience. (Might the compunction come from not being completely sure that they are insentient?)

While some common ethical convictions seem to lean in the direction of attributing interests to nonsentient beings, I believe that the bulk of our ethical convictions are better accounted for if we require sentience. Moreover, many of the recalcitrant beliefs may lose their intuitive grip when alternative explanations for their presence are offered (for example, that it is difficult to imagine destroying natural wonders without affecting any sentient beings' interests). Their power is further diminished when it becomes apparent that no satisfying theoretical account supports them, as I intend to show later. As argued in Chapter 2, we must not be lax intuitionists ready to pander to all of our pretheoretical convictions. We should strive for various theoretical virtues, including argumentative support and global illumination, which require a developed account of prudential value.

Some have argued that all and only living beings have *a good of their own* and therefore interests. Robin Attfield defends this thesis in what may be the clearest and best argued work in environmental ethics.[35] More specifically, Attfield argues that all living creatures have a general "interest in flourishing after their kind by developing their own specific capacities."[36] But the fact that nonsentient beings lack the capacity for enjoyments and pleasure justifies granting them *less* moral significance:

---

[35] *The Ethics of Environmental Concern,* 2nd ed. (Athens, GA: University of Georgia Press, 1991). See also Paul W. Taylor, *Respect for Nature* (Princeton: Princeton University Press, 1986); and Gary E. Varner, "Biological Functions and Biological Interests," *Southern Journal of Philosophy* 28 (1990): 251–70.

[36] *The Ethics of Environmental Concern,* p. 168

[Plants and bacteria] could have a moral standing and yet have an almost infinitesimal moral significance, so that even large aggregations of them did not outweigh the significance of sentient beings in cases of conflict. It could be that their moral significance only makes a difference when all other claims and considerations are equal (or nonexistent).[37]

That all living things have some moral standing is believed by Attfield and like-minded theorists to explain many of our considered beliefs (including some canvassed earlier in this text).

What are we to make of such views? Note, first, that objective value theories for humans, by dropping the Experience Requirement, open the door for a view like Attfield's. Dropping the Experience Requirement means that some things may affect a person's good without affecting her consciousness. Well, why can't there be beings whose good is *in each case* affected without their consciousness being affected (since they have no consciousness)? If a slave's well-being can be lowered by lack of freedom even if (due to lowered expectations) his situation does not make him less happy, why can't a fly be harmed by being put in a bottle and thereby prevented from doing what flies are meant to do?

While objective theories open the door to nonsentient beings, this door should be shut. The concession that while nonsentient beings have standing, their interests are much less weighty than those of sentient animals, hints that something is theoretically amiss. We can put pressure on this position.

A natural question is, "If plants and bacteria have interests, why not artifacts like tractors and natural objects like canyons?" Attfield asserts that only living things have *a good of their own*. The claim that nonliving things lack a good of their own might seem plausible in the case of artifacts, since they were made with *instrumental* purposes in mind. Of course, the fact that something *has* instrumental value doesn't mean it lacks a good of its own—think of teachers, pets, and teachers' pets. And through breeding and genetic engineering, we can *create* sentient beings for instrumental pruposes. So even being made for others' purposes does not disqualify something from having a good of its own. It is unclear to me why cars and buildings lack a good of their own, if having one does not require sentience. And if sentience is not required, the claim that ecosystems, waterfalls, and canyons have a good of their own is at least as strong. For that matter, why not blackholes, mud puddles, and positrons?[38]

For the sake of argument, suppose we were convinced that only living creatures were serious candidates for having interests—perhaps

---

[37] ibid, p. 154
[38] This paragraph bears the influence of Sumner, *Welfare and Welfarism*, ch. 3.

for reasons connected with biological functioning.[39] The claim that they have an interest in *flourishing after their kind* suggests a *natural-kinds metaphysic* and a *perfectionistic value theory*. Regarding the metaphysic, if the interests of a living thing are tied to its *kind*, why don't nonliving things have interests? Surely, if there are natural kinds for living things, there are natural kinds for natural nonliving objects. But there may be good reason to doubt the natural-kinds metaphysic, as suggested by Sumner:

> Even if we had adequate rules for determining what is to count as a kind, it is obvious that every particular thing belongs to many, perhaps infinitely many, such kinds. I am a human being, to be sure, but I am also a spatio-temporal object, an organism, an animal, a vertebrate, a biped, a parent, a philosopher, a baseball fan, and heaven knows what else. . . . Is my level of perfection [or flourishing] to be determined by just one favored standard? If so, how is this to be selected? Or is it to be determined by all of them?[40]

The perfectionistic value theory is also problematic. Why think flourishing after one's kind is a better measure of well-being than a more subjective standard? The two standards can conflict. Now maybe human flourishing would be explicated in a partly subjective way, reducing conflicts. We are, after all, autonomous and sentient (as well as other kinds of) creatures. But perfectionism seems to gain plausibility here—in effect, by changing into a flexible objective view—only by relinquishing the natural-kinds metaphysic. For it is doubtful that human beings constitute a unique kind that accounts for the plurality of items, including subjective ones, likely to be on an objective list.

This might be disputed. It might be claimed that our unique kind is that of *Homo sapiens*—a social animal with the capacity for autonomy, creativity, knowledge, and enjoyment. But species evolve gradually. If *Homo sapiens* is a unique kind, did our hominid ancestors jump from kind to kind—say, from *Homo habilis* to *Homo erectus,* and from *Homo erectus* to *Homo sapiens?* If so, at what points in the gradual evolution process did these jumps occur? No possible answer seems credible. Or were there almost innumerable natural kinds represented along the way, say, a new one for each mutation? If so, then do not today's *Homo sapiens* represent many different kinds? Understanding humans as a unique natural kind does not fit comfortably with the facts of evolution. That goes for other animals as well.

The case that certain nonsentient beings have interests has not been established. Without the support of a convincing account of prudential

---

[39] See Varner, "Biological Functions and Biological Interests."
[40] "Two Theories of the Good," p. 9

value, this position appears less coherent than one that adopts the common-sensical sentience requirement.

Two judgments creating a puzzle

All and only sentient animals have interests. But what interests do different sentient animals have? (For brevity, I will often just say *animals*, although it is important to remember that the referents are sentient.) Do they have an interest in staying alive? As we will see, this question quickly leads to a puzzle.

In ordinary circumstances, animals have an interest in staying alive, at least because the process of dying typically involves aversive mental states such as pain, fear, and suffering. But what if dying occurs in the absence of such mental states, as when an animal is unwittingly and painlessly killed in her sleep? Does she have, other things being equal, a life interest that is thwarted by death? The only plausible answer in the case of normal humans is "yes." If I died tonight without my knowledge and without any diminishing of the quality of my experiences, I would ipso facto be harmed to a great degree. All of my opportunities—for future enjoyments, accomplishments, loving relationships, whatever has ultimate value—would be squelched. Unless very good reason is given to abandon the intuition that, ordinarily, a normal human being is harmed by unwitting, painless death, a plausible value theory needs to accommodate it.

That's the paradigm case. How is it explained? By the fact that humans ordinarily have a very powerful desire to live? Well, viable value theories include subjective theories adopting the Experience Requirement and flexible objective theories. Neither seems to allow that a desire whose fulfillment reaches out beyond experience (remember, unwitting death) counts as *basic*. There are several possible directions in which to go. A subjective view needs to allow that opportunities for future satisfaction, enjoyments, and the like matter in their own right.[41] This option requires qualifying, or liberally interpreting, the Experience Requirement: Losing the possibility of future experiences counts as affecting experience in the required way. An objective view can either hold that opportunities for future goods count, or allow that conscious life (or just life) itself has intrinsic value. (The value of life on either account can, of course, be overwhelmed by evils faced in particular cases, such as the prospect of terrible suffering.)

---

[41] While it is unclear whether Regan's value theory is subjective, objective, or mixed, it understands the harm of death in terms of lost opportunities (*The Case for Animal Rights*, pp. 99–103). Sapontzis defends this opportunities thesis within a subjective theory (*Morals, Reason, and Animals*, pp. 159–75).

Do animals have life interests? Suppose healthy puppies with good prospects for satisfying lives are painlessly killed. Intuitively, it seems that the puppies are harmed and that the harm has to do with lost opportunities. Similar judgments in parallel cases involving apes and dolphins would seem at least as secure. Moreover, as just suggested (but see also the subsection, "Deny that Death Harms . . ."), *any viable way of accounting for the judgment that painless death ordinarily harms humans will imply that many animals have life interests.* For animals, too, can be deprived of future satisfactions, goods, or conscious life.

It is noteworthy that the strength of our conviction that death can harm an animal might vary depending on the sort of animal involved. Indeed, this brings us to the second judgment setting up our puzzle: Assuming that some animals are harmed by death, death seems to harm some morally considerable beings more than others. Consider Regan's famous lifeboat case:

> There are five survivors: four normal adults and a dog. The boat has room enough only for four. Someone must go or else all will perish. Who should it be? . . . [T]he harm that death is, is a function of the opportunities for satisfaction it forecloses, and no reasonable person would deny that the death of any of the four humans would be a greater prima facie loss, and thus a greater prima facie harm, than would be true in the case of the dog.[42]

Later we will consider Regan's rationale for the judgment. For now, only the judgment is important: A dog is harmed less by death than is a normal human in ordinary circumstances. This is a very strong conviction (although we must be mindful of the possibility of pro-human bias).[43]

Now for the problem. It seems very plausible to assert that *(1) death harms many nonhuman animals* (maybe all sentient ones—why would some be excluded?), but also that *(2) death ordinarily harms normal representatives of some species more than normal representatives of other species.* (I will generally drop the awkward "normal representatives" qualification.) Assertion (2) is strengthened by the intuition that chimps lose more from death than do, say, squirrels; there is no reason to think that differences appear only between humans and other animals. The problem is that it is *extremely* difficult to account for both (1) and (2) in a coherent way, as we will see next. Why does that matter?

---

[42] *The Case for Animal Rights*, p. 324
[43] A distinct, even stronger intuition is that it is morally worse, generally, to kill a human than to kill a dog.

Why this indicates a fundamental problem in value theory

Let us assume that there is a prima facie duty not to harm that applies, naturally enough, to all who can be harmed. (Here and hereafter, I mean *harm* in a morally relevant sense, not in the broader sense in which flowers can be harmed; similarly for *benefit*.) Then the foregoing assertion (1) implies that we have a prima facie duty not to *kill* many animals.[44] But then, unless (2) is vindicated, our prima facie duty not to kill these animals will be just as strong as our prima facie duty not to kill humans (setting aside certain social considerations that will be picked up later). This is very hard to believe; even Regan's strong animal-rights view does not go this far. This egalitarian thesis is even more difficult to believe in the case of animals considerably "lower" than dogs, such as mice, birds, lizards, and salmon. Then again, maybe there is an argument that would justify limiting the scope of (1) to some subset of sentient animals.

A principle of equal consideration—granting equal moral weight to relevantly similar interests—was defended in Chapter 3. If a human and lizard lose equally much from death, they have relevantly similar life interests meriting equal moral weight. It is clear how ethics needs prudential value theory here. For A's interest X and B's interest Y to be relevantly similar, A and B must have, in some sense, *the same thing at stake* with X and Y. Value theory provides criteria for when the same thing is at stake, by clarifying what harms and what benefits individuals, and how much.

The reason that life might differ in value for different individuals is that, whether or not life has any ultimate or intrinsic prudential value, it has great *instrumental* value. (Maybe conscious life is what is crucial, but I will ignore this complication, not least because one must be alive to be consciously alive.) Life is the precondition of nearly everything that has ultimate value for individuals. I say "nearly" because in certain cases, life can obstruct the realization of important values, such as the exercise of autonomy and freedom from suffering. Ordinarily, life has great instrumental value; the possibility that the ultimate goods that life allows vary in value indicates the possibility of relevantly different life interests.

There are also other goods that may vary in instrumental value in the way that life might. Two major examples are *freedom* (in the negative sense of absence of external constraints) and *functioning*. These are not

---

[44] It is often naively thought that painlessly killing animals eliminates all possible harm to them. This view is suggested in Department of Health and Human Services, *Guide for the Care and Use of Laboratory Animals* (National Institutes of Health Publication No. 85–23, 1985). This document regards the causing of suffering, but not killing, as demanding justification.

quite as sweeping in instrumental scope as life is. One might be able to have meaningful relationships, live to some degree autonomously, and accomplish things, with significant satisfactions, even if one is in prison or has lost some important bodily functions. Nevertheless, freedom and functioning are very important instrumental goods, permitting much of what we value. If the goods that my freedom permits are, on the whole, more prudentially valuable than what a bird's freedom permits, then equal consideration does not confer equal moral weight on my freedom and the bird's.

Most leaders in animal ethics have stated, or implied, that equal consideration does not imply that all lives are of equal prudential value.[45] None, to my knowledge, has noted that analogous moves might be made with other major instrumental goods, such as freedom and functioning.[46] For convenience, let us call all such comparative claims, made in the context of assuming equal consideration, *life moves* (understanding that life is only the most sweeping of the instrumental goods covered by the term).

I have the audacity to suggest that whether life moves can be justified is the most fundamental problem of interspecific value theory. As noted in Chapter 3, leaders in animal ethics tend to agree—correctly—that the avoidance of aversive mental states (taken in terms of aversiveness, not instrumentally) is a relevantly similar interest, no matter who has it: "Pain is pain." Equal consideration requires giving equal moral weight to this interest and (as explained in Chapter 9) doing so has far-reaching practical consequences. But we do not have much of a value theory covering animals if we do not know what to say about the comparative values of lives and other instrumental goods. And any reasonably complete animal ethics—even one denying equal consideration—depends on having such a value theory, which will underlie assumptions about the nature of harm and how to compare harms. One of the most common harms that we inflict on animals today is that of killing them. To get clearer on how much harm is caused by killing, or by death in general, it would seem helpful to approach the question (in part) comparatively, using the more familiar human case as a point of departure. So let us

---

[45] In addition to the works of philosophers cited later, see Feinberg, *Rights, Justice, and the Bounds of Liberty*, p. 200; Christina Hoff, "Immoral and Moral Uses of Animals," *New England Journal of Medicine* 302 (1980): 115–18; L. W. Sumner, "Animal Welfare and Animal Rights," *Journal of Medicine and Philosophy* 13 (1988), pp. 169–70; and Donald VanDeVeer, "Interspecific Justice and Animal Slaughter," in Harlan B. Miller and William H. Williams (eds.), *Ethics and Animals* (Clifton, NJ: Humana, 1983), pp. 147–62.
[46] I noted this possibility in "The Distinction Between Equality in Moral Status and Deserving Equal Consideration," *Between the Species* 7 (1991): 73–77.

turn to several attempts to handle the puzzle posed by claims (1) and (2), some of which try to justify life moves.

Attempts to manage the puzzle

1. Deny that death harms those who lack a concept of death. One way to manage the puzzle is to deny that death harms individuals who lack a concept of death. This move tries to reduce the tension between (1) and (2) by greatly limiting the scope of (1). Proponents of this approach assume that few animals have the concept of death. They also assume that one must have this concept in order to have a desire not to die, and that one must have such a desire in order to have a life interest.

But it is very difficult to determine which animals have the concept of death. Not only is this issue difficult empirically; conceptually, it is not at all clear what having this concept amounts to. One might say that having a concept of death involves having a sense of oneself existing over time—with the idea that this excludes most animals. But even "lower" vertebrates can experience fear (see Chapter 5), which involves perceiving something as threatening, which in turn involves some sense of oneself as subject to future harm (implying existence over time). If a more robust sort of self-awareness is required, the specific requirement needs to be defended. (We saw in Chapter 7 that self-awareness admits of different kinds and degrees.) This empirical and conceptual uncertainty places proponents of this approach on slippery ground.

Moreover, our examination of value-theory options established that desire satisfaction per se is not constitutive of well-being. Thus, as noted earlier, it is *not* simply thwarting the desire to live that constitutes the harm of death. How might proponents of this approach respond? Perhaps as follows:

> Notwithstanding the niceties of our examination of value-theory options, the fact that certain individuals care deeply about staying alive must have some weight. It would help to explain our intuition that killing humans is ordinarily a monstrous business, whereas the painless killing of, say, chickens does not seem problematic at all. We might allow that certain animals—surely this is arbitrary, but let us say apes, monkeys, elephants, dolphins, and other whales—appear to have a decent grasp of death and probably care about avoiding it. That they are harmed by death is not implausible. The criterion of caring about staying alive does a reasonable job of accounting for our beliefs.

The idea that caring deeply about staying alive helps to ground a life interest has considerable intuitive plausibility. Accommodating some nonhuman animals strengthens this position; it is hard to believe that chimps, for example, have no life interest while humans do. Still, this position is untenable.

First, we cannot forget the difficulties associated with deciding who has a desire to avoid death; stating the argument in terms of caring does not seem to change the issue. At least it seems appropriate to place an onus on the defender of this view, such that he or she must do the following: (1) explain what having a desire to live in the relevant sense amounts to; (2) explain why having this desire in this sense is the crucial threshold (our value-theoretic conclusions notwithstanding); and (3) provide a reasonable amount of empirical evidence that certain animals but not others meet the criteria.

Second, the intuition that caring about staying alive is relevant to life interests can be accounted for without claiming that the mere satisfaction of this desire has intrinsic value. In most cases of human death, dying is not unwitting and painless. We succumb to cancer or some other disease and suffer greatly in the process. *Our caring about staying alive is part of the reason we suffer.* We have many unpleasant feelings as a result of wanting to hang on to life, such as sadness, anger, dread, perhaps a sense of isolation. Even in relatively "clean" cases of death— such as dying in a plane crash, or drowning after being pushed off Regan's lifeboat—significant suffering must be the norm. Thus, in ordinary circumstances, our caring deeply about staying alive helps to ground our life interests, since this caring usually means misery when we are losing the battle against death. So the strong desire for life provides a *nonbasic* ground of our life interests *in normal cases*. From a subjective or flexible-objective view, *the quality of experiences* to which this caring is connected is a *basic* ground of our life interests (i.e., a ground that appeals directly to the terms of the value theory, such as enjoyment and suffering).

So far no connection has been established between desiring life and being harmed in the exceptional cases of unwitting, painless death. Plausible subjective views include the Experience Requirement, which we interpreted such that death, by ending experiences, counts as affecting them. This covers even cases of unwitting, painless death. In such cases, desire satisfaction is not basic. Opportunities for experience are basic. And this way of understanding the harm of death opens the door to many more animals than the present approach was supposed to include. Plausible objective views count either opportunities for future goods, or conscious life itself, as having value and as explaining the harm of death. Neither interpretation shuts out animals.

Moreover, the present strategy for managing our puzzle has some odd implications. Maybe it is not odd to say that a chicken is unharmed by painless death. But recall the puppies. Whatever animals are included in the tight circle of life-desirers in the present approach, dogs are presumably out.[47] But, intuitively, a painless, unwitting death would seem to be a loss for a contented, healthy dog—in virtue of lost opportunities for the satisfactions and activities characterizing her life.

Consider certain humans as well. On any robust set of criteria for having a desire for life, criteria that would exclude most animals, human infants would not qualify. It strikes me as very odd to assert that a healthy baby with reasonable prospects for a good life is not harmed by having her opportunities stolen by death. Some will reply that the baby's *potential* distinguishes her from most animals. But that reply will not do, because it amounts to abandoning the claim that desires ground life interests and adopting an opportunities-based view. Others will simply allow the implication: Normal human babies with decent prospects are not harmed by unwitting, painless death. One wonders what they would say about certain other humans. Consider a moderately retarded child who, for whatever reason, fails the criteria for having a desire for life, but whose life has a decent balance of enjoyments over suffering. Do his opportunities not have prudential weight?

Finally, let us remember that desire theorists are wrong that the mere desire to live is the basis for life interests even in the paradigmatic case of normal adult human beings. Thus, they cannot vindicate even the idea that such humans are harmed by unwitting, painless death. To make room for that conviction would vindicate the thesis that many animals have life interests—throwing a great deal of weight on the comparative thesis (2).

2. Quantitative solutions within subjective accounts. The first approach concentrated on claim (1), arguing, unsuccessfully, that very few animals have what it takes to have a life interest. The next few approaches grant that many animals have life interests. The part of the puzzle on which they focus is (2), the claim that death harms some animals more than others. Their strategy is to vindicate this claim.

As noted earlier, many leaders in animal ethics have maintained that lives can differ in prudential value. Specifically, they have held that the lives of mentally more sophisticated beings are generally more valuable than those of mentally less sophisticated beings. While not implausible, this thesis requires defense. But none of these theorists has defended it in any depth. Thus, it is often unclear how to interpret their *life moves*.

---

[47]See, e.g., Allen E. Buchanan and Dan W. Brock, *Deciding for Others: The Ethics of Surrogate Decision Making* (Cambridge: Cambridge University Press, 1989), pp. 197–99.

Sometimes they use quantitative language, which seems to fit well with subjective views: A life with more of whatever experiences have value could be argued to have greater prudential value than a life with less of these experiences.

Recall Regan's defense of his life move. The harm of death is said to be "a function of the opportunities for satisfaction it forecloses, and [clearly] the death of any of the four humans would be a greater prima facie loss, and thus a greater prima facie harm, than would be true in the case of the dog." By speaking of opportunities for satisfaction, Regan's assertion sounds like a quantitative claim within a subjective theory. Another seemingly quantitative claim comes from James Rachels: "[W]hen a mentally sophisticated being dies, there are more reasons why the death is a bad thing."[48] Perhaps these reasons are connected with opportunities for satisfaction.

In what way, exactly, are more opportunities thwarted by a human death than by an animal death? Perhaps the claim should be taken literally: Human lives generally contain, *numerically,* more opportunities for satisfaction than do animal lives. But this claim is problematic. First, it needs a nonarbitrary way of *individuating* opportunities (or interests, or reasons why death is bad) to support the quantitative claim. This method of individuating need not be very precise, just precise enough to support the comparison definitively.

Second, the approach neglects the complication that there are some opportunities for satisfaction that certain animals have but that humans lack. For example, death robs the dolphin, but not the human, of the pleasures of echolocation (sonar), and robs canines, but not us, of an immense olfactory world. At the very least, the tenability of this approach depends on an extraordinarily complex task. For it must determine for normal members of a particular species—not nonhuman animals generally!—which satisfaction opportunities they have that humans lack, and it must compare that number to the number of such opportunities possessed by humans but not members of that species. And how do we know in advance which side will have more?

Our literal interpretation of Regan's statement may have been uncharitable. Instead of *more opportunities* for satisfaction, maybe we should think of opportunities for *more satisfaction,* an idea that better fits a plausible subjective theory. Rather than getting hung up on the problem of individuating opportunities or anything else, we might interpret *more* in a natural, mental-statist way. We often speak of more, or less, satisfaction, enjoyment, or pleasure. The claim, then, is that human lives

---

[48] "Do Animals Have a Right to Life?," in Miller and Williams, *Ethics and Animals,* p. 254

typically contain a greater balance of attractive mental states over aversive ones than animal lives contain.

Sapontzis spells out the position this way:

> It is often claimed that humans can experience enjoyment, fulfillment, distress, and frustration of a greater variety and sublety than can animals. The animals' range of experience is (supposedly) limited by their limited intelligence to matters of sensation, digestion, and reproduction, while, thanks to our superior intellect, we are capable of appreciating fine art, conceptual matters, moral fulfillment, flights of imagination, remembrance and anticipation, and so on in addition to what animals can experience.[49]

While this position is more natural and intelligible than the previous one, it proves highly problematic upon inspection.

Sapontzis' criticisms explain why. First, as noted in Chapter 5, available evidence suggests that animals are capable of a much wider variety of feelings than we have traditionally granted them, and most differences are differences of degree. Moreover, again, many animals are capable of sources of satisfaction of which we are incapable. Singer argues that humans' enriched sense of time allows a greater range of feelings, including hope and regret. If true, this might suggest that animal feelings are *more intense* than ours:

> [T]he distress and frustration experienced by a human prisoner of war can be alleviated by recollections of past freedom and hope for future release, while a dog trapped in a laboratory cage (supposedly) has no recollection or hope to ease its distress and frustration. Similarly, humans are notorious for not getting full enjoyment from present pleasures because they have fixated on past sorrows or are fretting about future difficulties, while animals, like dogs playing on the beach, do not seem to have their present enjoyment thus diluted. Now, if animal feelings are more intense than ours, then this extra intensity could counterbalance the extra feelings our extensive temporal capacity provides us.[50]

On the other hand, as Mill argued, if humans' greater mental complexity really did permit greater ranges and depths of satisfaction, humans should also be capable of more extensive and deeper *suffering*.[51] On a subjective view, this capacity would count negatively for the value

---

[49] *Morals, Reason, and Animals*, p. 218
[50] ibid, p. 220. In this discussion (pp. 220–21), Sapontzis cites Peter Singer, *Practical Ethics* (Cambridge: Cambridge University Press, 1979), ch. 4; and, on the possibility of animals' having more intense feelings, Bernard Rollin, *Animal Rights and Human Morality* (Buffalo: Prometheus, 1981), p. 33.
[51] John Stuart Mill, *Utilitarianism*, George Sher, ed. (Indianapolis, IN: Hackett, 1979; first published 1861), p. 9

of a life. So let us suppose that the subjective theorist can make the comparative claim stick for certain animals. Maybe we cannot say that human life typically includes more satisfaction than dolphin, dog, and eagle life due to their special sensitivities that we lack and numerous other complications. But, surely, we can confidently claim that our lives have more satisfaction than, say, snake and goldfish lives. Even granting a great deal of uncertainty about the specifics of different animals' lives, reptiles and fish are so neurologically simple that we can safely assume that their mental lives are far less lively than our own. Let us grant this eminently reasonable-sounding claim. It doesn't seem to help the subjective theorist, because humans are obviously capable of far more suffering than are snakes and goldfish.

To see it from another angle, subjective theorists can embrace this line of argument in justifying their life moves, but, apparently, only at a serious cost: They would seem to have to allow that a human life characterized by somewhat more suffering than satisfaction has *less* prudential value than the contented life of a snake! The lifeboat move apparently works but only for happy human beings in comparison to relatively primitive vertebrates. I suspect that few subjective theorists have this sort of result in mind.

It might be objected that I have wrongly assumed that the quantitative measure appropriate to the present sort of life move is *aggregative* rather than *distributive*. A distributive measure of total well-being could give *greater weight* to "higher highs" (the greater satisfactions or joys available to mentally complex beings) than to "lower lows" (the profound sufferings of which such beings are capable).[52] Such a weighting would help to justify life moves, since the lives of normal humans and perhaps some other "higher" animals would receive higher scores. While intuitively attractive, this move seems ad hoc and arbitrary. Without a compelling argument to support this type of quantitative scale, it looks suspiciously like a product of species bias. It seems analogous to the claim of an unorthodox "utilitarian" that in maximizing the good, we should give greater weight to the good of members of *his or her* group. (Further reflections later on, however, may put quantitative life moves back in business.)

3. Solutions appealing to hypothetical choice. Solutions appealing to hypothetical choice also attempt to vindicate claim (2), but they are less clearly attached to either subjective or objective theories. Mill is famous for arguing that some pleasures may be qualitatively superior to others, deserving greater weight in measuring well-being.[53] The pleasures of

---

[52] Sumner pointed out this possibility to me.
[53] *Utilitarianism*, p. 8

cultivating one's mind and character have a higher quality than those of getting drunk and fornicating. His value theory is notoriously open to interpretations covering both subjective and objective ground. But his stated basis for the thesis of differential quality is the choice or preference of individuals well acquainted with the options: "Of two pleasures, if there be one to which all or almost all who have experience of both give a decided preference, irrespective of any feeling of moral obligation to prefer it, that is the more desirable pleasure."[54] Applying this standard to the issue of the comparative value of whole lives, he states that "[f]ew human creatures would consent to be changed into any of the lower animals for a promise of the fullest allowance of the beast's pleasures. . . . "[55]

Mill's conclusion is noteworthy for several reasons. First, he apparently distinguishes himself from the quantitative approach by asserting the superiority of human life even where an animal's life is assumed to be chock full of the pleasures of which the animal is capable; he did not limit the comparison to cases in which the humans would be relatively happy.

Second, if Mill's use of *few* is taken literally, his statement leaves open the possibility that some humans might prefer an animal's life. No doubt some rare humans—even ones who are not miserable—would. There are two ways to interpret Mill at this point. We could understand him to assume that even the lives of these recalcitrant humans have more value than animal lives; he did base the superiority of certain pleasures on the preference of all *or almost all*. In that case, there is a problem of justification (one facing objective theories generally): Why isn't the recalcitrant human's preference authoritative in her own case (especially when the criteria for superiority are supposedly based on preferences)?

On the other hand, we could read Mill as liberally allowing that the eccentric's life is *not* more prudentially valuable than that of an animal with whom she would trade places. That seems consistent with much of the spirit of subjectivism, but it has an implication that some (not all) would find troubling: The lives of certain *cognitively normal* humans who are not miserable are less prudentially valuable than those of some animals. For those who would find this implication damaging, the damage it causes is mitigated by the fact that it would probably apply to very few actual humans.

Speaking of actual humans, Mill's approach has another curious feature. In a certain sense, no human is competently acquainted with both human pleasures *and* animal pleasures. True, we must use our

---

[54] ibid
[55] ibid, p. 9

imaginations and extrapolate from our experiences as best we can. We can have some idea of how pigs feel eating, resting, and having sex, based on our experiences. But the limits of our experience are significant regarding certain details, a point noted earlier in connection with the canine olfactory world and the dolphin's echolocation. Even in the case of a pig, we can't simply imagine ourselves wallowing in the mud to judge the desirability of this pleasure; we really have to imagine *being pigs*, with thick skins and other pig characteristics, wallowing around. This point may seem obvious. But it is easy in practice to underestimate the desirability of certain experiences as a result of not trying hard enough to grasp what they are like for those having them.

Singer is clearer than Mill that the choice in question is a *hypothetical* one, requiring imagination and not just a comparison of certain experiences that we have already had. He imagines that special powers allow him to live the life of a human, literally transform him into a horse and live that life for a while, before entering a third, speciesless state in which he can remember and reflect on his human and equine experiences. Offered the chance to live another life, that of a human or a horse living about as well as either can live on this planet, he suggests that he (and we) would choose the human existence, implying a value judgment about the respective values of these lives.[56] Singer tentatively concludes as follows:

> In general it does seem that the more highly developed the conscious life of the being, the greater the degree of self-awareness and rationality and the broader the range of possible experiences, the more one would prefer that kind of life, if one were choosing between it and a being at a lower level of awareness.[57]

How well does this life move hold up?

While intriguing, this proposal has significant difficulties. First, it has Mill's problem of clear-thinking persons with oddball preferences. Such a person is either wrong or not wrong. If she is wrong, I suspect that the only way to defend that judgment is to move to an objective theory, obscuring or perhaps eliminating the role of choice. (Maybe we could

[56] *Practical Ethics*, 2nd ed. (Cambridge: Cambridge University Press, 1993), pp. 105–7
[57] ibid, p. 107. In the following chapter (ch. 5), Singer discusses the ethics of taking animal life and places great weight on whether the animals in question are *persons*. The discussion seems terribly confused, partly due to the dubious role given to personhood, but also because he takes personhood to be based on rationality and self-consciousness, and he apparently takes self-consciousness to be all-or-nothing (or nearly so). He writes "[i]t is notoriously difficult to establish when another being is self-conscious" and wonders whether dogs and cats and perhaps "lower" animals are persons (p. 119)! His treatment of self-consciousness entirely misses the fact that it comes both in degrees and in different forms, as we saw in Chapter 7.

make sense of her being wrong within subjectivism. But why would one have an informed preference for an animal life that offers less satisfaction than one's actual life, as implied by the idea of a wrong choice within subjectivism?) If she is not wrong, then, again, we cannot assert that *her* life is more valuable than that of a horse, an implication that some will find unpalatable.

Additionally, Singer's approach might not even be intelligible. To avoid human bias, I must really get into the horse's hoofs in conducting the thought-experiment. But to be sufficiently neutral, I must, presumably, not bring anything peculiar to my mental life into my new evaluations. But it is not obvious that evaluations can even be made from a standpoint of such radical neutrality. It is not enough to imagine being a horse having equine experiences (no minor epistemological feat). I must compare these experiences to a human's. Is there enough of a self—indeed any self—left to make comparisons? On what basis are they to be made, if none of my particular preferences can get them off the ground? Since we are to imagine having excellent human and horse lives, I cannot compare what it is like to be a human having a nice time and a horse being brutally whipped; I should imagine being a horse frolicking with other horses, drinking from a pond on a hot day, eating sugar cane, and the like. Unless I start with certain preferences or values, how can I judge one life to be preferable to the other?

I suspect that the hypothetical choice approach either falls into indeterminacy or begs questions by starting from a nonneutral position assuming certain preferences or values. If the latter, the position may well collapse into a version of the next approach.

4. Qualitative solutions within objective theories. The difficulties of justifying life moves within a subjective theory of value constitute one motivation for approaching our puzzle from an objective theory. The objective theories discussed previously were developed as accounts of *human* value. But they could be employed in the interspecific arena. The idea would be that certain features of normal human lives are objectively valuable and are either absent or severely diminished in animal lives. While many of his writings suggest that he rejects objective theories, Frey here sounds like a proponent:

> To be sure, part of the richness of our lives involves activities we have in common with animals; but the truth is that we engage in a whole host of activities—falling in love, marrying, helping our children and young people to grow in numerous ways, working well and achieving job satisfaction, developing our minds in ways our relations never thought possible, acquiring cultural and intellectual interests, as well as hobbies . . . — that immeasurably deepen the texture of our lives. . . . [T]he value of a

life is a function of its quality, its quality a function of its richness, and its
richness a function of its scope or potentiality for enrichment. . . .[58]

For Frey, the greater *richness* of the lives of normal humans somehow
confers greater value upon them. *Richness* could be interpreted as a
dimension of satisfaction, within a subjective account. But my sense is
that Frey, and others invoking richness, give *special weight* to certain
characteristically human activities (so that a semi-unhappy human engaging in many such activities will have a more valuable life than, say, a
flourishing cat). On the views under consideration, certain activities are
thought to be of a *higher quality*—much as Mill thought but divorced
from Millian claims about actual or hypothetical choice.

One advantage of this qualitative strategy is that it accommodates
many of our intuitions about the value of lives across species. It also
overcomes the difficulty of the hypothetical-choice approach regarding
persons with recalcitrant preferences, by assuming that certain features
of normal human lives are objectively valuable (and therefore not dependent for their value on anyone's preferences).

Qualitative solutions to our puzzle are likely to divide over the ways
in which they justify their claim that certain features of lives are objectively valuable. As I use the term, those favoring *intersubjective* justification will cite human value judgments, conventions, practices, or even
nature, as at least part of what makes their value claims true or correct.
But it is very unclear that such an appeal can justify claims about the
comparative value of human and animal lives. Take autonomy as an
item on a proposed list. How is broad agreement (or whatever) *among
humans*—who are typically autonomous beings—about the value of
autonomy relevant to comparisons between humans and nonautonomous animals? (For that matter, of what relevance is such broad
agreement to those very rare humans who, on reflection, do not value
autonomy? Like any objective value theory, an interspecific one faces
the charge of not being flexible enough—a problem analogous to that of
persons with recalcitrant preferences, which problem faces hypothetical-choice theories.)

In addition to seeing the problem from the angle of bias, we can
consider it from that of generality. To make the supposedly objective
value of something depend on the characteristics of the beings whose
well-being is in question is to fail to have a sufficiently general account
of prudential value.[59] Such a theory should explain the nature of well-
being at its most basic; the theory is inadequate if its validity is rela-
tivized to beings with certain traits. Maybe close relationships are im-

---

[58] R. G. Frey, "Animal Parts, Human Wholes," in James M. Humber and Robert F.
Almeder (eds.), *Biomedical Ethics Reviews 1987* (Clifton, NJ: Humana, 1987), p. 93
[59] Sumner, *Welfare and Welfarism*, ch. 3

portant not just for humans but for dolphins, certain apes, and elephants. But it is plausible to think that the value of close relationships depends on being a social animal. What sense would it make to say that an animal solitary by nature is worse off for not having close relationships?

These points cannot rule out what I call *radically objective* justification—which does not implicate human judgments, conventions, practices, or nature (or any other animals' natures) as part of what makes the value claims true or correct. The challenge to these theorists is to justify the claims about the special value of the items on the list, and about the greater value of lives containing those items, in a way that is explicit, coherent, and plausible.

To my knowledge, the only philosopher to make a serious start in developing an objective interspecific theory is Robin Attfield. As we saw earlier, Attfield holds that living creatures have an interest in flourishing after their kind. Although this thesis proved to be problematic, it will be useful to consider Attfield's position as a strategy for justifying life moves. He argues that the losses of animals painlessly killed are best understood in terms of their being deprived of their potentials.[60] But different animals have different potentials or capacities, and the exercise of some—those of greater complexity—is more valuable than that of others. Thus, "because of the good which the creatures concerned stand to gain or lose, lives in which some capacities are realized are more valuable than those in which they are not or cannot be. . . . "[61]

Unfortunately, Attfield never *defends* his comparative-value thesis in any tolerably explicit way. *Why* do some capacities count more than others in assessing the values of different lives? What is the *relevance* of complexity to prudential value? Maybe the only arguments that can be given are something like these.

First, certain features of most human lives—such as enjoyments, autonomy, understanding, accomplishment, and deep personal relationships—would seem to have value in *any* life that contained them; they seem to have an *enriching* quality. Some will disagree, of course, raising doubts such as those about the value of close relationships to solitary animals. A theorist might respond, however, that *complexity itself* is what counts, the specific goods just mentioned being typical human manifestations of this general value. This move probably retains whatever intuitive plausibility with which the position began. It also avoids the charge of insufficient generality while making it harder to charge speciesism, since nonhuman animals could manifest complexity in their own ways (such as echolocation).

---

[60] *The Ethics of Environmental Concern*, p. 172
[61] ibid, p. 176

However it is formulated, the first argument is a direct intuitive argument. The second is indirect: Since human lives generally have much more of these goods (or of complexity) than do animal lives, and since some animal lives have more of some of these goods (or of complexity) than do other animals' lives, the value assumption in question accounts well for our convictions about the comparative value of different kinds of lives.

The possibility of objective accounts of interspecific value raises an important issue that merits a brief detour from our study of the comparative value of different lives: *Do objective views adequately account for an individual animal's well-being?* Such views assess the well-being of an animal in terms of objective criteria determined by the animal's natural capacities. To be plausible, such an account will have to be flexible, that is, partly subjective, not allowing too sharp a deviation from assessments based on the animal's mental life. Rollin's view appears to imply a flexible objective approach:

> It is plausible to suggest that happiness resides in the satisfaction of the unique set of needs and interests, physical and psychological, which make up what I have called the *telos,* or nature, of the animal in question. Each animal has a nature which is genetically and environmentally constrained, from which flow certain interests and needs, whose fulfillment or lack of it *matter* to the animal.[62]

Here, Rollin emphasizes the convergence of subjective and objective criteria of well-being: Violating an animal's nature tends to cause her unhappiness (a point vindicated by evolutionary reasoning).

Elsewhere, Rollin notes that subjective and objective criteria can diverge. He contends that it would seem clearly wrong to capture a gazelle, tiger, or eagle, and condition her to prefer living in a tiny cage and to abhor open places—even if she lived with no pain and considerable pleasure. The wrongness consists of violating the animal's nature.[63]

This is an outstanding test case. Rollin is rather quick to side with objective criteria, however. In the real world, capturing and conditioning an animal to hate her natural habitat would probably involve the infliction of significant suffering; part of the intuitive power of Rollin's example may derive from the assumption that this is so. But let us add details to preserve the point of the case: The animal is captured while sleeping, given a drug keeping her unconscious, and then subjected to brain surgery that reverses the hard-wiring that motivates roaming in

---

[62]Bernard E. Rollin, *The Unheeded Cry: Animal Consciousness, Animal Pain and Science* (Oxford: Oxford University Press, 1989), p. 203
[63]*Animal Rights and Human Morality*, pp. 34–35

the wild. (Assume that she preserves presurgery memories so that there is no question about whether she is the same animal.) One might continue to feel the intuitive pull of objective criteria (I do), but it is hard to get one's mind around the clamor of spontaneous reality checks ("There is no way all this could be done while making the animal happier!").

Suppose, instead, that a tiger is living in rough conditions that are unlikely to improve and that entail much suffering. Prey is scarce; bad weather is worsening due to a changing climate. And instead of brain surgery, kind treatment and a strong tranquilizer in the tiger's food are what make her more content. Might the tiger be better off, overall? Intuitions still seem likely to differ, a fact that may reflect lack of closure in the subjective–objective debate.

5. Egalitarian response: Deny the comparative claim. Our puzzle arises out of a tension produced by the claim that many animals have life interests, the claim that their lives can differ in prudential value, and the difficulty of justifying the second claim. As we have seen, some try to reduce the tension by denying that many (if any) nonhuman animals have life interests, obviating the need for further support for the second claim. Others accept the first claim and defend the problematic second claim. The *egalitarian* strategy is to deny the second claim.

The egalitarian approach tends to be more negatively than positively argued. Proponents sometimes discredit factual claims invoked to support one of the other approaches. For example, Sapontzis contests any facile assumption that what a dog enjoys is less satisfying than what humans enjoy. Like defenders of the quantitative arguments explored above, Sapontzis works from a subjective-value theory. He reminds us that from this standpoint, what matters is how satisfying a life is *for the subject*—and argues that we have no basis for asserting greater quantities on the human side. Animals might be shut off from some of our sources of enjoyment due to their lesser intelligence. At the same time, "we cannot enjoy the life of a dog, a bird, a bat, or a dolphin. Consequently, we cannot appreciate the subtleties of smell, sight, sound, and touch that these animals can apparently appreciate. Here we are the boors."[64]

Another common tack is to dispute not the factual assumptions but their alleged implications for interspecific value comparisons. In particular, suppose we could determine that our lives typically had more satisfaction than, say, beaver lives. Still, a beaver's life is all she has. It is,

---

[64] *Morals, Reason, and Animals*, p. 219. For a fuller development of his value theory, see "Groundwork for a Subjective Theory of Ethics," *American Philosophical Quarterly* 27 (1990): 27–38.

therefore, in a sense, incomparably valuable to the beaver, so there is no basis for saying that it is less valuable than a human life.[65]

The egalitarian approach features another negative aspect. It is not argued that we have compelling reasons to assert that the lives of normal humans, monkeys, bluejays, and lizards are equal in value. Rather, it is claimed that *we should regard them as equal*—for lack of good reason to regard them as unequal. On the side of this approach is the principle of universalizability, which enjoins us not to treat cases differently unless a relevant difference between them is identified.[66] Therefore, the present position might be regarded as a default view that wins unless defeated by a compelling argument in favor of some other view.

Is there such a compelling argument? For many philosophers, the consideration that may loom largest here is the stubborn conviction that the lives of normal humans *must* be of greater value than the lives of many, if not all, nonhuman animals. Perhaps that conviction is unjustified; it has not yet been very satisfyingly defended. In either case, that conviction probably constitutes the single most forceful counter to the egalitarian approach. Whether it shifts the burden of proof to that approach, or leaves it with the others, is not at all obvious.

Does this puzzle motivate reexamining equal consideration?

The approaches discussed earlier have had difficulty managing our puzzle. The claim that few, or no, animals have life interests because they lack a desire for life has numerous odd implications, mistakenly takes desire satisfaction to be the basic ground of human life interests, and ends up being unable to ground the latter. Quantitative solutions within subjective theories try to justify the claim that some life interests are weightier than others, but apparently at the cost of implying that contented lower vertebrates would lose more from death than would slightly discontented normal humans. Qualitative solutions within ob-

---

[65] I think Sapontzis makes this point (*Morals, Reason, and Animals*, p. 220), but his discussion seems to shift from one argumentive strategy to another without clearly distinguishing them. (Moreover, Sapontzis begs questions by never noting the possibility of a life move within an objective value theory.) See also Edward Johnson, "Life, Death, and Animals," in Miller and Williams, *Ethics and Animals*, pp. 123–33.
[66] One might charge that the egalitarian approach claims too much of universalizability (as Jorge Garcia pointed out to me). That principle enjoins us to treat relevantly similar cases similarly and relevantly different cases differently. Nothing strictly follows about how we should treat *cases about which we are uncertain whether they are relevantly similar or different;* any presumption about those cases would be a methodological principle, whereas universalizability is logical. But as argued in Chapter 3 in justifying a presumption in favor of equal consideration, various normative considerations can be marshalled to remove any serious doubt about whether there should be a presumption in favor of equality.

jective theories can vindicate the comparative thesis (2) only if they strive for radically objective justification; in any case, this approach has never been supported by developed arguments. The egalitarian approach abandons the comparative claim, thereby avoiding the foregoing problems, but arguably abandons too much: It is very hard to believe that normal humans lose no more in dying than do fish and reptiles (even if we can forgo prudential comparisons with certain "higher" animals). None of these positions is entirely happy. This whole area is quite baffling.

One possible response to this dialectic is to reexamine equal consideration. Perhaps, after all, it should be abandoned. The stubbornness of the comparative thesis may point not to the need to accommodate it *within value theory* but to make room for it by making adjustments *in ethical theory*.[67] If so, maybe ethical theoretical changes should be made at the most basic level by supporting a gradualist principle of *unequal* consideration: Roughly, *the greater a being's cognitive complexity, the more moral weight her interests should receive.* This would cover not only life interests and other instrumental interests but all interests. Pain—taken simply in terms of its phenomenological badness—would have greater moral weight if a normal human had it than if a dog had it, and similarly between a dog and a hummingbird. Such a gradualist picture of unequal consideration would no doubt fit many of our comparative intuitions (notably, those about different life interests).[68]

As noted in Chapter 3, I do not think unequal consideration is obviously incorrect and deserving of quick dismissal. But, again, it does not appear to hold up to close and careful scrutiny. Unequal consideration is less *coherent* (in our broad sense of the term—see Chapter 2) than equal consideration. It has problems with humans whose capacities confer lower standing, in any consistent use of the criteria governing how much consideration one is to receive. Not only do their life interests count less in principle; all of their interests do. Interspecifically, this position handles some intuitions nicely but others much less well. It has no difficulty comparing the weight of different life interests. But, as just noted, it suggests that some beings' pain (taken intrinsically) counts more than others'. How can one's intelligence, sensitivity, and the like be relevant to *how much a certain amount of pain or suffering matters?* (We are talking about the same amount of aversiveness here, by hypothesis.) On a more global level, the champion of unequal consideration has no clear way to defend the *relevance* of cognitive criteria in determining

---

[67] Cf. Peter Carruthers, *The Animals Issue: Moral Theory in Practice* (Cambridge: Cambridge University Press, 1992), ch. 4.
[68] Invoking numerous capacities she believes to be morally relevant, Lilly Russow defends a gradualist position in a promising book in progress.

how much weight one's interests are to receive. Finally, there is a very conspicuous possibility of *pro-human bias* lurking behind the metaphysical-sounding claim that the interests of normal humans just naturally have greater moral weight than others' relevantly similar interests. (On a historical note, it is fascinating how often unverifiable metaphysical theses have been made in the name of treating some as naturally less deserving than others. Might we smell a residue of feudalism or racism here?[69])

At the same time, the foregoing dialectic about interspecific value theory may provide the strongest case in favor of unequal consideration. And a proponent of unequal consideration can point out that anyone who assumes equal consideration but tries to justify a life move within an *objective* theory is also making a metaphysical-sounding claim. For the latter theorist claims that certain criteria can sometimes override an individual's judgment about her own good, even when she is not making obvious cognitive errors. Surely some account is needed as a basis for such a view of well-being. Claims of objective value attaching to different capacities across species have a loud metaphysical ring.

According to the gradualist, then, if the choice is between a gradualist view of unequal consideration, and equal consideration plus a life move within an objective-value theory, the choice is not *whether* to "go metaphysical" but *at what theoretical point* to do so. And that *is* the choice, the gradualist might continue, because life moves within subjective theories come at way too high a price, and hypothetical-choice approaches seem to collapse into objective theories (if they make sense at all). Assuming we don't want to go the rather incredible egalitarian route, we need to go metaphysical at some point to justify some morally interesting differences between us and turtles. Doing it at the level of basic principle is the most sensible, all things considered.

Again, for reasons already stated, I disagree. But I want to bring out the power of this theoretical back door move toward unequal consideration. Champions of equal consideration have not acknowledged its power, perhaps because they have contented themselves with highly superficial life moves.

Further reflections

To make the options vivid, here is a summary:

1. Abandon equal consideration;
2. Base life move on desire-for-life argument;
3. Base life move on hypothetical choice;

[69] See Sapontzis, *Morals, Reason, and Animals*, p. 226.

4. Make quantitative life move within subjective theory;
5. Make qualitative life move within objective theory;
6. Reject life moves in favor of egalitarianism.

I have argued against (1) and (2). I reject (3) because, if there is anything to this thought-experiment, it reduces to another approach, probably (5). That leaves (4), (5), and (6). Can we go further?

Let us first examine egalitarianism and its implications more closely. To begin, when egalitarianism is considered in the context of "Whom would you save?" scenarios, such as Regan's lifeboat case, this view looks almost crazy. Who could really believe that one should not save a normal human over a dog, not to mention such "lower" vertebrates as a tortoise or snake? But these scenarios are complicated by the possibility that ethical factors quite independent of prudential value influence our convictions.

For example, human beings are capable of doing more good for the world than are other animals (although they also can do far more evil, a point sometimes overlooked); the belief that the human, if saved, is likely to do more good is a moral consideration extraneous to the value theory question. More convincing perhaps is the fact that the death of a human, especially one who has not yet reached old age, usually causes a great deal of misery among family and other loved ones. Ordinarily, we can assume that the misery caused would be much greater than that caused by the death of an alligator or seagull. (That is no excuse for ignoring the great misery that the death of a highly social animal, such as a whale or ape, is likely to cause to members of her group.) Furthermore, close relationships presumably justify partiality in the lifeboat. One shudders to think that one's spouse might pass one up for a dog! Much of the value of human lives (and probably those of other highly social, intelligent animals) derives from the deep commitments into which individuals enter, regardless of how this value is analyzed theoretically. These and perhaps other moral considerations may lead us to conclude that a human should be saved, without shedding clear light on interspecific value.

Let us set aside "Whom would you save?" scenarios and remember our more basic value question: Does death harm some sentient animals (including humans) more than others? I cannot help but believe that the answer is "yes"—although I am far from clear on *how many* such comparisons of normal species representatives can be justified. I am quite prepared to reject egalitarianism's refusal to judge that normal humans lose more, in dying, than do, say, fish, amphibians, and reptiles. I am tempted to go much further, but, as a check against bias, I will wait to see what can be justified with argument.

My willingness to support *any* life moves entails a rejection of the idea that, since an animal's life is all she has, its prudential value is beyond cross-individual comparison. That a lizard's life is all she has, in other words, does not rule out the possibility that a flourishing kangaroo would lose more from dying. But I must stress that the reflections that follow are very tentative. The theoretical territory has barely been trod upon, and we cannot hope to settle it overnight. Fellow settlers are most welcome.

I think that quantitative life moves within subjective theories can fare better than might at first be thought (as in our earlier discussion). We have to keep in mind that we are talking about *amounts* of satisfaction and the like; there is no room in this approach for giving special weight to certain *kinds* of satisfaction. Still, it seems likely that, in the vast majority of cases, a human's death wipes out greater opportunities for satisfaction than does the life of a trout, lizard, or alligator. The mental lives of these animals are presumably pretty dim. Of course, that means they suffer less, a point with which we need to come to terms.

Let us take on the exceptional cases that are so challenging to this position. We can allow that *some* humans' well-being is lower than that of contented lower vertebrates. Some humans are in such terrible straits, with such poor prospects, that their suicides would not be irrational.[70] They would lose less from death than would many animals. But note, first, that this comparative value judgment by no means entails that the presumption against killing these humans is less strong than the presumption against killing the animals. As we saw earlier, there are many moral considerations, independent of prudential value, that enter into moral judgments regarding killing. Among the most prominent is the impact of one's actions on the community, including effects on trust, the creation of fear, and the causing of sadness. And, generally, the autonomy of autonomous beings—a group that includes many of the humans in question—should be respected.

Notice also that we cannot, on a subjective view, just assume that the semi-unhappy person is less well-off than a contented animal. The harm of death is a function of opportunities. The opportunities of a semi-unhappy person are usually, in fact, quite considerable, even if things aren't going so well at the moment. *People often turn things around.* That is one reason semi-unhappy people (in contrast to totally miserable people lacking hope) generally do not want to die. Another

---

[70] That is not to assume that they are, much less should be, suicidal. Fear of death (deeply rooted in us as a result of natural selection) can prevent the miserable person who has very poor prospects—as judged from her own values—from desiring death. So can a noble desire to be available to others who are in need. These and other factors make clear that the presence or absence of a desire to die is not a reliable measure of how one's life is going.

likely reason is that *they often value trying*, irrespective of how things will actually turn out. Since we are talking about *satisfaction*—which takes into account an individual's own values—the life of someone who values trying will receive a higher prudential score than if we attempted simply to sum up her expected pains and pleasures. (Expected satisfaction is still taken as an aggregate, but one complicated by factoring in the individual's values.) To be sure, often semi-unhappy people do not turn things around. But even factoring in *probability*, it is plausible to think that the expected level of satisfaction of such people—including the satisfaction that comes from trying—is greater than that of many contented "lower" vertebrates.

Now consider the human for whom life is going reasonably well and who is not yet very old. Compare a flourishing member of any species that does not have a very long life span. In most cases, the human is likely to live a lot longer than the animal. If the lives of both are going well, other things being equal, the human has more to lose in dying. A middle-aged dog loses between five to ten good years; a middle-aged human, say, twenty to fifty good years. There is no denying that such comparisons are significant from a quantitative outlook. Admittedly, this argument does not support life moves with respect to animals with very long life spans, such as elephants and certain tortoises.

Overall, subjective theories appear to permit some plausible life moves. Which? I am fairly certain that the combination of arguments just given justifies the following assertion within a subjective approach: Generally, human lives have greater prudential value than the lives of fish, amphibians, reptiles, and birds. I suspect, but am unsure, that the same considerations could be plausibly extended to "lower," shorter-living mammals. At some point—as we consider animals more like humans in terms of cognition, conation, and life span—the subjective theorist has to tip her hat to egalitarianism. And that point will probably be considerably short of what our bare intuitions might suggest, since they tend to support life moves with respect to all, or nearly all, animals. (But intuitions here may well be distorted by bias.) Moreover, the subjective theorist is required to acknowledge that, in some cases, it would be better to be a pig satisfied than a human unsatisfied.

In contrast, qualitative life moves within objective theories are likely to be intuitively more satisfying but theoretically more in debt. If certain kinds of mental functioning, deep personal relationships, autonomous living, and accomplishment have greater prudential weight than equally satisfying conditions and activities of other animals, the theorist can cover most of our comparative intuitions. Who knows? Maybe even a truly miserable, hopeless person will turn out to be better off than a hog in hog heaven (although I would be highly suspicious of such a radical divorce from subjective criteria). In any event, there is no clear reason why normal human life would not count as prudentially higher than the lives of at least most animals, including most mammals. (Open-minded theorists might be highly impressed by the caring relationships, accomplishments, and other sources of satisfaction of dolphins, apes, and other impressive animals.)

This approach would also seem to permit fewer exceptions to rules of thumb about the comparative value of different kinds of lives: "This oddball might prefer to be a feline pleasure-monger, but he doesn't realize how valuable his interpersonal relationships and accomplishments are." For many, this feature will add to the theory's intuitive attractiveness.

On the other hand, an objective approach owes us some reasonable account of what capacities have special weight and why they have special weight. If all special weight is a function of complexity, this claim needs to be argued in depth—and defended against reasonable challenges (such as cases in which complexity conflicts with felt satisfaction). Because the approach overrides the authority of individuals in certain cases, and waxes "metaphysical" while subjectivism stays down to earth, the story had better be a good one. The fact that qualitative life moves within objective accounts are *so* convenient (given what we want to believe) heightens the feeling of need, in any honest mind, for further argumentation of a high quality. The intuitions supporting these life moves certainly do not count as considered judgments (see Chapter 2).

In conclusion, if the preceding arguments have been correct, a full-blown egalitarianism leaves too much to be desired, raising the question of what life moves can be justified. I believe that just as subjective and objective accounts are both contenders in the human arena, life moves within such accounts extended to animals are also both contenders. (I incline in the direction of subjectivism but am far from certain.) Yes, normal humans who are not thoroughly miserable and hopeless lose more from dying than do many animals with moral status (at least from fish through birds, I think). But for what range of species this can honestly be asserted, and with what sorts of exceptions, cannot be determined without buying into one approach or another.

Thoughts about other instrumental goods and conclusion

In this chapter, we have explored interspecific value mainly through the lens of life moves—so named because the comparisons in question have traditionally been couched in terms of life and distinguished from experiential well-being. But life moves can in principle also be made for other major instrumental values, such as freedom and functioning, even experiential well-being taken instrumentally. I will close this chapter with some brief comments about major instrumental values other than life, followed by general remarks about our findings.

Freedom, taken negatively as lack of external constraints, and *functioning*, both mental and physical, may well count as intrinsic values on an objective theory. On both subjective and objective theories, these goods have great instrumental value in almost all circumstances. Their loss typically entails great frustration and distress, as well as the inability to do many things we could otherwise do. Any theory must also recognize *the instrumental role of experiential well-being:* When we suffer, we tend to be distracted and somewhat debilitated. Regarding our dealings with animals, the latter instrumental good is relevant wherever we might cause pain, distress, or suffering to animals. Freedom becomes important when we confine animals, functioning when we cause them injury or disability.

When two beings A and B are confined, disabled, or distracted by suffering, are the magnitudes of their losses affected not only by their circumstances but by what kinds of beings they are? Let us consider freedom and consider a normal human, a dog, and a frog each confined in a cage that is small in proportion to their bodies. Take subjective theories first. The human's loss is a function of experiential well-being (with possible qualifications, depending on the theory, that need not concern us here). People don't generally like to be confined; they become angry, frustrated, afraid, and saddened. Other animals' losses from confinement are also a function of effects on experiential well-being.[71]

Note that, on a subjective theory, it is not immediately obvious that a human loses more than a dog by being confined, even in ordinary circumstances. Either can be made quite miserable. The human might gain more from comprehending hope and moral consolation but lose more from anticipatory dread and deeper sadness. The only factor that seems to tilt fairly consistently toward the conclusion that humans lose more is their considerably longer life expectancies. This difference is erased in the case of a puppy or even middle-aged dog and a very old human. In comparison to a frog, however, humans will lose much more in anything like ordinary circumstances due to their greater capacities for satisfaction, their ability to turn bad situations around, and their vastly longer life spans.

On objective accounts, as they are likely to be developed, freedom interests will differ importantly in a wider array of comparisons. Note, by the way, that the human's loss from confinement can diverge from

---

[71] See James Rachels, "Why Animals Have a Right to Liberty," in Tom Regan and Peter Singer (eds.), *Animal Rights and Human Obligations,* 2nd ed. (Englewood Cliffs, NJ: Prentice Hall, 1989), pp. 122–31.

that measured by subjective criteria. The person may lose hope and lower his expectations, or may be conditioned to do so, in which case his level of contentment may not be a good measure of what he has lost. Dogs, too, can give up hope and lower their expectations, although I am doubtful that frogs are so emotionally complex. As for comparisons, an objective theory could easily assert that a human ordinarily loses much more than a dog from confinement due to the greater objective value of what is lost—potential accomplishments, time with loved ones, the chance to complete a life plan, and so on. As with life interests, objective theories can confidently compare freedom interests in many cases in which subjective theories cannot, or at least have trouble doing so (say, with "middling" mammals). Naturally, objective theories have no trouble making such comparisons in dealing with such "low" vertebrates as frogs.

How about comparisons with respect to functioning interests, say, in cases where a human and another animal are crippled or rendered brain-damaged? For the most part, comparisons here would seem to track those involving freedom. The same would appear to be true of experiential well-being, considered instrumentally. After all, what varies in each case is the intrinsic value of whatever is blocked by the relevant impediment (confinement, impairment, distraction). The differences can be traced, then, to the theory of value rather than the instrumental interest in question.

What can we conclude from our investigations of interspecific value, or well-being across species? On both of the contending general approaches to prudential value, subjective and objective accounts, there are some morally interesting differences among beings with moral status. For example, exceptional circumstances aside, it seems correct to assert that a normal human life has greater prudential value than a life of a fish, an amphibian, a reptile, or a bird. How far "up" one can move and make such confident comparisons depends on whether one works within a subjective or an objective theory. Objective theories vindicate a much wider range of life moves, placing normal human life above all or nearly all nonhuman animal life (and similarly with other major instrumental values).

Now we *could* capture such theoretically confirmed differences by speaking of *differences in moral status*.[72] For, presumably, the prudential differences will sometimes have moral relevance. For example, a starving person with no access to edible vegetation should kill and eat a catfish before a pig, and should go after a duck before considering

---

[72] I argued that a principle of equal consideration and differences in moral status were logically consistent in "Equal Consideration and Unequal Moral Status," *Southern Journal of Philosophy* 31 (1993): 17–31.

cannibalism (although additional moral complexities enter into the latter). And suppose that your two pets, a snake and a chimp, are each hell bent on having access to the basement but would likely harm each other there. (Set aside the question, taken up in Chapter 9, of whether people should own wild animals at all.) Other things being equal, it would be better to limit the snake's ability to move freely than the chimp's.

While we could summarily collect morally interesting differences by speaking of unequal moral status, this language is so likely to be misunderstood and misused that it might be best to drop it. Assuming that we retain a principle of equal consideration, morally interesting differences that flow from considerations of prudential value are *much* less extensive than has been traditionally thought, especially if we opt for a subjective approach. I have found that many people are disposed to understand talk of unequal moral status as describing radical differences in how much consideration different beings are owed. Even if they can be convinced that such talk is recommended within the confines of equal consideration, it seems to tempt them to overgeneralize and think in terms of absolute prioritizing of, say, human life interests over animal life interests. While, conceptually, there is no objection to speaking of differences in moral status (properly understood), this usage is liable to be confusing and subject to so many qualifications as hardly to seem worthwhile. What we must not do is jump from the premise that there are some morally interesting differences to the conclusion that they justify all sorts of exploitation of "inferior" animals by humans. Certainly not all that we may justifiably do or not do is a direct consequence of prudential-value comparisons like those discussed previously. To understand our obligations to animals—what they are and how they are limited—we have to pick up our value-theory acquisitions and return to ethics.

Chapter 9

Back to animal ethics

The principle of equal consideration defended in Chapter 3 is somewhat vague and abstract. It requires giving equal moral weight or importance to relevantly similar interests, no matter who has them. A critic might charge that this principle is purely formal or empty. In a sense that is right, because equal consideration *by itself* settles no ethical issue. A nihilist might give all relevantly similar interests the same moral weight by giving all of them none! But those who stress equal consideration in animal ethics do so with the understanding that humans (or their interests) are to be taken seriously. An ethical view developed within the framework of equal consideration for animals is substantiated by an adequate ethics regarding our treatment of human beings.

Several implications of equal consideration (given plausible principles covering humans) will be fleshed out in this final chapter. But it is worth mentioning up front that most of the specified principles and other conclusions reached in this chapter do not strictly depend on (fully) equal consideration for animals. Quite a few of these conclusions flow from the uncontroversial assumption that we have a prima facie duty not to harm—combined with insights about the ways in which sentient animals can be harmed (as explored in Chapter 8) and the premise (defended in Chapter 3) that animals have moral status so that their interests matter morally. Thus, these and several other conclusions seem to depend only on giving animals *serious*—not necessarily *equal*—consideration. (That most of these conclusions are at odds with prevailing ways of treating animals says much about the status quo.) But some of our findings will be clearly tied to equal consideration.

This chapter begins by exploring obligations concerning the causing of harm, proceeds to an examination of possible obligations to benefit and to respect autonomy, and concludes with discussions of eating animals and keeping them in zoos.

GENERAL OBLIGATIONS OF NONMALEFICENCE

Among ethical principles that are clearly substantive and not just formal, one stands out as a considered judgment so basic and indisputable that any system of thought not honoring it would probably not be a system of ethics. This is *the principle of nonmaleficence,* which states a prima facie duty not to harm. Its indubitability, however, may depend on leaving it vague and not specifying its scope. Debate begins once we ask to whom it applies. Some today might be inclined to assume that nonmaleficence applies only to humans.

If so, such individuals will not be able to sustain their position for long. As argued in Chapter 3, and elaborated in subsequent chapters, animals have interests that matter morally in their own right. Indeed, after some of the garbage generated by prejudice and unsound argumentation is swept away, the principle of nonmaleficence *extended to sentient animals*—who can, after all, be harmed—continues to stand as a considered judgment.

We can specify nonmaleficence into *principles* or *rules* (I will use the first term) for animal ethics. First, we can generate a principle that, while sounding modest enough, has important consequences for animals: *Don't cause unnecessary harm.* (If this is just a restatement of nonmaleficence, it focuses it in a useful way.) Now that it is clear that animals can be harmed, we can see that this principle might go somewhere. It does not claim, controversially, that we may never harm animals, or humans, just that we must not do so needlessly. Harming requires adequate justification. One might object that the pliability of *unnecessary* empties this norm of content: "One can claim that any harm is necessary!" Yes, one can, but not plausibly. And *even if we never state precise conditions for which harms are necessary, principles that make sense of our judgments about clear cases of unnecessary harm will prove to have some far-reaching consequences for our treatment of animals.*

Reasonable people will agree that kicking a cat hard in the face, on a whim, is an example of causing unnecessary harm.[1] There are any number of cases of clearly unnecessary harms to animals. But what if we consider cases in which one does not *cause* harm but *strongly encourages it,* thereby making it more likely? Does the spirit of nonmaleficence, or do other moral considerations, support moral judgments regarding such actions?

Suppose you didn't kick anyone, but, on a whim, paid a friend a modest sum to kick a cat in the face. Assuming you didn't force your

---

[1]Some of the ideas in the following discussion were stimulated by a thought-experiment in Robert Nozick, *Anarchy, State, and Utopia* (New York: Basic Books, 1974), p. 37.

friend, it seems correct to say that you did not cause the harm in question; your friend did. But both of you acted wrongly—your friend, for causing the needless harm, *and* you, for encouraging and commissioning it. That you did not cause the harm does not absolve you from all moral responsibility for it. (Those who, in disagreement with me, would argue that by paying for the kicking, you actually *cause* the harm will have, if anything, more reason to accept the principle at which I am driving.)

Now suppose that there is a whole institution of cat kicking, carried out by a small portion of the population but made possible by regular payments by you and others. You derive a great deal of satisfaction from watching the kicks or even just contemplating them. You're no sadist. What pleases you is *not* the fact that the kicking causes great pain, fear, and suffering to the cats, that it rearranges their faces, or that it eventually kills them; in fact, you consider these regrettable side-effects. You like watching, or contemplating, the display of skill put on by the better kickers. (We are beyond mere whim here.) There is a well-developed tradition of standards that counts certain kicks as especially on target; other kicks are warmly appreciated for the style of the kicking motion itself (roundabout, sidekick, forward snapkick, and so on). It can take years to get really good at cat kicking, and some never get it; many lacking talent keep at it because they enjoy the challenge (not to mention being outdoors in the elements, with other kickers and their dogs).

I assume that it would be wrong to help keep this institution in business through regular financial support. You are not doing the clearly gratuitous harming but are commissioning others to do it. One striking feature of this imaginary case is how frivolous the harming is. (On the other hand, it is not obvious what *principled* difference there is between such cat kicking and hunting for sport or bullfighting. Indeed, I would argue that the three activities are wrong for roughly the same reasons.[2]) The harm's frivolity motivates a general consideration of morally salient features of harms. For starters, a harm can be characterized by (1) its *magnitude* (by which I mean to include both the amount of a harm, if it occurs, and the likelihood of its occurring) and, if the harm is intended, (2) *the significance of its purpose* (e.g., hoped-for bene-

---

[2]Some argue that hunting for sport is justified by the need to cull animals to reduce overpopulation. Although I cannot enter into the complexities of this issue here, I would (1) caution against the use of this argument as a rationalization for indulging the (rather unadmirable) pleasures of hunting, (2) raise the question of whether animals threatened by possible starvation are not, on the whole, better off left alone (at least in some instances), and (3) argue that there are far more humane ways to "euthanize" animals than by gunning them down.

fits taking into account their likelihood, the prospect of averting harm). Both factors bear on judgments about the justifiability of specific harmful actions—whether they are reasonably considered *necessary*—and of actions supporting such harm.

But before we can state a principle about actions supporting institutions that wrongly harm, we must consider a further complexity. Each of us should avoid causing unnecessary harm. We should also make reasonable efforts not to support others' unnecessary harming. But as our *causal proximity* to such harming decreases, so does our moral responsibility for it, other things being equal. Thus, in addition to (1) a harm's magnitude, and (2) the significance of its purpose—both of which bear on whether the harm is necessary—a third factor becomes conspicuous when we do not cause the harm in question: (3) our causal proximity to it.

Because causal distance can diminish responsibility, the factors of seriousness of purpose and magnitude of harm come into play again, this time in determining our moral responsibility for some unnecessary harm. For convenience, let us call the combination of the latter two factors the *net badness* of the unnecessary harm. How is net badness relevant? Well, if we are causally distant from some unnecessary harm, we are not so clearly responsible for it as when we are causally very close to the harm. Net badness can tip the scales from it being unreasonable to consider one responsible for the harm to it being reasonable to hold one responsible. If you patronize a pizza company that is known to pollute the environment in a way that probably causes a negligible amount of unnecessary harm, it is doubtful that your patronage is ipso facto morally wrong. Suppose, however, that you know the company to be owned by a local chapter of the Ku Klux Klan infamous for several recent lynchings of blacks. Surely you should buy pizza elsewhere. Here, net badness varies while causal proximity remains constant.

When net badness is constant, causal proximity can vary in a way that affects responsibility. Suppose that we are wondering whether to rent a Disney video from a store that we know rents child pornography. I assume that the making of child pornography involves extreme likelihood of great (and unnecessary) harm. But the video store doesn't make the movies; it only buys them from people who make them. So we are twice removed from the production of such videos. Still, by patronizing a company that patronizes the terrible institution of child pornography, we seem to do wrong; we seem close enough, given the net badness, to have moral responsibility. Suppose, on the other hand, that we buy groceries from a store that employs someone who, we happen to know, sometimes rents videos of this kind. Here, our purchase of groceries is causally quite remote from the harm that concerns us. (We support a store that supports a person who supports another store that buys videos from a company that perpetrates the harm.) It would seem unreasonable to condemn shopping at this grocery store.

The trick is to state a principle that makes sense of the idea that we often have moral responsibility for the actions we support (here, focusing on financial support) without claiming too much. What I do claim is that the following is a defensible principle within the spirit of nonmaleficence: *Make every reasonable effort not to provide financial support for institutions or practices that cause or support unnecessary harm.* "Reasonable" here is very rough but not useless. It makes room for the factors of one's causal proximity to unnecessary harm as well as its net badness, without imposing an artificial ordering to these factors.

This principle might worry some utilitarians, because it might sometimes require one to abstain, boycott, or divest without its being clear that doing so will actually lead to good results. But, if so, that is a knock against the version of utilitarianism in question, not against the principle. To worry to such an extent about whether good results will be forthcoming is to doom many potential social reforms from the start. Think where South Africa would be with apartheid if the first groups to divest from that country had instead thought like the hesitant utilitarian. (Actually, there is probably considerable utility in the foregoing principle. But it need not rest on so uncertain a basis as utilitarianism.)

While exploring in the following sections specific aspects of nonmaleficence, I will focus on what sorts of actions amount to the causing of unnecessary harm. Throughout the discussion, we can bear in mind the moral link we have just established between *causing* such harm and *wrongfully supporting* those who do. I will not explicitly formulate for each principle about the causing of some type of harm another principle about financially supporting that kind of harm.

OBLIGATIONS NOT TO CAUSE UNNECESSARY SUFFERING

The most obvious way in which animals can be harmed is by being made to *suffer*. In Chapter 5, suffering was characterized as a highly unpleasant emotional state associated with more-than-minimal pain or distress. On any plausible value theory, suffering is something that, in itself, makes one less well-off. In terms of suffering's intrinsic aversiveness (as opposed to its instrumental disvalue), the avoidance of suffering is a relevantly similar interest for any potential sufferer. Thus, equal consideration implies that we should give equal moral weight to a certain amount of suffering, no matter who has it.

The following principle should therefore be fairly secure: *Don't cause significant suffering for the sake of your or others' enjoyment.* Let me explain the qualifications. I limit the principle to "significant" suffering to increase its plausibility. Perhaps twenty unexpected people shouting "Surprise!" at a surprise party would cause an acutely self-conscious person to suffer a little, but it is not clear that doing so would be wrong. Why "for the sake of *your or others'* enjoyment"? It may sometimes be right to cause suffering for *the sufferer's* own future enjoyment, with his or her, or an appropriate proxy's, consent. For example, a trainer or physician might justifiably cause great pain in rehabilitating a patient so that he can again do things he enjoys.[3] Why pick on enjoyment? Unlike self-defense or legitimate punishment, the goal of enjoyment does not seem weighty enough to justify causing someone else to experience significant suffering. (In terms of the features of harm discussed previously, the purpose is not significant enough given the magnitude of the harm.)

But the hard-core utilitarian might challenge this claim. Imagine a huge colosseum filled with people who delight in watching two animals (or human slaves) fighting to the death. At least one of the combatants will suffer greatly, but, according to the utilitarian, at some point the spectators' enjoyment must compensate for the harm done. I tend to disagree in principle. I strongly disagree *in practice*. The general acceptance of a norm that invites the causing of significant suffering for others' enjoyment, no matter how carefully the norm is circumscribed, is so likely to lead to injustice that we are better off without it. We had best regard enjoyment as simply not weighty enough to justify the infliction of significant suffering.[4]

Causing significant suffering in the name of *a very important purpose* (e.g., major benefits, the averting of great harm) has not been ruled out; a weighty enough purpose might make such suffering necessary. It is commonly assumed that a nation may sometimes conscript young persons in its defense, although this involves coercion and predictably results in considerable suffering for many of the conscripts. I would argue that if all reasonable efforts to amass an adequate volunteer army have failed, and the nation is *justly* entering a state of war, conscription

---

[3] With appropriate consent, it might even be justified to cause significant suffering for your or others' enjoyment—say, in realistically portraying suffering in making a movie. If so, we could reword the principle to refer to *significant nonconsensual suffering*. But the question of whether this qualification is appropriate is practically irrelevant for animal ethics, and qualifying every harm-related principle with *nonconsensual* is likely to cause more confusion than clarity.

[4] This argument against accepting such a norm for general public use could be made by a rule-utilitarian (see, e.g., R. B. Brandt, *A Theory of the Good and the Right* [Oxford: Clarendon, 1979]) or any utilitarian distinguishing the norms we can justify in times of leisurely reflection and those we should disseminate for educating children and on-the-spot decision making (see, e.g., R. M. Hare, *Moral Thinking: Its Levels, Method, and Point* [Oxford: Clarendon, 1981]).

is justified. (How often these conditions are met is another question.) Many people believe that causing substantial suffering to animals can be justified when necessary for the pursuit of significant biomedical research, which, if successful, will lead to future benefits. (It is a fascinating historical fact that in this country, conscription for military service is widely accepted, whereas the proposal that humans be conscripted for biomedical research would likely provoke horror and indignation.)

Some might contend that coercing innocent individuals to undergo significant suffering, even for a very important purpose, is always wrong. As my view about conscription shows, I am not prepared to go that far. Can we articulate any more meaningful principles about the causing of suffering, then? Equal consideration suggests one rather directly: *Apply equally any standards that allow the causing of suffering.* (Here, again, we are considering suffering in terms of its aversiveness; the complication that suffering can also be instrumentally bad will be considered later.) As with equal consideration, this principle is, in itself, purely formal. But coupled with reasonable assumptions about the ethical treatment of humans, it has very far-reaching implications for animals.

For example, it would imply that any harm–benefit standard invoked in the name of making a research animal suffer is acceptable only if applying the same standard to human subjects would be acceptable. This idea might be taken to provoke the problem of marginal cases, as discussed in Chapter 3. But the chief evil of suffering—what we most hate it for—is precisely its aversiveness, which is the same for the animals and humans in question, by hypothesis. Therefore, the cognitive capacities of the human are irrelevant here (although they might be relevant to a consideration of instrumental goods). In any event, it is clear that in practice, giving equal weight to (equal amounts of) human and animal suffering would tend very strongly in the direction of animal liberation. When animals are no longer treated as resources to be exploited, and when making them suffer is contemplated as solemnly as is causing human suffering, most of our current animal-exploiting practices will be history. In addition to hunting for sport, bullfights, and several practices discussed later, plausible examples include cosmetics testing, rodeos, poaching for ivory or skins, whaling, and trapping for fur.

PRESUMPTIONS AGAINST KILLING

Since we should not cause unnecessary harm, and sentient animals are generally harmed by death (see Chapter 8), there is a presumption against killing sentient animals. But sometimes this presumption can be overridden, when circumstances are such that killing is necessary—for example, when killing is a last resort in self-defense. In any event, the presumption against killing is not equally strong for all animals, in large part because the magnitude of harm entailed by death is not the same for all animals (see Chapter 8). The presumption against killing catfish is weaker than that against killing dolphins or humans. (I use *dolphin* to include members of the family Delphinidae and porpoises, members of the family Phocoenidae.) How one understands the strength of the presumption against killing normal members of a particular species will depend, to some extent, on one's interspecific value theory. But before we go for details, let us formulate the general presumption as a principle: *Don't kill sentient animals unnecessarily.* We can understand the strength of the presumption against killing particular animals as varying with the criteria for what counts as necessary killing; the stronger the presumption, the more stringent the criteria.

Let us begin with common views about killing humans. To avoid distracting controversy, let us consider postinfancy humans who are glad to be alive. I assume that the presumption against killing them is nearly absolute. There are *some* circumstances in which such humans may be permissibly killed: when there is no other way to stop them from killing you or innocent others, or if they are military personnel on the opposing side of a war that your country has justifiably entered. No doubt there are others. But the presumption against killing these paradigm holders of a right to life is so strong that most of us will never be in a situation in which we should override it. To contend that any nonhuman animals enjoy such a strong presumption against being killed would be very revisionary indeed.

I want to contend just that. In Chapters 6 and 7, we considered numerous capacities that (1) are often tied to the concept of personhood (which I believe to be too vague and contentious to be useful in animal ethics), and (2) might plausibly be considered relevant to whether a being enjoys a robust right to life within the more exclusive frameworks of objective value theories: agency (as manifested in intentional action), rationality (thinking or reasoning), sociability, self-awareness, moral agency, and autonomy. Data about Great Apes and dolphins that emerged in exploring these capacities—and phenomena that sometimes implicate them (as evidence of reasoning emerged in our investigations of deception and language)—suggest that these animals possess as much of these capacities as do many humans. (That is so even if no nonhuman animal meets the threshold for autonomy.) Some of these humans, such as typical autistic three-year-olds, would presumably meet any reasonable set of conditions for a robust right to life. The presumption against killing these humans, I assume, should be the same as that against killing you or me.

As noted in Chapter 8, the strength of a presumption against killing is not purely a function of the harm of death to the one who dies. One must also consider the effects of a policy of permissible killing, and of particular acts of killing, on the fabric of the moral community: Will inhibitions against killing humans be generally weakened? Also important is the resultant misery of loved ones. These additional factors tend to strengthen the presumption for human "borderline persons" (for those who insist on personhood language). For we do seem to be in a community with other humans in a way in which we are not with nonhuman animals; and the misery caused by an untimely human death is typically very extensive.

But let us not content ourselves with facile distinctions. True, we do not have the sorts of community ties with dolphins and apes (by which I will here mean only Great Apes, not gibbons and siamangs) that we at least think of ourselves as having with other humans. (One might question the depth of one's ties to people living a completely different way of life in an island country that one has never heard of, but let us ignore this complication.) At the same time, the misery caused by the untimely death of an ape, or a dolphin, to her group must be very considerable; these animals are highly social, not to mention intelligent and sensitive. The misery would probably include both sadness over the loss and fear for their security.

Furthermore, I would not want to hold that the presumption against killing humans like the autistic three-year-old should be appreciably weakened in the (perhaps imaginary) case that their deaths would not cause much misery and would not weaken community bonds. That is because I believe they possess enough of whatever capacities might be relevant for a robust right to life. Having not argued fully for this assertion, however, I will not be dogmatic about it. (But see, in Chapter 3, the critique of Carruthers' efforts to handle the problem of marginal cases.)

It is difficult to see why the presumption against killing apes and dolphins should be regarded differently. There is no plausible way to ground a life move in comparing these animals and humans within a subjective theory (see Chapter 8). The prospects for doing so within an objective theory are only marginally better. One would presumably give special weight to deep personal relationships, accomplishment, autonomous living, and understanding. (These goods depend on capacities such as those canvassed earlier; for example, autonomous living depends on autonomy.) Whether or not the deep relationships among apes and among dolphins are *personal* relationships (assuming that is given some clear meaning), they are complex, long term, and emotionally deep. And a watchful eye would find accomplishments among these creatures—say, overcoming one's fears and becoming top chimp, or escaping from potentially fatal tuna nets. We don't know whether these animals live autonomously, but we do know that many humans, including many adult humans, do not. And while human understanding no doubt averages higher than ape and dolphin understanding, it is important to remember that we are dealing with degrees. I submit that any consistent appeal to objective criteria in an attempt to justify a life move against apes and dolphins will have disturbing consequences for quite a few humans (some of whom we would generally consider normal), who accomplish little, have weak relationships, never question their motivations and values, or the like. Moreover, the significant likelihood that bias drives the claim of objective goods and the weight given them in interspecific comparisons should arouse our suspicions that the life move is unjustified. Certainly, no adequate working out of such a life move has yet been achieved.

I conclude, therefore, that *the presumption against killing humans, Great Apes, and dolphins is virtually absolute.* In a robust, though not absolute, sense of the word *right,* humans, apes, and dolphins have a right to life. How strong is the presumption against killing sentient animals "lower" than apes and dolphins? Here matters get very complex, in part because of the divergence of subjective and objective value theories. But a few worthwhile points can be made.

First, *for a large class of sentient animals—at least fish, herpetofauna (amphibians and reptiles), and birds—the presumption against killing these animals is ordinarily weaker than that against killing humans, Great Apes, and dolphins.* This thesis is reasonably drawn from the fact that valid life moves can be made with respect to the former class of animals within both subjective and objective value theories. Certainly, such additional factors as effects on the fabric of the moral community, and the misery caused by the loss of loved ones, reinforce this thesis (although the first factor might concern only the killing of humans).

How strong is the presumption against killing *mammals* "lower" than apes and dolphins? This is harder to assess, and one's answer will be affected by the details of one's value theory. Intuitively, it might seem that the presumption against taking such mammals' lives is weaker than taking human life. But we must be very careful with self-serving intuitions in the absence of a theoretically sound framework in which to make sense of them. To some extent, the effects-on-moral-community and misery-caused factors may support a stronger presumption against taking human life. But this is so only if the presumption against taking the animal lives starts off lower than that for humans, by virtue of a valid life move. (If these animals enjoy a virtually absolute presumption against being killed, how can additional factors matter?) This is most likely to be so with the cognitively least complex and shortest-living mammals, perhaps rodents.

However tempting it may be to jump on the life move bandwagon for "lower" and "middling" mammals, our enthusiasm should be tempered by the problem of marginal cases. Take a familiar example of a "middling" mammal, dogs. There are many handicapped human beings whose opportunities for satisfaction (on a subjective view) or for partaking in specially weighted activities (on an objective view) are less, or at least no greater, than a normal dog's opportunities of the same kind. (Indeed, as noted in Chapter 8, even normal humans do not appear to have greater opportunities for satisfaction than do "middling" mammals, except to the extent that they are expected to live longer—a factor that applies usually but by no means in every case.)

It is not at all straightforward that value theory vindicates a life move with such animals. If it does, whatever criteria are invoked will exclude certain humans—not only anencephalics and permanently comatose patients, but some severely retarded persons, persons with advanced Alzheimer's, and others. And appeals to the negative effects of killing on the moral community, and on the victim's loved ones, may be of limited comfort. To invoke such factors in justifying laxer standards for taking, say, canine life is to imply that these lax standards would be appropriate for these disadvantaged humans, were it not for certain social contingencies. Some will find that implausible.

Whatever live moves ultimately support presumptions against killing certain animals that are weaker than presumptions against killing humans, apes, and dolphins, these life moves are relevant *in principle* to major instrumental goods other than life. What they might amount to in practice is another question.[5]

NEGATIVE OBLIGATIONS REGARDING OTHER MAJOR INSTRUMENTAL GOODS

Let us turn to obligations, flowing from nonmaleficence, regarding other major instrumental goods: freedom (or liberty, the lack of external

---

[5] For some reason, leaders in animal ethics tend to miss this complexity, apparently thinking that the only major goods worth distinguishing are experiential well-being (as an intrinsic good) and life. Singer, for example, seems unaware of the instrumental roles of freedom, functioning, and experiential well-being:

> While self-awareness, the capacity to think ahead and have hopes and aspirations for the future, the capacity for meaningful relations with others and so on are not relevant to the question of inflicting pain—since pain is pain, whatever capacities, beyond the capacity to feel pain, the being may have— these capacities are relevant to the question of taking life. . . . The evil of pain is, in itself, unaffected by the other characteristics of the being who feels the pain; the value of life is affected by these other characteristics. (*Animal Liberation*, 2nd ed. [New York: New York Review, 1990], pp. 20–21)

constraints), functioning, and experiential well-being considered instrumentally.

Freedom is generally valuable to sentient animals due to its instrumental role in allowing lives that (1) are satisfying (on subjective views) or (2) permit the animal to exercise her natural capacities (on objective views). Confinement, then, generally harms sentient animals to the extent that it interferes with their living a good life (in the prudential sense). But confinement is a tricky concept. Is a well cared for dog confined if she cannot escape a square-acre backyard? Is a human baby confined if enclosed in a playpen, the ground floor of a house, or a fenced-in backyard? By *confinement*, I will mean *the imposition of external constraints on movement that significantly interfere with one's ability to live a good life*. Thus, fenced-in backyards, playpens, and the like do not necessarily confine in the sense relevant here; the devil is in the details.

We can now state this principle: *Don't confine sentient animals unnecessarily*. This does not imply that we should not have pets. For having pets does not confine animals in the relevant sense unless restrictions of their liberty practically preclude their having a good life.[6] Confinements in our sense are justified only when necessary. (As we will see later, zoos often confine animals unnecessarily.)

Confinement of *dangerous* animals—in particular, animals dangerous to humans—is sometimes necessary. My family once had a dog who bit a human child and, on another occasion, knocked down a different child. Neither was seriously injured, but the dog was clearly somewhat dangerous. She was taken away and exterminated—a case of killing that was wrong because unnecessary. Restricting her liberty to prevent her from injuring children would have been justified, however. (This might have been accomplished without confining her in our sense; proper use of leashes would probably have been quite compatible with her having a good life. But perhaps the dog was tormented by children who did not know any better, in which case educating the children would have been helpful.)

Of course, confinement of dangerous animals is often unnecessary. Sharks are dangerous but will not harm you if you never get near them. The point that it is sometimes necessary to confine dangerous animals concerns those who are likely to interact with us and cannot feasibly be returned to the wild (where they would not endanger us). So the fact that lions are dangerous would not justify confining them in zoos.

---

[6] Although I have not defended the claim that having pets is ethically defensible—a claim some animal-rights people deny—I cannot see how having pets, if they are treated well enough, could be objectionable. Here I assume we are talking about animals incapable of autonomous action; as explained later, any animals capable of acting autonomously would provoke distinct ethical considerations.

Clearly, *there is a strong presumption against confining nondangerous sentient animals.* But sometimes confining such animals *for their own safety* is justified; the expected benefit may compensate for the harm. But restricting an animal's liberty to ensure her safety is usually entirely compatible with her having a good life, in which case the restrictions are not confinements in the relevant sense.

The foregoing presumption is, of course, extremely strong in the case of normal humans. Taking away a person's freedom is a serious matter, whether she is imprisoned for life or detained temporarily in the interest of national security or her own safety. For reasons parallel to those stated in relation to killing, the presumption against confining beings like our autistic three-year-old should be as strong as that against confining normal humans. But this thesis crosses species lines: *The presumption against confining innocent humans, Great Apes, and dolphins is virtually absolute.* They have a very strong, although not absolute, right to liberty (or to restrictions of liberty that do not significantly obstruct their having good lives, as with reasonable restrictions of children's liberty). The qualification "innocent" is meant broadly here. It serves to indicate that the presumption against confining can be overridden for those who are dangerous and those (humans) whom it would be justifiable to incarcerate.

In cases where a nondangerous animal's safety is not a factor, when, if ever, might it be necessary to confine such an animal? One debatable possibility is a situation in which confining several animals appears to be the only way to procure desperately needed medical benefits. Is the case for confining an animal in such situations stronger than that for confining a normal human, due to the former's losing less from confinement? Can a life move be made regarding confinement?

Note, first, that on a subjective value theory, considerations of freedom are redundant, given those about experiential well-being. The harm of confinement reduces to the suffering, and loss of satisfaction, that it causes. And while confinement may have a greater experiential impact on humans than it does on animals with much duller mental lives—fish, herpetofauna, and birds—the case regarding mammals is far more dubious, and almost certainly bogus in the case of "middling" and "higher" mammals. On objective value theories, life moves regarding confinement are possible, in principle, even with most mammals. But they are difficult to separate from other considerations, because confinement generally lowers experiential well-being (a component of well-being on plausible objective views). In any event, *to the extent that we can separate out freedom interests in practice, for a large class of sentient animals—at least fish, herpetofauna, and birds—the presumption against confining them is ordinarily weaker than that against confining humans, Great Apes, and dolphins.* That by no means implies that confinement is not a serious moral matter with regard to the former animals. Confinement not only typically lowers experiential well-being; it can be fatal when the animal's needs are not well understood or are ignored.

Thus, in taking seriously the freedom interests of sentient animals, we must consider not just whether confinement is justified in a particular case, but also the conditions and duration of confinement. Just as we should confine only when necessary, we should confine only *to the extent* that is necessary. This means that pigeons confined for some necessary purpose should not be kept for a month if keeping them a week would suffice for that purpose (and they are capable of returning to the wild). More interestingly, in practice, *the conditions of any justified confinement must be responsive to the animal's needs.* If it is feasible to allow pigeons to fly around for parts of the day, that opportunity should be provided to them. Social needs are not met when, for example, monkeys are forced to live in isolation. (Whether it is ever justified to confine monkeys in the first place is hardly obvious. But, if so, permitting them meaningful interactions with conspecifics would be a high priority, perhaps a nearly absolute requirement.)

Functioning has an instrumental role very similar to that of freedom (see Chapter 8). Disabling, making an individual less able to function, is the corresponding harm. But has a hike disabled me, in any interesting sense, if it has so tuckered me out that for an hour I can't walk? Let me stipulate a more restricted use. By "disabling" I will mean *damaging someone's ability to function in a way that significantly interferes with her ability to live a good life.* On subjective views, the instrumental impact of disabling reduces to effects on experiential well-being. But disabling is ordinarily an extensive harm that does little or no good for anyone. So it would seem very hard to justify many cases of disabling, regardless of one's value theory. Now stopping the attack of a dangerous animal— say, a rabid dog or an alligator—might justifiably involve disabling her. However, *given our equal-consideration framework,* it is difficult to think of other circumstances justifying the disabling of sentient animals, even if doing so could bring substantial benefits. Hence, a strong conclusion: *There is a presumption against disabling sentient animals (that is, damaging their ability to function in ways that significantly interfere with their ability to live a good life), and, if such animals are nondangerous, the presumption is virtually absolute.* If this is correct, it rules out most or all research that disables animals, such as studies that involve fracturing live monkeys' skulls to study the head trauma sustained in automobile accidents.

What about experiential well-being taken instrumentally? On subjective value theories, experiential well-being would be instrumental to activities, pursuits, and conditions that are satisfying and enjoyable— that is, to experiential well-being! So there is little or no sense in trying to separate out an instrumental role for this good on subjective theories.

In principle, it is possible to do so within an objective theory. Then, theoretically, we might be able to justify a lesser presumption against causing suffering to certain kinds of animals—insofar as suffering is taken only instrumentally.

It does not seem worthwhile to try to put this theoretical possibility into practice. First, there would have to be a way of reconciling this life move with the fact that (a given amount of) suffering, *taken as an intrinsic evil,* gets equal moral weight no matter who has it. How, in practice, do you extricate suffering as an instrumental evil from suffering as an intrinsic evil? Maybe this problem is not insuperable, but there are others as well. For we would also have to deal with the fact that equal consideration suggests, at first glance, that a lowered presumption against causing suffering to certain animals implies a lowered presumption for similarly situated, handicapped humans. Naturally, one might try to soften this moral blow by appealing to effects on the moral community and loved ones. But this appeal is weaker here than in the case of killing, for at least the reason that causing temporary suffering for some very important benefit is unlikely to cause as much misery to loved ones as would killing. Finally, this theoretical possibility is intelligible only from objective views. (And, of course, they still owe us a theoretically deep account of comparative prudential value—although this concern is hardly unique to the present life move). I therefore favor simply taking the avoidance of suffering as a relevantly similar interest, whoever the interest-bearer is.

Beginning with the very general principle of nonmaleficence, a considered judgment, we have reasoned our way to a number of principles and other conclusions regarding the treatment of sentient animals. At this point, we will turn to ethical issues that start from much less certain ground than nonmaleficence: obligations to benefit and obligations to respect autonomy.

OBLIGATIONS TO BENEFIT

The problem introduced

In this section, we confront what I call *the problem of positive obligations,* a challenge to any ethics that takes animals seriously. Positive obligations are obligations to take active means to benefit, or prevent harm to, others. For convenience, let us use *benefit* or *help* to cover all such actions. Negative obligations, in contrast, require *not* doing certain kinds of things, such as harming or interfering with autonomous decisions. (There may be cases in which it is unclear whether an obligation should be classified as positive or negative, but this complication does not importantly affect our discussion.) The problem of positive obligations is best stated in the form of a *reductio ad absurdum*—an argument that tries to refute a position by showing that it implies something absurd.

Let us formulate the problem in a way that presents our final challenge to the extension of equal consideration to animals:

(1) Equal consideration, extended to animals, implies that we have positive obligations to animals that are as extensive as our positive obligations to humans; (2) Our positive obligations to humans are at least moderately extensive; therefore (3) Equal consideration, extended to animals, implies that we have at least moderately extensive positive obligations to animals; (4) That we have such positive obligations to animals implies that we should be aggressively engaged in their habitats, trying to save them from all manner of natural dangers; (5) The last thesis is absurd; therefore (6) We do not have moderately extensive positive obligations to animals; and therefore (7) Equal consideration, extended to animals, is mistaken.

This important challenge can be met.

To begin, although (2) will be disputed by libertarians and others who do not take humans very seriously, I grant it both for the sake of argument and because I believe it to be true. Premise (2) neither asserts that we have extremely strong positive obligations to humans nor question-beggingly precludes such obligations, which are asserted by some thinkers.[7] Still, the reductio argument falters at several points.

To begin with a relatively simple point, (4) is incorrect. It is consistent with the claim that we have moderately extensive positive obligations to animals that such obligations are limited to actions necessary to eliminate unnecessary harm to animals *caused by humans*. To abstain from and boycott such practices and institutions is most naturally understood as the stuff of negative duties. But *to take active means* to bring them down is a form of benefit or removal of harm, the stuff of positive obligations. Actions that seek to put an end to human abuse of animals

---

[7] For arguments in favor of extremely strong positive obligations to humans, see Peter Singer, "Famine, Affluence, and Morality," *Philosophy and Public Affairs* 1 (1972): 229–43; and Shelly Kagan, *The Limits of Morality* (Oxford: Clarendon, 1989). For a fascinating recent debate about whether *extremism* is tenable, see Jeremy Waldron, "Kagan on Requirements: Mill on Sanctions," *Ethics* 104 (1994): 310–24; Michael E. Bratman, "Kagan on 'The Appeal to Costs'," *Ethics* 104 (1994): 325–32; and Shelly Kagan, "Defending Options," *Ethics* 104 (1994): 333–51. For other stimulating contributions to this debate, see Fred Feldman, *Doing the Best We Can* (Dordrecht: Reidel, 1986); Samuel Scheffler, *Human Morality* (Oxford: Oxford University Press, 1992); Brad Hooker, "Rule-Consequentialism," *Mind* 99 (1990): 67–77; and Thomas L. Carson, "A Note on Hooker's 'Rule Consequentialism'," *Mind* 100 (1991): 117–21.

do not, at least in most cases, require aggressive engagement in animals' habitats. Think of protests against factory farms and bullfights.[8]

Our limited positive obligations to animals

Given other things we believe, equal consideration does imply that we have some positive obligations to animals (even if these obligations do not strictly depend on equal consideration). First, *special relationships with animals*, as with humans, are a basis of positive obligations.[9] By taking on pets (by initiating owner–pet relationships), owners assume a duty to take good care of their pets, to administer responsibly to their well-being. A pet owner who allows her cat to starve has violated this duty. I am prepared to defend the following principle, which states two necessary conditions: *Provide for the basic physical and psychological needs of your pet, and ensure that she has a comparably good life to what she would likely have if she were not a pet.*

The first clause—*a basic-needs requirement*—sets a floor of well-being for pets, since it condemns all failures to provide for their essential needs (including psychological needs, which are often neglected). It is justified by (1) the assumption of responsibility inherent in the act of taking on a pet, and, perhaps more intuitively, (2) considerations of basic decency on the understanding that animals have moral status. The second clause—*a comparable-life requirement*—is justified by the claim that animals should not be made worse off for becoming a pet, since making them worse off would be an unnecessary harm.[10] This requirement might be hard to engage in certain cases, since it requires information and imagination about what might have been. And sometimes it will offer little protection. A hopelessly domesticated poodle might simply starve if she were not a pet—in which case, a pretty crummy domesticated life could meet this standard. But the first clause picks up the ethical slack when the second is lax. The second clause protects animals from being forced to have an appreciably less good life

---

[8] Tom Mappes made me aware that (4) in the reductio argument can be challenged in this way.

[9] I do not mean to suggest that relationships are necessarily the *ultimate* basis for these obligations; perhaps a deeper basis could be found in consequentialist considerations or reasonable social expectations.

[10] If it were objected that sometimes having pets, even where this condition is not met, is important enough to count as necessary, I would be strongly inclined to disagree (except *possibly* in exceptional cases such as seeing-eye dogs for the blind). Anyway, equal consideration could be invoked to justify the comparable-life condition. We would not accept, for example, removing a child from a foster home if we knew she would end up worse off with her adoptive parents.

than they could otherwise have, just for their owners' sakes. A flourishing monkey, for example, might lose a lot by being captured and domesticated, even if her basic needs were met and she ended up being fairly well off, overall.

Positive obligations to animals can also be based on *voluntary agreements* that are independent of special relationships. If I begin a job with the Humane Society, I incur whatever obligations to animals my position is understood to involve. Joining an animal-protection organization may commit one to help animals in various specific ways. But neither positive obligations stemming from voluntary agreements nor those flowing from special relationships are very controversial.

The major source of controversy is the claim that we have an obligation to contribute to the general good of animals. While morality requires that we contribute, to some extent, to the general good, the extension of equal consideration to animals probably does not specifically require us to contribute to the general good *of animals;* or, if it does, it certainly does not generate moderately extensive positive obligations and, in particular, an obligation to be aggressively engaged in animals' habitats in order to protect them from dangers. [Premise (1) in the foregoing argument is incorrect, as is the conclusion (3); and, again, premise (4) is mistaken.] Let me explain.

First, outside of special relationships and voluntary agreements, our positive obligations are in an important sense *discretionary.* They are discretionary in the sense that we may *choose,* amid the deafening roar of urgent calls for help, to which we will respond. Start with humans. I know that there are many very weighty needs calling for our attention: people starving in Sudan, Indian girls sold into spousal slavery by their parents, impoverished Russian women hoodwinked by the promise of a job into coming to Europe and then forced into prostitution or pornography, Thai children sold into prostitution, African girls mutilated for the sexual satisfaction of tribesmen, South Africans butchered in racial and tribal conflicts, Salvadoran peasants randomly murdered by government-sponsored death squads, innocent blacks executed in the American south due to the incompetence and lack of interest of court-appointed lawyers, Washington DC children killed as they walk to school by the erratic gunfire of drug-addicted gang members, people dying of AIDS everywhere—among many, many, seemingly endlessly many more. I know that each of these causes is worthy and that I should help to alleviate suffering. At the same time, I am not obliged to contribute to *any one particular* cause. I should select some causes (and perhaps pray on behalf of others). Suppose that I do not contribute to the cause of Salvadoran peasants or Thai children. I have not thereby failed to give them equal consideration. I can grant the importance of their needs, but I cannot—and am not obliged even to try to—attend to every good cause. Equal consideration does not demand my contribution to any particular cause making up part of the general good.[11]

Now surely the needs of unknown animals are part of the common good, to which we should contribute. Still, even if every cause to which I contribute is a human cause, I probably have not failed to live up to equal consideration extended to animals. For, again, we have discretion about where and to whom to lend a hand. Moreover, we know the world of humans much better than that of animals and, for that reason, are likely to be much more effective feeding the human hungry than feeding starving wolves, with unknown effects on their ecological niche. True, we could learn more, and perhaps should—but even this investment would take time and other resources that could be devoted more directly to answering needs.

Some might object that a strikingly one-sided pattern of beneficence—say, all the causes to which one contributes are American, or tied to some religion—reveals a bias against the importance of certain other needs. Similarly, if I never lift a finger for animal causes, I show speciesist colors and fail to give equal consideration. I am doubtful about this argument, but let us grant it for now. It does not in any clear way imply that we have *moderately extensive* obligations to animals. Even less does it imply that we should be zooming through nature trying to protect animals against natural disasters, predators, and the like.

As explained previously, we can benefit animals in need not only by meddling in nature but by meddling with our current animal-abusing practices and institutions. Someone devoting a certain amount of time, energy, and money trying to contribute to the general animal good would almost certainly accomplish more by contributing to animal-protection groups, writing to congresspersons, participating in protests, supporting the study of alternatives to animal research, joining action committees, and the like, than by looking for animals in the wild and trying to help them.[12] Now there might be exceptions. Well-organized, knowledgeable groups such as Greenpeace do a lot of good for animals in their natural habitats. Then again, maybe their work is only a partial

[11] One might wonder, then, why we should grant premise (2), which claims that we have at least moderately extensive positive obligations *to humans*. If our positive obligations are discretionary, could one not ethically decide to contribute only to animal causes? But the idea of discretion is that one is not obliged to contribute to any one particular cause, an idea consistent with the claim that we are obliged to contribute to at least some human causes (leaving open which ones). What the ground might be of such an unspecific obligation to help humans is another matter. I simply assumed that this premise of the reductio argument was correct.

[12] See S. F. Sapontzis, *Morals, Reason, and Animals* (Philadelphia: Temple University Press, 1987), p. 247.

exception. Perhaps when they succeed in protecting individual animals in their habitat, they protect them from our animal-abusing practices, such as whaling.

Both proponents and critics of the reductio argument presented earlier sometimes ask whether equal consideration for animals (or some other animal-respecting principle) specifically implies that we should protect animals in the wild *from predators*. Even if we were required to meddle in nature, protecting animals from predators would not be a high priority—if it would be sensible at all. Better that we help whales stuck in ice or protect animals threatened by a natural disaster. Predators are, with very few exceptions (such as humans), exclusively or primarily carnivores, being unable to survive without meat. To protect the gazelle from the lion, or the elephant from the hyena, would be to save one but doom the other. It seems very doubtful that we are obliged to pick sides here (even if shooting a lion might cause the lion less suffering than what her gazelle victims would experience). Nature really seems to be "red in tooth and claw" when it comes to carnivores.[13] (While many steak-loving humans like to regard themselves as part of this vast chain of carnivorousness, they neglect the fact that omnivores do not need meat to survive with good health. Indeed, overall, meat may do us more harm than good.)

In conclusion, the reductio argument concerning positive obligations to animals fails. Contrary to that argument, if the combination of equal

---

[13] Nevertheless, Sapontzis takes the issue of interfering with predators very seriously. One reason is that he understands morality to involve three basic moral goals: a utilitarian one, fairness, and the development of character (ibid, p. 89). Even though utilitarian thinking is but one prong of his system, it leads him in the direction of serious interventionism. Sapontzis concludes as follows:

> D1: We are morally obligated to alleviate unjustified animal suffering that it is in our power to prevent without occasioning as much or more unjustified suffering.
> D2: Innocent animals suffer when they are preyed upon by other animals.
> D3: Therefore, we are morally obligated to prevent predation whenever we can do so without occasioning as much or more unjustified suffering than the predation would create, and we are also morally obligated to attempt to expand the number of such cases (p. 247).

This argument is problematic. D1 qualifies the animal suffering we should alleviate as *unjustified*. While D2 makes no mention of this qualification, Sapontzis assumes that causing the innocent to suffer is unjustified (personal communication). But, because most predators need meat to survive, I would argue that the suffering that they cause in doing what they have to do is not unjustified, in which case the obligation stated in D1 does not apply to most predation. Anyway, Sapontzis blunts the practical impact of D3 by making the good point that we can do more good by trying to end human abuse of animals, with the exception of preventing predation by animals under our control, such as our pets (p. 247).

consideration and our obligations to humans supports any positive obligations to animals, these obligations prove to be plausible ones.

IS RESPECT FOR AUTONOMY RELEVANT TO ANIMAL ETHICS?

We have now considered obligations not to harm animals in various ways and obligations to benefit them. Turning to another major ethical principle, does *respect for autonomy* generate any obligations to animals? In Chapter 7, evidence was found to be inconclusive as to whether any nonhuman animals meet the criteria for autonomous action. The need for critical self-reflection inherent in autonomy makes it doubtful that many animals could qualify. The most likely candidates are, naturally, language-trained apes and dolphins. Among the languageless, the most likely candidates are untrained apes and dolphins due to their overall cognitive sophistication.

Suppose that a series of ethological studies provided convincing evidence that chimpanzees and dolphins were capable of autonomous action. This development would complicate our obligations to them, for beneficence might now conflict with respect for autonomy. Imagine that a chimp colony in the wild is hit with a devastating disease that threatens to wipe out many of its members. A group of ethologists who had established a rapport with the chimps and earned their trust somehow manages to convey their desire to help. They have a promising treatment. But the chimps, appearing to understand their options, reject the offer of assistance. Should their refusal be paternalistically overridden in an effort to help the chimps?

Imagine that some dolphins well acquainted with kind and trusted scientists are having trouble surviving in the ocean. Several of these dolphins, when sick in the past, had been captured, restored to good health in benign captivity, and returned to the sea. The experiences of the formerly captive dolphins have been, in some rough way, communicated to the other dolphins. The scientists now succeed in communicating their offer of help, but the dolphins prefer to go it alone. Would paternalism be justified? (Assume in both scenarios that the humans have a prima facie obligation to benefit the animals, based on a longstanding professional commitment.)

Admittedly, this is not a pressing issue. For one thing, the cases are hypothetical on two major counts. We do not know that these animals are autonomous, and it is unclear that we could communicate so well with them. Even if one of these almost sci-fi scenarios became actual, the choice between an enlightened effort to help these animals and respecting their autonomy would not be a tragic choice. No one could be strongly criticized in such a case for either respecting autonomy or paternalistically intervening in a way that was very likely to be beneficial. Much more pressing are issues concerning our obligations to benefit in the absence of conflict and, even more, obligations not to harm.

Having said that, let me put forward a conditional promissory note of a principle: *If there appears to be a genuine conflict between benefiting an animal and respecting her autonomy, unless the expected benefit is very great and the apparent infringement of autonomy very marginal, respect autonomy.* This principle is sensible for two reasons.

For one, we generally favor autonomy in the human case, and there is no obvious reason why, in principle, we should treat any truly autonomous animals differently. Second, the difficulty of deeply understanding an animal's way of life makes it likely that, in practice, we could often be *mistaken* about what would benefit her, all things considered, especially when she appears to make an informed refusal of help. In judging what would benefit highly complex animals, one must take into account any known idiosyncratic likes and dislikes, even any values that they may have, since plausible value theories are at least partly subjective. Such individualized information could make a difference in certain cases—even if, in many other cases, it is fairly obvious what would bring benefit.

In cases in which an autonomous animal does not seem to understand the nature of her options, and it is quite clear (to humans) what would benefit her, there is the possibility of *presumed consent*. This is, in fact, a more likely scenario, due to the complications of interspecific communication. The animal's refusal might be based on an assumption of hostility on the part of concerned humans, a failure to understand her medical predicament, or fear. Such factors tend to undermine autonomy. Thus, it may be that although a dolphin does not want an intervention, she would want it if adequately informed about what was going on, not overcome by fear, and so on—in which case respecting autonomy and beneficence would converge.

RECAPITUATION

Before turning to the issues of eating animals and keeping them in zoos, let us list together the various principles and other conclusions reached thus far in this chapter.

1. Don't cause unnecessary harm.
2. Make every reasonable effort not to provide financial support for institutions that cause or support unnecessary harm. (For each of the following principles about the causing of some type of harm, we could—but will not here—formulate another principle about financial support of that kind of harm.)

3. Don't cause significant suffering for the sake of your or others' enjoyment.
4. Apply equally any standards allowing the causing of suffering.
5. Don't kill sentient animals unnecessarily.
6. The presumption against killing humans, Great Apes, and dolphins is virtually absolute.
7. For a large class of sentient animals—at least fish, herpetofauna (amphibians and reptiles), and birds—the presumption against killing these animals is ordinarily weaker than that against killing humans, Great Apes, and dolphins.
8. Don't confine sentient animals unnecessarily (where "confinement" is understood as the imposition of external constraints on movement that significantly interfere with one's ability to live a good life).
9. There is a strong presumption against confining nondangerous sentient animals.
10. The presumption against confining innocent humans, Great Apes, and dolphins is virtually absolute.
11. To the extent that we can separate out freedom interests in practice, for a large class of sentient animals—at least fish, herpetofauna, and birds—the presumption against confining them is ordinarily weaker than that against confining humans, Great Apes, and dolphins.
12. The conditions of any justified confinement must be responsive to the animal's needs.
13. There is a presumption against disabling sentient animals (that is, damaging their ability to function in ways that significantly interfere with their ability to live a good life) and, if they are nondangerous, the presumption is virtually absolute.
14. Provide for the basic physical and psychological needs of your pet, and ensure that she has a comparably good life to what she would likely have if she were not a pet.
15. If (hypothetically) there appears to be a genuine conflict between benefiting an animal and respecting her autonomy, unless the expected benefit is very great and the apparent infringement of autonomy very marginal, respect autonomy.

As mentioned previously, *most of these principles and conclusions do not seem to depend on the relatively strong assumption that equal consideration should be extended to animals.* Many grow out of the uncontroversial idea that we have a prima facie duty not to harm, in combination with insights about the ways in which sentient animals can be harmed. Moreover, I have been somewhat cautious methodologically. In numerous cases, I preferred to risk erring on the side of understatement in order to increase certainty while stating norms that would prove to have important practical consequences.

Of course, I have argued that equal consideration for animals is more reasonable than its denial, given the failure of opponents of equal consideration to meet their burden of proof. Perhaps the burden of proof will be met someday (although I wouldn't hold my breath). Anyway, those who doubt that animals should be extended *equal* consideration should note that a commitment to giving animals *serious* consideration would be enough to support most of the foregoing conclusions. In particular, I believe (although I will not argue here) that only conclusions 4 and 13 clearly depend on equal consideration, and that, of the others, only 6, 10, and 14 might depend on this assumption. Let us turn now to some additional practical consequences of the present view.

THE ISSUE OF MEAT EATING

The ethics of meat eating is the most important ethical issue involving our treatment of animals. No other human practice comes close in its impact on animals, considering the numbers of animals harmed and the extent of harm. In the United States more than 100 million mammals are slaughtered each year for food; the number of birds is an astounding 5 billion yearly. (Harms other than death will be discussed later.) Factory farming—the institution of intensive animal-rearing methods that produces most of the meat we consume—is a true ethical oddity. As we will see, there is probably no practice that is more commonly accepted yet so difficult to defend (cogently) than that of purchasing and eating factory-farmed meat. Still, meat eating is not an area of ethical absolutes. Eating meat is not intrinsically wrong. Meat eating is wrong when it is due to the relationship between one's actions and the causing of unnecessary harm to animals.

Factory farming

1. Description. Since World War II, factory farms—which try to raise as many animals as possible in the smallest possible space in order to maximize profits—have largely replaced traditional family farms, 3 million of which have gone out of business. The single-minded pursuit of profit has the corollary that animals are nothing but meat-producing objects. They have been treated as such. Increasingly intensive rearing conditions have guaranteed that *death* is not the only harm to which factory-farmed animals are subjected. They are *confined* (in our sense), sometimes *disabled* by injury, and caused to have such unpleasant experiences as pain, fear, anxiety, and boredom. It is safe to say that factory-farmed animals typically experience considerable *suffering* in their lives, as we will see in the regrettably brief summary that follows.[14]

After hatching, *broiler chickens* are moved to enclosed sheds containing automatic feeders and waterers. From 10,000 to 75,000 birds are kept in a single shed, which becomes increasingly crowded as they grow at an abnormally fast rate. Crowding often leads to cannibalism and other aggressive behaviors; another occurrence is panic-driven piling on top of one another, sometimes causing suffocation. Concerns about the possibility of aggression have led many farmers to debeak their chickens, apparently through sensitive tissue. By slaughter time, chickens have as little as six-tenths of a square foot of space apiece. There is typically little ventilation, and the never-cleaned droppings produce air thick with ammonia, dust, and bacteria.

Laying hens live their lives in "battery" cages made entirely of wire. Cages are so crowded that hens can seldom fully stretch their wings; debeaking is common practice to limit the damage of hens' pecking cagemates. For hours before laying an egg, a hen, deprived of any nest, paces anxiously amid the mob; at egg-laying time, she must stand on a sloped, uncomfortable wire floor that precludes the instinctual behaviors of scratching, dust bathing, and pecking for food. Unnatural conditions, lack of normal exercise, and demands for high egg production cause bone weakness. Some hens undergo forced molting, stimulated by up to twelve days without food. When considered spent, hens are stuffed into crates and transported in uncovered trucks for slaughter; during handling and transport, many (over two-thirds in one study) incur broken bones. Laying hens and broiler chickens have the same fate: They are shackled upside down, fully conscious, on conveyor belts before their throats are cut by an automated knife. (Hens' brothers have short lives due to their commercial uselessness. After hatching, they are gassed, dumped into plastic sacks and left to suffocate, or ground up while still alive to make feed for their sisters.)

Hogs, a highly intelligent and social species, have virtually nothing to do in factory farms except stand up, lie down, eat, and sleep. Usually deprived of straw or other sources of amusement, and separated from

[14]My description of factory farms draws broadly from Michael W. Fox, *Farm Animals: Husbandry, Behavior, and Veterinary Practice* (Baltimore, MD: University Park Press, 1984), Part I; Jim Mason and Peter Singer, *Animal Factories* (New York: Crown, 1980), chs. 1–3; Singer, *Animal Liberation*, ch. 3 (which draws mainly from trade journals and magazines of the farm industry); Melanie Adcock and Mary Finelli, "The Dairy Cow: America's 'Foster Mother'," *HSUS News* (Winter 1995); Melanie Adcock, "The Truth Behind 'A Hen's Life'," *HSUS News* (Spring 1993); and the following brochures from the Humane Society of the United States: "Farm Animals and Intensive Confinement" (1994), "Questions and Answers About Veal" (1990), "Fact Sheet on Hogs" (1983), and "Fact Sheet on Broiler Chickens" (1983).

each other by iron bars in small crates, hogs appear to suffer greatly from boredom. Sometimes they amuse themselves by biting a tail in the next crate. Industry's increasingly common response is to cut off their tails—a procedure that, like castration of males, is usually done without anesthesia. Hogs stand on either wire mesh, slatted floors, or concrete floors—all highly unnatural footings. Poor ventilation and accumulating waste products cause powerful fumes. Hogs are often abused at the loading and unloading stages of transport, particularly at the slaughterhouse. Rough handling sometimes includes the use of whips and electrical "hot shots."

Veal calves are probably worse off than other farm animals. Shortly after birth, they are taken from their mothers and transported considerable distances—often with rough handling, exposure to the elements, and no food or rest. At the veal barn, they are confined in solitary crates too small to allow them to turn around or even sleep in a natural position. Denied solid food and water, they are given a liquid milk replacer deficient in iron (in order to produce the gourmet white flesh), resulting in anemia. Because it is drunk from buckets, rather than suckled, the liquid food often enters the rumen rather than the true stomach, causing diarrhea and indigestion. The combination of deprivations sometimes result in such neurotic behaviors as sucking the boards of crates and stereotyped tongue rolling.

Like their veal-calf siblings, many *dairy cows*, as calves, never receive colostrum—the milk produced by their mothers, which helps to fight diseases. More and more they are confined either indoors or in overcrowded drylots (which have no grass). Unanesthetized tail docking is increasingly performed. In order to produce some twenty times the amount of milk a calf would need, dairy cows are fed a diet heavy in grain—as opposed to the roughages for which their digestive tracts are suited—creating health problems that include painful lameness and metabolic disorders, which are exacerbated by confinement. About half the U.S. dairy cows at any one time have mastitis, a painful udder inflammation. Many cows today are given daily injections of Bovine Growth Hormone to stimulate additional growth and increase milk production (despite a surplus of dairy products). Although their natural life span is about twenty to twenty-five years, at about age four, dairy cows become unable to maintain production levels and are transported for slaughter. Most processed beef comes from them.

Cattle raised specifically for beef are, on the whole, better off than the other farm animals already described. Many of the cattle get to roam in the outdoors for about six months. Then they are transported long distances to feedlots, where they are fattened up on grain rather than grass. Craving roughage, the cattle often lick their own and other cattle's coats; the hair that enters the rumen sometimes causes abscesses.

Most feedlots do not confine intensively. Their major sources of distress are the boredom likely to result from a barren environment, unrelieved exposure to the elements, dehorning (which cuts through arteries and other tissue), branding, the cutting of ears into special shapes for identification purposes, and unanesthetized castration (which involves pinning the animal, cutting his scrotum, and ripping out each testicle).

Transporting hogs and cattle for slaughter—which can entail up to three days without food, water, or rest—typically results in conspicuous weight loss and other signs of deprivation. Pneumonia, broken limbs, and death are common occurrences. The slaughtering process itself is likely to cause fear. The animals are transported on a conveyor belt or goaded up a ramp in the stench of their fellows' blood. In the best of circumstances, animals are rendered unconscious by a captive-bolt gun or electric shock before their throats are slit.

2. Moral evaluation. With these facts in view, it is clear that the institution of factory farming, which causes massive harm for trivial purposes, is ethically indefensible. So is the practice of supporting factory farms by purchasing their products. Let me elaborate.

Factory farms violate the following conclusions, stated earlier: (3) Don't cause significant suffering for the sake of your or others' enjoyment; (5) Don't kill sentient animals unnecessarily; (8) Don't confine sentient animals unnecessarily; and (13) There is a presumption against disabling sentient animals and, if they are nondangerous, the presumption is virtually absolute. Besides killing sentient animals, factory farming also causes them significant suffering and restricts their liberty in ways incompatible with their living well (beef cattle being a possible exception in the months when they are free to roam). In many cases, animals are also seriously disabled through injury.

The crucial insight in evaluating factory farms is that none of the inflicted harms can plausibly be regarded as *necessary*. That is because we do not need to eat meat to be healthy, much less to survive. (Even if a very unusual person, or someone in dire circumstances, needed meat to survive, he or she presumably would not need factory-farmed meat in particular.) The chief benefit of meat to the consumer is enjoyment. Meat tastes good. For those who cannot with experience come to enjoy nonmeat foods as much as meat, meat eating represents *additional enjoyment*—enjoyment beyond what a meatless diet would bring them. Factory farms wrongly cause significant suffering to procure this extra enjoyment (3). And this benefit can hardly be thought to justify the killing (5), confining (8), and (when applicable) disabling (13) of sentient animals. (If one claimed that the basic purpose of factory-farmed meat were not enjoyment but rather something else, such as convenience or tradition, it would be appropriate to respond that no purpose plausibly ascribed to meat eating could justify the harms described.)

Some who are interested in animal welfare have the intuition that the factory farming of chickens is less morally problematic than that of hogs and cattle. Now recall these conclusions: (7) For a large class of sentient animals—at least fish, herpetofauna, and birds—the presumption against killing these animals is ordinarily weaker than that against killing humans, Great Apes, and dolphins; and (11) To the extent that we can separate out freedom interests in practice, for a large class of sentient animals—at least fish, herpetofauna, and birds—the presumption against confining them is ordinarily weaker than that against confining humans, Great Apes, and dolphins. If comparable amounts of suffering are caused to factory-farmed animals, there may be some basis for distinguishing the cases of chickens and the other animals. Chickens are birds, and perhaps life moves can be made with respect to birds and the mammals in question (even though our conclusions make comparisons between the "highest" mammals—not hogs and cattle—and birds). On the other hand, chickens may suffer much more than cattle raised specifically for beef due to their different lots in farm life. Moreover, no plausible argument can be made that the fate of factory-farmed chickens is necessary, only that the way chickens are treated may be less bad.

Factory farming is an ethically indefensible institution. But is it wrong to buy and eat its products? Earlier we reasoned carefully to this conclusion: (2) Make every reasonable effort not to provide financial support for institutions that cause or support unnecessary harm.[15] Factory farms stay in business only as long as people buy their products. Given the terrible harms they inflict—and the fact that consuming their products is not needed for life, health, or enjoyment[16]—one who regularly patronizes factory farms (as most American consumers do) can hardly be described as making every reasonable effort not to support

---

[15] I believe that this principle is more easily applied than the principle of utility favored by Singer, who struggles somewhat in trying to show why we should be vegetarians in *Animal Liberation* (pp. 163–64). In an article, Singer forges a more convincing link between utilitarianism and vegetarianism ("Utilitarianism and Vegetarianism," *Philosophy and Public Affairs* 9 [1980]: 325–37). Also, unlike Tom Regan's approach (*The Case for Animal Rights* [Berkeley: University of California Press, 1983], mine does not require the assertion of nearly absolute rights for animals—an assertion reasonably debated and underdetermined by Regan's arguments.

[16] Even if, contrary to my assumption, someone could not enjoy food *at all* without meat, that would be no more reason to gratify his tastes than would the fact that someone could enjoy only child pornography be a reason to satisfy his tastes. See Singer, *Animal Liberation*, ch. 4, for details about the viability of vegetarianism as a life style.

them. Meat consumers commonly feel psychologically distant from the activities of factory farms, but morally they are close enough to share responsibility for these activities. Could someone who largely abstains from meat but occasionally makes an exception (say, when visiting parents on a holiday) be described as making every reasonable effort—or as doing her share—not to support factory farms? Perhaps, and it seems wise not to quibble about the finer points. The important idea is that people should recognize the wrongness of supporting factory farms and act accordingly.

Our case for the duty to boycott factory farms has been based on conclusions focusing on our obligations to animals. Perhaps surprisingly, this case is strengthened when we focus on human welfare. Here I will simply summarize some leading considerations.

First, *factory farming has had a terrible impact on the environment in terms of pollution and the consumption and inefficient use of soil, energy, and water.*[17] Second, *factory farming has a pernicious effect on the global distribution of food for humans.* For example, it takes twenty-one pounds of protein to feed a calf to produce one pound of beef for humans. Somewhat less inefficiently, it takes about eight pounds of protein in hog feed to generate a pound of pork. Humans are affected by such extraordinary inefficiency. The American demand for meat requires devoting close to ninety percent of our oats, soybeans, sorghum, corn, and barley—and half our cropland—to feeding farm animals, who return about one-seventh as much in edible meat. Meanwhile, wealthy countries' demand for meat makes plant proteins too costly for the masses in countries touched by starvation. There is easily enough grain protein, if used appropriately, to feed every human on earth.[18] Third, *factory farming in the United States has greatly harmed family farmers and rural communities by putting some 3 million farms out of business.* The American meat industry is now dominated by a relatively small number of large corporations (which receive the greater share of government farm subsidies). These companies have misled the public by promoting an image of gentle, traditional farming methods and by distorting information about the dietary impact of meat.[19] Finally, *meat eating, especially at average American rates, is associated with several health problems.* Americans consume about 2.5 times as much protein as they need and too little carbohydrates and fiber, with higher rates of coronary heart disease, stroke,

---

[17] See, e.g., Humane Society of the United States, "Environmental Fact Sheet" (1994); and Mason and Singer, *Animal Factories*, ch. 6.

[18] See Mason and Singer, *Animal Factories*, pp. 71–81, 116; and Frances Moore Lappe and Joseph Collins, *World Hunger: Twelve Myths* (New York: Grove, 1986).

[19] See, e.g., Humane Society, "Farm Animals and Intensive Confinement"; and Mason and Singer, *Animal Factories*, ch. 7.

diabetes, atherosclerosis, and certain cancers.[20] Part of the problem may be inadequate policies for inspecting factory farms.[21] Contrary to common concerns, vegetarianism is not associated with health problems; indeed, some phenomenal athletes with huge protein needs have been vegetarians.[22] At the same time, it cannot be inferred from these data that a diet that includes a modest amount of meat is less healthful than a vegetarian diet.[23]

In conclusion, the case for a duty to boycott factory farms is overwhelmingly strong. All things considered, perhaps the only major beneficiaries of factory farms are large agribusinesses. Gradually putting them out of business by boycotting their products would have at least short-term costs—for the business owners, their employees, and maybe local economies. Concerns about such costs have motivated utilitarian efforts to justify the status quo.[24] But five points should demonstrate that these costs do not negate the duty to boycott. First, the costs in question would be borne only once, whereas the costs to the animals will continue indefinitely if factory farms stay in business. Second, ending factory farms (assuming that they are not simply replaced by less intensive meat-production methods) would free up massive amounts of currently wasted protein, which could be used to feed hungry humans. Third, harmful effects on the environment and (for those who quit meat generally, not just factory-farmed meat) on human health would be avoided.[25] Fourth, the demise of factory farms should permit more family farms—including ones producing no meat—to go into business, reducing if not fully counterbalancing the costs in question. Fifth, my argument for the duty to boycott does not depend on utilitarianism—stemming instead from the principles mentioned previously—so it is not vulnerable to utilitarian refutation.

It may be heartening to know that several countries have begun to institute reforms that curb some of the excesses of factory farming.[26] But in a country as dominated by big business as the United States is, it would be naive to wait for the government to act to protect animals. Consumer initiative is the only way.

---

[20] Humane Society of the United States, "Human Health Fact Sheet" (1994)
[21] ibid; Orville Schell, *Modern Meat* (New York: Random House, 1978), pp. 323–27
[22] Singer, *Animal Liberation*, pp. 179–83
[23] This point is made in Michael P. T. Leahy, *Against Liberation: Putting Animals in Perspective* (London: Routledge, 1991), p. 213.
[24] See R. G. Frey, *Rights, Killing, and Suffering* (Oxford: Blackwell, 1983), pp. 197–203; and Leahy, *Against Liberation*, pp. 214–15.
[25] Roughly these three utilitarian counterarguments are made in Singer, "Utilitarianism and Vegetarianism," pp. 333–34.
[26] See Fox, *Farm Animals*, ch. 7; and Singer, *Animal Liberation*, pp. 112–13, 136, 142–44.

Traditional family farms

Because the vast majority of animals we eat come from factory farms, most of our discussion of eating animals has concerned this institution. But people also eat animals who come from other sources. One of these is the traditional family farm.

Family farms cause much less suffering to animals than do factory farms due to their far less intensive rearing conditions. Indeed, some animals may not even be confined in our sense; the restraints on their liberty may not significantly interfere with their living well. But, no matter how innocuous the living conditions, animals must die to become meat, so they cannot escape harm.

The moral case for family farms is much stronger than that for factory farms. Still, in the final analysis, the institution of family farming and our financial support of it seem ethically indefensible. For one thing, the killing of sentient animals in family farms is unnecessary, since meat eating is (in all but the most extreme circumstances) unnecessary. Moreover, certain aspects of family farming do cause significant suffering. Beef producers brand, dehorn, and castrate cattle. Almost all family farming methods involve the separation of mothers from their young at an early age—presumably distressing such animals as cattle and hogs, probably even chickens.[27] There are also harms involved in slaughter and, where applicable, prior handling and transport.

Most of these harms are, or can be, escaped by chickens and turkeys on family farms. (Unfortunately, an increasing proportion of turkeys are being raised in factory farms.) If a chicken or turkey were never abused and were allowed to live a pleasant life (say, with families intact) before being instantaneously killed, death would be the only relevant harm. Although my view condemns unnecessary killing, I have argued that birds are harmed less by death, ordinarily, than are the "highest" mammals. Those who, in disagreement with me, hold that death does not harm birds at all might find no grounds to condemn this part of family farming.

Seafood

Many of the animals we eat come from the sea. Consider, first, *fish and cephalopods (squid and octopi)*. In Chapter 5, we concluded that these animals are sentient, subject to pain and distress. Whether their consciousness is complex enough for them to suffer was left somewhat more open. Catching fish and cephalopods involves hooking or netting them and causing them to suffocate—clearly causing unpleasant feel-

[27]Singer, *Animal Liberation*, p. 146

ings. Traditional fishing methods do not involve confinement, since the animals are free to live in their natural environment. Of course, fish and cephalopods die in order to become food. I have argued that death harms sentient animals, even such "low" animals as trout. But those who might disagree in the case of birds are even more likely to do so in the case of fish.

In a best-case scenario, then, fish or cephalopods might be harmed very little. Those who believe that these creatures are not harmed by death, and who doubt they suffer, might hold that the minor harm of short-term unpleasant feelings are compensated for by the gains to humans: health, convenience, pleasure, and employment for fishers.[28] My thesis that death harms the sentient, and my inclination to give fish and cephalopods the benefit of any doubt regarding suffering, lead me to a different view. I hold that fishing is probably not justified (assuming that other foods are available and adequate, as they may *not* be for some people around the world). At the same time, I have argued that we must make every *reasonable*—not every *possible*—effort not to support unjustified institutions and practices. It might be argued that someone who has boycotted factory farms and family farms but occasionally eats fish has met this standard. I *suspect* that we are obliged to boycott fish, but certainly buying fish is much less morally problematic than buying factory-farmed or even family-farmed meat.

I have neglected a complexity: Many fish today are raised in fish farms, which entail terrific crowding of fish. These conditions amount to confinement and no doubt add to the unpleasantness of the fish's lives. When fish have been raised in this way, the case for a duty to boycott becomes stronger.

Shrimp, crabs, lobsters, and other invertebrates (other than cephalopods) are another form of seafood. As discussed in Chapter 5, available evidence does not make a strong case that these animals are sentient, although the issue is hardly settled. If they are not sentient, nothing we do to them harms them at all. Highly virtuous people may wish to give them the benefit of the doubt and abstain from eating them. My view does not condemn eating these animals.

There is one more case that deserves mention. For many years, the nets used to catch tuna (a kind of fish) frequently ensnared and killed *dolphins*. But recall this conclusion: (6) The presumption against killing humans, Great Apes, and dolphins is virtually absolute. Fortunately, public outcry about the killing of dolphins motivated tuna catchers to adopt dolphin-safe nets, which allow dolphins to escape through spe-

---

[28] Of course, a strong animal-rights view, such as Regan's, would not yield this result because the gains to some could not justify harming others (except in rare circumstances that do not apply here).

cial holes—a nice example of the difference that protest and boycotting can make. While supporting the tuna industry is itself morally problematic, buying tuna from companies that regularly doom dolphins is about as grave a matter as supporting factory farms.

THE ISSUE OF ZOOS

The ethics of keeping animals in zoos has received comparatively little attention in the literature. But as the public becomes more interested in animal welfare, the ethical adequacy of zoos is increasingly questioned. In contrast to factory farms—which by their nature are extremely intensive and harmful to animals—zoos *can*, I will argue, meet appropriate ethical requirements, even if few presently do. The issue of zoos differs from that of meat eating generally because zoo-going is for most people an occasional activity that costs little or nothing, leaving scarce room for boycott. The ethical focus is better placed on zoo owners and directors and on legislators.

Description of zoos[29]

Animals have been collected and kept for many years, dating back at least to ancient Egypt and ancient China. The modern era of zoos, or zoological parks—parks that exhibit animals, chiefly for entertainment or educational purposes—apparently begins in 1827 with what is now known as the London Zoo, which, like many modern zoos, also proclaimed scientific objectives.

Zoos could not exist if animals were never taken from the wild. Both historically and typically today, the process of keeping animals in zoos begins with humans entering the wild and capturing animals, transporting them (sometimes intercontinentally) to a zoo, and introducing them to a new, captive existence. In many cases, an additional step is that of trading and dealing in wild animals, a step that often includes considerable cruelty and neglect. Not surprisingly, the rigors of this extended process kill many animals. Death may come from an arduous journey (which may include mistreatment), deadly infections, or im-

[29] My description of zoos draws broadly from Stephen St C. Bostock, *Zoos and Animal Rights* (London: Routledge, 1993), chs. 5–7; Jeremy Cherfas, *Zoo 2000* (London: British Broadcasting Co., 1984); John W. Grandy, "Zoos: A Critical Reevaluation," *HSUS News* (Summer 1992); John W. Grandy, "Captive Breeding in Zoos," *HSUS News* (Summer 1989); H. Hediger, *Wild Animals in Captivity* (New York: Dover, 1964); Humane Society of the United States, "Zoos" (1984); Dale Jamieson, "Against Zoos," in Peter Singer (ed.), *In Defense of Animals* (Oxford: Blackwell, 1985), pp. 108–9; and Linda Koebner, *Zoo Book: The Evolution of Wildlife Conservation Centers* (New York: Forge, 1994).

proper adaptation in the new zoo environment. In addition, family members of captured animals are often killed to facilitate capture; a well-known example is the slaughter of chimpanzee mothers in order to obtain infant chimps. Naturally, the potentially lethal events and conditions sometimes injure and cause disability. In the case of animals who live in families or other social units, groups are broken up by the process of capture and delivery (unless the entire family or group is captured and kept together).

An alternative to capturing animals for zoos today is to breed animals from those already in captivity. Breeding animals of an endangered species may even be among the stated purposes of a zoo. Some zoos breed in order to sell surplus animals. Breeding may occur simply because fertile animals are caged together, or it may be the result of managed breeding programs. In the very best of cases, breeding programs attend to the need for genetic diversity (to avoid health problems associated with inbreeding), avoid creating animals beyond the number that can be adequately cared for, and release some of the animals to the wild.

Regarding life for the captive animal, zoos vary enormously. The continuum includes "zoos" that are not literally zoological parks; the most squalid are road-side menageries, often featuring a single caged animal to attract passersby to a gas station or gift shop. Some larger menageries (usually called *zoos*) share in none of the major purposes of zoos except possibly entertainment; animals are housed in small, barren cages, and visitors are neither educated about the animals nor encouraged to respect them. But even zoological parks proper vary a great deal. Some are little better than the larger menageries just described. Many, such as the National Zoo in Washington, DC, have some good exhibits, with adequate space and enrichment given the animals' needs, as well as some very poor exhibits. The best have a great deal of space and in some instances nearly reproduce animals' natural habitats. My (quite fallible, literature-based) impression is that some of the best zoos are the San Diego Wild Animal Park, Zoo Atlanta, Brookfield Zoo in Chicago (the world's largest indoor exhibit), the Bronx Zoo, and the Edinburgh Zoo and Glasgow Zoo in Scotland.

Ethical evaluation

1. Taking animals from the wild. Let us begin our ethical evaluation of zoos by considering the taking of animals from the wild. We know that capture and transport often kill animals and that many die soon after arriving at zoos. Even the best-intentioned efforts cannot prevent all such deaths, given what is involved in capture and transport as well as the innumerable potential harms that threaten stressed creatures entering an alien environment. Based on what we know about the mental life of vertebrate animals—since the vast majority of zoo exhibits display vertebrates—capture can be assumed commonly to inflict pain, fear, anxiety, and suffering. In the case of highly social animals, breaking up families or other groups presumably causes sadness and feelings of missing loved ones. During transport, animals also endure temporary confinement in our sense: They do not live well during passage. And disability is at least occasionally an outcome. The harms of unpleasant feelings and temporary confinement (which are predictable), disability (at least occasional), and death (common) together set a very strong presumption against capturing wild animals. (See especially the foregoing conclusions 1, 4, 5, 8, and 13.)

Can this presumption be overridden for the commonly cited benefits of entertainment, education, research, or species preservation? Might the harms involved in capturing animals for zoos be considered necessary? In the case of the first three benefits, we are clearly concerned with benefits *to humans* (although some benefit may eventually redound to certain animals following successful research). I believe that the goals of entertainment, education, and research cannot justify the harms in question—at least in the case of mammals, the chief interest of zoogoers. Entertainment is simply not a serious enough benefit to justify such harms; principle 3 prohibits causing significant suffering for the sake of people's enjoyment. Education and research are weightier goals, but zoos are not necessary for education about animals in our multimedia world, while at least most research does not depend on the existence of zoos.[30] Even if some research does depend on zoos, and the research itself is reasonably considered necessary (no small assumption!), there are already many animals in zoos. Given the alternative of breeding, further capture of animals from the wild is clearly unnecessary, for any of these three goals.

Can the goal of species preservation justify the likely harms of capturing wild animals? Perhaps for public-relations reasons, many zoos portray themselves as promoting the protection of endangered species. Yet, of over 900 endangered species, no more than 15 have been bred in zoos for return to their natural habitats. Breeding commonly produces surplus animals who are auctioned off or otherwise disposed of; they may end up in roadside menageries or at game ranches where they are hunted as trophies. Moreover, animals who are returned to the wild may be unequipped if they were not parented by their own species.[31]

---

[30] See Jamieson, "Against Zoos," pp. 111–13; and Grandy, "Zoos: A Critical Evaluation." On the other side, Bostock argues that some educational and scientific benefits do require zoos (*Zoos and Animal Rights,* chs. 10 and 11).
[31] Grandy, "Captive Breeding in Zoos"

Poor record keeping in zoos often leads to inbreeding, producing young animals who perish more easily from environmental stresses and diseases.[32] At the same time, some zoos *are* doing good species-preservation work. But usually this is done at breeding facilities remote from the public, not at the zoos themselves, casting further doubt on the need for zoos—much less the capturing of new animals—to protect endangered species.[33]

Another reason to doubt that species preservation justifies capturing wild animals, or even keeping animals in zoos, is the debatable value of the goal. When preserving species is compatible with treating individual animals sufficiently well, the goal is laudibly pursued. But if species preservation and animal welfare *conflict*—say, if preserving a monkey species required capturing several monkeys, keeping them in conditions that made them miserable, and forcing them to mate—I cannot see any justification for sacrificing the individuals' interests.[34] No doubt some humans would be very pleased to know that a species had been saved, but their pleasure would not justify causing serious harm to the monkeys. Moreover, there is no being corresponding to the words *nature, biosphere,* or *the environment* who would benefit. And I do not find plausible the assertion that the discontinuation of a single species out of the innumerable species on earth can inflict terrible damage on the ecosystem.

In conclusion, *at least in the case of mammals, wild animals should not be captured for zoo exhibits.* (A reasonable exception in principle is the case of a particular animal who would be better off being captured and cared for. But I would not be optimistic about the results of giving people the discretion to make such a judgment.) Our discussion has mostly focussed on mammals, the main draw for zoos. In the case of "lower" animals, some of the harms involved in capture may be smaller in degree. Conclusions 7 and 11 state that the presumptions against killing and confining are ordinarily weaker in the case of a large class of species—at least the "submammalian" ones—than in the case of apes, dolphins, and humans; a detailed value theory may permit more specific life moves that would be relevant in this context. Furthermore, the

---

[32]Cherfas, *Zoo 2000*, p. 113; Jamieson, "Against Zoos," p. 114

[33]It might be claimed that zoos are necessary to maintain public support for the breeding facilities, making zoos indirectly necessary for species-preservation projects. This seems possible but quite speculative in the absence of evidence. Anyway, I don't think this possibility crucially affects my position in light of the other considerations under discussion.

[34]Bostock claims to reconcile animal rights and environmental ethics by allowing that sentient animals should be respected both as sentient individuals and as remarkable things worthy of preservation (*Zoos and Animal Rights*, p. 135). But he never explores the value claims of environmental ethics in any depth or even notes how the two approaches can conflict.

fact that "submammalian" animals generally have less rich mental lives and less emotionally close ties to conspecifics means that, other things being equal, their capture is likely to involve less harm in the way of unpleasant feelings. Perhaps in some cases the associated harms could be kept to a near-zero level. I therefore leave open the possibility that the goals of education, research, and species preservation justify capturing some "submammalian" animals, but the case for doing so would be greatly weakened where captive breeding is feasible.

2. Keeping animals in zoos. Regarding animals already in zoos, is it morally justified to keep them in zoos at all? If so, under what conditions? If asked what harm is likely to befall the best-treated zoo animals—who ideally live full, pleasant lives—we are likely to think of captivity itself. But captivity is not necessarily a harm. *Not all captivity is confinement in our sense of restrictions of liberty that significantly interfere with an animal's ability to live a good life.* If a lizard, robin, groundhog, or cheetah is not confined in our sense, captivity per se does not harm her.

Conclusion 14, which states criteria for appropriate pet keeping, suggests two reasonable criteria for keeping zoo animals: *Provide for the basic physical and psychological needs of the zoo animal, and ensure that she has a comparably good life to what she would likely have if in the wild.* Thus, as with pets, we have basic-needs and comparable-life conditions, both of which must be met.[35] If the basic needs of a dolphin are met, but barely, and the dolphin would be doing much better in the wild, keeping her is wrong. If some of a hyena's basic needs are not met in captivity, keeping her in those conditions is unjustified even if she would probably be worse off in the wild due to limited food supplies and bitter weather. (In cases like this last one, it may be better to try to improve conditions so as to meet the animal's basic needs rather than return her to the wild.)

Some may disagree that any conditions can justify captivity—perhaps for reasons relating to respect. But if an animal's needs are met and her life is at least as good as it otherwise would be, I can see no more reason to object to keeping her than there are reasons to oppose restricting human children's liberty in certain familiar ways. Preventing a five-year-old from drinking whiskey, or from living at a neighbor's house, and keeping a bird in a way that meets the foregoing two conditions are examples of restricting liberty that are *not* instances of

[35] I am unsure whether taking an animal from the wild or keeping her in a zoo is analogous to taking on a pet in terms of assuming the responsibilities of a special relationship. If not, then the basic-needs condition is justified solely by an argument from decency on the assumption that animals have moral status. (See the earlier discussion of pets.)

disrespecting autonomy. In neither case is there autonomy to disrespect (see Chapter 7).

While the present view does not oppose all keeping of animals in zoos, the two necessary conditions constitute a very challenging standard. Apparently, only a small fraction of zoo exhibits currently meet this standard,[36] but it can be met—at least with most animals. With highly social animals, such as elephants and primates, meeting this standard may require family preservation, given the likely psychological harms of breaking up families.

In the case of most species, a really good zoo exhibit can meet animals' needs and offer them a good alternative to the wild by promising certain benefits. Life in the wild can be "nasty, brutish, and short." While we must not underestimate harms that are likely to attend certain conditions of captivity, neither should we naively glorify the wild. Some animals have very high death rates in the wild. *But if death is a harm, then longer life is a benefit*—one that top-notch zoos might offer. Regular feeding is not guaranteed in the wild. Mild states of ill health can cause prolonged discomfort to wild animals without killing them. Thus, the availability of competent veterinary care in a zoo constitutes a benefit.[37]

But even zoos that offer good veterinary care and long lives for animals frequently neglect their psychological needs. Social animals deprived of family members, or even a reasonable number of companions, are depressingly commonplace. Intelligent animals given nothing to do are condemned to lives of boredom and listlessness. Many elephant and ape exhibits combine these forms of inexcusable neglect. Meeting the psychological needs of animals requires creative enrichment of their environment or, better, something approaching their natural habitats.

These goals are challenging and expensive but not impossible. An intriguing example of enrichment are conditions that require, or at least allow, intelligent animals to work for food or use their ingenuity to obtain it. These arrangements can make life more interesting, invigorating, and perhaps healthful. One may find chimpanzees "fishing" with sticks for termites at the Edinburgh Zoo, orangutans digging with twigs for honey at the San Diego Zoo, or carnivores searching, climbing, or leaping for food at Glasgow Zoo.[38] Presently, the National Zoo in Washington, DC, is creating an exhibit called "Think Tank," which will feature numerous interactive games designed to be stimulating for

---

[36] See, e.g., Grandy, "Zoos: A Critical Reevaluation."
[37] For reminders of the darker side of the wild, see, e.g., Hediger, *Wild Animals in Captivity*, ch. 4; and Bostock, *Zoos and Animal Rights*, ch. 5.
[38] These examples come respectively from Cherfas, *Zoo 2000*, p. 130; Koebner, *Zoo Book*, p. 88; and Bostock, *Zoos and Animal Rights*, p. 69.

monkeys while educating the public about monkeys' cognitive capacities. As for zoos providing something close to animals' natural habitats—minus the more deadly elements—my (again, literature-based) impression is that the San Diego Zoo, Zoo Atlanta, the Bronx Zoo, the Edinburgh Zoo, and Glasgow Zoo demonstrate what can be achieved with sufficient dedication and investment.

Some zoos can meet the basic-needs and comparable-life conditions for many animals. *Zoos that cannot or will not improve enough to meet these conditions should close.* But should both conditions apply to *all* animals? Conclusion 11 states that there is a weaker presumption against confining numerous species (at least "submammalian" ones) than there is against confining apes, dolphins, and humans. Perhaps the goals of education, research, and species preservation can justify some exceptions to these conditions in the case of some "lower" vertebrates. I recommend sticking to the two conditions, however. On the whole, they should be easier to satisfy in the case of "lower" vertebrates, whose needs are generally simpler. And an invitation to make exceptions would seem too open to self-serving abuse. (Also, it is unclear to what extent we can even separate out freedom interests in practice—see conclusion 11.)

The basic-needs and comparable-life standards, which should apply to all exhibits, are sufficiently demanding that probably few zoos could meet them. Menageries cannot meet them and therefore should be banned. Individuals probably should not own wild animals (as opposed to domesticated pet species) because the animals' complex needs are too likely to be neglected and enforcement of appropriate standards would be impossible. It would probably be wisest to prohibit private zoos as well. The profit motive seems very likely to lead to mistreated animals. (In the United States, the Department of Agriculture currently appears to have little interest in enforcing the extremely minimal provisions of the Animal Welfare Act in zoos, circuses, and menageries.) If all this is correct, the only justifiable zoos are top-notch public ones.

A final point about education and the cultivation of attitudes is in order. It is paramount that zoos not reinforce the common attitude that animals are essentially objects for our amusement and use.[39] This attitude is reinforced by most zoos today. Think of gorillas languishing in sterile, jail-like exhibits with no place to hide from jeering crowds. Any acceptable zoo will not only furnish valuable information about animals but will inspire admiration and respect for them. Maybe, in the

---

[39] Cf. Jamieson, "Against Zoos," p. 117. Even if no animals are harmed as a result of reinforcing this disrespectful attitude, the attitude itself, and reinforcing it, seem criticizable. See the discussion in Chapter 8 of external goods.

end, this can be accomplished only by doing a good job of simulating animals' natural habitats.

3. A few special cases. Although I have argued that the basic-needs and comparable-life conditions should apply to all prospective zoo animals, a few special cases merit additional comment. First, the conditions, in effect, apply only to animals with interests; animals lacking interests have no needs (in any sense relevant to morality) and cannot be provided or deprived of a good life. There would therefore appear to be no coherent case against keeping nonsentient animals in zoos. Nor are there ethical restrictions on how they are kept (except that attitudes of disrespect for animals generally should not be promoted, say, by using sea urchins as dartboards). At present, of course, we are unsure which animals are nonsentient. (I argued in Chapter 5 that insects are nonsentient without taking a position on where to draw a line between them and cephalopods.) But the fact that not all animals have interests provides an additional reason to reject a liberation ethic that opposes all keeping of animals in zoos.

On the other end of the nonhuman scale are apes and dolphins. In light of the evidence about their mental complexity (see Chapter 7), it would seem that meeting their basic needs would be so challenging as to set a very strong presumption against keeping such animals in zoos or aquatic exhibits. Species preservation, an admirable goal, especially animates us in the case of our nearest relatives, the apes. But this goal should be pursued only within the constraints of our two conditions. This would seem to entail family preservation, a great deal of space, and very enriched environments affording ample opportunities for climbing, exploring, problem solving, and playing.

On the other hand, I doubt we should keep any dolphins in aquatic exhibits. For us land animals to provide a comparably good life seems an impossible task in view of their marine habitat and rich social organization. I doubt we could come close to reproducing that, or anything as good.

Index

Note: This index does not contain entries for all of the authors cited in the text.

Adams, David, 95n, 99n, 100, 108–9, 110n
Adcock, Melanie, 282n
Allen, Colin, 82–3, 85n, 151, 152, 156n, 157n
animal-rights view, 5–6, 46, 52, 233, 269n, 285n, 289n. *See also* Regan, Tom
anxiety: concept of, 119–20; evidence for, in animals, 120–2; qualitative differences in, 122–3; relation to fear, 117–18
aquatic exhibits, 297
Aristotle, 50, 126, 153n, 217
Artificial Intelligence (A.I.), 90–1
Attfield, Robin, 228–9, 245
autonomy: concept of, 204–7; possibility of, in animals, 207–10

Baier, Annette, 28n
Baier, Kurt, 27
Bateson, Patrick, 109n, 111n
Beauchamp, Tom L., 20n, 34n, 57, 206n
behaviorism, 85, 86–7, 89, 91, 95, 105
Bekoff, Marc, 82n, 85n, 86n, 87n, 183n
Bennett, Jonathan, 168
Bentham, Jeremy, 45, 214n
Bitterman, M. E., 132–3, 141
blindsight, 104–5, 113–14
Blustein, Jeffrey, 29n
Bostock, Stephen St C, 290n, 292n, 293n, 295n
Boyd, Kenneth M., 108n, 109n, 110n, 112n, 122n, 123n, 135n
Brandt, R. B., 20, 215n, 216, 219–20
Brock, Dan W., 218n, 237n
Buchanan, Allen E., 237n
bullfights, 260, 264, 274

Carruthers, Peter, 9, 22n, 43n, 54–6, 111n, 112–15, 249n

casuistry, 28, 31, 33. *See also* inductivism
Cavalieri, Paola, 183n
Chantek, 179, 197–8
character, moral. *See* virtue, moral
Cheney, Dorothy L., 81–2, 160–1, 177, 184
Cherfas, Jeremy, 290n, 293n, 295n
Childress, Jim, 34n
Christman, John, 206
Churchland, Patricia, 92
Churchland, Paul, 92, 102n
Clarke, Stephen R. L., 199n
cognitive ethology, 84–5; strong cognitive ethology (SCE), 87, 143; weak cognitive ethology (WCE), 87, 132, 148
cognitive psychology, 85, 89, 92
Cohen, Carl, 36–7n, 65n
coherence, concept of, 14–17, 18–19, 23
Collins, Joseph, 286n
commonsense psychology. *See* folk psychology
communication, 183–5. *See also* language
conation, 129–31, 136, 142
concepts: different conceptions of, 150–3; relation to beliefs, 150, 152–3
confinement, concept of, 269
consciousness: concept of, 101, 114–15; distinguished from self-consciousness, 101, 115, 175; question of its function, 103–5; relation to desires, 131; relation to nature, 102; relation to other mental states, 101–2
considered judgment, concept of, 20
contractarianism. *See* contract theories
contract theories, 45, 46, 52, 53–6, 66
Copp, David, 20n, 218n
cosmetics testing, 45, 55, 264. *See also* research, harmful use of animals in
Crick, Francis, 102n
Crisp, Roger, 87n

Daniels, Norman, 13n, 21, 23–4
Darwin, Charles, 85, 91
Davidson, Donald, 13n, 141n, 146–50,
    154, 155, 163, 172n
Dawkins, Marian Stamp, 81, 104n, 11n,
    133–4, 139, 162n, 164–5, 185–6, 187n,
    200
deception, 161–3
deductivism, 11, 13, 16, 22, 27, 31, 32. *See
    also* foundationalism; rationalism
"deep ecologists," 49–50
DeGrazia, David, 2n, 32n, 36n, 37n, 47n,
    100n, 107n, 108n, 109n, 116n, 121n,
    204n, 234n, 256n
Dennett, Daniel C., 79n, 82n, 86, 89n,
    102n, 103n, 105n, 114, 137n, 145, 163,
    166–7
Descartes, René, 17, 79, 88, 97, 150n, 163
desire-satisfaction theory, defined, 214
de Waal, Frans, 200, 202
Dewey, John, 13n, 71, 72n
disabling, concept of, 271
distress, concept of, 116–17
Dostoevski, Fyodor, 41n
Dretske, Fred, 139n
dualism: property dualism, 88; substance
    dualism, 88, 89
Dworkin, Gerald, 205

eliminative materialism, 92
enjoyment: concept of, 125, 126, 221–2; in
    animals, 127
environmental ethics, 228, 293
ethics of care, 28. *See also* Gilligan, Carol

factory farming, 45, 274, 281; description
    of, 281–4; effects on humans, 286–7;
    moral evaluation of, 284–6
family farms, 288
fear: concept of, 118–19; relation to anx-
    iety, 117–18; relation to pain, 118
Feinberg, Joel, 47, 234n
feminist ethics, 25, 28, 31
Feyerabend, Paul, 92
Finelli, Mary, 282n
Flanagan, Owen E., Jr., 30, 71, 77n, 102n,
    103, 104n, 105n
Fleishman, Steve, 78n
Fodor, Jerry, 79n, 132
folk psychology, 78–9, 92, 132, 141, 163,
    172
foundationalism, 11, 16, 17n, 22. *See also*
    deductivism; rationalism
Fouts, Roger S. and Deborah H., 171n,
    195
Fox, Michael W., 282n, 287n
Frankfurt, Harry, 205n

freedom, instrumental value of, 255–6
Freud, Sigmund, 97, 150n, 164
Frey, R. G., 3–4, 6, 47, 53, 140, 143n, 212–
    13, 243–4, 287n
functionalism, 90–1
functioning, instrumental value of, 255,
    256
future, sense of. *See* temporality

Gallup, Gordon G., Jr., 93–5, 173
Garcia, Jorge, 51n, 248n
Gardner, Beatrix T. and R. Allen, 170–1,
    180n, 185
Gauthier, David, 214n, 216n
Gaylin, Willard, 59n
Gert, Bernard, 27, 218n
Gibbard, Allan, 19, 82n
Gilligan, Carol, 28, 30
Goodall, Jane, 171n, 177n, 178n, 179n,
    180n, 184n, 197n, 200n, 202
Goodman, Nelson, 13n
Grandy, John W., 290n, 292n, 295n
Griffin, Donald, 85–6, 159n, 172–3, 176n,
    184n, 190, 193
Griffin, James, 214n, 215n, 216n, 217n
Griffith, William B., 45n

happiness: concept of, 125–6; in animals,
    127
Hare, R. M., 12, 20n, 50, 216n
Harrison, Peter, 108n, 112n
Hauser, Marc D., 82–3, 85n, 151, 152
Hediger, H., 290n, 295n
Herman, Louis R., 171, 179n, 184n, 187–9,
    192, 193, 198
Herrnstein, R. J., 151–2
Hoff (Sommers), Christina, 30n, 47, 234n
Holmgren, Margaret, 24n
hominid species, 58–9, 230
Humane Society, 275, 282n, 286n, 287n,
    290n
hunting, 45, 260, 264

identity theory, 89, 90–1
impartiality. *See* universalizability
indirect duty view, 41–3, 44, 54
inductivism, 13, 31. *See also* casuistry
inherent value, 5, 66, 68n
insects, 91, 99, 105, 108, 110, 111–12, 133
intentional action: concept of, 171–2; rela-
    tion to agency, 172; relation to self-
    awareness, 174–5
intentional stance, 86–7, 147–8
interests: concept of, 39; idea of relevant
    similarity of, 47–8, 51, 233–4; place in
    ethics, 39; possessed by sentient ani-
    mals, 226–31
intuitive balancing, 32–5

Jackson, Kathryn, 30
James, William, 71
Jamieson, Dale, 6n, 85n, 86n, 87n, 183n, 290n, 292n, 296n

Kagan, Shelly, 15, 63n, 214n, 223–6, 273n
Kant, Immanuel, 41, 50, 66, 168
Kanzi, 188, 190, 191n
Kitcher, Patricia, 79n
Koch, Christof, 102n
Koebner, Linda, 290n, 295n
Koko, 173, 180–1, 190, 196–7, 208, 209
Kripke, Saul A., 155n

LaFollette, Hugh, 82n
language: concept of, 185; necessary for certain concepts, 158
language studies with apes: apparent apologies, 208–9; early claims and reaction, 185–7; recent, 194–8
language studies with dolphins, 188–9, 193; self-awareness suggested in, 180–1
Lappe, Frances Moore, 286n
Leahy, Michael P. T., 2n, 112n, 287n
libertarianism, 45–6, 52, 273
life, instrumental value of, 231–2
life move: defined, 234; problem of justifying, 234–5
Lorenz, Konrad, 85
Lycan, William G., 85n, 90

Mappes, Tom, 274n
marginal cases, problem of, 55–6, 70–1, 73, 264, 268
Mason, Jim, 282n, 286n
McGinn, Colin, 150, 152, 176
memory, 159–60. *See also* temporality
mental state, concept of, 97–9
mental statism, defined, 214
Midgley, Mary, 7, 37n, 42n, 61–5, 169, 170n
Miles, H. Lyn White, 179n, 197–8
Mill, John Stuart, 45, 239, 240–2
Mitchell, Robert, 203n
moral agency: argument from, 65–71; full-fledged, 203–4; not all-or-nothing, 204. *See also* virtue, moral
Morrel-Samuels, Palmer, 187
Morris, Christopher W., 212n

Nagel, Thomas, 101n, 145
Nielsen, Kai, 13n, 24n
nociception, 99–100, 107, 109
Nozick, Robert, 42, 45–6, 124n, 214n, 222, 259n

objective theory, defined, 216

pain: basic facts about, in humans, 107–8; concept of, 105–7; evidence for, in animals, 108–12
Parfit, Derek, 213n, 215n
Pears, David, 150n
Peirce, C. S., 13n, 71
perfectionistic theory, defined, 217
personhood, 210n, 242n, 265, 266
pets, 269, 274–5, 294
physicalism, 88, 89
pleasure: concept of, 124–5; in animals, 126–7
poaching, 264
Powers, Madison, 63n
pragmatism, 18, 19; classical, 19, 71–2
predators, 277
Premack, David, 185, 186–7, 189
propositional attitudes, 137–8, 144, 146, 148, 153, 163

Quine, W. V., 13n, 24

Rachels, James, 26n, 47, 60n, 69n, 70n, 73n, 77n, 164, 199n, 238, 255n
rationalism, 11, 15, 16, 17, 22, 29, 57. *See also* deductivism; foundationalism
Rawls, John, 13n, 19–20, 21, 23, 27, 54, 216n
Raz, Joseph, 20n, 218n
reasoning, practical, 141, 142–3, 164. *See also* thinking
relevance, problem of, 67–9
Regan, Tom, 5–6, 39, 46, 47, 52, 53, 68, 140n, 155n, 174–5, 212, 231n, 232, 238, 285n, 289n. *See also* animal-rights view
research, harmful use of animals in, 81, 264, 270, 271, 276. *See also* cosmetics testing
Richardson, Henry S., 32–4
rights, 45–6; to liberty, 270; to life, 265–7. *See also* animal-rights view; rights theories
rights theories, 39, 64. *See also* animal-rights view; rights
Rodd, Rosemary, 8, 59, 60n, 71n, 174n, 178, 179n, 182–3, 184n, 191, 192n, 201–2
rodeos, 264
Rollin, Bernard E., 2n, 77n, 80n, 93n, 99–100, 107n, 109n, 110n, 126n, 246–7, 239n
Rorty, Richard, 13n, 103n
Rose, Margaret, 95n, 99n, 100, 108–9, 110n
Ross, W. D., 11n, 12, 34, 66n
Rowan, Andrew, 100n, 107n, 108n, 109n, 111n, 112n, 116n, 121n, 122n
Russow, Lilly, 249n

Sapontzis, S. F., 7–8, 70n, 140n, 199, 201, 203n, 213, 227n, 231n, 239, 247, 248n, 250n, 276n, 277n
Savage-Rumbaugh, E. Sue, 173n, 183n, 184n, 188, 189–90, 190–1, 192, 194–5
Scanlon, Thomas, 54, 213n, 214n, 217n, 219–20
Schell, Orville, 287n
Searle, John R., 101, 132, 134, 137n, 138, 143–4, 152, 158, 164
self-awareness: admitting of types and degrees, 181–3; bodily self-awareness a type, 172–4; introspective awareness a type, 176; relation to intentional action, 174–5; relation to temporality, 174; social self-awareness a type, 176–8; suggested by imitation, 178–80
Sellars, Wilfred, 13n
Sen, Amartya, 215n, 218n
sentience, 3, 57, 69, 93, 99, 101, 136, 142, 226–31
Seyfarth, Robert M., 81–2, 160–1, 177, 184
Sidgwick, Henry, 124, 214
Singer, Peter, 2–3, 6, 20n, 38, 44–5, 47, 53, 69n, 88n, 183n, 212, 227n, 239, 242–3, 268n, 273n, 282n, 285n, 286n, 287n, 288n
Smith, Jane A., 108n, 109n, 110n, 112n, 122n, 123n, 135n
social bondedness, argument from, 61–5
social relations thesis, 174, 175
Sorabji, Richard, 153n
speciesism, 28, 31, 276
specification, 32–5
Stich, Stephen, 144–6, 154
subjective theory, defined, 216
suffering: concept of, 116; widespread, in animals, 123
Sumner, L. W., 47, 106n, 124n, 125n, 126n, 127n, 210n, 213n, 217n, 221–2, 227, 229n, 230, 234n, 240n, 244n
surprise, 148–9

Taylor, Paul W., 228n
temporality, 167–71
Terrace, Herb, 186, 189–90, 194–5n
thinking, 163–5. *See also* practical reasoning
thought. *See* thinking
Tinbergen, Niko, 85
trapping, 45, 264

universalizability, 27–31, 50–1, 248
utilitarianism, 3, 4, 5, 6, 12, 39, 45, 46, 52, 63, 126, 213, 262, 263, 277n, 287
utility-versus-rights debate, 6, 9

value theory, defined, 211
VanDeVeer, Donald, 47, 234n
Varner, Gary, 133n, 135n, 138n, 141–2, 228n, 230n
virtue, moral, 41–3, 54; concept of, 199; possibility of, in animals, 199–203. *See also* moral agency; virtue ethics
virtue ethics, 28. *See also* moral agency; virtue, moral

Washoe, 170, 179–80, 185, 186, 195, 199–200
well-being, experiential: concept of, 211; instrumental value of, 255, 256
whaling, 264, 277
White, Morton, 13n
White, Robert, 41, 44
Wittgenstein, Ludwig, 13n, 57n, 89–90, 150n

zoos: description of, 290–1; issue of keeping animals in, 290, 294–7; issue of taking wild animals for, 291–4